THE
SUMERIAN SWINDLE

BOOKS FROM SSPRESS
— www.sspress.shop —

White Power, by George Lincoln Rockwell
The Monsters of Babylon (2 vols.), by Gregory Delaney

THE
SUMERIAN SWINDLE

How the Jews Betrayed Mankind

Gregory Delaney

sspress

— 2025 —

SSPress, LLC

Special Services Press, LLC, is a non-profit educational publisher.
www.sspress.store / www.sspress.online

Library of Congress Cataloging-in-Publication Data

Delaney, Gregory
The Sumerian Swindle: How the Jews Betrayed Mankind
Edited version of 2014 edition

p. cm.
Includes bibliographical references

ISBN 978-1963-1433-31
(pbk.: alk. paper)

1. Jews, history of
2. Anti-Semitism, history of

Printing number: 9 8 7 6 5 4 3 2 1

Printed in the United States of America on acid-free paper.

ACKNOWLEDGMENT

The editor would like to thank O. G. for his extensive assistance in the preparation of this text.

CONTENTS

EDITOR'S PREFACE

This book is about the origins of the Jews—the most malevolent people ever to walk the Earth, in the view of the author. But to explain this, the author, Gregory Delaney, must expend a large effort examining the pre-history of the Jews: of the 'proto-Jews' or 'pre-Jews,' if you will. Thus, most of this book is dedicated to the period of time from 3000 BC in ancient Mesopotamia, until the appearance of Abraham, which Delaney places about 1550 BC. At that point, he says, "real" Jews appeared, along with the so-called religion of Judaism.

But of course, the people and ancestors of Abraham would have been 'ethnic Jews' for thousands of years prior to that date—Jews in all but name. Hence, Delaney takes us on an extended tour of the history of Mesopotamia, Sumeria, Babylon, and all related peoples, places, and events. Civilization began with the Caucasoid Sumerians around 3300 BC, but the troubles began when they imported Semitic Amorites, circa 2900 BC. These Semites were the genealogical predecessors to modern Jews; they *were* Jews, in a biological sense, although Delaney doesn't call them that. And it was they who set mankind on a path of destruction.

To anticipate the text to come, Delaney observes that the key innovation leading to the destruction of civilization was *lending money at interest*—and especially, at *compound* interest. This apparently simple and innocent financial tool allowed certain individuals to acquire vast wealth, and hence to impoverish other peoples, to corrupt rulers, and to drive nations into war. The Sumerians invented this idea—hence the "Sumerian Swindle"—but the Semites/Jews perfected it and deployed it as a weapon against humanity. (Perhaps he should have called it the "Semitic Swindle," but he didn't.) These Semites proceeded to develop what the author calls the 21 Secret Frauds of the Sumerian Swindle (chapter 4), and they then used these tactics to defraud and dispossess people all over the ancient world, and on in to the present day. It is a fascinating story of debauchery, kleptocracy, greed, and outright evil.

And all along, Delaney deploys his usual mix of humor, sarcasm, and moral outrage, crafting a compelling, readable, but still scholarly study of the Jews and how they "betrayed mankind" to their own benefit. There are no footnotes in this edition, although all of the author's facts have been checked and confirmed to be correct. Delaney has a remarkably vast knowledge of the ancient world, and he is exceptionally courageous in his critical analysis of the Jews. No one else has ever written a comparable work.

This book was originally intended as Volume One to a series entitled "How the Jews Betrayed Mankind." The second volume is the book *The Monsters of Babylon*; both were apparently written circa 2010 and underwent at least three revised editions. But they were apparently never published in hard copy, likely because no mainstream publisher would touch them. But the books appeared online as full PDF files, which is how most people read them today, even though both files are large and un-wieldy, and in need of professional editing.

Then in 2024, a new imprint, SSPress, edited and published a new, clean edition of *Monsters*, in two large volumes. And now, in 2025, the same editors have released the prior work, *Sumerian Swindle*. This present work is again edited for clarity and conciseness, and text deletions have been made throughout to tighten the work and maintain a focus on the central points. The chapter structure has also been altered, again for read-ability and better flow of ideas. But both books deserve to be read together, beginning here and moving on to *Monsters of Babylon*; it is one, long, continuous story—a story with profound lessons for the present day. In fact, these two works, in (now) three volumes, are more relevant than ever, with the ongoing Israeli genocide in Palestine and the ongoing Jewish-inspired war in the Ukraine. The reader will surely find many fascinating parallels, even from millennia past.

Delaney, sadly, died in 2020 at the age of 68. He was unable to complete his original vision of a four-volume set of books. But fortunately, he has left us with some true masterpieces of writing and critical analysis, and these two books will surely stand the test of time as irreplaceable contributions toward understanding the broader Jewish Question.

This book is a work of history—but it is *real* history, living history, the kind of history that you always wish you learned in school but never did. No one else has yet had the requisite combination of skill and bravery to compose a book such as this. We are hugely fortunate that Gregory Delaney (aka Banjo Billy, aka G_d), was able to dedicate the time and effort needed to construct this book and its sequel, *Monsters of Babylon*. May we have the wisdom to absorb and act upon its message.

THE
SUMERIAN SWINDLE

PART ONE

Origins of the Sumerian Swindle

MAFIA, THUGS, AND JEWS

For several hundred years in India, a similar people to the Jews used to live in family and clan villages. And they made their living as murderers and thieves. They called themselves Thugs or Thuggees. The Thugees of India were a secret society whose so-called "religion" was based upon murder and theft. They lived among their fellow Indians as rug weavers and artisans. To look at them, their fellow Indians could not tell that they were any different from themselves. They spoke the same language, wore the same clothes, and ate the same food.

But the Thugees worshipped the Hindu demon goddess, Kali. It was the Thugee belief that this demon goddess demanded that victims be sacrificed to her without shedding their blood—that is, the victims must first be strangled.

For one month every year, during the travel season in India when the weather was good and there were many travelers and pilgrims on the roads, the Thugees would make some excuse to their employers and acquaintances and take a leave of absence from their regular occupations as merchants or weavers or restaurateurs or farmers. Saying that they had to go to a distant wedding or to visit an ailing relative or using whatever excuse that they could invent, they would leave their villages and go to meet other Thugees for a month of murder and theft, all devoted to their goddess Kali whom they believed would welcome them into the Hereafter.

Known among themselves as "masters of deceit," (a term that American FBI director Herbert Hoover would use to describe the Jews of the 20th century), the Thugees befriended rich travelers to whom they perfidiously offered their services as protectors and guides. But once they were in an out-of-the-way location, they would fall upon the travelers and strangle them. This was the one and the only method of murder decreed by their demon goddess, to strangle their victims, never to knife or bludgeon them.

As they tightened the garrote around the neck of their victims, they whispered into their ears, "See, oh Kali! Look, oh Kali!," calling their goddess to witness the crime. Then, the Thugs stole all of their victim's possessions, mangled their faces so that they could never be identified, and buried them deeply so that they could never be found. Their victims simply disappeared into the mystery of India. And when the travel season was over, the Thugees would return to their home villages with their newly acquired wealth and continue their lives as rug weavers and merchants, though richer than they had been before.

The religious belief of the Thuggees was that they were the servants of their goddess. And just like the Jews, they served their deity by preying upon the people among whom they lived. And just like the Jews, their secret fraternity had their own secret language, secret meetings, and secret rituals. Indeed, because of the criminal nature of their practices, just like the Jews, they kept their actions hidden from outsiders. And just like the Jews, without practicing secrecy and deceit they could not have perpetuated their wicked ways for so many centuries.

Regardless of their alleged "religion" of Kali-worship, the Thugees knew that if they were caught in their crimes, that they would be punished. So, like all other criminal gangs, everything that they did was plagued with the fear of discovery and exposure. Everything that they did was masked with deceit and the utmost secrecy. In these ways, they were not at all different from the Jews.

India is home to many diverse religions. And Hinduism is very tolerant of all of them. Even though the Indian people and Hinduism in general are accepting of all manner of religious activities and beliefs, no one in India would have accepted among themselves a secret group of murderers whose religious practice was to stealthily murder everyone whom they met and to steal their property. So, to practice their so-called "religion" without being executed for their crimes, secrecy and deceit were their most important tactics. When they murdered people who were traveling in large groups, they murdered everyone in the entire group and left no one alive as witness, just like the Jews.

As organized gangs, during the three hundred years of the known history of this Thugee cult, it has been estimated that the Thugees murdered between one million and three million people in India, stole their belongings and buried their corpses. These millions of Indian people simply disappeared, never to be heard of again. Then, the Thugees would return to their villages and lead lives of simple folks who often had extra money to help their fellow villagers and thus gain prestige for themselves—just like the Jews.

Each and every year, this same routine was repeated as the secrets of the Thugees were passed down to sons and passed down to grandsons without the people of India ever having heard of this cult—such was their secrecy. That the Thugees of India did not last for even longer than three hundred years was strictly due to the perseverance of the British in rooting them out. And the man who was primarily responsible for exterminating the Thuggees from India in the early 1800s was Major General Sir William Henry Sleeman.

In the book *Thug: A Million Murders*, you can read a first-hand account of this great British hero's description of the Thugs of India in the words of his biographer and great-grandson, Colonel James L. Sleeman. And remember, his description is of just one, sweet-looking old Indian man. As you read his words, realize that we are studying here an even more diabolical sect of Jews who are similar to but far more evil than the Thugees.

Because these Thugees were a hereditary conspiracy, Major General Sleeman was able to extinguish these crime families by executing and imprisoning the fathers and imprisoning for life the sons. Thus, no Thugees were allowed to pass their evil teachings down to succeeding generations. And so, Thugee vanished from India, thanks to the British.

Once you understand that crime families and their teachings are both hereditary and cultural, whether inherited from Mafia families or Thugee families, you are ready to study the origins of the most secretive sect of bandits and genocidal maniacs to have ever walked the earth. Like the Thugees, these also hide behind a mask of religion. In modern times, these most horrible of monsters are known as Jews.

CHAPTER 1

THE LAND OF MESOPOTAMIA, CRADLE OF CIVILIZATION

Today, you might think that there is something new under the scorching, desert sun of Iraq. In the early 21st century AD, the dry soil was blown into dust by the bombs of F-16 fighter jets. Huge tracts of the dry and fertile soil, groves of date palms, the flowing water of the Tigris and Euphrates Rivers, and the towns and villages were poisoned with depleted uranium ordinance while pilotless robot killer drones flew high overhead, being piloted via satellite from half a world away. So, you might think that there is something new in the 14,000-year-old history of Mesopotamia, but you would be wrong. Of course, the tools for killing and the methods of destruction and genocide are far more advanced today, but the land is just the same and the people are just the same as they were in 12,000 BC.

The most striking difference to a modern observer visiting 12,000 BC would have been the scarcity of humans. People lived just about everywhere, from the farthest southern reaches of today's Chile to the Norse tundra, but they would have been hard to find, living in small and isolated bands. They had to be scattered, because the human animal is an omnivorous carnivore, and large carnivores surviving off the land require a large range—about 5,000 acres per person, in the case of carnivore Homo sapiens. Depending on local conditions, a band of just 25 hunter-gatherers could require more than a thousand square miles. By 8000 BC, the world probably supported fewer than 4 million human beings, roughly the population of contemporary Kentucky. By 8000 BC, humans already had fully developed languages, the most advanced of which expressed ideas and emotions with precision. It was a pure and natural world because Jews did not exist in 8000 BC.

Ancient Mesopotamia was located in what is today the modern country of Iraq [see Map 1]. The wars that are tearing that land apart today are really being fought for the same reasons that wars were fought in Mesopotamia at the dawn of civilization—for natural resources, money, and tribal territory. The actors, the tools, and the war machines are different, but the reasons for bloodshed are the same—wealth and political power. The sun, the wind, the water, the mud, and the stars are all the same. The greed and the evil in the hearts of ruthless men, are just the same. The corruption of the political leaders and the avarice of the moneylenders is just the same as it has always been. The only difference is found in this book that you are reading.

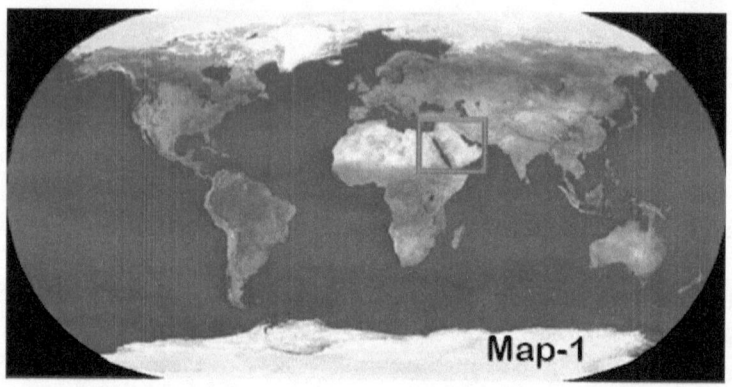

Map-1

Although over 5,000 years have passed since the Sumerians first began what has become our modern civilization, the geography and weather of modern Iraq is nearly identical to what it was during those earlier times. The climate is extremely hot and dry. Temperatures in central and southern Iraq can reach 120 degrees Fahrenheit (49 degrees Celsius). The soil is arid and wind swept. Mostly the land is rather flat with low, undulating mounds and hillocks. In the course of millions of years, the Tigris and Euphrates Rivers have meandered throughout the Mesopotamian Basin, uncovering and re-depositing the clay and silt soils of the region and producing a river-made land of mud, clay, and silt with almost no stone and no minerals. It is a land of dust and dirt and mud and hot sun. [see Map 2]

MIDDLE EAST
Map-2

Except in the mountains, there were no trees in ancient Mesopotamia but there were giant reeds around the rivers and in the southern marshes [see Map 3]. What geological variety there was in the somewhat flat landscape consisted of desert, foothills, steppes, and marshes with no rainfall in the summer months. The higher elevation steppe lands in those ancient times were grasslands, almost treeless with an average rainfall of ten inches. In the foothills and mountains, oak, pine, terebinth trees, grasses, wild barley, and wild wheat could grow. The flood season of the Tigris and Euphrates Rivers is between April and June, which is too early for winter crops and not long enough for summer crops.

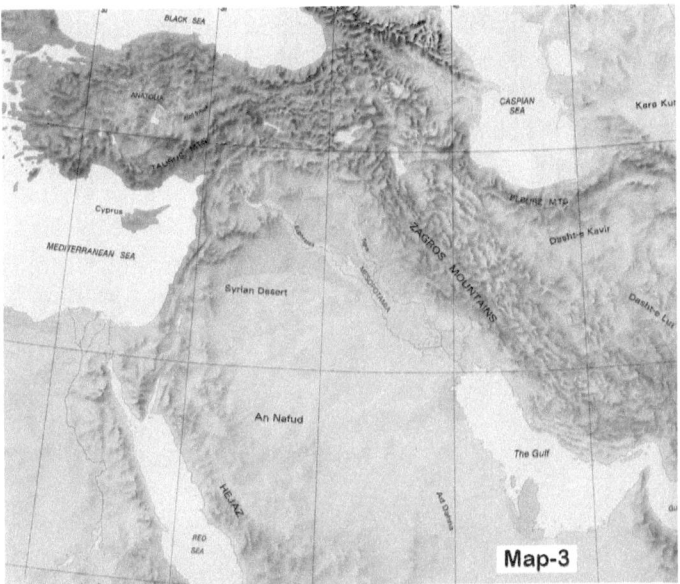

Map-3

So, by appearances, you might at first think that such a desolate place could not possibly produce the world's first civilization. But Mesopotamia is where civilization began. And it was a civilization that grew up out of the water, the mud, and the hot, scorching sun, which were the perfect conditions for growing grains and vegetables when irrigation ditches were dug.

As the Ice Age was ending, the hunter-gatherer people of 12,000 BC learned that they could make a living by gathering the seeds of the wild grasses that grew throughout the region. What few people there were in the world at that time, lived in open-air camps or in caves or in huts built of reeds. As hunters, they had found a good companion with another hunter, the wolves. These became the first domesticated animal by 11,000 BC.

And the dog has been man's best friend ever since those Stone Age times. Both man and dog hunted by running down their prey. The cross-country running ability of man was (and is) greater than any other creature on earth. Not the fastest but the most enduring of runners, mankind could run for days and chase down any animal to exhaustion and kill it with stone-tipped spears. The cross-country running hunters could leave their panting dogs far behind; or by working in partnership with their dogs, they could surround prey of any size or ferocity.

By about 9,000 BC, the people had learned how to make mud bricks. They developed weaving and craft specializations. They carried on long-distance trade in obsidian and copper. As hunters who had killed the adult nanny goats and who had raised and tamed the kids, they were able to domesticate the goat by 8,500 BC. With milk goats, these Stone Age people didn't have to go hungry from scarce game because, by that time, they could use their hunting skills in protecting their herds from predators. By 8,000 BC, they had also domesticated the sheep which provided them with woolen clothes as well as meat. [see Map 4]

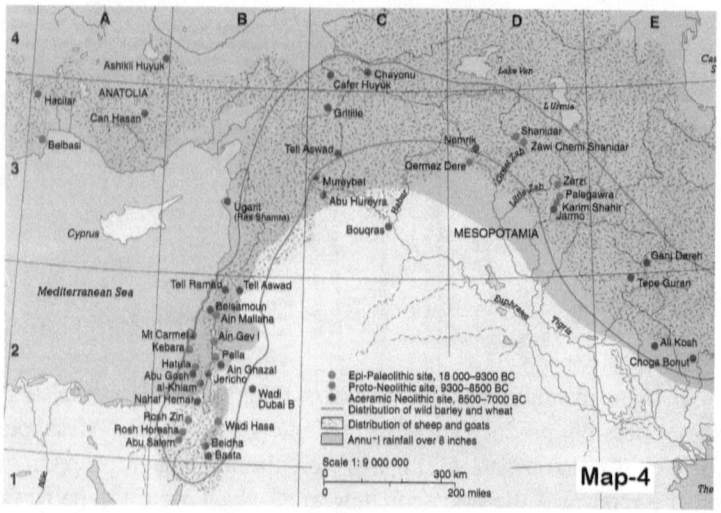

As the Ice Age retreated and the weather warmed, all across the grassy hills of the Ancient Near East, the people discovered that if they could gather and store enough grass seeds that they didn't have to wander about with their goats and sheep; they could stay in one location, where the wild grasses provided food both for them as well as for their flocks. These grasses grew in such abundance on the hillsides that even a single person working for two weeks with an obsidian blade could harvest enough to feed a family of four for a year. When an entire family or a village cooperated with such a harvest, there was plenty of food for everybody. Because grain does not decay if it is kept dry; it can last for decades. A reliable food supply allowed for the establishment of permanent camps, allowing the wandering hunter-gatherers to settle down into villages where, by 7500 BC, they domesticated the wild pig. By 7000 BC, cattle and the always useful rodent-catching cat were domesticated. And they discovered how to make pottery for cooking and for protecting stored grain from insects and rodents.

All of the peoples living throughout this entire Fertile Crescent region, stretching in an arch from the Mediterranean Sea to the Persian Gulf, gathered these wild grasses. These grasses sustained a scattering of small, permanent villages for 3,000 years of small farming. But it was in the land between the two rivers of the Euphrates and Tigris Rivers with their copious and reliable water supplies that farming was able to blossom into the foundation for civilized life. [see Map 5]

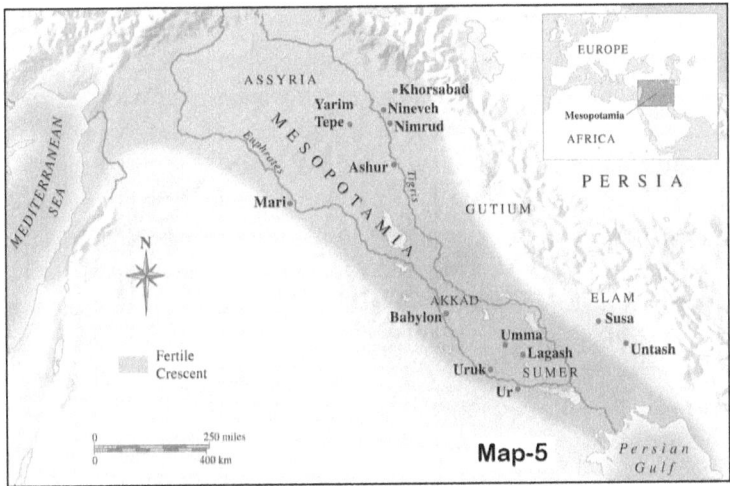

The long Zagros Mountains chain divides Mesopotamia from Persia. The arid plain of the Two Rivers and a sand desert, is broken down at its southern end by the watershed of the Karun River. Here is "Elam" (the "East"), an alluvial plain closed in on all sides by the Zagros Mountains, except on the western side where it is open to Mesopotamia and the Persian Gulf. Geographically, it is a part of Mesopotamia rather than Persia.

The vast deposits of silt carried down by the Karun River from Elam, formed a bar across the upper end of the Persian Gulf which held up the flood waters of the Tigris and Euphrates so that their silt was deposited against the bar instead of being swept out into the Gulf. With the slackened current, much silt gradually filled in the marshes, forming dry land through which the Euphrates cut its bed. Also flowing into this delta region in ancient times, but now dried up, was a fourth river out of Arabia which created the area known to us as Eden, the land of the four rivers.

The dry, sedimentary soil from these rivers was immensely fertile when watered under the hot sun, so it invited settlement. But rich as the soil was, and easy as was the tillage, yet to profit by its richness required much labor on a large scale. It was not a land in which the isolated farmer could prosper. The grain had to be sown, of course, in winter. But in the spring, just as the young grain sprouted, the river came down from the mountains in flood, overran and scoured out the fields and destroyed all hopes of harvest. The river had to be kept in check by artificial banks. The land, if it was to yield a second crop, had to be irrigated by canals. The enormous labor required to solve such difficult farming problems was obvious, but the task was beyond the powers of any one landowner.

To grow grain in the dry soils of southern Mesopotamia, the farmers dug ditches to carry water from the rivers to the dry fields. This soil, this *river-made* soil, washed down from the mountains and washed about by the meandering rivers over millions of years, once it was irrigated, proved to be very fertile; it produced tremendous crops beneath the bright sun. With plenty of food, with mud bricks for building their homes and clay pottery for cooking and storing their foods, civilization began in southern Iraq—all based upon water, dirt, sun, grain, and intense physical labor.

We call these earliest non-Semitic people in Mesopotamia, "Ubaidians" after Tell al-Ubaid where their pottery was first discovered by modern archeologists. Although they were a Stone Age people, using flint, obsidian, bone, and wood for their tools, the modern reader should not look down upon those ancient people with disdain. All of those ancient people were of the same species of Homo Sapiens as we are, ourselves. So, it is important to remember that they had the same feelings, the same love for their children, the same social ambitions, and the same intelligence that we have in our own modern lives. Of course, they did not have the same knowledge and understanding about the world around them or the same educational level as we do, knowledge which we have only acquired from the people who came before us. They were less knowledgeable than we are but they were just as intelligent. Indeed, the knowledge that we, ourselves, have today is built upon the very knowledge that those early people developed. So, we should look upon those ancient people more as our very own great-great-great-grandparents rather than as some distant and dusty barbarians to whom we owe nothing.

That being said, you will find it profitable to keep the humanity of those people in mind during this study so that you can better understand the theme of this book. What we call "modern civilization" is a direct result of what those early people invented. Even the foundation for the very words that you are now reading were developed by the inhabitants of Mesopotamia when they invented writing over 5,000 years ago. Five thousand years is not very much time compared to the four-billion-year age of the earth. It is like only yesterday. Thus, although the theme of this history deals with ancient people, they were really the same people as we are today. So, what you are reading is not ancient history; it is the history of today because many of the very same events are happening today even though they are rooted in ancient times.

At 9,000 BC, as the last of the Ice Age was disappearing, the Ubaidians went about their lives of sowing and reaping grains and domesticating animals. They left behind for us to dig up and to wonder about, tools such as hoes, obsidian adzes and knives, sickles, mud bricks and baked bricks, spindle whorls, loom weights, sculpture, painted pottery, and the plow. They marked their possessions with clay stamps and cylinder seals. But they also built canals and irrigation ditches and dedicated large mud-brick temples to their gods. And for such architecture, calculation skills in arithmetic were required, as well as a basic knowledge of geometry. They used water clocks—clay bowls with a small hole in the bottom, which were floated in a basin of water so that they could mark time by how long it took for the bowl to sink. With these clocks, their village chiefs and town governors were able to regulate the amount of irrigation water each field was allowed.

Although they had no written records, they relied upon what all the ancient peoples relied upon, and of which we modern people have limited abilities—their *memories*. With no written records with which to store information about their past, they used the well-developed faculties of their human brains to memorize the events of their times and to pass along to their children the stories of their past. They began their stories by claiming that their entire civilization got its start at the town of Eridu in the southern part of the country. And these stories were passed along to the people who came after the Ubaidians.

It is important for you to identify with those ancient people as fellow humans so that you can fully understand the theme of this present history. They were just as human in every way as you are. In their clay sculptures, we can see how the Ubaidians saw themselves [see Figure 1]. And it is here that I want you to understand some secrets that the archeologists and scientists have overlooked—the real humanity of those ancient people. You must not look at their sculptures in the same way as do the archeologists, who egotistically consider themselves more modern and therefore more advanced in their own humanity. By doing so, the scientists blind themselves to the advanced knowledge of those ancient people.

Figure - 1

It is often remarked how reptilian and alien the Ubaidian sculptures are. And it is difficult for the archeologists (or almost anybody else) to imagine how a people could look so extra-terrestrial and odd. But this is because the modern scientists do not perceive those ancient people through human eyes but only through cold scientific lenses. They look only at the hard data and forget that the cold pottery and clay sculptures reflect the workmanship of living people who, although they could not read or write their ideas, could sculpt them.

To understand the secret knowledge that the Ubaidian sculptors were expressing, you need only to ask yourself the question: "Who am I?" Or ask the question: "What am I?" And then, try to make a sculpture of yourself, or of your friends or family, in answer to that question. This is what the Ubaidian sculptors did. And this is why their features look so odd because what they were showing was not just their outer appearance but their *inner Being*. In this respect, they were expressing something far in advance of what most modern people understand about themselves. In those sculptures, they were expressing their true selves, not as individual person-alities but as living, breathing Beings looking outward from an inner reality.

Lower your own eyelids, look outward through lowered eyelids, and ask yourself, "Who am I? What am I?" Then, look inside yourself at the living One who is asking this question. Do you understand, now? Their sculptures reflect their Inner Being looking outward. They reflect your own inner Self as living Human Beings.

Certainly, the Ubaidians did not look into mirrors, because there were no mirrors other than pools of standing water. They knew what they looked like reflected in water so their sculptures of themselves were expressing something other than that. They were not fooled in the same way that modern people are fooled by the exact and reverse image of themselves looking back from a mirrored glass which does not waver like a pool of water.

Most modern people think that what they see in a mirror, is a reflection of their true selves. But they are wrong. In a mirror, you are only looking at the reverse reflection of your outside appearance and not looking at your Inner Being. Thus, you are being misled by the technology into thinking that what you see on the outside—your face, your clothes—is who you are on the inside. Can you deny that you exist inside of yourself as well as outside of yourself? Isn't there something inside of you that makes you a Human Being? You cannot see your inner self, your True Self, in a mirror. For that, you must see with your inner eye in order to perceive yourself on the inside! To see your false and temporary self in a mirror, you must open your eyes; to see your True Self within, you must close your eyes.

To understand the Ubaidian sculptures, and to actually see one of those people with your very own eyes, you must see what they saw. Ask yourself the question, "Who am I?" and then breathe gently and look out from your eyes. But do not look out too far, rather look through just the slits of your eyes so as to view yourself in the living act of looking outward. Breathe gently and lower your eyelids. Ask yourself, "Who am I?" and close your eyes slightly and breathe gently and look within yourself at how your face is shaped on the inside, at how your nose breathes life from the inside, at how you can see and feel what you are like on the inside. And why? Because this is the living spirit of you looking out from the inside. This is not the same as looking at a cold and distant reflected image of yourself in a mirror. This is being alive exactly where you are right now.

And so, the view that the ancient Ubaidians had of themselves is true, while the view that modern people have of themselves is false. How can you say that you are superior to the Ancient People if your views are false? You know now what they looked like reflected in yourself. This is the meaning of the clay models that the Ubaidians made of themselves. They were then as you are now: a living Being looking inward through half-closed eyes.

*****

As the Ubaidians grew in numbers through the success of their agricultural efforts, they began to organize themselves around their priests and temples. The ancient peoples looked to their priests for guidance, and *all* of the ancient peoples believed in the gods. This is important to remember: *all* of the ancient peoples believed in the gods. There were no atheists in ancient times. There were no Communists, Jews, Humanists, or Feminists telling them that they were nothing but animals. There were no scientists telling them that they were nothing but monkeys descended from more primitive monkeys. They wouldn't have believed such fables because they were in many ways more intelligent than modern scientists because they had common sense.

You can understand the ancient people if you think like a child who is awed by Creation. For example, that hot, yellow, blinding disk that rises and sets every day, and lights up and heats the entire world! How fantastic! But what is it? What could it be? You can look directly at it by rolling up your index finger and peeking through the tiny hole that is formed within the finger's embrace. When the clouds partly cover it, it looks like a great bright wheel that rolls across the sky. Is it a chariot wheel of a god? Or maybe it is a great eye in the sky looking down upon mankind. Without the technology of telescopes, one's imagination of what the sun really is or what the moon is, were all theories of equal validity. For who could deny that the crescent moon was not a great boat floating across the sky? No one in the ancient world could prove otherwise. In its crescent, it looks like a shining reed boat, just like the reed boats then plying the Euphrates; so it must be a boat. What else could it be? No one could prove otherwise. So, with no opposing theory, the moon remained a heavenly boat for the next four thousand years!

And of course, the world was flat because you could see that it was laid out as a vast plain with mountains and rivers and a great starry sky full of twinkling, shining gods that circled about overhead. Of course the stars circled the Earth because you could see them move, yourself! And the Earth was solid and immovable because you could feel it under your feet as such. And that cool, white, full moon that rises and sets in the night sky! It gradually changes from dark moon to bright moon. What is it? A great goddess in the sky, looking down upon mankind?

Of course, the Ancient Ones had no telescopes to tell them that the moon is a rocky sphere orbiting in space or that the sun is a ball of nuclear gasses. But if you look at the world as they saw it, you will see that the bright thing that waxes and wanes in the night sky resembles a disk. The disk changes into horns like on a cow. Or perhaps it looks more like a reed boat in the sky. And of course, that great sea of stars is a Milky Way highway, a path through the sky that leads off into distant lands where the gods live and where mankind may someday journey.

Or clouds and rainbows! Birds and beasts! Rivers and oceans! Rain and wind and lightning and thunder! Look again, O Modern Man! Look at all the natural phenomenon that we modern people take for granted! Look at Nature again with innocent eyes! All those things are still just as fresh and full of wonder as they were 12,000 years ago. The only thing that has changed is the dulling of perceptive astuteness of the modern people of today who consider themselves superior to the Ancient Ones who built the foundations of our very own culture.

To understand those ancient people, you must empty your mind of the modern theories of scientists who have lost touch with True Reality and look at the world around you with the mind of child. A child knows nothing, but is willing to see and hear and learn everything. Only then can you understand what the ancient people knew and what the ancient people are still trying to tell us, if we will only listen.

Each of the hundred billion neurons in our brains are, on average, connected to seven thousand other neurons, in a dense web of more than 150,000 kilometers of nerve fibers. This is a ridiculous number—it's more than enough nerve fiber to wrap around the earth three times. Our neurons can connect any neuron to any other in six jumps or less. The ancient people were no different from us in this respect. They, too, were Homo sapiens, just like us, only less educated.

So, look carefully because the Ancient Ones have secrets to tell us. But most of us are too arrogant in our knowledge and conceited in our wealth to listen to the murmurs from the dusty past. In this book, I will tell you some of those long-lost secrets that have not been told since civilization was young.

*****

The Ubaidians lived in Iraq for over 1,000 years without knowing how to how to read and write. But they figured out how to drain the marshes for agriculture, develop trade, and establish industries such as weaving, leather work, metalwork, masonry, and pottery.

Writing would come with the arrival of a Caucasian people from Anatolia some time before 3300 BC. These were called *Sumerians*. Their language became the prevailing language of the territory. They introduced a number of technological and cultural contributions, including the first wheeled vehicles and potter's wheels; the first system of writing (cuneiform); the first codes of law. They built cities of mud bricks with monumental architecture, city walls, and the first city-states.

The Sumerians invented the wheel by about 3500 BC. They formulated the earliest concepts in algebra and geometry. They developed a system of weights and measures which served the ancient world until the Roman period. Their money was based on shekel weights of silver. Many of the constellations were mapped by the Sumerians. They created the zodiac still in use today. The symbols and names have changed only slightly but remain true to the originals, with one symbol for each planet they believed to exist. They developed a system of mathematics based on the number 60 which is still used in the measurement of time, today. They invented a calendar system still used by the Jews to this day.

The Sumerians developed a complex system of sewers and flush toilets to rid cities of waste and the unhealthy effects of swamps. They smelted metals and invented bronze. They mined precious metals with which they created any number of fine works of art. They made cylinder seals which were used to make images by rolling them across damp clay, often to tell a story. They had schools for their children. They created laws to regulate society. They wrote the first Farmer's Almanac.

Many of the Sumerian texts tell stories which were later plagiarized by the Jews, who thereby used such pilfered fables to deceive and betray the Christians and to mislead and deceive the Muslims—see *Monsters of Babylon*. Such stories as: the creation of man from a lump of clay by a Jewish god; the resurrection of a divine son of a Jewish god; Adam in the garden of Eden where Eve is seduced by a snake; the Flood caused by a wrathful Jewish god in which a giant boat—an impossibly enormous boat—was used to save from drowning two of every critter on Earth; and the super-strong Jew Samson, among other tall tales. These were all invented 2,000 years before there were any lying Jews to tell them!

And most important of all: The Sumerians inherited a greatly destructive ancient weapon from the Ubaidians and refined it into the Sumerian Swindle. With this ancient invention, anyone who wielded this weapon could destroy entire nations, annihilate entire populations, enslave all of mankind, and own for their personal possession the entire planet, along with all of its wealth.

The Sumerian Swindle was so secret that even today's scientists and modern scholars have been unable to understand its workings or to correctly recognize its destructive power. Modern scholars are just like the ancient people who could see the ravages of the bubonic plague, where millions of people perished and entire countries were desolated, while they attributed that disease to demons or to the wrath of God. Likewise, our modern scholars also can see the ravages wrought by the Sumerian Swindle but are blind as to its causal vector. The results of its destructive power are obvious but its cause is invisible to them.

Throughout history, this ancient and terrible weapon has destroyed entire countries, snuffed out the lives of hundreds of millions of people worldwide, created starvation, disease, warfare, and ecological doom, with very few people learning the true cause of such disasters. The Sumerian Swindle actually has the power to *destroy the entire world*. And it is being used today for just that purpose by the same ancient monsters who perfected it.

So really, how can you think that the ancient people were so dumb if we modern people, and even our greatest scientists, still cannot understand the knowledge or the inventions of Ancient Man? Better think again and ask yourself, "How smart are our modern scientists and philosophers today, if they don't understand even the simplest inventions from antiquity? How smart are our political and religious leaders if the inventions of 3500 BC are too complicated for them?"

You should have some respect for the intellectual achievements of Ancient Man because his inventions have not only shaped our modern world, but those same inventions also threaten to destroy it. I am not referring to destroying the world with nuclear bombs or genetically-modified germs. I am referring to destroying the world with the very ancient and very top-secret mechanisms of the Sumerian Swindle.

CHAPTER 2

THE SUMERIAN SWINDLE:
THE ANCIENT SECRET OF
WEALTH AND POWER

You readers who are bankers or Jews or other assorted thieves and con artists might want to skip this chapter since you already know how to betray your country and defraud your people. But for those of you who don't like being enslaved and impoverished, learning something about how the Jews do it can save your health, your wealth, your family, your people and your nation from poverty and destruction.

First, we must understand some basic cogs in the machinery that make the Sumerian Swindle work. I am writing down these secrets for the very first time in history so if you didn't think of them first, yourself, then perhaps it is because you have taken them for granted because they "have always been here."

The Sumerian Swindle started like this: If you are on good terms with your next-door neighbor, and you run short of some flour or eggs in the middle of cooking supper, a neighborly thing to do is to run next door or send your children next door to borrow what you need until you can go to the market and restock supplies. After shopping, you will repay your neighbor for the borrowed food.

Such borrowing among neighbors has been going on ever since people began living together in groups—that is, for the past ten or twenty million years. Borrowing and repaying, is a way to build friendships and to sustain society. Borrowing and repaying, is a vital mechanism in every human society. But it became corrupted among the Ubaidian money-lenders. Something about this natural human relationship changed. Perhaps one neighbor got tired of constantly lending out grain to another neighbor who was slow to repay. So, it happened that at a certain time, the lending neighbor agreed to lend out a measure of grain only if the borrower agreed to repay a measure and a handful; or perhaps a basket of grain was lent out in return for a basket-and-a-half in repayment; or perhaps, sensing the reluctance of a neighbor to loan, the borrower, himself, out of charitable good will and personal need, offered to repay two baskets of grain for one loaned. Whatever the actual origin of the mechanism, the Sumerians evolved a system that we today call, "interest on a loan."

Central grain storehouses were a part of every town. And in every town and village, individual grain storage space was a part of every house. So, when the larder was empty, borrowing from a neighbor kept starvation from the door and promoted friendly relations among neighbors in a harmonious society of give and take.

But something else occurred in the actual understanding of this development in the minds of both the borrower and the lender. A borrower who repays the loan has nothing left in his hands to contemplate. But the lender who gains back the loan plus interest has more than he started with to contemplate. The poor man becomes even poorer than he originally was and the rich man becomes even is richer than he was. The actual physical ownership of the grain plus interest enabled the lender to accumulate an ever-increasing store of goods. In addition to what he started with, both the returned loan as well as the interest could be loaned out at interest. And that interest when repaid could again be loaned out in a spiraling increase in total wealth.

This was the beginning of the Sumerian Swindle, the charging of simple interest on a loan. Two baskets of grain on loan at 50% interest brought back three baskets. These three could again be loaned at 50% interest to bring back four-and-a-half. These four-and-a-half could again be loaned to bring back six and three-quarters. In a short time, those original two baskets produced an additional four and three-quarters baskets of grain for free. And so on, and so on, as an increasing spiral of profits accumu-lated for free and for doing no work other than making loans. As the size and number of loans increased, the total wealth of the grain lender began to increase far beyond the wealth of his neighbors.

Then, a magical and mysterious thing happened. Once a certain profit point had been reached where the lender was loaning out not his original grain but the grain that he had previously received as interest, then everything that he profited from that point onward was wealth given to him for free. The grain that he received as interest-on-the-loan had cost him nothing. And when he loaned out that same grain at interest, both it and its returning interest were free grain that had also cost him nothing. This free grain continued to multiply over time as it was loaned out again and again. Huge mountains of grain filling his storerooms to the rafters began to accumulate, free grain which had cost him absolutely nothing more than charging interest-on-a-loan.

In those days, a man's wealth was measured by how much land and grain he had and by how many goats and sheep that he owned. Very soon, those Ubaidian grain lenders were enjoying vast fortunes. Thanks to the arithmetic deception of lending-at-interest, they were loaning out at interest what they had gotten for free.

Eventually, using that free grain in barter for other goods, everything that they owned actually had cost them absolutely nothing at all!

The lender found that by loaning out a basket of grain, he got back two baskets instead. Of course, a light bulb did not go off in his head because it was still the Stone Age, seven thousand years before Benjamin Franklin and Thomas Edison, but certainly the very first loan shark had a major brainstorm! Without working under the hot sun, without lifting a single load in a basket upon his head, without walking a single step, two baskets of grain were delivered to his door. And the one who delivered the grain was glad to do it since the loan had helped him through a difficult time. After all, they were all fellow villagers and all on good relations with one another.

The hatred would come later.

Grain could be bartered for goats, and goats traded for woven cloth and boats; and boats and goats and grain could be exchanged for houses and irrigated land, etc. By loaning out grain at interest and using the interest-income to barter for other goods, a clever trader could leverage his way to more wealth than any of his neighbors even though all of them had started off at the same level in society. Like the modern bankers who pile up their swindled wealth into skyscrapers, yachts, private jets, investments in war and cornering the commodities market, the Ubaidian moneylenders began to pile up wealth in grain, silver, and land. Whether as an ancient grain dealer or as a modern banker, they got all this swindled wealth for free! By getting something for nothing simply by charging interest on a loan, they had discovered Secret Fraud #1 of the Sumerian Swindle: *"All interest on the loan of money is a swindle."*

It might seem odd, but the fact is that all of the excessive wealth of modern-day bankers, financiers, loan sharks, Jews, and related swindlers, is based upon nothing more than two baskets of barley creating three. Secret Fraud #1 of the Sumerian Swindle was based upon what people all over the world had been doing for tens of thousands of years. If one member of a village or tribe was short of supplies, other members would give or loan him what he needed. And when he was able, he would return the borrowed goods or else return goods of equal value. But to insist that he return more than he had borrowed—that was the swindle.

*****

In all farming communities, drought, insects, fire, rain, flooding, and a myriad of woes plague farmers. So, there are always farmers who need a loan to get through the bad spell. Lending and paying back, borrowing and returning, have always been a part of normal human society. If a farmer needed a basket of grain for his family, he would borrow it from a neighbor. And when the harvest came in, he would repay what he had borrowed.

This was a natural and a balanced exchange system; no one profited and no one lost. And, the entire community benefited so civilization thrived in a natural way. Goods were distributed in an equitable way which was good and natural and fair to everybody.

However, once a lender asked for more in return than what he had lent, an unnatural imbalance was introduced into society. No longer were men equal and dependent upon their work for their material rewards in life. Interest-on-a-loan created the inequality of those who became *rich* without actually working for their wealth and those who became *poor* in spite of incessant labor. In other words, charging interest-on-a-loan automatically created a diseased situation in society where the rich sucked the life out of the poor. It created two social classes, one class of financial vampires living off of the blood and sweat of a permanently impoverished laboring class.

But lending at interest has been going on for longer than anyone can remember. So, why is lending-at-interest an unnatural phenomenon? That it is unnatural, can be seen by looking at Mother Nature, herself. Making loans by those who "have" to those who "do not have," is a natural attribute of all sentient beings who live in social groups. No matter what creatures or even what forms of symbiotic animal or plant life that you care to study, you will find that lending and paying back, is one of the characteristics that keep societies of social creatures both strong and prosperous.

Ants and bees create huge societies of individual members who make loans to one another as a part of their daily life. Indeed, without loans the bee and ant colonies would have died out hundreds of millions of years ago. When an ant is hungry, she approaches another member of her colony, taps a few appropriate messages with her antenna against the antenna of her sister ant, and if this sister ant has food in her stomach, she will regurgitate a portion and give it to the hungry one to eat. In this manner, enormous amounts of labor and time are saved since the hungry ant does not have to travel back to the colony for a meal but can approach the lunch wagon no farther than the nearest worker. Thus, the colony can extend its power over a greater scavenging area through this mutual system of colony-wide food distribution and sharing. In many more ways, this loaning of food between ants gives the entire colony more power, success, and prosperity. Later, after she has eaten her fill back at the colony food larder or from scavenged foods found in the field, the borrowing ant eventually returns food from its stomach to whichever hungry sister ant that asks. The same is true for bees.

Thus, it can be seen that "loaning" and "borrowing" and "paying back" are all part of animal social groups that increase the prosperity and survivability of the entire colony. No individual loses and no individual gains because it is a balanced and a natural system in which all members benefit. Not a single one of those humble insects ever asks for more than it needs, nor does it amass for itself a special hoard of crumbs or honey stashed in a private and secret hideaway that is a result of them taking but not giving back. The ants and bees have been making interest-free loans to one another for a billion years and they have thrived as social creatures while we modern people have had greedy bankers and moneylenders since only about 3500 BC and yet our societies fail and crumble with wars and want. Is this example too complicated for you Readers who are swindling bankers, thieving financiers, and lying economists?

Ancient man, also, has borrowed and loaned and paid back. As a result, everybody has benefited and everybody has survived. But modern man has been charging interest on loans for the past 5,000 years and we are racked and ruined with warfare, famine, disease, ecological destruction and many other social catastrophes while the fat bankers preen themselves in their luxury chalets and counting houses. This is all a result of the Sumerian Swindle. Even a lowly lichen adhering to a rock is a higher and more natural life form than is a moneylender, financier, or banker.

Mankind is a social creature who makes loans to his fellows. Perhaps the hunt for game one day was unlucky for one family group so they would share in the roasted antelope that their neighbor had caught that day. And when they were lucky in the hunt, they would share their fresh deer meat with that same neighbor who had not been lucky or else share a basket of grain or acorns or berries. In this way, mankind, as a social creature, was able to thrive through the power of mutual helpfulness and sharing. Making loans to one another and paying back, gave the entire tribe more resiliency and strength. If one had food, all had food. In this way, everybody survived through mutual help and no one died through neglect.

But woe to the greedy or selfish tribe members who were anti-social by refusing to share what they had! Woe to those who borrowed but did not give back! They became ignored and ostracized. They were known as "takers." They only took but did not give back. And if they didn't get the social message when their own wants were rebuffed, then eventually they became outcasts and perished alone in the wilderness with no tribe to sustain them. In this way, natural selection improved mankind as a social creature. Like the ants and bees who shared in mutual prosperity, mankind was also at one with Nature as he used loans and sharing for greater group strength and solidarity. Love of one's neighbor was expressed through giving. And through giving and sharing, strong personal and social bonds were forged, providing the ancient people with strength against all adversaries.

To fully understand the Sumerian Swindle, throw aside your conditioning and your "take-it-for-granted" state of mind and understand from a new perspective this system of "interest-on-a-loan." The First Secret Fraud of the Sumerian Swindle is: "All interest on the loan of money is a swindle." That's right. Every banker and moneylender is a deceiving thief and a cruel swindler although he tries to keep this fact hidden. So, to make it easy to understand—simplify, simplify.

In modern times, the Sumerian Swindle is like the old shell game of hiding a pea under a shell. This game is so simple: just one pea and three walnut shells. And yet the pea gets lost from view both by the quick moving and mixing up of the walnut shells by the deft manipulations of the huckster using sleight-of-hand. A good street hustler using nothing but three walnut shells and a pea, can separate the gawking suckers from their money in a short time if they place their bets on the wrong shell because he can always make sure that it is the wrong shell.

Bankers and moneylenders also use sleight-of-hand in concealing their thefts but theirs is a sleight-of-hand by juggling numbers. This was something beyond the knowledge of the majority of the Ubaidian people but very well understood by the lenders.

All interest on the loan of money is a swindle. The modern moneylenders and bankers are all criminals. Part of the trick in their black art, is that moneylenders have been around since Mesopotamian times so that these parasites have been taken for granted and accepted as a "normal" part of society. But bankers are not at all normal. They are all crooks. However well-dressed and honest they pretend to be, the bankers are no different than a street hustler manipulating a pea among walnut shells. But to make the game more to their benefit, they manipulate trillions of peas between billions of walnut shells so that no one seems to be able to keep track of where all the money goes except themselves. That all of the money disappears into the bankers' pockets isn't noticed in the confusion caused by some winners and some losers milling about and wondering what happened to the economy.

For the sake of unraveling this ancient mystery in a simple way, let's assume that there is only one moneylender in the whole world and only two pieces of money. The two pieces of money can be lumps of gold or silver, pennies, francs, yuan, marks, dollars, whatever name you wish to use for them—but there are only two of them. I could use two dollars for this example or even two pennies but because the Mesopotamians used shekel weights of silver in their system of exchange, let's do the same for this example as well as for the examples given later. A shekel of silver was about one-third ounce or about eight grams—roughly the weight of one paperclip. Let's assume that there are only two shekels of silver in the whole world.

Now suppose that there are two men who want to borrow from the moneylender one shekel of silver each. Either they are merchants or farmers or perhaps only a parent wishing to have a big wedding party and dowry for a beloved daughter. Each man goes to the moneylender to borrow one shekel of silver, which is loaned at 50% interest for one year with their farms and personal property offered as security that the loan would be repaid.

Now, remember (for the sake of this illustration) there are only two shekels of silver in the entire world. At 50% interest for each shekel, that means that each borrower must return one-and-a-half shekels to the banker at the end of the year. If each man returns to the banker one and a half shekels, that adds up to a total of three shekels that the banker will have in his hands. But remember, there are only two shekels of silver in the entire world! So, how can these borrowers return to the banker three shekels of silver? In fact, it is impossible.

Because they could not repay the interest on the loan, the moneylender could seize their farms and personal goods which were worth far more than the loan, itself. They were swindled out of their valuable properties because repaying the interest is impossible because the amount of money necessary to do so, does not exist. And it can never exist because the interest added to the loans are mere numbers and not real money.

We can see the workings of the Sumerian Swindle when the problem is simplified like this. But this swindle is hidden from the average man because in reality, the amounts of money are so large and they involve so many borrowers that the swindle is not so easily perceived. And yet, there is always less money available in reality than what the banker demands because the arithmetic creates something that is not really there—*phantom money*, an extra shekel out of thin air. You can say that it is all just simple arithmetic but the ancient moneylenders called it quite simply, "A miracle!" Real money that appears from out of the imaginary numbers on a ledger book!

At first, the ethics of the Ubaidian moneylenders was not much different than that of their own people. Small towns keep their individual people adhering to society's norms through social pressures and gossip. In the small villages where everybody knew everybody else, it was very rare for one neighbor to steal from or to swindle another without everybody finding out about it. Retribution was either exacted with fisticuffs or death, or the neighborly aggressor would be called before the council of elders or the village chief and the disagreements would come under public scrutiny. It was social pressure alone that kept those who loaned-at-interest within a reasonableness that was conducive to social harmony. These are the facts of small village life. If people are to get along, then one citizen cannot be allowed to prey upon another.

Strangely enough, for such a dishonest system, money lending depends upon the goodness and honesty of mankind. It posits the proposition that anyone who borrows is obligated by the honor of his name and the holiness of his promise sworn before the gods, to repay the principal and interest on the loan. This is where the swindle gets most of its power because *it relies upon the borrower being honest.* It relies upon the borrower being honorable. It relies upon the borrower being god-fearing and true to his word. But it does not depend upon the lender of money to be any of these things. Thus, Secret Fraud #2 was incorporated at an early time: *"Loans rely on the honesty of the borrower but not the honesty of the lender."*

By 4000 BC, not only had the Ubaidians developed small towns and an organized society but they had also developed into two social classes which were later named by the Sumerians as the *awilum* (the Haves) and the *muskenum* (the Have-Nots). This system of getting back more than they lent out, developed over a period of more than a thousand years. So, the incremental change in the wealth and power of the awilum (the Haves) over the muskenum (the Have-Nots) was not noticed since it was so gradually accomplished. Through many generations, rich fathers taught their sons how to parasitize their neighbors and the poor fathers taught their sons that, after borrowing grain from the awilum (the Haves), then the honest thing to do was to pay back that grain plus interest because "that's how it has always been." Instead of lending-at-interest being recognized as an aberration and a swindle, the system itself began to be accepted as normal because "it has always been here."

For the awilum (the Haves), this loan-plus-interest became an asset that could be passed along to his sons. And the original loan that had cost them nothing and which brought them more wealth for free in interest payments, could also be passed from one generation to the next as grain- and silver-lending families bequeathed to their descendants the fruits of usury as ongoing accounts. Eventually, the wealthy families and wealthy individuals arose who, through greed and acquisitive barter, were able to gain a large share of the total wealth of the community. Over many generations, those families became owners of large properties and the employers of many laborers to work those properties. Farms, silver, grain, land, and slaves, all became theirs. And they got it all for free.

Lending-at-interest became commonly accepted as an ordinary part of the pre-literate Mesopotamian society simply because it "has always been here." The rich insisted on their "rights of ownership" and the poor accepted their poverty since it was brought upon them so gradually by the subtle swindle of constantly paying out more than they owed, that they didn't notice the decline of their well-being.

Later, a new fraud was developed when the farmers could see no reason to pay back loans of grain to lenders who already had more than they needed. As fellow citizens, it didn't seem fair that a rich grain lender would demand payment from a poor farmer who barely had enough to eat. So, the farmers, being honest and fair folks, began to only pay back the principal but not the interest on the loan. In response, the lenders began to demand that loans-at-interest be secured with property. As a result, loans which were not repaid plus the interest, forfeited the farm. In this way, the lenders began to acquire not only more grain and silver for free but also free farms, as they enforced Secret Fraud #3: *"Collateral that is worth more than the loan, is the banker's greatest asset."*

Social upheaval did not occur immediately because there was still vacant land that could be settled, so there was still a place for the dispossessed to move to. Through the loaning of grain or silver at interest and then being dispossessed of their farms, the People were forced to dig new irrigation systems and build up the raw land located farther from the rivers. Although loans-at-interest had worked its inevitable evil, the effects were diluted because there was still places for the people to go. The poor did not rise up and kill the rich but a greater social distance developed between the rich and the poor. As villages grew into cities, and there was a greater social distance and impersonality between the wealthy who lent money and the poor who borrowed from them, a more callous, ruthless attitude developed in the rich and a more seething hatred developed in the poor.

Once society accepted the legitimacy of collecting interest-on-a-loan and once the cities grew into more impersonal sizes, the moneylenders were free to take whatever profits they could, even by resorting to force. And force was often necessary when the moneylender wanted to dispossess a family from their lands and possessions. Pulling a struggling child from the arms of a fighting and screaming mother and father required force. Pushing entire families off their farms required force. And with increased wealth, the moneylenders who did not have enough strong sons and male relatives, became the employers of guards and goons and strong-armed gangs of enforcers. There were no laws in those days to prevent a moneylender from physically enforcing his dispossession of a debtor's property.

The moneylenders could get away with their swindles because they were swindling honest people who mistakenly assumed that the moneylenders also were honest and their loans were legitimate. Recall Secret Fraud #2 of the Sumerian Swindle is: "Loans rely on the honesty of the borrower but not the honesty of the lender."

*****

If you have ever inspected a modern credit card contract or any other banking document, there is always "fine print". In addition to the tiny print that is difficult to read, it is often printed with gray ink, making it even more difficult to decipher. Have you ever wondered why this is so? If the modern bankers and credit card companies are honest businessmen, then why do they use tricks and deceit in order to trick you into entering into one of their fraudulent contracts? Basically, bankers and credit card companies are all swindlers. Their entire industry is criminal in nature, so secrecy, tricks, and deceit are part and parcel of the bankers' business methods.

The methods of modern bankers are built upon the exact same methods employed by the ancient moneylenders of Sumeria. The bankers are all crooks trying to swindle you out of your property, but they demand that you, yourself, must be honest and true to your word. They present you with a fraudulent contract to sign which stipulates how they are going to steal from you. And they expect you to keep the agreement, honestly and true, even though they, themselves, are neither honest nor true. The moneylenders demand that you honestly repay to them with interest what they have dishonestly defrauded from you. This is what modern moneylenders and bankers do to you but it was worse for the people of ancient Mesopotamia.

Just as a modern banker can have the sheriff throw you into the street and seize your personal property, for the ancient Mesopotamians the prospect of slavery was an additional punishment. And so, Secret Fraud #2 of the Sumerian Swindle is also one of its best kept secrets. Although the moneylenders are all crooks who defraud you out of your possessions, they hypocritically demand that you, who are their victims, be honest and pay them your money. Bankers refuse to loan money to thieving crooks because they are the thieving crooks who only make loans to honest people.

Life was good and profitable for the awilum (the Haves) as they gained more and more properties and goods through lending-at-interest. Those with great wealth tend to demand luxury since they can afford the extra expense. It became fashionable for people with wealth to buy the best of garments, which in those days was merely a wrap-around, and the fanciest of trinkets.

Bartering for goods and equating goods to baskets of grain, began a system where trade could be accomplished between a variety of mixed goods merely by equating each of them to an agreed upon amount of grain, then trading each of the goods by their value in grain.

And there was something else among all of the dusty trade goods in that dusty and dry country of ancient Iraq that was also desirable. The silver metal that was too soft for anything except ornaments or shiny cups and trinkets, had a trade value also. Silver was rarer than baskets of grain and had to be imported from distant lands. Because of its rarity and durability, a small amount of silver could be traded for a large amount of grain or for goats or lands or houses. The trade ratio between this shiny metal and what people were willing to trade for it was quite high.

Soon it was accepted that a purse containing a few shekels of silver was equal to huge piles of grain, numerous goats and sheep, oxen, fields of barley, houses and any other thing for which men and women bartered and traded. Thus, silver became a useful and relatively light weight method for exchanging goods. Although not a true form of money, silver became a type of commodity money. Silver was not valuable because of any intrinsic value in and by itself, but simply because men and women desired to have it for what could be bartered for or bought with it. As a shiny metal commodity, it could be made into a ring or a bracelet and carried about and traded in that form. Or it could be an in-between trade good such as in trading a goat for some silver in one town and then trading that same silver for some jars of beer in another town. Because it could be used to buy anything, it became the most desirable of all things because it could be traded for all things. In ancient Sumeria, silver could be traded for anything.

All metals like silver and gold came from outside of Mesopotamia. These imports were much in demand for jewelry and for the decoration of the temples. Because of their relative scarcity when compared with other goods, it took many commodities to trade for very small quantities of either silver or gold. It was not that silver and gold had any value of their own, but their relative scarcity allowed small amounts of them to be traded for large amounts of other things. It was this scarcity in ratio to the abundance of other things that gave them their value. So the awilum (the Haves) who wore silver and gold rings and bracelets and broaches, displayed their wealth not only as jewelry but as the large amounts of grain and the many goats that such jewelry could buy. A silver bracelet that had cost many goats, was an impressive piece of shiny metal to every farmer who only owned a few goats. Such silver rings, bracelets and necklaces were instantly recognized by everybody for the large amount of commodities they could buy, thus giving high social status to the wealthy ones who wore them.

A rich man or one of his wives could flaunt their wealth by wearing a silver necklace weighing 12 shekels of silver [96 grams or 4 ounces] which was the value of a plow ox or the value of 18 goats or the value of hiring 15 farm hands for the entire day. The same amount if silver could hire more than 30 strong-arm goons to help in evicting a farm family from their foreclosed property. For the moneylenders, that silver necklace had cost them *nothing* because they had purchased it from the silversmith with silver that they had gotten for free from their moneylending business. Strutting around wearing valuable jewelry that had cost them nothing, buying or foreclosing on farms and houses that had cost them nothing, eating the best of foods that cost them nothing, wearing the best of garments that cost them nothing, living in homes that had cost them nothing, these moneylenders very soon developed a rather "lordly" attitude toward the people around them. The merchant- moneylenders lived like gods without effort and in great style while the people from whom they swindled, had to work laboriously from sunrise to sunset just for enough to eat.

Although the basic system of commerce in Mesopotamia was barter, silver became in all respects the money of the ancient Near East. It was bartered in shekel weights, and each shekel weighed about eight grams. Using these weights and measures and the clay tablet accounting records which they wrote, we know what the wages and prices were in those ancient times.

Silver was a barter commodity that evolved into a kind of commodity money that could be used as a medium of exchange for everything. A farmer might refuse to trade his grain for a hundred-weight of raw wool but he would gladly trade it for a few shekel-weights of silver. He could then trade the silver for some new garments and a new mortar and pestle for his wife and the baby goats that he really wanted.

One lump of gold is of no use in commerce because the entire society cannot do business trading among themselves with one lump of gold. So, except between kings and bullion merchants and money changers who dealt in very large amounts, gold's extreme rarity limited its usefulness as a type of money. Silver, however, is rare but not so rare that it wasn't plentiful enough to be used as a medium of exchange. Although one lump of gold is useless in business, a thousand lumps of silver begin to make the wheels of business turn, as they were traded back and forth between buyers and sellers. Thus, silver became the basis of the monetary systems that developed in the ancient Near East.

Silver, itself, is as worthless as sand because whatever value it has, is given to it by the mutual agreement of men. As a metal, it lasts for ages and does not deteriorate like cloth or cooking oil or grain or even the land, itself. As long as it could be traded for anything in addition to acting as a form of money, it also became a method to store wealth. A ton of grain could be sold for silver. A parcel of land could be sold for silver. A slave could be sold for silver. A house could be sold for silver. And years later, when the grain was eaten, the land washed away by the river, the slave dead of old age and the house fallen down in an earthquake, the silver could be taken out of its hiding place and fresh grain, more land, a young slave and a new house could be bought with that silver. Silver, thus became a very valuable and useful commodity metal that was recognized very early as useful both as a medium of exchange and as a storage of wealth. Anything could be sold for silver and that silver could then buy anything else.

*****

Great wealth also brought problems for the wealthy. Through lending-at-interest and then dispossessing the borrower, the awilum (the Haves) began to acquire more land than they or their relatives could possibly farm. They acquired more foreclosed houses and fish ponds and boats and farm animals than they could possibly manage themselves. Human resentments being what they are, the moneylenders found it difficult to hire a farmer to work on the same field that they had swindled from him. Farmers who had lost their land to the grain and silver lenders preferred to start afresh by digging new irrigation ditches and cultivating new fields farther out in the arid lands.

To solve his problem of too many foreclosed properties and untended flocks, the Ubaidian moneylenders began to hire laborers from the north of Mesopotamia. Those Northerners (Subarians) were poor hunter- gatherers without farms or farming skills. In exchange for the usual wages of grain and oil, woven cloth, and beer, they became the cheap immigrant laborers of pre-literate Mesopotamia. Using carefully controlled wages and strong-arm tactics from his foremen and enforcers, the awilum (the Haves) were able to keep these poor people hard at work. The Ubaidian word for "slave" became "Subarian."

Although the cuneiform archives name them as Subarians—a name which meant "slave"—in fact these names were not ethnic or tribal references at all. The four directions named in Sumerian were North (Subar), South (Sumer), West (Amurru), and East (Elam) and the city of Babylon later became the center of it all. Thus, the names of these people that have come down to us indicate, not their ethnicity or country of origin, but the direction in which they resided.

As the moneylenders hired more and more Subarians from the north to work the land, the displaced and foreclosed poor Ubaidians were forced to seek refuge in the temples as servants or to hire themselves out as muskenum (the Have-Nots) laborers or to work on the land as tenant farmers. Once-proud landowning farmers who had been among the class of awilum (the Haves), were reduced to being landless paupers working for a daily bowl of barley porridge. They had been swindled of their land to become the slaves of those who had lent to them at interest. This led to a great deal of rebelliousness among these displaced workers and resent-ments toward the *tamkarum* (merchant-moneylenders) who had taken their farms and enslaved their children. Grumbling and threatening mobs of hungry muskenum (Have-Nots) were a growing threat to the money-lenders' personal security.

The moneylenders found that they could increase their profits by importing large numbers of foreign workers from the Subar (the North) to work the lands. These poor Subarians did not ask so much for their pay since they were happy to merely have a bowl of barley porridge and a pot of beer for their labor. And if the moneylending landlord gave them enough barley and beer to also support a wife, then he could hire a devoted worker. Surrounded by cheap immigrant labor, the displaced Ubaidian farmers became more docile when they found, to their great terror, that if they did not work for the awilum (the Haves) as cheaply as the immigrants and without grumbling, then they would starve to death as the foreign workers displaced them in the fields and in the brick yards. Cheap labor was the ever-desired goal of the awilum (Haves), who greedily always wanted more by taking it away from those who had less. This is still seen in modern times where immigrant labor is used by the wealthy (the Haves) to defraud, swindle, dispossess, and betray the very people among whom they are allowed to live without getting hanged for it.

And so, huge tracts of land were worked both by foreign Subarians whom the moneylenders brought in from the North and by the impoverished Ubaidians who worked the estates of the temple and of the King.

*****

Thus, through money lending, the Ubaidian people were defrauded of their homes and were displaced by hired immigrant labor. The farmers became servants on their own lands. Because this would be a recurring theme throughout the history of the entire world, it should be studied in detail here.

How can less-developed and more-primitive foreign people displace the more advanced citizens of a country? There are *three stages* to this displacement, beginning with treason from above found in the greed of the tamkarum (merchant-moneylenders).

First, cheap foreign laborers are brought in by the moneylenders and landlords under the protection of their own high social status and their fraudulent "ownership" of the land. The Ubaidian people accepted the ancient "ownership swindle" in which the awilum (the Haves) can "do what they want with their own property." This attitude was also accepted by the Ubaidian landowners whose property was next to the foreign tenant farmers, working the foreclosed properties owned by the moneylenders, simply because they saw no danger in denying what they considered to be their own rights as property owners, themselves. This attitude was also accepted by the grumbling itinerant workers and debt-slaves because they didn't have any choice. They were the voiceless and powerless "Have-Nots."

Thus, using the smokescreen of land ownership—that is, "this is my property and I will do with it as I please no matter how many people I harm"—the awilum (the Haves) moved foreign workers into the country to work cheaply and increase their personal profits, while forcing the displaced workers of their own country and of their own city-state, into silence by threat of unemployment and starvation.

Second, when foreign people live as minorities among any population where they are outnumbered, they usually assume a very friendly, cheerful, and helpful attitude toward the majority population in an effort to be accepted and to blend into society. Through continuing friendliness, they tend to disarm the populace of any distrust and resentment of their un-asked-for presence. Through persistent friendliness, the danger that they pose is overlooked and forgotten.

And *third*, once this foreign population has reproduced and immigrated to a number that approaches a nearly equal or superior number to the host population, they give up their previously cheerful and friendly attitude and begin to assert a more aggressive and acquisitive character as they strive to take for themselves the land and properties that are owned or rented by the original population. This is subversion and disenfran-chisement from below. This is something that the devious moneylenders recognized at a very early stage in their success as parasites. And this is a three-stage pattern that you will see repeated over the next 7,000 years, right up to the present times as the merchant-moneylenders betray and impoverish their own people by hiring cheap, foreign labor.

Unlike small tribal societies where personal loyalties are of paramount importance, the distance that great wealth created between the rich and the poor, gave the rich an impersonal interest in the poor. The Ubaidian moneylenders, shrewdly peering through their slit-like, half-closed eyelids, swindled the land away from and created a sub-class of the working poor among their own people. To further enrich themselves, they hired the cheaper Subarian laborers who undercut the pay scale of the workers. As more and more Subarians were immigrated into the country, the wages paid by the awilum (the Haves) decreased because they could hire foreigners at a cheaper price.

So, through foreign immigration, the social distance between the rich and the poor grew even wider and more impersonal. The Ubaidian land owners thought nothing of hiring foreigners while their own people either starved or worked for starvation wages. There were no laws against it in those ancient times, so as long as they profited in shekels of silver, then it was all okay. Why should they care?

As wages fell through cheap immigration, the wealth of the tamkarum (merchant-moneylenders) increased. So, they bought up and re-sold vast properties to a foreign Caucasian people from the Iranian plateau. These people entered Mesopotamia from the South, from Sumer. So, they were called Sumerians. They brought with them abundant silver to buy up the foreclosed properties from the Ubaidian moneylenders who were only too happy to sell their surplus lands to these foreigners from the south.

But the Sumerians were not fools. They asked the Ubaidian moneylenders, "Why do you betray your own people to us by selling us their land? They are your own people?"

The Ubaidian moneylenders were born and raised in Mesopotamia. They had lived there all their lives. So, one might think that if they were not filled with a patriotic enthusiasm toward the good of their country, then at least they would have a neighborly warmth in their hearts toward their fellow citizens. Shrewdly peering through their slit-like, half-closed eyelids as they sized up their questioners, those wily merchant-moneylenders, those "gentlemen" and expert salesmen that they were, gave a reply that has become a standard throughout the ages.

"What are those people to us? They are not our friends because they hate us and wish to do us harm. We have loaned them silver and helped them to buy land and purchase property. As the great god Enlil is our witness, we have done everything that we can to loan them silver and help them buy the best farms and the finest orchards.

But still they hate us for our goodness and generosity because they are full of bigotry and hatred. But you are our friends. You can protect us from those who hate us. So, we will give our friends a good deal in buying whatever goods and properties you want because we own much lands and will make you a good bargain. We will loan you silver in any amount at low interest rates because you are our friends. And to further show our friendship, we have many fine daughters who will make fine wives for your sons."

Thus, the Ubaidian moneylenders sold their foreclosed farms to people from outside of Mesopotamia, to foreigners from the south (Sumer) and east (Elam) who had silver in abundance. These people are known to us as Sumerians simply because they arrived in Mesopotamia from the south, from "the Sumer."

The Sumerians were a much more intelligent people than the poor Subarians (the "northerners"). They knew a bargain when they saw it; and the agricultural abundance of Mesopotamia was what they wanted. The Sumerians were not interested in becoming the paid servants and the poor laborers of the Ubaidian landlords like the Subarians were. So, they traded their silver bangles and rings for the farms and fields which the awilum (the Haves) had owned.

And like blood-sucking fleas, the moneylenders jumped from their old victims who hated them, onto their new victims who innocently accepted the moneylenders as their friends and guides and mentors. The ancient snake, with soft words and low interest rates, coiled around its prey. Its bite would come later.

Of course, as the Ubaidian moneylenders saw it, they were the "owners" of the land and had a right to sell it to whomever they chose. But in actual fact, nearly every shekel of silver and every parcel of land that they had, was a result of defrauding their own people through the swindles of moneylending and the confiscation of pledged collateral. They were robber-barons selling off their loot.

Because this system of lending-at-interest had existed long before the Sumerians had arrived, they accepted the Swindle without a second thought because "it had always been here." After all, by the time the Sumerians had arrived, the cities and towns of Mesopotamia were already over 3,000 years old. So, they accepted the entire system without question. The interest-on-a-loan, the Sumerians called *"mas,"* a word used for both calves and interest. So, this idea that interest could increase magically like the birth of a calf, concealed the Swindle during its earliest inception. That the interest was a swindle was known only to the moneylenders.

As the new landowners, the Sumerians brought in more and more of their relatives from the South until they became so numerous that the Ubaidian inhabitants of Mesopotamia entirely disappeared as an ethnic group and the land came under the complete domination and power of the Sumerians. These people greatly improved upon what the Ubaidians had developed and they produced inventions of their own. The Sumerians are credited as being the founders of civilization. In addition to their many positive contributions to mankind, they developed the Sumerian Swindle to its highest level of fraud and passed it along to the modern world as the demonic invention known as *compound interest.*

With their keen intelligence, they could see the potential of what the Ubaidians had built. They transformed the crude scratches on clay which the Ubaidians had used to count cows and baskets of grain, into a robust system of writing and mathematical calculation.

Writing, however, was not invented to record great poetry, epic myths, or novels. Writing was not invented to write down prayers and songs in praise of the gods. For millennia, poetry and epic tales of the Gods and Heroes had been transmitted orally by the bards, storytellers, and singers. So, there was no "necessity" to invent writing for that. What was needed was a method for recording the baskets of grain, the pots of beer, the numbers of ducks, and the various other commodities that were traded among the merchants and farmers. And writing was needed to record sales agreements and loan contracts. Thus, writing was originally invented as an accounting tool.

As early as 10,000 BC, the Ubaidians had used tokens of clay shaped as spheres, cones, rods, and discs the size of small marbles for simple household and market bookkeeping. This system worked well enough for six thousand years in Mesopotamia, developing with a variety of squiggles on the sides of the disks to record numbers.

During those six thousand years, the Ubaidians built large mud-brick towns and towering mud-brick temples while not even one person knew how to read or write. Six thousand years is a long time to be illiterate. And before that, as hunter-gatherers, Mankind did quite well for several millions of years without reading or writing a single word. *But to keep track of their pots of beer!* Now that was something about which no one wanted to lose count!

Around 3500 BC, the Sumerians discovered that those commodities that were represented by clay "things" could more easily be represented as scratches incised upon wet clay. Instead of having a heavy basketful of clay disks that represented the sacks of wool and pots of beer and baskets of grain that were owned by a temple or by a rich merchant, those commodities were found to be more efficiently recorded by a few squiggles and lines on a tablet of clay no bigger than one's open palm. With this invention, a thirty-kilogram basket of clay disks and spheres was replaced by a one-eighth kilogram clay tablet with markings on it that could record a whole city-full of baskets filled with clay markers.

When the Sumerians realized the potential power and usefulness of those scratches on wet clay, they improved upon them and created a complete writing and counting system known to us as cuneiform, meaning "wedge-shaped" [see Figure 2]. Writing was invented, not by novelists and poets in need of expressing their artistic urges, but by the bean counters in need of keeping track of their beans.

With the invention of writing, both time and distance were changed in relation to mankind. Distances were made shorter and time was made irrelevant. The simple clay writing tablets of the Sumerians erased the destructive influence of time, itself, because even the faintest markings on the clay tablets could carry the written ideas across the millennia to where our present-day scholars can read the very words and know the very thoughts of those ancient people.

With the invention of writing, contracts and treaties could be stored for eons without losing a single word of the original agreement. Distant kings could communicate with one another in words that could not be changed by either forgetfulness or distance. Without having to make perilous journeys, merchants could order exact amounts of goods with agreed upon prices from suppliers in distant countries. Contracts for the sale and rental of fields and farms with agreed upon payments and time schedules could be written down as proof of any business arrangement, and these could be stored for centuries without losing a single word in the contract or the smallest grain of silver in the payment. With writing, the Sumerians were able to weld the small villages and towns of Mesopotamia into powerful states aided by this new the power of communication. And all of this was accomplished with marks made upon wet clay without a single Jewish television program or Hollywood movie to corrupt their cultural progress. There were no Jews in the earliest civilizations, but they had moneylenders.

However great the invention of writing was for making complex civilizations possible, it was *the people who controlled the writing* who also controlled those complex civilizations. Since writing was actually invented by the merchants, then the merchants were the ones who first and foremost benefited from writing. And if a merchant did not know how to read and write, he could always hire a scribe to do it for him.

But here is a curious fact. However great an invention that writing is, how much attention do you give to it? Every day, do you look at some written words and sigh great "oohs" and "ahhs" at the very wonderfulness of written words? Or do you think nothing at all of reading and writing whatsoever? When you want to read or write something, you merely read and write. Don't you take for granted the reading-and-writing because you have been familiar with it for your entire life? I am setting up a trap here, so be careful.

The same can be said of the invention of the wheel. This simple device, which was also invented in Mesopotamia, carries the entire modern world. We would not have an industrial or even an efficient rural society without the wheel to drive our vehicles and turn our machinery. But do you stop in awe and stare in wonder every time an automobile drives by and point your finger in excitement at the rolling wheels and say, "Oh, look! A wheel! Look! A whole bunch of wheels!" Of course not! Wheels are so common. And they have been around since before we were born. So, we take them for granted as an ordinary part of life. I am setting up a trick here, so be careful.

Those things which have existed since before we were born, is something that everybody takes for granted. Automobiles, glass windows, forks and spoons, telephones, and millions of other items are examples of things to which we don't give a second thought since they have "always been here." We all grew from a baby to an adult with these inventions all around us. Right? Now, be careful, I am setting up a trick here.

But you know from your study of history, that automobiles, glass windows, telephones, etc., have not been here forever. You may even know from your modern collection of trivial information the names of the people who invented these things and even the dates when they were invented. But what could the ancient Mesopotamians know about the inventions of their own people? Literally, they could know nothing at all because all of their inventions were made before writing was developed.

Thanks to the archeologists, we know that between the first small Ubaidian villages and the beginnings of genuine civilization with the Sumerians, an amazing 6,000 years had gone by. Six thousand years of people sowing and reaping, raising their families and dying and not a one of them being able to read or write! I am setting up a trick here. So be careful and think about this a bit.

In relation to your own life, think about your own country and its history. Think about your own relatives and your own family and put this into perspective. If your parents are still living, do you remember your grandparents? What about your great-grand-parents? Can you remember them? Aside from some old photographs, what can you really say about your great-grand-parents? And certainly there is very little if anything that you can remember about your great-great-grand-parents since they died before you were born. And what can you know about your distant relatives from a hundred years ago? And even though you can read and write, what can you say about your relatives who lived five thousand years ago? Five thousand years ago you had living relatives! You exist, so certainly they did too. But there is absolutely nothing that you can say about any of them, dust as they are, blowing in the wind and imaginary spooks conjured up in your own mind. Be careful. There is a trick coming up here.

*****

"Time is money," or so say the modern capitalists and financiers who daily use both time and money to increase their profits and betray the world. So, of course, it is important to understand Time if you want to understand the people who use time to swindle you out of your money.

Five thousand years is really a very short time. But to modern people at the beginning of the 21st century AD, five thousand years seems to be ancient and remote. Because everything changes so much in modern times, we tend to view a hundred years ago as quaintly antique while 5,000 years ago seems impossibly ancient. Five thousand years is beyond the modern human's comprehension. However, it is important to understand why a few thousand years is really a very short time because, as I show you the secrets of the Jews and moneylenders, you must understand that long periods of time are not a barrier to conspiracies of family origin.

If you look at the entire known universe and put all of that time into a ratio of a single calendar year, you can begin to get an idea of how relatively recent is five thousand years ago. That is, if you count the very beginning of the universe as starting on January 1st and the end of that calendar year as ending December 31st, you can get an excellent idea of the relatively short time that five thousand years really is.

Beginning with the Big Bang of expanding gases on January 1st, the Earth didn't form until September 14—more than three-quarters of the way through the year. The oldest fossils of green algae and bacteria weren't laid down until October 9, and the first photosynthetic plants were formed by about November 12. And by December 1st, oxygen began to infuse the Earth's atmosphere. The first worms began to form by December 16. The first fishes began by December 19. The first trees and reptiles began about December 23, and the first dinosaurs by December 24. The first mammals began by December 26, and the first birds by December 27. The dinosaurs become extinct by December 28. And by December 29 the first primates evolve. And by December 31 the first humans appear by about 10:30 PM.

By 11:00 PM on December 31, people learn to use stone tools. And by 11:46 PM we learn to use fire. By 11:59 PM, the hunters of Europe begin drawing pictures on their cave walls. By 11:59 PM and 20 seconds, agriculture is invented. And at 11:59 PM and 50 seconds, recorded history at Sumeria begins. And thus, as a ratio of man's life on Earth against the age of the universe, all of our recorded history since writing was invented has taken place within just *the last ten seconds*. But of course, this is just a ratio and in no way can make one comprehend even small lengths of time such as a mere 5,000 years. I am setting up a trick here, so be careful.

It is important to realize how very recent a time span five thousand years is and to not be deceived into assuming that people are any different today than they were then. In all of that time, we have invented into our daily lives both material things and intellectual ideas that are just as useful to us today as they were to the people of five thousand years ago.

The wheel was invented about 5,500 years ago, and what would we do without it? Because wheels are such ancient technology, should we throw them aside and never ride bicycles or automobiles or trains because as "modern people" such ancient relics are too old for us? How absurd!

And writing was invented 5,000 years ago, but since you are reading this, you know that such an ancient invention is too useful to do without. How could we carry on our civilized lives without reading and writing?

We are really quite young, we Human Beings. The span of our lives against the vastness of Creation is very small. The whirling and wheeling of the galaxies in limitless space do little for us and certainly take no heed of our existence. It is the life that we lead in the present moment that means anything at all. Of what use is it to know the distance to Alpha Centauri or the speed of light around a black hole? None of this matters at all in our daily lives. But how fast a wheel spins that carries us along a freeway, or what time the train arrives to carry us to work, means quite a lot because these things, in real time and in real space, directly impact our very lives. I am setting up a trick here, so be careful.

Can you begin to understand the incredible time frames that we are dealing with? Your inability to say anything about your own relatives of five thousand years ago is no different than the problem that the Mesopotamians had in saying anything about their own relatives. In fact, you probably know more than they did since genealogy and photography and archeology and writing have preserved enough that you can at least make a guess.

So, let's solve the problem of the tricks that I have set. In trying to remember your distant relatives, you can now understand the impossible problem of trying to remember people whom you have never met. Furthermore, by taking for granted the man-made inventions in our daily lives, we tend to forget that these things are here today but they were not always here. Were wheels always here? No. Were telephones always here? No. Was writing always here? No. But it is easy to take them for granted because they are so familiar in our daily lives. We don't think twice about seeing a spoon or a fork or a pair of chopsticks, an automobile or an airplane or a book because they have been here since before we were born. We take them for granted. So, here is the trick.

Understand this about the Sumerian Swindle: *It was not always here.* The Ubaidians of 5000 BC invented it and the Sumerians took it up and, through writing and mathematics, increased its power a trillion-fold. The Sumerian Swindle is an ancient secret that modern scientists totally fail to understand and yet it has already been used throughout history to destroy entire nations and extinguish the lives of millions of people.

The ancient Sumerian Swindle is being used today by the Jews and financiers and bankers to destroy entire countries, to swindle generations of people out of their wealth, to create despotic tyrannies that crush freedom, to enslave mankind, and to destroy all knowledge of God. Under the control of these greedy and evil people, the Sumerian Swindle has that kind of power. It has that kind of power, and yet modern man takes it for granted as a "normal" part of life rather than the criminal fraud that it is simply because we erroneously assume that "it has always been here." Since it "has always been here," why not allow it to continue to ravage mankind, impoverish entire countries, bring warfare into every town? And so mankind allows those evil monsters who control the Sumerian Swindle to prosper while all that is Good and True and Holy is allowed to be destroyed by them.

The Sumerian Swindle was invented in Mesopotamia, yet it is overlooked by archeology, misunderstood by politicians, and invisible to the common man simply because we take it for granted "because it has always been here." The secrets of the Sumerian Swindle have been closely guarded for over 7,000 years by those who profit from stealing the wealth of mankind. And these secrets are still being held in the greedy and power-mad hands of some of the evilest fiends ever to have walked the Earth.

This super-secret invention of the Sumerians was not nuclear weapons or jet fighter planes, nothing as amazing as that. The super-secret Sumerian Swindle is quite simply the loaning of money at both simple and compound interest. Take care! There's a trick here. This boring subject of lending-at-interest has created and destroyed individual people and entire nations for the past 7,000 years. Hundreds of millions of people have starved to death, wars have ravaged the nations of mankind, diseases have spread, hundreds of millions of people have been enslaved and worked to death, entire nations have arisen to great heights of culture and have been laid waste with fire and pestilence—all because of the Sumerian Swindle.

With such power inflicted upon us from ancient times, how can we not want to understand the very thing that destroys our families, robs us of our wealth, steals our jobs, forecloses our homes, pushes us into wars, betrays our country, and enslaves us?

You—O Modern Man—might think that you understand the modern world because you take the modern world for granted. But the modern world is in the grip of an ancient evil that arose long ago in the land of Sumeria. The Sumerian Swindle is practiced today by every thieving banker, perfidious Jew, and treasonous financier, but it has *not* always been here.

*****

You may wonder, "Ho hum! Boring! What's so secret about compound interest?" To get an appreciation for this power, consider the Parable of Joseph's Penny. The Parable goes like this: If, at the birth of Jesus, Joseph had loaned out *one penny* at a compound interest rate of 5% per year, how much would be in the account today if Jesus returned to collect on the investment?

The answer to this simple question has some very amazing results. If the interest was calculated yearly for 2,000 years, then Jesus would be able withdraw in dollars an amount equal to $24 times 10^{39}. That is, $24 with 39 zeros after it! Literally:

$24,000,000,000,000,000,000,000,000,000,000,000,000,000.

Very few people can even pronounce or read such a huge number, let alone comprehend such a stupendous amount of money. Or if the compound interest was calculated *daily*, then Jesus could withdraw in dollars $267 with 39 zeros after it.

These amounts of money would buy several spheres of gold the size of the planet Earth. It's hard to believe, but you can calculate it out for yourself to verify these numbers. That is the power of compound interest on just one penny!

But these numbers also reflect the banker's tricks with time. To look ahead a bit, Secret Fraud #10 of the Sumerian Swindle is: "*Time benefits the banker and betrays the borrower.*" So, perhaps some Readers can understand why the bankers claim that they are charging you, let's say, 15% interest on your credit card but they calculate the compound interest *daily* rather than yearly. You assume that you are paying 15% and they do, indeed, calculate your interest at 15%. But by calculating the interest daily, adding that to what you "owe" and then the next day calculating interest on top of that, the devil-bankers make over ten times more than what they can steal from you by calculating the interest yearly. Over ten times more, even though they are still allegedly charging you the same 15%!

Part of the equation is Time. At first, the amounts owed in interest are relatively small. But in compound interest, as the interest owed is added to the principal, and interest is then calculated upon that sum, the amounts skyrocket with an ever-steeper acceleration until it becomes absolutely impossible to pay off the huge debt and the debtor becomes bankrupt and enslaved. That's the Sumerian Swindle in its ultimate summation, using compound interest to betray and impoverish all of mankind. Any modern person who has fallen into house mortgage and credit card debt, has been swindled in this way.

Again, for comparison, what would be the amount of Joseph's Penny if, instead of compound interest as calculated above, the interest was calculated as *simple interest?* For the same penny, for the same 5% per year, for the same period of 2,000 years, the amount that Jesus would be able to withdraw would total *a mere $1.01* (or 101 pennies).

Do you understand the incredible grand larceny that was then, and is today, being committed by the moneylenders, bankers, and financiers? They are all swindling criminals without exception. The Sumerian Swindle has been used to betray both the people of the ancient world as well as the people of the modern world. Even the simple interest of lending out two baskets of grain to get back three, is a swindle.

Or for those modern people who have fallen into the banker's trap of buying a home on credit, here is something to think about. Even at simple interest of 5%, if you buy a $100,000 home on a 30-year mortgage, you will end up paying off the loan after 30 years for a total of $250,000. Even at simple interest, you are really not paying 5% to own a home, you are actually paying a total of 150% which is an extra $150,000 over the $100,000 price of the home. More than double the original price! The home does not increase in value, *rather, the money decreases in value through the automatic inflation created by the Sumerian Swindle.*

But home loans are calculated with *compound* interest. Using the same amounts at compound interest, a $100,000 home costs an extra $332,194 for a total of $432,194. In other words, you are actually paying over 400% for your home, not 5%. Thus, *inflation* is an automatic result of lending-at-interest. Prices keep going up because the bankers are allowed to swindle both the government and the people of our wealth. Such are the frauds of the modern bankers who use the ancient Sumerian Swindle to gain "ownership" of the entire world.

The above arithmetic shows the power of compound interest in creating huge debts that the people have to pay to the bankers who do no more to earn it than by holding out the palm of their hands. In a nutshell, the mechanics of the Sumerian Swindle works this way: Numbers are infinite. You can multiply and achieve infinite sums quickly. But real things are finite. It is impossible for infinite numbers to equal real things in quantity because real things are not infinite. So, when a banker uses infinite numbers to multiply real things, he is swindling you because he is asking the impossible—he is asking you to give him more real things than actually exist. A loan of $10 times 50% means that the numbers claim that they have multiplied and created a real thing by 50%, but that's impossible.

Yes, you can say that if I loan you two apples at 50% interest, that you owe me three apples. And you can pay me the three apples from the millions of other apples that exist. But this does not mean that this business math equation is true. It is a mathematical and physical impossibility because one cannot multiply real things by imaginary numbers and end up with more real things. The error is concealed among the indefinitely large number of apples that exist in the world.

Prove it yourself. Sit down in a closed room with two apples, a pencil and a piece of paper and write this equation: 1.5 x 2 apples = 3 apples. Does another apple magically appear? No. But the lying numbers on paper say that it does.

The same is true when multiplying lumps of silver with numbers. Although the numbers increase, the lumps of silver remain constant. Thus, the ancient people were forever looking for silver mines to balance their accounting tablets because there never was enough silver to equal what the numbers claimed that should exist.

Even though the amount of silver on the planet Earth is indefinitely large, it is not infinite in amount because the Earth, itself, is not infinite in amount. The total amount of silver on the entire planet is still not large enough to pay off the interest rate of the loans based on silver and claimed to be owed by the accounting numbers.

Multiplying money by numbers does not make more money; it only makes an illusory debt that is impossible to repay because there is never enough money in existence to equal the lying numbers. When the people could not repay the impossible demands of the moneylenders, the Ubaidian moneylenders confiscated their farms, their goods, and even their wives and children. Then, they sold their country right out from under them and gave it to foreigners—all while peering shrewdly through their slit-like, lowered eyelids.

The wealthy Ubaidian moneylenders taught their swindle to the Sumerians and married their stinking daughters into the highest levels of Sumerian society. And this society became the founders of a civilization that was trying to balance the totally impossible amounts of silver and gold that their fraudulent and inflated accounting records claimed to be "Past Due," by going to war with their neighbors.

CHAPTER 3

THE SUMERIANS AND THE
BEGINNING OF CIVILIZATION

During the 3,000 years before the birth of Christ, there flourished in Mesopotamia one of the most enduring and significant civilizations which the world has known. Its chronological extent very much exceeded that of the ancient Hebrews, while the mass of texts which survive are at least twenty times longer than the whole of the Old Testament. This mass of texts from Mesopotamia were buried for 5,000 years beneath the rubble of their abandoned and destroyed cities. Written on clay tablets that were baked into impervious bricks, the cuneiform writings of these long-vanished civilizations were not translated until the later part of the nineteenth and the beginnings of the twentieth centuries AD. These ancient documents contain the proof that the Jews have been telling lies to all of mankind for the past 3,500 years. And they provide a repeating template for all historical events, even into modern times: that is, the great difference between historical facts and the word of the Jews.

Modern Western civilization has been very negatively affected by the lies of the Jews simply because we have not had access to the original cuneiform records, and have had to rely upon the fraudulent Jewish writings, beginning with the Hebrew Bible (a.k.a., Old Testament). When you only get one side of a story, what else can you do except to believe the story for lack of any other evidence? And so, with their multitudinous prevarications and forgeries, the Jewish version of history has very much colored and twisted our ideas about the people and events in the Ancient Near East. It is only through the modern work of archaeologists that a truer picture of those ancient times has emerged.

Long before the insignificant kingdoms of Judah and Israel were invented, great empires were established in the Middle East. The first of these were, of course, Sumeria and Egypt, beginning sometime before 3000 BC. It should be noted that what we know of those ancient times has only been discovered in the past 150 years or so. Although the Old Persian script had been deciphered by 1840 AD, it has been the accumulated knowledge found not only in the Assyrian and Sumerian royal archives but also in the stone inscriptions and papyrus writings of the Egyptians that give us a more balanced picture of those times—a picture that is far more accurate than can be found in the slanders and fictions that the Jews wrote in the Old Testament. Digging through the ancient rubble of destroyed cities, the archeologists of today have been able to piece together the history of those long-vanished civilizations using the actual records and the very words left by those people. And that history is very much different than what is found in the plagiarized, Old Testament hoaxes of the Jews. We must listen to what those ancient people had to say about themselves before considering the fables of the upstart Jews and their self-serving, mythological fantasies.

Although the peoples whom we call the Ubaidians first began the Mesopotamian Culture, the real credit for establishing civilization goes to the Sumerians. Because their agglutinative language group resembled that of the peoples from south of the Caspian Sea, they may have originally emigrated from that area. They would have traveled through Iran, avoided the Zagros Mountains, and entered Mesopotamia from the south. According to their own tradition, they came from the South. In the Sumerian language, "*subar*" means "north," "*elam*" means "east," "*ammuru*" means "west," and "*sumer*" means "south." And so, as a people from the South, they were called Sumerians.

They entered Mesopotamia gradually sometime between 3200 and 3100 BC when the open sea of the Persian Gulf was 250 kilometers (155 miles) further north than it is today. They soon became the masters of the entire region. Modern archeologists claim that they probably came from the Iranian plateau and so they would have an Aryan origin. The records that they left show that the Sumerians were an intelligent people with common sense and a pragmatic view of life. They prized wealth and possessions, farms filled with rich harvests and many cattle, successful hunting in the outback, bursting granaries, and nets full of fish. Their many legal documents show that they were very conscious of their personal rights and were not shy about dragging into the law courts those who encroached upon those rights. And their literature shows how much they valued honor and recognition and prestige and pre-eminence. What they brought to the existing culture of the Ubaidian land-owners and Subarian workers was an acute intelligence that allowed them to take the pre-existing inventions and ideas and improve upon them while adding inventions of their own.

The earliest names of Mesopotamian kings were Sumerian names. They dominated every aspect of Mesopotamian life and their Sumerian language became the only language spoken. And they are credited with the invention of writing, since it was during their dominance that this technology achieved its full potential—from a mere accounting method to a fully functioning technology for transmitting and recording human thought.

With writing and the use of written mathematical calculations, the Sumerian Swindle was perfected. The simple interest of the Ubaidians was super-charged into the grand larceny known today as compound interest. Actually, both simple and compound interest are swindles. Yet, with writing the numbers on wet clay, compound interest became an engine generating incredible wealth for those who controlled it, while creating great poverty and destruction for those who suffered under it.

Although the entire Mesopotamian riverine region is deficient in most of the basic materials of civilized existence, such as hard timber, stone, and metal ores; even so, the Sumerians turned an agricultural community— whose only three assets were water, sunshine, and mud—into an advanced and literate culture.

They devised such useful tools, skills, and techniques as the potter's wheel, the wagon wheel, the plow, the sailboat, the arch, the vault, the dome, casting in copper and bronze, riveting, brazing and soldering, sculpture in stone, engraving, and inlay. Their cuneiform system of writing on clay was borrowed by other peoples and used all across the Near East for some two thousand years. Almost all that we know of the early history of western Asia comes from the thousands of clay documents inscribed in the cuneiform script developed by the Sumerians and excavated by archeologists only in the past 150 years.

Although the majority of early archeology digs were commenced for the purpose of verifying Biblical histories, it soon became apparent from both physical artifacts and the cuneiform and hieroglyphic translations that the vast majority of Old Testament stories—that is, those Jewish fables which were not complete lies—were inaccurate myths at best. And yet, even though Jesus had warned that the Jews are liars and deceivers, and even though modern science proves that Jesus told the truth about the Jews, the Christians of today still believe the lies of the Jews.

This past 150 years of archeological rooting around marks a period of enlightenment in our modern world. Until the archeological remains of the Sumerians and the later Assyrians were excavated from the Mesopotamian dust, our only knowledge of those ancient people was what could be gleaned from a few paragraphs of excoriations and curses written about them by the rabbis in the Old Testament. What the West has known about a culture whose chronological extent very much exceeded that of the

Hebrew people by several thousands of years, was close to zero. It was as if the actual history of mankind had been purposely erased from the historical record!

The Jews tell their stories from their religious bias that the cultures of the Sumerians, Babylonians, Assyrians, and Egyptians were all evil, while the culture of the Jews is pure and good. But rather than trust what the lying Jews have to say on the subject, we can read for ourselves from the cuneiform clay tablets what the Sumerians, Babylonians, and Assyrians wrote. We can read from the hieroglyphics what the Egyptians wrote. This will help us to understand the evil lies and great hoaxes that the Jews have perpetuated upon all of mankind in this essential area of knowledge about God and the true history of mankind, two areas of human concern which the ancient people cherished but which the Jews purposely concealed and destroyed.

Those readers who are atheists should be warned that just because this book shows the Jews to be liars, frauds, and swindlers, does not mean that religion, itself, is false. And those readers who are religious should be warned that this book in no way attacks your belief in God. But you will find that what you believe will be greatly altered and made much stronger, even as your views undergo a change in perception.

It may seem odd to the casual reader to begin a history of the Betrayers of Mankind with an essay on religion. But in order to understand the power that religion had on the ancient people as well as its uses in the modern political landscape, this is where we must begin. Please understand, especially you readers who have religious beliefs, that this history in no way is an attack against religious faith or belief in God. You will see from what follows that there is a God, and He is good, but that there is no god in Israel. To understand this, let us consider the gods that were worshipped 2,000 years before the Jews began to tell their lies. In this way, we will have the background necessary to perceive Semitic hoaxes and avoid them.

The Gods of Sumeria

For the Sumerians, everything good and holy began at the city of Eridu located near the Persian Gulf.

Although the Ubaidians founded Eridu, it was the Sumerians who began their culture there. It was the Sumerians who wrote down the ancient stories and myths that had been committed to memory for three thousand years and which thereby became part of the culture of the Sumerians. So, they wrote that all culture came forth from Eridu.

Modern people have a variety of religions, atheistic ideas, agnostic ideas as well as no ideas at all about religion. To a modern reader, it may seem odd to think about this, but you must understand that all of the ancient peoples were very religious. All of them believed in the gods. Regardless of whether you, yourself, believe in God or not, you must understand this. There were no atheists among the ancient peoples.

They did not have our modern scientist's views of the universe, scientists who can see distant galaxies floating in empty space but who cannot see God. They did not have a modern scientist's quantum mechanical views of the universe, scientists who can theorize subatomic particles vibrating in yet more empty sub-atomic space but who still cannot see God. They did not have the modern politician's view that their actions were immune to any power outside of their own abilities to cajole and persuade. To the ancient peoples, God and the gods were everywhere evident, controlling and always observant of the actions of man. Religion was the very basis of Sumerian life, and everything in their society revolved around their religious beliefs.

The Sumerians asked the simple questions of religion such as: "Where did mankind come from?" They did not have modern scientists lying to them and telling them that they had descended from monkeys. They looked about and honestly answered this eternal question and said, "Obviously, we were created by the gods."

They asked other questions such as, "What is the purpose of life?" They did not have communists and capitalists and atheist Jews telling them that they were only animals who would do best by serving the corporate state as slaves and as mindless consumers of manufactured products. They answered this question with the only answer that made sense: "The purpose of life is to serve God." Regardless of what the lying rabbis claim about those people, this and this alone was the primary guiding point for all of the various religions of Mesopotamia. Their own words written with cuneiform characters on fire-hardened clay, prove this.

From the poorest laborer to the mightiest king, everyone in Sumerian society began and ended their daily life in prayer to the gods, aware of mortal man's humble purpose in life. For what other purpose was man created but to serve the gods? What power could a puny and mortal man have against the thunderclap, the burning sun, the fierce wind, against disease and, especially, against the cold inevitability of death? The

Sumerians knew the answer to these questions and practiced their lives as a daily devotion to the gods.

In the modern world, we try to make clear-cut distinctions between the various categories of fortune-telling, magic, religion, theology, and ethics. Such distinctions are not always easy to maintain even in the modern world, and in ancient times such distinctions would have been almost meaningless. In the ancient world, all these elements were parts of one great whole. The transit of the sun, moon, and stars, the rains and winds, the heat of the day and the cold of the night, were all a part of the vast fabric of Reality with which the Sumerians built their religion and their civilization. As members of one great entity, they communed with their gods through devotion, prayers, and sacrifice; and they received answers to their prayers through dreams, omens, direct conversations with God, and through priestly wisdom.

A modern reader may scoff at the gods. But whether you believe in a god or not, is really not important to this history. What is vitally important for you to understand is that the ancient people, each and every one of them, believed in the gods. To understand them and their culture and what their impact upon our own modern societies is, it is vital to understand what they believed. In this way, we can understand them more easily.

I will just briefly touch upon the gods of the Sumerians here as a background reference only. I will also tell some of the ancient secrets that have been hidden from modern scholars and scientists until now. Not wanting to bore the average atheistic reader or the average ignorant modern scientist or to horrify the average religious reader, this will be just a short survey. It is important to have an idea of the religion of the Sumerians of ancient times and their various gods so that you are neither deceived by the lies of the Jews nor by the ignorance of the modern scientists.

Firstly, the Sumerians had a working knowledge of the human aura. In more recent times, this spiritual radiation is often seen in old paintings of saints and gods. The human aura can be seen in others only by those who already perceive it in themselves. One of the earliest symbols for this radiant energy is found in what is today known as the Maltese cross [see Figures 3 & 3b].

The Maltese cross represents a man or woman standing with outstretched arms with their holy aura radiating from their bodies. The Maltese cross occurred as a religious symbol as early as the Jemdet Nasr period (~2900 BC) in precisely the form in which it is met with in Christian art. Although the later Christians would accept this ancient design as a symbol of the cross, its representation of the radiance of the human spirit was recognized by the Sumerians 3,000 years before Jesus taught about the Holy Spirit. However, the highest level of spiritual knowledge was not found among the Middle Easterners nor the Egyptians; it was found among the European people as expressed in their Stone Age art at places such as Newgrange, Ireland; Gavrinis, France; and at thousands of Celtic sites throughout Europe.

Figure - 3

Figure - 3b

As the ancient people knew, the very most important of the Eight Essentials of Life is air to breathe. Without air, men die in only a few minutes. The gods, themselves, as living gods, obviously also had to breathe. So, the most important of all the Sumerian gods was named *An*, the god of the heavens and the air, the god of the living breath, the god whose breath permeated the Universe and gave life to gods and men. This ancient name was practiced in the temples as a mantra which is still potent today, as you can understand by practicing it yourself.

From the earliest records, *Enlil* is known as "the father of the gods," "the king of heaven and earth," "the king of all the lands." Kings and rulers boasted that it was Enlil who had given them the kingship of the land, who had made the land prosperous for them, who had given them all the lands to conquer by his strength. It was Enlil who pronounced the king's name and gave him his scepter and looked upon him with a favorable eye. When we analyze their hymns and myths, we find Enlil glorified as a most friendly, fatherly deity who watched over the safety and well-being of all humans and particularly, of course, over the inhabitants of Sumeria.

The deep veneration of the Sumerians for the god Enlil and his temple, the Ekur in Nippur, can be sensed in a hymn which reads in part as follows:

Enlil, whose command is far-reaching, whose word is holy,
the lord whose pronouncement is unchangeable, who forever
decrees destinies, whose lifted eye scans the lands, whose
lifted beam searches the heart of all the lands; Enlil who sits

broadly on the white dais, on the lofty dais, who perfects the decrees of power, lordship, and princeship. The earth-gods bow down in fear before him. The heaven-gods humble themselves before him...

The city (Nippur), its appearance is fearsome and awesome. The unrighteous, evil oppressor, ... the informer, the arrogant, the agreement-violator, He does not tolerate their evil in the city. The great net ... He does not let the wicked and evil-doer escape its meshes.

Such goodness and positive virtue among the Sumerians belie the slanders and imprecations of the lying rabbis toward those ancient peoples. The Sumerians valued the righteous, the good, the trustworthy, the humble, and the honest. And they abhorred the wicked and the evil-doer. Remember this because it has vital importance to this history. The gods preferred the ethical and moral over the unethical and immoral, according to the Sumerian sages. Practically all the major deities of the Sumerian pantheon are extolled in their hymns as lovers of the good and the just, of truth and righteousness.

Indeed, there were several deities who had the supervision of the moral order as their main function: for example, the sun-god, Utu (who was later named Shamash). Another deity, the Lagash goddess named Nanshe, also played a significant role in the sphere of man's ethical and moral conduct. She is described in one of her hymns as the goddess...

... who knows the orphan, who knows the widow, knows the oppression of man over man, is the orphan's mother, Nanshe, who cares for the widow. Who seeks out justice for the poorest. The queen brings the refugee to her lap, finds shelter for the weak.

And so, these wicked evil-doers are listed in the Sumerian literature as "the unrighteous, evil oppressors, the informer (slandering gossip), the arrogant, the agreement-violator, the oppressor of orphans and widows, the oppressor of the poor and the weak, the refugee from war." Strangely enough, this description is very close to the words that Jesus would use to describe the Jews 3,000 years later.

Obviously, what the religious scriptures of the Sumerians preached was Goodness. Once again, the actual words of the Sumerians show what slandering liars the rabbis are because they have vilified these people throughout history and have gotten away with their lies for 5,000 years, until last 150 years when the science of archaeology proved the betrayals of the Jews to Truth.

Although the Sumerians recognized that their gods had certain physical attributes or that they were represented by special totems or symbols, none of their gods were as puny and weak and non-existent as the modern Jewish historians and rabbis claim them to be. Rather, the gods of the Sumerians were powerful and all-pervading. The slanders that are used by the Jewish writers are bald attempts to make the Jewish god appear to be mighty and the gods of other people to appear as myths or as cows or as crescent moons. But the gods of the Sumerians were actually more powerful than, and certainly not less powerful than, the Canaanite god that the Jews later claimed for their own.

The Sumerian god, Enlil, was described in the cuneiform scriptures as:

> Enlil, to bring forth the seed of the land from the ground, "Hastened to separate heaven from earth, hastened to separate earth from heaven...." The seed of the ground was Humankind as well as the growing plants. On other tablets it is written that: "Heaven was created of its own accord. Earth was created of its own accord. Heaven was an abyss, earth was an abyss."

This not only supersedes the Old Testament plagiarisms of the Jews by more than three thousand years, but also shows an understanding of the universe that is in no way less advanced than the latest modern theories and observations of astrophysics. Indeed, the Universe truly is a great abyss. The earth was a great abyss before mankind populated it and it is still today huge in comparison to the size of a man. It did not take a telescope orbiting in space for the Sumerians to understand this.

Unlike modern man, all the people on Earth could look up into the unpolluted night sky and see the glory of the Milky Way in all its brightness, an incredible view unhampered by the electric lights of the cities which glare all night, hiding the face of Heaven so as to enrich the electric company stockholders.

Just as human beings build civilization using a division of labor within a social hierarchy, so too did the Sumerians envision their gods as having similar attributes. Thus, there was not one all-powerful god who did all the work of maintaining the universe but, rather, there were multitudes of various gods who did their own work while being under the rule of one supreme god. Much as human society functioned with kings and priests giving orders to their subalterns who in turn passed along these orders to those lower on the hierarchy, so too did the gods of the Sumerians operate.

In the third millennium BC, a canonical list of the gods totaled almost 2,000 gods. Later, the Sumerians estimated that there were 3,600 gods (sixty times sixty). The holy family of the gods all descended from the sky. The sky god, Anu, controls the heavens and is above everything. His holy city was Uruk. He had two consorts, Ki and Nammu. With his consort, Ki the Earth goddess, they produced Enlil the air god, whose holy city was Nippur. Nippur was also the holy city of Ninlil the air goddess. Enlil and Ninlil produced Nanna (later called Sin) the Moon God, whose holy city was Ur.

But above them all was the sky god, Anu, to whom all things under heaven and earth bowed because his command was "the foundation of heaven and earth." And as the ultimate source of all authority, Anu was associated with the king, the highest authority on Earth whom he designated as ruler.

It should be noted here that the Sumerians practiced something which gave them great bliss and spiritual knowledge through the meditation technique of the mantra. Through the repetition of the name of God—in this manner, "An, An, An, An"—the Sumerian priests and people found both spiritual sustenance and food for the soul. They found peace and tranquility of mind and happiness in the heart. And so, the name of the original god of mankind was An, and certainly not Yahweh nor Jehovah.

Also, this An mantra is used even to this very day, as the Om syllable—in this manner, "Om, Om, Om, Om." Try it and you will like it. God is no farther away than the repetition of His name. And though He has many names, more is the pity for those who do not know even one of them. But such are the modern-day politicians, financiers, and Jews! These three godless creatures make such a mess of the world!

The undisputed religious center of Sumeria was the city of Nippur where Enlil's temple of Ekur was located. Ekur was the paramount shrine in all of Sumeria, and tradition points to Nippur as the place of assembly for the "election" of the supreme ruler. The king was nominated for office by his own city-god in an assembly of gods meeting at Nippur. These gods were represented by the chief priests from the temples of Sumeria. Nippur was never directly involved in the petty squabbles that characterized the relationships between the other cities of Sumeria, nor was it the titular capital of any dynasty. But possession of the holy city of Nippur entitled a Babylonian king to adopt titles that implied at least theoretical hegemony over the country. This power over kings was later usurped by Babylon and its god, Marduk.

The Sumerians were a happy people, and the bliss and joy they found in worshipping their gods clearly shows on the statues of their priests and worshippers who all wear smiles of bliss and have eyes filled full of awe. [see Figures 4a, b, c]

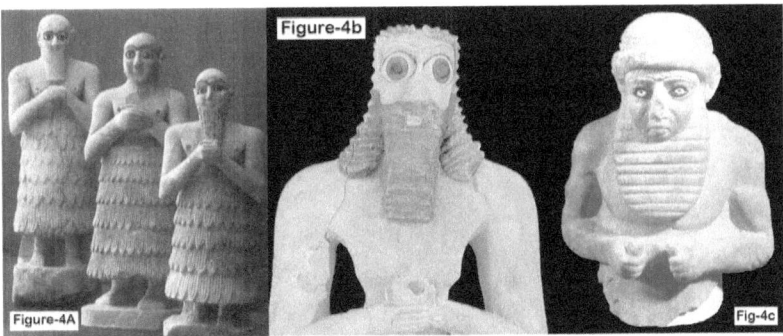

But there was a Great Evil rampant in the Land of the Two Rivers. This Evil was intent upon changing the contented smiles and awe-filled eyes of these first civilized people into grimaces of hard labor and eyes full of tears. This evil was found in the hearts of those who practiced the Sumerian Swindle.

The Temple

For the ancient Sumerians, the temple was the center of Sumerian society quite simply because God was the center of Sumerian society. The Sumerians did not pray to some wind god or fire god, but rather, they were praying to God, Himself, the highest power of which they could conceive. These gods appeared to the Sumerian People in the wind or the fire or whatever physical manifestation seemed imbued with holy power. But they did not pray to the wind or the fire, they prayed to *the god* who was within the wind and the fire.

> O Shamash, king of heaven and earth, judge above and below; Light of the gods, guide of Mankind; who judges the cases of the great gods! I turn to you; seek you out.

Such prayers to the sun god transmit through the millennia the heart-felt and fervent piety of these people. They were praying to God, the All-Father who listens to all prayers directed to him. Do the lying Jews and the insane Muslims and the deluded Christians of modern times really believe that God does not hear the prayers of those who turn to Him no matter what name they use to call him? Shamash the sun god rises and sets every day. But his power was not restricted merely to an orb in the sky because the power of this god radiated to all parts of heaven and earth. Whether a child calls his father "Da!" or "Daddy!" or "Pater!" or "Pere!" or "Shamish!", his father turns to him in response because his father knows the call of his own child, no matter what name the child uses to get the attention of the father.

It is a great defect in modern perceptions to take the dull scientific view that the sun is an exploding sphere of nuclear gases held together by its own gravity. This explains the physical phenomenon while hiding its ethereal nature. A scientist may say this and brush aside the fantastically amazing reality of the blindingly immaculate sun, but his explanation would not make the sun any less awesome of a radiant entity.

There is a great difference in quality between an ancient person who, with love in his heart, prays to the sun as his god, compared with a modern scientist who, with nothing but cold calculations in his heart, reduces the sun to mathematical symbols on a blackboard. Which of these two people are enlightened and which is dwelling in darkness? The universe is alive, the entire world is alive, but modern science claims that everything is dead, merely composed of chemicals and empty space. Thus, they do not perceive the Life Force within them and the Life Force without them. There is no childlike awe in their dark eyes.

Modern people are being misled by science if they throw away the wonderfulness of our world only to accept the boring, dull, misleading descriptions of science. With your very own eyes, you can see the amazing wonder of the world. You can smell the life-giving power in the air. You can feel your aura radiate and embrace your soul. If you look, you will see.

Why ignore this incredible beauty and spiritual power by sticking your head into a scientific textbook explanation which ignores Life while celebrating Death? The mystical view of the universe is observed through your own mind, heart, and soul—the most subtle, insightful, and precise of instruments—and not through a telescope or microscope. The ancient people used their own minds and perceptions to discover realms that are still unknown my modern man. Some of these realms will be indicated in later chapters and volumes.

If the Sumerians were farmers, they prayed to a storm god because it was upon the rain clouds that their crops and herds depended, and it was from the wind and storms that their crops could be destroyed and their herds scattered. Because the storm god also delivered his water by the rivers, then the river god was also vitally important. And of course, one couldn't very well ignore the sun god because only with his all-seeing eye could the world be illumined and the crops grow. This seems ridiculous to the modern person, praying to the storm clouds and rivers and the sun. But it was all part of mankind's efforts to gain some control over his environment and not be buffeted about by the powers of Nature.

So, the people prayed to these manifestations of our great and beautiful world because everything in creation is essential to one's life and prosperity and happiness, just as it is today. Everything in creation is holy. The entire universe is holy, for it is a pristine masterpiece of perfection, exquisite in every atom. And it is all connected as a single skein of many vibrations. Prayer is one of those vibrations which powers and protects humanity, and which drives human societies. It is type of a vibration that enters the cosmos and the cosmos responds to that vibration.

The Sumerians did not have modern scientists telling them that they were ignorant fools for believing in non-existent gods because they could see with their own eyes the beauty and majesty of the holy sun rising above another day of life for them. They could smell the sweet nectar of the air; they could feel the buoyant and silken majesty of the water; and they could feel their own spiritual Life Force radiating as an aura around them. They had no communist Jews telling them that they were nothing but animals because the Sumerians could see with their own eyes the human spiritual radiance shining within the love of their wives and the laughter of their children. They could see the aura radiating from their holy men and priests. And when the spirit left the body of a loved-one at death, they could see it hovering about and returning to either haunt or to console them.

Our modern scientists are the real fools who blindly cannot observe and appreciate these things that are evident even to a child. When a scientist draws a single line on a blackboard, the molecules of chalk vibrate and break off of the chalk-stick and cling to the slate chalkboard with noisy shrieks of protest. It is not a dead and empty event because he (or she) who directs the hand which draws the line is a Living Entity. And it is that human being residing within the muscles and bones of that scientist, who directs the muscles and bones and chalk stick to draw that line. And it is that human being—invisible, ethereal, thinner than mist—whom the scientist does not see simply because he does not look within himself.

Thus, he is blind to his True Self and blind to the True Nature of the universe.

Beneath the radiant blue sky, the Sumerians were a happy people. The fertile plains of Sumeria gave them food. The mud bricks of the earth and the reeds of the marshes gave them shelter. With hard work and the blessings of the gods for good crops, good cattle, and good health, then and only then, could they and their families and their gods be well-supplied with everything. They depended upon the blessings of their gods and their gods depended upon the offerings and prayers of their people. As long as they served their gods by working in the fields, fishing in the rivers, hunting in the outback and offering a portion of their handiwork to their gods through the priests of the temples, the Sumerians experienced the fullness of life, peace and plenty. Sumeria was a happy land. And the Sumerians were, in general, a happy people. And why not? They had in abundance everything that life has to offer. They were blessed by the gods and they knew it—and other people knew it, too. Other people who lived in the rocky terrain or in the desert wastes knew how fertile and bountiful was Sumeria. And those people coveted that food-filled land.

Because of the discoveries of modern archeology, we can throw aside the Jewish lies that the ancient people were evil sinners just because they didn't pray to the Jewish god who hated all of mankind. All of the slanders that the rabbis wrote about them in the Old Testament are proven false by the cuneiform texts that the Mesopotamians have left us as records of their histories as well as records of their very thoughts.

If they made an idol of their sun god in a temple, it was no more or less of an idol than the idol that the demon Jews make of their Torah scroll of dead goat skins, which they adore and kiss and march around all dressed up in tapestries with a crown on its head.

The lies that the Jews have always told about these religious people are easily proved to be lies by the prayers of the Mesopotamian peoples, themselves. This prayer to the sun god is just as valid as any prayer offered up by Christians or Muslims today because the All-Father knows the sound of his own children:

> O Shamash, … judge of heaven and earth. … who establishes light for the people; Shamash, when you set, light is withdrawn from the people ....
>
> When you come forth, all Mankind becomes warm. The cattle and living things that go out on the steppe land, they come towards you, you give them life. You judge the

case of the wronged man and wronged woman; you give them a just decision.

...You take care of all the people of the lands; Everything that Ea, the king, the counselor, has brought into being is wholly entrusted to you. Whatever has breath, you shepherd equally; You are their keeper, above and below....

You give the crooked judge experience of prison; The person who perverts justice for a bribe, You make to bear punishment. He who does not accept a bribe but takes the part of the weak Is pleasing to Shamash, who will give him long life.

Such prayers tell us of the devotion and love these people had in their hearts. But they also tell us about certain criminals who ravaged their societies. The "crooked judge," the lawyer who "perverts justice for a bribe," were very much a part of Sumerian society because they "have always been here." And because they "have always been here," we in modern times must learn from history and root them out entirely. Such prayers as these identify crooks in high places. At the same time, their prayers prove the goodness and ethical foundation of the priests and temples. The Sumerian priests could see very clearly the good and evil in men. They preached against those who took advantage of the poor and the weak. The temples were places of solace and refuge.

However, one must not assume that the ancient Sumerians had the idea that their god would save them in a heavenly paradise after death in exchange for the service and devotion of the suppliant. Such ideas would have to await the Aryan Hindu and Aryan Buddha and the Celtic-Druidic observations and the teachings of Jesus several thousand years later. For the Mesopotamian, who saw the purpose of life to be only as a servant of the gods, what After-Life there was for him, was nothing but the gloom of the Underworld. They had not yet found that Narrow Path to Enlightenment.

And so, the Sumerians made the most of every single day, both with joyful appreciation and with deep prayer. They did not view their gods as being particularly bounded by moral justice because gods could do what they wanted. As a servant of the gods, mortal man was of no significance. And so, personal ambition and personal greed were accepted as legitimate character traits. But these traits were to be tempered with morality and goodness and honesty because this was how the gods wanted their people to be, followers of justice, of the "straight way."

Always, among all of the ancient peoples, there were priests. Perhaps they did not start their careers as priests, but they became priests, nevertheless. Sitting around a fire at night, contemplating the stars or perhaps offering wise counsel to their fellows, certain people became respected through their wisdom and advice. Or perhaps looking into the future and wondering about the coming season's prosperity, and calculating the moon phases and star crossings, gave them a certain skill for helping their people prepare for the proper times for sowing and planting.

Some people became priests merely because they could see the futility of pursuing any other occupation because wealth and power are temporary while infinite time and space are immortal. And against infinite time and the temporary nature of life, what other help does mankind have other than that from the gods? And what better way to understand eternity and to help the people than to be a priest?

Modern scientists may scoff before they are shoveled into their graves, but the ancient people discovered something amazing about a life devoted to realization of godhead. The discoverers of these mysteries were the priests who maintained the temples of the gods. And the beneficiaries of these mysteries were the people, themselves, who devoted their love and their lives to the gods. It is with devotion and love that human society is made strong.

Beneath the starry skies, beneath the brilliant sun, upon the wide and beautiful Earth, the ancient Sumerians asked the question: "What is the purpose of life?" And they realized the answer: "The purpose of life is to serve God." And when they worked together toward that purpose, life became abundant and joyful to them. It was truly a wonderful mystery that such was so.

One of the great discoveries of the Sumerians was that every man and woman could attain an actual realization of God. Certainly, they prayed and made sacrifice to their deities, but they also received solace in return. Like any modern religious person who feels good and holy through their daily genuflections and prayers, so too did the Sumerians feel the bliss and confidence that comes to those who fulfill their duties in the service of God. No atheist or agnostic can understand the peaceful bliss that is experienced when knowledge of God enters a person's heart.

Ancient Mesopotamians believed that man was created to serve the gods. This principle was interpreted literally, so the idols of the gods were cared for, fed, and clothed. They expressed their adoration of the god by serving the image of the god. The temple administration included the chief priest, various kinds of exorcists, singers, musicians, scribes, and the staff who supervised the temple businesses.

According to a detailed text from the much later Seleucid period, although certainly valid also for Sumerian times, the divine statues in the temple of Uruk were served two meals daily. The first meal was served in the morning when the temple opened, and the other was served at night, immediately before the doors of the sanctuary were closed. Each meal included two courses, called "main" and "second."

From descriptions of divine meals, the following sequence can be reconstructed. First, a table was placed before the image. Water for washing was offered in a bowl (even the gods had to wash up before eating!). Then a variety of beverages, special cuts of meat, and fruits were brought to the table. When the gods ate, they were hidden from both priests and the common people. Whatever was left over (which, of course, was everything), the priests and their families would eat.

This religious ritual was simply a means of providing a physical service to a spiritual god. Like modern people saying a prayer before meals, first the god eats and then the people eat. Just as man is a physical being who houses a holy spirit within him, the Sumerians used a physical representation of their god in the form of an idol to serve as a house and a resting place for the god. Thus, the statues and images of the various ancient peoples were never believed to be the actual god, himself. These images were physical places into which the gods were believed to invisibly enter. So, an ancient person would look at the image of a god and know that his god was inside of that image looking out at him.

To the ancient people, the gods were real. To modern people, the gods are imaginary. But since modern people cannot even see something as simple and common place as their own divine and holy spirits—or their own Qi—how can they expect to understand God? Modern people have been led away from the knowledge of God. Why and by whom? You shall learn.

But whether or not you believe that a god actually lives inside of the statues, doesn't matter anymore than whether you believe that God created the world in six days. If you want to understand the ancient people, what you believe doesn't matter. What the ancient people believed, is all that matters for you to understand them. And it is *their* beliefs, not your beliefs, which shaped their history and their culture—and then shaped your history and your culture today because they were your ancestors.

*****

No less than modern man, they asked themselves the Grand Questions of life. The results of their philosophical pondering were written in cuneiform classics such as the Epic of Gilgamesh. The Epic was first written onto clay tablets at the turn of the Second Millennium or earlier (around 2,000 BC). It was popular among the Sumerians, as well as later among the Babylonians, Assyrians, Hittites, and Hurrians who no doubt read it to the illiterate and numerous other peoples of the Near East. The Epic itself is, of course, much older.

For generations, the folk memory of the Sumerian people passed along poems and stories by word of mouth. Only after many generations were such stories preserved by poets in written form. These poems contained great wisdom. The great problems of mankind were cited and pondered and wise conclusions were attained for the mysteries of life, death, and the hereafter.

That the Epic of Gilgamesh was a popular poem, is attested by the numerous fragments of copies scattered all over the Fertile Crescent region and beyond. Thus, this ancient refrain from The Epic of Gilgamesh is often repeated in the literature of all peoples:

> Gilgamesh opened his mouth, saying to Enkidu: "Who, my friend, can scale heaven? Only the gods live forever under the sun. As for Mankind, numbered are their days. Whatever they achieve, is but the wind."

Do these words sound familiar to those of you who have read the Bible or the Dhammapada or the Bhagavad-gita? These are the observations of the wise men of all peoples. These longings, these hopes that life is not a passing phase never to return but is merely one step in an eternal procession, were thoughts written down by many peoples who were far older than the lying, perfidious Jews.

> Shamash was distraught, as he betook himself to him; He says to Gilgamesh: "Gilgamesh, whither rovest thou? The life thou pursuest, thou shalt not find." Gilgamesh says to him, to valiant Shamash; "After marching and roving over the steppe, Must I lay my head in the heart of the earth That I may sleep through all the years? Let mine eyes behold the sun That I may have my fill of the light! Darkness withdraws when there is enough light. May one who indeed is dead behold yet the radiance of the sun!"

Do these themes not sound familiar to you readers of the Old Testament? The writer of Ecclesiastes was familiar with the Epic of Gilgamesh as is reflected numerous times in Ecclesiastes 2:24 and in 5:18, 8:15 and 9:8-10. And the Epic continues:

> Siduri the tavern-keeper said to Gilgamesh: "Gilgamesh, whither rovest thou? The life thou pursuest, thou shalt not find. When the gods created Mankind, Death for Mankind they set aside, Life in their own hands retaining. Thou, Gilgamesh, let full be thy belly, Make thou merry by day and by night. Of each day make thou a feast of rejoicing, Day and night dance thou and play!
>
> Let thy garments be sparkling fresh, Thy head be washed, bathe thou in water. Pay heed to the little one that holds on to thy hand, Let thy spouse delight in thy bosom! For this is the task of Mankind."

And as in Ecclesiastes 2:16 and 9:5, so too in Gilgamesh:

> "Since the days of yore there has been no permanence; The resting and the dead, how alike they are! Do they not compose a picture of death, The commoner and the noble, Once they are near to their fate?"

As expressions of their sincere devotion and piety, the Sumerians built great temples to their gods in all of their cities. Those rectangular temples were constructed of mud bricks and decorated with gold and silver and precious stones. They built high ziggurat towers of three levels with the god's house at the top and all of it enclosed by the walls of the temple grounds.

That the temples were the largest and tallest buildings in a Mesopotamian city very significantly indicates that the most important and most powerful persons in those ancient societies were the priests who served their gods of creation and their gods of the universe. This is an identical correlation to European societies up until the 18th centuries AD, where the cathedrals built to celebrate God and Christ were the biggest buildings.

However, in all the modern cities today, the biggest and tallest buildings in a city are not the temples or churches. The biggest and tallest buildings are owned by the bankers and moneylenders. The banks are presided over by the mighty dwarfs of finance who serve their God of

Money. Those who bow to the gods, are servants of the gods; those who bow to money, are betrayers of the gods. The ancient people followed the example and advice of the priests, while modern people follow the example and advice of the bankers and merchants who make their profits when mankind forgets about God and embraces money.

Because the Sumerians devoted their lives to serving the gods, their temples were more than mere places of worship. Since the purpose of life was to serve the gods, every aspect of life was an act of service and devotion to god. So, the temples were also centers of manufacture and trade. As the "estates" of the gods, the temple grounds were where the business of a vibrant society was transacted. Temples were places of worship as well as places for doing business and conducting trade.

The temples managed the cultivation of grain and vegetables and fruit trees. The temple shepherds took care of the herds of sheep, goats, and cattle. Inside of the temple grounds and in outlying cottages, the temple staff supervised a spinning and weaving industry. Cloth, clothing, leather, wooden and pottery objects were all manufactured for use by the temples both on the temple grounds and in outlying properties. These goods were used for domestic and foreign trade. And for all these activities, storerooms, granaries, workshops, and living quarters were required.

Because of their profits from manufacturing and trade, as well as being the beneficiaries of the goods and properties bequeathed to them from pious devotees, the temples grew in wealth and in landed property. They were not only the center for the lives of the Sumerian peoples but were their nurturing and protecting element as well. In times of famine, the temples gave interest-free loans of grain to the people. The temples provided a refuge for orphans and illegitimate children. Parents who were being hounded by the moneylenders, could sell their beloved children to the temple for service to God rather than sell them to the moneylenders as lifelong slaves and prostitutes.

In addition to the main temple in the city, every town and village had its own small sanctuaries; every house had its own little alcove that housed a statue or a talisman of the family god. Along the roads, the canals, and the thoroughfares, were wayside shrines where a farmer or boatman could pause for a quick blessing from the god and where merchants and travelers could ask for divine protection or to offer thanks for a safe return. Without doubt and with all certainty, the people of Mesopotamia were a religious people. They were not the knaves that the lying Jews and ignorant Christians and maniacal Muslims claim that they were. They were a religious people who honored the gods and who lived their lives as nobly as they could.

To understand the power and wealth that the Sumerian people enjoyed, you cannot use money or gold as a measure of wealth. Money, as you will see, is mainly (though not entirely) a fraudulent delusion. It is better to understand *the goods that money can buy,* since these goods are no different today than they were 5,000 years ago. A cow is a cow, no matter if you can buy one for a penny or for a thousand dollars. And even though a tiny grain of silver no larger than a barleycorn means no more to a modern person than a handful of paper money would have meant to a Sumerian, a cow is still a cow today just as it was in ancient times. Only the money that it takes to buy the cow is different.

If a Mesopotamian worker of 3000 BC could fill his stomach for a penny's worth of barley porridge bought from a roadside shop while a modern office worker pays ten dollars for the same-sized bowl of porridge bought from a fancy restaurant, both the ancient man and the modern man are filled up on a bowl of porridge and are satisfied. The bowl of porridge is no different, only the amount of money to purchase them is different. How can anyone say that a copper penny is less valuable than a paper ten-dollar bill, if they both can only buy the same bowl of porridge? Physical things are constant while money is as variable as a mirage.

Be careful, the Sumerian Swindle is at work here. I will repeat these arguments later, but it will be useful to you to begin thinking about and understanding these ancient concepts now because modern people are being swindled out of our physical goods in exchange for a mirage. The Sumerian Swindle is just the same and so are the modern swindlers.

To get an idea of the scale of wealth that flowed through Meso-potamia in 3000 BC, let's look at just the food that was required by a Sumerian temple in just one day. Enormous amounts of food were provided to temple administrators and craftsmen. For example, one text listed a *daily total* of more than 500 kilograms of bread, 40 sheep, two bulls, one bullock, eight lambs, 70 birds and ducks, four wild boars, three ostrich eggs, dates, figs, raisins, and 54 containers of beer and wine, in addition to other offerings.

The best agricultural products and the best food animals were sent to the temple, to be used in three different ways: as daily food served to the divine image, as income or rations for the temple staff who supervised and prepared the divine meals, and as savings accumulated for future use or for trade. The temple also relied on funds supplied by the royal house, by wealthy citizens, and, occasionally, from shares of war booty. The temple represented the communal identity of each city. The temple was usually located in the center of the city and was both the largest and tallest building.

Until recently it was generally believed that in the early Sumerian period the temple owned all the land of the city-state; but it has now been shown that the temple share amounted to perhaps no more than one-eighth of the whole. The rest of the land was owned by families or clans collectively, and could only be sold by agreement of all the prominent members of the family or clan. The buyers of such land would be members of what was becoming the ruling class or nobility, and these people thereby came to own land as *private* property in addition to what they held as *family* property. Their lands were worked by poor landless freemen.

In a normal society, there are four general classes or castes. This social pyramid is formed by the priests at the top who guide society. They are followed by the king and administrators who protect society. These are served by the merchants and traders who manage the goods created by society, while all of society is supported by the farmers and laborers. These four classes make up society—that is, these four classes make up all normally-evolving societies. Originally, this, too, was the normal and natural arrangement in Mesopotamian society in its earliest stages. The natural order was clearly observable within the earliest archeological record but was later sublimated behind a super-imposed "wealth factor."

At a very early stage, this "wealth factor" began to corrupt the natural order of society. As money flowed into their coffers through the Sumerian Swindle and as their wealth increased, this normally-evolving human society of *priest-king-merchant-and-farmer*, devolved instead to the beginnings of what we have today in modern society.

The corrupted system of society that we have today is composed of *banker-merchant-politician-and-slave*. The priest has been almost entirely vilified and abandoned. This corruption was not apparent to the Sumerians any more than it has been apparent to the modern archeologists because it has evolved so slowly and insidiously that the Sumerians didn't notice the subtle changes, any more than modern people do. The corruption of society has been overlooked by the modern archeologists simply because "it has always been here," because that is as far back as they can remember.

And so, a modern society, having cast aside its priests, suffers under the godless and perverse criminals who operate the Sumerian Swindle today—the bankers, the merchants, and the financial speculators. And where the godless rule, devils play.

Sumeria's entire social structure became gradually corrupted, from being centered on God to being centered on ownership of material goods and properties. As noted above, Sumerian society was divided into two groups, those who owned landed property—the *awilum* (the Haves)—and those who were dependent upon the wealthy—the *muskenum* (the Have-Nots). Thus, from a very early time in the earliest history of civilization, a perversion occurred in the natural order of mankind, and this perversion was carried along through successive eras as an accepted practice simply because "it has always been here."

While the ancient people were serving their gods in the temples, and while the priests and kings were serving their gods and nurturing their people throughout the country, and while society was evolving normally and joyfully, in the dark and dismal mud-brick houses of the money-lenders, the great evil of the Sumerian Swindle arose, secretly, with only the moneylenders profiting from the destruction of the people.

Ancient Egypt

We will study more about ancient Egypt in later chapters. But to focus on the theme of this book, a short mention is here in order.

Many modern people assume that Egypt is older than Mesopotamia. This is due to the fact that the ancient Egyptians built with enduring stone while the Sumerians and Babylonians built with mud bricks. So, Egyptian tombs and monuments are still present today while the mud-brick temples and palaces of ancient Sumeria, Babylonia, and Assyria are little more than mounds of dirt. Also, the high water-table in Sumeria destroyed all organic evidence, while the drier conditions of Egypt preserved even hair, bone, and linens.

The Egyptian civilization was old but not as old as Sumeria. And it was not even as spiritually advanced as the Stone Age people of Europe, but its stone monuments were far more impressive. As the Ice Age declined and the earth warmed from its long winter, the vast grasslands of the Saharan Plain—which had been a rich hunting ground that was filled with zebras, giraffes, and antelope—dried up and turned into desert. The dark-skinned peoples who had hunted those grasslands moved on to more hospitable environs toward central Africa, while the Caucasian people who had colonized the Mediterranean Basin and North Africa moved to the fringes of the Mediterranean Sea and into the Nile valley.

By 2700 BC—three centuries after Sumerian culture had blossomed—the Old Kingdom period of Egypt began. As isolated as Egypt was, surrounded by inhospitable deserts, 300 years is plenty of time for such inventions as writing and agriculture to spread to Egypt from Sumeria. The ideas spread but not the culture that fostered them. So, Egypt evolved its own unique culture, though some of the ideas that it had borrowed from Sumeria were ideas that grew into uniquely Egyptian expressions.

There are three important differences between Sumeria and Egypt that should be noted. *First*, while the Sumerians believed that the king was the servant of the gods, the Egyptians believed that the king was, himself, a god incarnate. The Sumerians lived to serve the gods while the Egyptians lived to serve the Pharaoh. By serving the Pharaoh-god-incarnate, they served the gods. *Second*, in Sumeria, the lands originally belonged to the temple of each city-state to be worked in service to the gods. In Egypt, the lands and all of Egypt belonged to Pharaoh. And *third*, the Egyptians never made use of a money system—at least it wasn't a money system that could be manipulated by greedy merchants. All business and services in Egypt were accomplished through barter and food rations. Workers were paid in rations of grain and oil and cloth. The only markers that could be used as a sort of money were scarabs. And since these carved dung beetles were not made of precious metals, they couldn't be falsified by weight or mixed with base metals. They were simply tally scarabs allowing their exchange for a ration payment. Thus, they had *local* but *not international* value.

Money tends to free people to more easily trade the necessities of life among themselves. Barter tends to restrict people to a lifestyle that cannot be easily divorced from the land. For example, a rich farmer in Sumeria, after selling his grain for silver, could hide his silver under a rock. Thus, a huge pile of grain could be concealed by being turned into silver and then hidden. But a successful farmer in Egypt, after growing the same amount of grain as the Sumerian, needed to store his grain in a large storehouse where his wealth was easily observed and counted by Pharaoh's scribes.

Barter tended to keep people tied to their land and to their crafts since whatever they did for a living could only be turned into a profit by trading for an equally bulky and heavy pile of trade goods. This tended to add to the Egyptians' isolation as a people because the limited travel that there was in those early days, was not easily accomplished by people whose wealth was stored as bulky and heavy sacks of grain rather than as relatively light and concealable purses of silver.

Also, with barter, much more wealth can be concentrated at the top of the social pyramid when a laborer's pay is in food rather than silver. A hungry worker is glad to have a handful of food as his pay and is less likely to run away when his food is limited by how much grain he can carry. And when everyone gets the same ration of food or clothing, there is not much incentive for individual achievement.

And so, Egypt attained a high level of culture and a unique civilization but its achievements leveled off after the first thousand years because, by then, they had developed everything that such an agrarian society required to maintain their ancient way of life.

Because of the relative security provided by its surrounding deserts, Egypt was able to enjoy a more peaceful cultural evolution than the constantly warring Mesopotamia. Sumeria was surrounded by a variety of different peoples and had no natural barriers against attack. So, Sumeria underwent far greater social changes over time than did Egypt.

Culture always progresses during times of peace. So, the several thousand years of peace that Egypt enjoyed found expression in everything from the pyramids and temples to the daily life of a happy and contented people. Thus, the religious and spiritual knowledge that most ancient people experience, was fostered in the peaceful lands of ancient Egypt. There, great religious mysteries were attained. And yet, the Egyptians never attained the high spiritual abilities of the ancient European people who built Newgrange Ireland and Gavrinis, France.

Modern science has no knowledge or concept of what the ancient Egyptians had achieved on the religious and spiritual level. Knowledge of auras, the spiritual body, the dynamics of the bioelectric energy field (Qi), super-human strength, out-of-body travel, meditational transcendence, and communion with God, were all common knowledge to the Egyptian priests and people, although such knowledge is still a mystery to the hunch-backed and diseased modern scientists. I explain these subjects more thoroughly in *The Monsters of Babylon*.

Although Egypt was growing to the greatness for which it is justifiably famous, it was an isolated kingdom that had little effect upon the early history of Mesopotamia or of anywhere else in the world beyond the Nile River margins. That being said, let's return to the history of Sumeria.

CHAPTER 4
DAILY LIFE IN SUMERIA

The quality of life in any country can be best understood by whether or not the people have for themselves the Eight Essentials of Life. This is an ancient knowledge but one that you can use to question the quality of your own life and the success of your own race and your own country. These Eight Essentials of Life may seem like a simplistic way of looking at civilization and at happiness, but why make things complicated when happiness is so easy to understand and attain?

The Eight Essentials of Life are: *Air, Water, Food, Clothing, Shelter, Spouse, Children,* and *God.* When people have all of these, then life is good and the people are happy. You can measure the quality of your own life by considering these Eight Essentials and whether or not you, yourself, have them. But for now, let's just see how these affected the people of Sumeria and the other peoples of the Ancient Near East.

There was not much problem with the Sumerians having enough good air to breathe. Not having air pollution to contend with as we do in modern times, they had plenty of fresh air every day, unless of course a dust storm blew in from the desert. So, both the "Haves" and the "Have-Nots" were equal in this regard. Although not everyone knew the priestly and religious secrets of meditational breathing, everyone at least had fresh and unpolluted air to breath.

Also, water was not much of a problem. Although they lived in the semi-arid and desert conditions of the Fertile Crescent, the water of the Euphrates and Tigris rivers and their tributaries provided plenty of water. And the water-table was high enough for wells to be dug. However, not knowing of water-borne diseases or of bacteria, all levels of society suffered from such things as dysentery and a variety of infections and lung ailments. After all, these were farming communities always in close contact with dirty animals and the bacteria and toxic mold spores from dung piles. And their houses were made of mud-bricks, so filthy conditions where a small scratch could lead to severe infections were a constant part of life. Their average life span was just 40 years—a figure which is skewed by the loss of many infants in the first year of life.

Food is the third Essential of Life. However, this is where the awilum (the Haves] and the muskenum (the Have-Nots) began to experience different qualities of life. As most people will agree, food is not just a necessity but it is also one of the pleasures of life, since the delicious flavors that can be derived from good cooking are so nice. Much can be deduced about any people by studying the food that they ate.

In Mesopotamia of 3000 BC, with its hot sun and fertile soil, two crops per year of a large variety of foods were grown. Compare what you find at your local supermarket with the foods enjoyed by these ancient people and you will see that they had nearly as great a variety, and much healthier foods, than do modern people. Although modern foods seem to be of great variety and/or wholesomeness, this is mainly a result of the deception of the merchants; they increase their profit margins by dealing in unripened, tasteless fruits and vegetables, genetically modified organisms (GMOs), synthetically fertilized plants, steroid-hormone-vaccinated farm animals and all manner of meats, fish, fruits, vegetables and factory-produced "junk foods" which have been shipped from around the world in cans, plastic packages, and frozen cartons, all in mummified and out-of-season states of decomposition.

So, basically, the people of 3000 BC Mesopotamia ate healthier food than do modern people. And their teeth prove it because, with rare exception, they did not have any dental cavities, since they did not eat either refined flour or refined cane sugar. The exceptions were among the awilum (the Haves), who could afford to eat large amounts of honey and date sugar. The Sumerians did not use refined sugar; instead, they enjoyed fruit juices, particularly grape and date juice. And so, their teeth were not rotten like the teeth of modern people, who suffer from the Jewish Medical Swindles. Only the very rich could afford honey, which was imported. "Mountain honey" as well as "dark," "red," and "white" honey were mentioned in the cuneiform texts.

The basic food of all Sumerians was, of course, grain. Barley was the chief grain of Sumeria primarily because it could grow in a more alkaline soil than could wheat. Wheat was grown in the higher elevations, but for the irrigated lands of Mesopotamia where the evaporating and percolating irrigation water raised the salt content of the soil, barley was the staple crop. Other cereals eaten, besides barley and wheat, were millet and rye. These were eaten as unleavened breads that were either baked or roasted as thin disks upon a hot griddle (as is still done in the Middle East today), or cooked into thick porridges. Rice was not cultivated until the first millennium BC.

Onions, leeks, shallots, and garlic were basic to the ancient diet. Their savory flavors and healthful qualities were as much appreciated then as they are today. Onions were described in the cuneiform texts as being sharp, sweet, or those "which have a strong odor."

In their extensive gardens, the farmers also grew lettuce and endive, melons and gourds, lentils, beets, carrot-like plants, and fennel bulbs. Lentils, beans, and chickpeas were plentiful and when eaten with the various grains, provided a balanced and wholesome diet. Other vegetables included a variety of lettuces, cabbage, summer and winter cucumbers (described as either sweet or bitter), radishes, beets, and a kind of turnip. Fresh vegetables were eaten raw or boiled in water.

Many herbs and spices were available, such as salt, coriander, black and white cumin, mustard, fennel, marjoram, thyme, basil, mint, rosemary, fenugreek, watercress, saffron, and rue (an acrid, green leafy plant). Dates were an important part of the common diet, while the palm also provided date sugar and date wine, as well as a celery-like delicacy cut from the growing heart of the male palm. They made sweet date syrup from the dates. And of course, because dates are easily dried and preserved, they were a valuable trade commodity with foreign lands.

Other fruits commonly grown were apples, pears, grapes, figs, quince, plums, apricots, cherries, mulberries, melons, medlar, peach, pomegranates, as well as pistachios.

Meat was also a part of the ancient Mesopotamian diet. Massive reed barns housed numerous flocks and herds, which were then redistributed for sustenance and cult needs. The animals were delivered alive and then slaughtered by a butcher. But some animals were dead on arrival. Both types of meat were considered fit for human consumption because both were same-day fresh. The meat from already-dead animals was fed to soldiers, messengers, and cult personnel. Dead asses were used only as dog meat.

Poultry, geese, and ducks were raised for meat and eggs. Chickens were was introduced from India in the first millennium BC, along with rice culture. Mutton and, less commonly, beef, were eaten at festivals, and in the earliest times, offerings of goats were a regular feature of peasant worship and an equally regular part of peasant diet. But as the merchants and moneylenders increased their wealth, there was a corresponding reduction in the wealth of the people. So, the ordinary peasant could less afford goat meat in his diet because the pay for his labor was reduced so much.

Pig meat was regularly eaten, since wild pigs were found in the southern marshes, and domestic pigs were raised in large herds. As omnivorous scavengers, they could eat anything and barley was provided them as a supplement. Since fat is usually in short supply in primitive diets, fat pork was considered a delicacy. A Sumerian proverb makes the point that it was too good for slave girls, who had to make do with the lean ham.

The Sumerians also drank milk: cow's milk, goat's milk, and ewe's milk. Milk soured quickly in the hot climate of southern Iraq. Ghee (clarified butter) was less perishable than milk, as was the round, chalky cheese, which could be transformed back to sour milk by grating it and adding water. The texts do not mention the processing of sheep's milk before the Persian period, at which time it was made into a kind of cottage cheese. Other dairy products included yogurt and butter. Many kinds of cheeses were produced: a white cheese (for the king's table), "fresh" cheese, and flavored, sweetened, and sharp cheeses.

The rivers were filled with fish and turtles. Turtle eggs and frogs could be found along the river banks. There were no synthetic fertilizers or pesticides in those days to poison the water and kill them all. A Sumerian text (~ 2000 BC) described the habits and appearance of 18 species of fish including carp, sturgeon, catfish, and eels. Fish was an important source of protein in the diet.

In addition to beer and date wine, grape wine was known as early as the Proto-literate period (3200-2900 BC), probably as an import from the highlands. In that early period, it was not a drink in everyday use. Such fermented beverages, which probably contained a good deal of lees, were imbibed from a common vat through hollow reeds, of which the end was perforated with small holes to form a kind of filter.

Beer was an important part of the Sumerian diet and there were many varieties. The literal translation was "barley beer." The Sumerians at Ur enjoyed dark beer, clear beer, freshly brewed beer, and well-aged beer as well as sweet and bitter beers. They did not use hops for flavoring. Ration lists for palace employees recorded the distribution of one quart to one gallon of beer a day, depending on the rank of the recipient.

Throughout Mesopotamian history, brewing was in the hands of women, for this craft is the only one which was under the protection of female divinities, while the ale-wife is specifically mentioned in the laws of Hammurabi.

Unlike beer, wine could be made only once a year, when the grapes ripened, but wine had a longer shelf life when stored in a sealed jar. It was referred to as a very expensive and rare commodity, found in areas of natural rainfall in the highlands. Many wines were named after their places of origin. Though wine consumption increased over time, it was still a luxury item, served only to the gods and to the wealthy. Only women ran the wine shops where certain priestesses were prohibited from entering upon penalty of death. Other products of the vine included grape juice, wine vinegar, and raisins.

As you can see, with all of this great variety of foods, the Mesopotamian peoples had everything that they needed to cook some delicious and healthful foods. Cereals were made into pastry, cakes, or biscuits by cooking the flour mixed with honey, ghee, sesame oil, milk, or various fruits. Soups were prepared with a starch or flour base of chick-peas, lentils, barley flour, emmer flour, onions, lentils, beans, mutton fat or oil, honey, or meat juice. The soups were thick and nourishing—a meal in a bowl.

Many foods were preserved for times of need. Grains were easy to keep and, when properly stored, could last for decades. Legumes could be dried in the sun. A variety of fruits were pressed into cakes. Fish and meat were preserved by salting, drying, and smoking. During the winter, ice was brought from the highlands, covered with straw, and stored in icehouses for cooling beverages, even during the hottest summers.

Thus, it can be seen that the Sumerians and the people of Mesopotamia were well-stocked with food. Indeed, the bountiful harvests of the Fertile Crescent region are what supported those people in attaining the higher levels of civilization. With abundant food from an agricultural base, they were not restricted in their cultural advancement like their nomadic neighbors, who relied upon the unreliable hunting and gathering and the nomadic shepherding of goats.

The Sumerians ate two meals a day. They bragged about their highly developed cuisine and compared it to that of the desert nomads, whom they believed had no idea of the ways of civilized life. They described the nomads as eating raw food and not even knowing how to make a cake with flour, eggs, and honey. Such an abundance and variety of food caused the hungry goat-herders of the surrounding countries to covet those fruitful lands of Mesopotamia.

*****

With food, the Third Essential of Life, well-supplied, what did the Sumerians do for clothing? Spinning and weaving was an art known since Paleolithic times. Because the Sumerians kept sheep and goats, the wool clothing that they made kept them warm in the winter. And they grew flax that produced a light cloth for summer months. But since the generally hot weather required few clothes at all, Clothing, the Fourth Essential of Life, was also well-supplied to those people.

The Fifth Essential of Life is shelter. Again, this was easily supplied by the natural surroundings. The people who lived in the marshes of Sumer, had learned how to build rather large and beautiful houses out of the giant reeds that grew there in abundance [see Figure 5]. These were used for housing, for barns for their small cattle, and as pens for ducks and geese. As the photograph shows, such reed houses are still used today in southern Iraq by the so-called "marsh Arabs."

Figure-5

And of course, Mesopotamia is famous for its large cities made entirely of mud bricks. As any child knows, mud can be made into many things besides mud pies. And when it dries, it is almost "as hard as rock." From mud bricks, huge temples were built, reaching 80 feet above the plains. Entire cities with double-storied houses, domed roofs and arches, sewer drainage systems, and town walls were made entirely from mud bricks—both sun-dried for common work and baked bricks for fortifications, drain pipes, and palace facades.

With food and shelter well-supplied, the Sumerians found that the Sixth Essential of Life, a spouse, was not difficult to find. Marriage (throughout the whole of Sumerian and Babylonian society) was monogamous in the sense that a man might have only one woman who ranked as a wife and who enjoyed a social status corresponding to his. But for a man to also go the Temple to enjoy "praying" with the temple prostitutes, was not something for an obedient wife to complain about.

Once the moneylenders had perverted society enough by turning the wives and children of their victims into whores and slaves, it became a normal part of Mesopotamian society to make use of the female slaves as sex slaves. The offspring of such unions were carefully legislated in the surviving law codes. With so much of everything necessary for a happy life, the Sixth Essential of Life, a spouse, was easy to find. There were few, if any, bachelors in Mesopotamia.

As you shall see, slavery grew because of the growing national and private debts of the people to the moneylenders. As slavery increased, sexual exploitation became an ever-increasing pleasure of the merchant-moneylenders (the Haves) who owned slaves.

The Seventh Essential of Life are children. Most civilizations know that children provide much help for the parents around the home and farm. Children are like a savings account toward one's later years, if they are raised right. With children, society is assured a strong and bright future. And with children, parents can experience the fulfillment and the immortal nature of their lives. And they can assure themselves of comfort in their old age.

Most people in those days could more easily make a living because children became workers in the fields and shops very early. The money-lenders made good use of children because they could hire a man and his boys to work the fields and pay only for the man.

However, even though civilization was successful in Mesopotamia, and even though the country had attained a population of one million by the third millennium BC, life expectancy was still rather short, when including infant mortality. The average life expectancy was about 40 years although many lived to be older; 50, 60, or even 90 years were not unknown.

In a wisdom text from the Syrian city of Emar, the gods allotted Man a maximum lifetime of 120 years. To see one's family in the fourth generation was considered the ultimate blessing of extreme old age. We know that the mother of King Nabonidus lived for 104 years—she told us so in her autobiography. Archives have shown that many individuals lived at least 70 years. But as the moneylenders manipulated the kings and their countries into wars, it was not old age but battle casualties that became the major cause of death among adult males.

Finally, the Eighth Essential of Life, with their God to protect and nurture them, the Sumerians had everything that life could offer. The fertile land produced abundant crops and there was enough food for everybody as well as a huge excess for trade. With their flocks of sheep and goats and fields of flax, there was enough wool and linen clothing to protect them from both heat and cold. The mud bricks and the reed houses gave them shelter. The work in the fields gave them food. Yes, there was enough for everybody. Thus, after so many hundred years, the Ubaidians were forgotten and stories began to circulate among the Sumerian storytellers, priests, and bards about a long-ago Garden of Eden to which they were all heirs. These stories were eventually written onto clay tablets, the tablets were baked into bricks, and the stone-hard bricks were dug up 5,000 years later by the archaeologists to prove that the Jews are liars. But in 3000 BC, there were no Jews, so there were a lot of happy people living in Sumeria.

That is, there was enough for everybody and the people were happy —except for the *tamkarum* (merchant-moneylenders) who already had more than they could ever use. For those greedy and voracious parasites, nothing could satisfy them because there was an entire world that they did not yet own.

Even though there was enough of everything for everybody, the food and the goods were not everywhere equally abundant because there were only two social classes that had evolved in this Cradle of Civilization, this Fertile Crescent, this land of Sumeria and Babylonia and Assyria, this land of Mesopotamia.

There was enough for everybody but not everybody had enough. This was because the people were divided into the two classes of the awilum (the Haves) and the muskenum (the Have-Nots). Mainly, the "Haves" got what they had by taking it either by force or by fraud from the "Have-Nots." Under a system where the Sumerian Swindle was allowed to be practiced, there could only be "Haves" and "Have-Nots" along with the resulting slaves from both classes who were enchained for not being able to pay their debts to the merchant-moneylenders. The fraudulent nature of lending-at-interest mathematically and automatically and relentlessly swindled from both rich and poor, routed all wealth into the greedy hands of the tamkarum (merchant-moneylenders). Those greedy bean-counters and accountants knew this from the very earliest times—their arithmetic proved it!

Under the unyielding calculations of the Sumerian Swindle, these members of the Treasonous Class were determined that for them to continue to be the "Haves," meant that everyone else would have to continue to be the "Have-Nots." The awilum (the Haves) got everything that they had from the labor of the muskenum (the Have-Nots). And to keep what they had, meant that they could not give any of it back. The muskenum (the Have-Nots) accepted this state of affairs because they did not understand the Sumerian Swindle for what it really is. They believed that owing more than you borrow was "a normal part of life." Because the Swindle had been a part of Sumerian society for longer than anyone could remember, implied that it "had always been here." So, why question it?

The only danger to the moneylenders' schemes were those ordinary, curious people who questioned why the moneylenders should be allowed to gain "ownership" of the entire world for free; to enslave the people upon it to do their bidding; and to keep what they had swindled without doing a smidgen of work other than to manipulate the numbers on an accounting tablet and only bothering to languidly push forward their upraised palms expecting to be paid. All of this without being hanged for it! But in Sumeria, there were no trees upon which to hang the moneylenders, so no one thought of such a simple solution to the problems which the tamkarum (merchant-moneylenders) were beginning to cause all of mankind.

Defrauding the Peasants

As population and land use increased, it was necessary for the various farms and gardens on arable land to be carefully plotted, measured, and the boundaries marked. Of course, the scribes were the only ones who knew how to calculate land sizes and to make measurements. They could also read and write on the clay tablets the sales contracts, mortgages, rentals, leases, and work agreements for all to see. A good memory was not enough once writing became the basis of contracts and agreements. If a peasant could not read, then he was dependent upon the scribes. However, trickery and deceit were valued talents in Mesopotamia. Those with the money, education, and avarice tended to oppress and dispossess those without those attributes. No matter how blatant the fraud, the poor had little defense from the ravages of the rich, just as in modern times.

The only protectors of the poor were *the priests*, who preached mercy for the muskenum (the Have-Nots) and who disapproved of the greed and the evils practiced by the awilum (the Haves). All of the gods of Meso-potamia wanted mankind to follow the "straight and true path." So, the priests of those gods were a great embarrassment to the tamkarum (merchant-moneylenders) when they accused them of crookedness and falsehood. And the priests were the cause of a loss in revenue when they preached to the lenders for mercy for the borrowers, when they implored the merchant-moneylenders to have mercy on the widows and orphans and not evict them from their homes or clap them into slave collars to work their lives away slaving for the moneylenders. It took a hard heart and an evil disposition to be a moneylender when there were such pesky priests confronting them at the temples and on the streets. But if they wanted to keep what they had swindled, the moneylenders learned to turn a blind eye and a deaf ear toward such busybodies.

Even though there was plenty of land available for crops, this land could not produce a harvest without huge expenditures of labor. Canals and irrigation ditches needed to be dug, the soil needed to be plowed, furrowed, harrowed, raked, watered, weeded, and tended, all meticulously with hand tools and an ox-drawn plow. Birds needed to be frightened away by the farmers' children. The investment in labor by the farmers was immense.

The house that they built out of mud bricks was both back-breaking labor and a labor of love by men who enjoy working on their own land with their own hands and raising a happy, well-fed family. Hard work did not mean that the work was without joy. Being close to Nature and close to God were some of the joys of farming, just as they are today—although the work in those days was more strenuous since it was all done with hand tools and with oxen or, for those too poor to hire an ox, with the wife and kids pulling a single-bladed plow, and everyone joining in the labor of digging and maintaining the irrigation ditches. In those days, it was work hard or starve with leisure. This huge amount of labor with hand tools and ox-drawn plows was necessary to turn raw desert into a bountiful farm. It was labor accomplished by the sweat of the entire farming family. Parents, children, grandparents, all did the work.

It was not just for a few shekels of silver which the moneylender wanted, but it was this huge amount of labor, the countless hours between sun up and sun down, the months and years laboring under the hot sun without pay but with the hope of a good harvest; it was this as well as the mud-brick houses and land itself which the moneylenders stole when they foreclosed a family farm. They did not foreclose on empty, undeveloped land. Just as the bankers do today, they waited until all of the work had been done and the crop ready to harvest before swindling the peasants out of their labor, their produce, and their property.

The man-years of labor plus the price of the land plus the cost of whatever mud-brick buildings that were on the farm, would make it too expensive for the moneylenders to buy and then resell for a profit. Farms were too expensive to buy for a fair price but they were not too expensive to steal for the price of a paltry loan.

Secret Fraud #3 of the Sumerian Swindle brought the moneylenders huge profits: "Collateral that is worth more than the loan, is the banker's greatest asset." In addition, Secret Fraud #3 went hand-in-claw with Secret Fraud #4 for stealing huge numbers of farms: "*Loans of silver repaid with goods and not with silver, forfeit the collateral.*" What did this mean to the victims of the moneylenders?

Returning to the example from above of only one banker in the world with only two pieces of money to loan, let's look deeper. The farmer and the merchant have both borrowed one shekel of silver and they must each repay a shekel and a half to the moneylender. If both the farmer and the merchant have a bad year and cannot repay even the shekel that they borrowed, the moneylender takes the farmer's farm and takes the merchant's shop as forfeiture. And so the moneylender gets an entire farm, a shop, and a house for only two shekels. These, he can sell for many shekels worth of grain and other goods. So, his profits are enormous. "Collateral that is worth more than the loan, is the banker's greatest asset," was a great swindle which is still being practiced today by modern bankers. It is a pawn-broker's method that is used by the big, modern bankers whose necks, even today, are not too big to fit into a noose.

This technique was used by the moneylenders of 3000 BC because even if they lost their principal, they gained even more by confiscating the collateral. Even if the principle was repaid, if the interest was not repaid, then they would not only get their principle back but they could additionally confiscate the property of the debtor as well! This was a powerful discovery! They could make money-on-a-loan and also make money even when the loan was not repaid! Indeed, because of the intrinsic fraud of the Sumerian Swindle of demanding more money than actually existed, some loans could never be repaid. And even then, the moneylender made money.

Under the relentless arithmetic of the Sumerian Swindle, it was difficult for a moneylender to lose when lending either grain or silver. The arithmetical numbers are eternally unwavering and the fate of mortal man is eternally at the mercy of both gods and moneylenders. When the principal and interest are repaid, there is a profit. And when the loan is not repaid, there is still a profit. But this was just the very simple beginnings of the business of legalized crime that has been passed down to modern man in the form of banking, mortgages, and credit card debt. This was just the beginnings of the Sumerian Swindle.

The following list does not make much sense now but each point is explained in the following chapters. The Sumerian Swindle has 21 secret frauds. The Twenty-One Secret Frauds of the Sumerian Swindle are:

#1: All interest on the loan of money is a swindle.

#2: Loans rely on the honesty of the borrower but not the honesty of the lender.

#3: Collateral that is worth more than the loan, is the banker's greatest asset.

#4: Loans of silver repaid with goods and not with silver, forfeit the collateral.

#5: The debtor is the slave of the lender.

#6: High morals impede profits, so debauching the virtuous destroys their moral superiority and pulls them below the depravity of the moneylender, who thereby masters them and bends them to his will.

#7: Monopoly gives wealth and power, but monopoly of money gives the greatest wealth and power.

#8: Large crime families are more successful than lone criminals or gangs; international crime families are the most successful of all.

#9: Only the most ruthless and greedy moneylenders survive; only the most corrupt bankers triumph.

#10: Time benefits the banker and betrays the borrower.

#11: Dispossessing the people brings wealth to the dispossessor, yielding the greatest profit for the bankers when the people are impoverished.

#12: All private individuals who control the public's money supply are swindling traitors to both people and country.

#13: To keep what we have swindled, our victims must be convinced that regaining ownership of what they have lost is never allowed. We must always take but they can never take back.

#14: Anyone who is allowed to lend-at-interest eventually owns the entire world.

#15: Loans to friends are power; loans to enemies are weapons.

#16: Labor is the source of wealth; control the source and you control the wealth, raise up labor and you can pull down kings.

#17: Kings are required to legitimatize a swindle, but once the fraud is legalized, those very kings may be assassinated or betrayed.

#18: When the source of goods is distant from the customers, profits are increased both by import and export.

#19: "Prestige" is a glittering robe for ennobling treason and blinding fools; the more it is used, the more it profits he who dresses in it.

#20: Champion the minority in order to dispossess the majority of their wealth and power, and then swindle the minority out of that wealth and power.

#21 As gatekeepers, control the choke points and master the body; strangle the choke points and kill the body.

*****

During the period of high Ubaidian Culture between 5000-4000 BC, while the Ubaidian people were founding the ancient cities of Adab, Eridu, Kish, Kullab, Lagash, Larsa, Nippur, and Ur, the Ubaidian moneylenders were busy defrauding and swindling their own people by using only simple interest. But the swindle did not really become a major power in the world until after the arrival of the Sumerians and the invention of writing and numbers. What had been a swindle at a local level using counting beads and clay markers became an incredibly profitable scam, supported by the invention of written agreements and arithmetic. With writing and arithmetic, compound interest became the main engine of the Sumerian Swindle. But before delving into this history, let's look at the metallic part of the Swindle more carefully.

In the ancient societies where silver was used as a form of money, manipulation of the availability of this commodity metal produced even greater profits. What happens when the farmer actually has a good year? He has borrowed one shekel of silver and must repay a total of one and a half shekels of silver. But there are only two shekels in the entire world and the banker has kept the second shekel hidden in his strong box and out of circulation. The farmer sells his goods in the market and returns to the moneylender saying, "Here is your one shekel back but I cannot find another half shekel of silver to pay you for interest on the loan. And so, I will pay the interest with produce from the farm." Thereby, the farmer tries to pay the banker with one shekel of silver and a half shekel's worth of barley. That seems fair, doesn't it?

But the moneylender, knowing that there are only two shekels and that he is hiding one of them, says, "Our agreement was to repay the loan of one shekel of silver with a shekel and a half of silver. The loan was for

silver and the repayment must also be in silver. Since you have paid back
the one-shekel principal in silver but not the half-shekel of interest in
silver, you forfeit your collateral. I will not accept repayment of the interest
in trade goods of equal value because the agreement was to repay the loan
all in silver." Because the banker had created a shortage of a commodity
metal such as silver, he was again asking the impossible. And when the
impossible could not be met, the moneylender seized the real property of
the debtor and got it for free, even though the debt could easily have been
repaid with trade goods of equal value. And so, Secret Fraud #4 of the
Sumerian Swindle is: "Loans of silver repaid with goods and not with
silver, forfeit the collateral."

The moneylender was able to seize the farmer's farm even when the
principal was repaid simply because the interest was not repaid in silver.
The banker demanded to be repaid one-half shekel which, in fact, did not
exist in circulation because he kept it hidden in his own vault. The debtor
believed that the shekel existed in circulation because the lying numbers on
the moneylender's loan agreement claimed that it existed and that he owed
it to the moneylender. The farmer believed that he had been unable to earn it
through his labor, because the world is so big that he cannot imagine that
its supply of silver is so small that it can be hoarded by just a few men.

And so, the people believe that what the moneylenders demand can
be met and so they believe that they still owe the bankers these impossible
sums. And since they believe that they owe the money, then they accept
the swindle as being an honest business error on their part. They blame
themselves for being unable to earn the silver, while the banker knows full
well that it is impossible to repay the loan. Either the money doesn't exist
because it is only lying numbers on an accounting tablet, or the banker is
keeping it hidden away in his strong room. Thus, the borrowers hand over
their property to the moneylender. The thieving moneylender is not in a
hurry to explain their error in judgement because no moneylender is an
honest businessman and every banker is a crook.

Of course, in reality there are many more pieces of silver in the world
than just two. So, in real life, not all the people are defrauded equally. But
the technique is the same. Even with many millions of pieces of silver,
there are always far fewer in circulation than what the account books claim
are due. Even though everybody in society is being swindled by the
bankers and moneylenders, those who are able to earn enough to repay
their loans, feel safe and superior to those who become impoverished.
When moneylenders are allowed to lend at interest, *everyone in society is a
loser*—except the moneylenders, as you shall see.

To continue with this example, let's say that the merchant has a good year and makes a shekel and a half of the two shekels in circulation, and the farmer has a bad year and only gains a half shekel. The merchant feels confident and successful in having repaid the loan, more so because he sees the farmer's land confiscated and the farmer's wife and children dragged off in slave's collars. With his profits, the merchant may even buy up the confiscated land from the moneylender and so become a part of the criminal enterprise. But regardless of how the wealth is distributed, whenever money is loaned-at-interest, it creates in a ledger book the lie and the delusion that there is more money to be repaid than is actually in existence. This was true in 3000 BC and it is true today. All bankers will lie to you and say, "Numbers do not lie." But what they don't tell you is that liars who write the numbers, *always* lie. And all bankers, loan sharks, financiers and moneylenders are liars who swindle with the lying numbers that they create.

The ancient money lenders discovered Secret Fraud #4 of the Sumerian Swindle: "Loans of silver repaid with goods and not with silver, forfeit the collateral." But what if the moneylenders, working in collusion, could make those loans to tens of thousands of people and then quietly withdraw silver from circulation by keeping it hidden in their safe houses or shipping it to another country or to another city-state? This would increase their profits and their land holdings by reducing the ability of the borrowers to repay the loans, by taking away the silver that the people needed to repay the loans plus the interest. Such cartels and guilds of moneylenders could influence the entire flow of history by enriching one state while impoverishing another state. And by doing so, their profits would be enormously increased not by waiting for profitable events to appear but to actually manipulate the economy of an entire country by smuggling silver between city-states. In such ways, the moneylenders of Sumeria devolved into parasites who did no actual work but siphoned away the wealth created by honest people.

Once the loans had been made, once the clay contracts had been written, once the agreements were presented to the gods and confirmed by the scribes, the honest borrowers were trapped by the dishonest money-lenders. By working in conspiring groups of moneylender guilds, they could claim both principal and interest in silver when there was not enough silver in circulation to pay off all agreements. There was not enough silver in circulation because the moneylenders were hiding it in their strong boxes, shipping it to other city-states, so as to disallow the debtors to pay off their debt. Hoarding silver was easy to do because the moneylenders got all their silver for free.

These ancient Sumerian moneylenders discovered the secret of using a commodity metal such as silver or gold as a form of money, so that they could swindle the wealth of their fellow men simply by controlling the abundance or dearth of these metals. By stipulating repayment *in silver*, the amount of which was both limited in quantity and could be hoarded out of circulation, they were able to rake the wealth of the ancient Near East into their own barns and counting houses.

My simple example of two pieces of money and only one banker holds true even when the amount of money is in the trillions and the number of swindling bankers is in the tens of thousands, as they are today. But the swindle and fraud of these techniques are still the same. Interest on a loan, even the tiniest interest in thousandths of one percent, still creates money on a ledger book that does not in reality exist. Whether we are discussing two farmers in ancient Mesopotamia or the millions of indebted farmers and homeowners around the world today, they are still being swindled by the bankers and moneylenders who use sleight-of-hand arithmetical tricks to create the illusion that what you pay back must be *more* than what you borrow.

Was all of this "legal"? Most of the traditions that were handed down to the people of Sumeria and Mesopotamia were just that, traditions. In those days, there were no codified laws that everybody followed. It was still a young and growing civilization of largely illiterate people who were led by literate thieves and swindlers who made their own rules as circumstances required. It was a civilization of awilum (the Haves) who made it a part of their "tradition" to take whatever they could from the muskenum (the Have-Nots) and to profit by enslaving them to the loansharking rackets called "debt" and "interest-on-a-loan."

If the defrauded peasant tried to get justice in the court system, he was in for a difficult time. In the first place, there was no court system as in modern times but, rather, an informal court presided over by a judge without jury. In Sumerian times, just as in modern times, the laws are as they "have always been," written by the awilum (the Haves) to protect what they have and written entirely for their own benefit. In the Mesopotamian courts of law, as Edward Chiera, Professor of Assyriology at the University of Chicago, wrote:

> The loser must either pay a sum of money or become the slave of the winner until such time as he does pay. It was a

very dangerous proceeding for peasants to bring their grievances to court because their chance of obtaining justice was slight, and most of them ended by losing their freedom. I have gone over these [cuneiform] contracts with great care, trying to find out whether the judges made any effort to apply the law and be wholly impartial.

Unfortunately, it is evident that they did not. The wealthy landlords kept their records in good order for generations, and quite often could produce a document duly signed by many witnesses, which attested their right to ownership and thereby closed the case. But the trouble was that the landlords had scribes of their own and a certain group of people who always acted as their witnesses. There was nothing easier, in view of the fact that the peasants did not know how to read, than to juggle a few figures or to alter measurements; the mistake would not be discovered for many years.

But these were the cases where the cuneiform records clearly showed the consistently fraudulent and biased nature of the Mesopotamian "law courts." If the cuneiform records were not sufficiently precise or if they were not adequate enough for a moneylender to swindle the peasant's property, then the moneylenders offered an ingenious swindle as an alternate choice. To "prove" their innocence and "prove" their honest piety before the gods, they offered to acquiesce to the will of the gods, if the peasant would accept the River Test.

A peasant could vow with the gods as his witness that the landlords and moneylenders were defrauding him. Or he could vow with the gods as his witness that he was telling the truth and that the moneylenders were liars. In such a case, he could claim his "right" to be subjected to the River Test. The event was timed with a water clock which consisted of a clay bowl with a tiny hole in the bottom, slowing sinking in a larger bowl of water. The peasant would be held underwater until the allotted time had passed and his bowl had completely sunk. If he didn't drown during that time, then the gods had sided with him and the landlord would have to give back the property or the money that was swindled.

At first, this might seem somewhat fair. The only problem was that the moneylenders controlled the size of the hole in the bottom of the bowl. So, a bowl with a tiny hole was given for the peasant's test. And since they usually drowned as a result, the peasants soon learned that it was better to refuse to take the test. Refusing the River Test implied that they did not have the gods behind them and that the moneylender was right in taking their property. It was an ingenious swindle in which the moneylenders were able to offer their own piety and trust in the gods as "proof." After all, *they* were willing to endure the River Test, too, just as long as the peasant tried it first. With the River Test as "proof," they could avoid accusations of fraud while stealing the lands of the muskenum (the Have-Nots) even as the superstitious and god-fearing people looked on in wonder.

This "legal" system of Sumeria was never questioned by those who lived under its thrall simply because it had "always been here." The rich had always enslaved the poor since before the Sumerians had arrived from the South. Money lending was a total fraud in every definition of the word, just as it is today. But it is only in modern times, after all of these millennia filled with the warfare, starvation, and disease purposely created by the moneylenders that we can ask: "Just because it has always been here, does this mean that fraud, swindling, and betrayal are legitimate ways for mankind to follow? If the rich got their wealth by stealing it from the poor, should they be allowed to keep it?" The awilum (the Haves) said, "Yes, it is mine!" And they continued to enslave their fellow men with usury and deceit while the muskenum (the Have-Nots) never thought about it simply because money-lending-at-interest has "always been here." Because it has "always been here," no one has ever asked, "Should it be allowed to continue?" or "Should the thieves be allowed to keep what they have stolen?" or "Why not hang the bankers and take back the wealth that they swindled?"

The Lifeline of the Canal System

Without water, the crusty and dusty soil of Mesopotamia could never have grown the world's first civilization. The flood season of the Tigris and Euphrates Rivers is between April and June, so it is not well-timed for planting. Yet, through irrigation ditches and canals, the two rivers were made to irrigate thousands of square miles of barley and wheat and green gardens [see Map 6]. With a dependable and carefully regulated irrigation system, Mesopotamia thrived.

It was this dependence upon the regulated flow of water that was most responsible for the necessity of civil government. Digging canals required well-ordered gangs of workers whose labor had to be evenly proportioned. Their food rations had to be equally weighed and fairly distributed. Proper amounts of water for each field had to be timed with the water clocks. The volume of water for each field had to be calculated. The canals and ditches had to be maintained against erosion and cleared of weed invasion. All of this, plus the numerous runners, cooks, suppliers, carpenters, rope-makers, boatmen, and ancillary workers of all kinds, had to be efficiently organized and administered. This was one of the major responsibilities of the city governments throughout Mesopotamia because without water and the resulting crops, everybody would die of starvation.

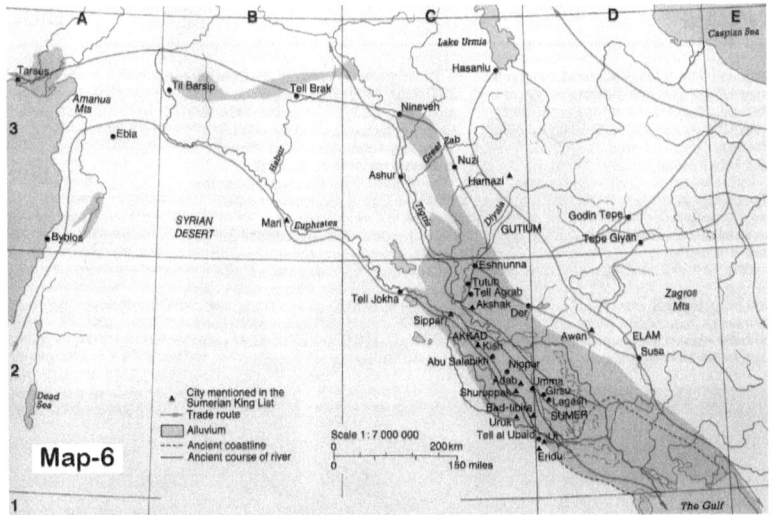

Map-6

These life-giving waterways were also important for trade. Indeed, trade was necessary for the very survival of these city-states because Mesopotamia lacked everything needed to build a civilization. Wood, metal, and stone could only be obtained from distant places, either through trade or by military force. And trade required transportation.

In ancient Mesopotamia, the most efficient way of transporting goods was by water. Most places in Mesopotamia could be reached by the Tigris and the Euphrates Rivers or along their tributary rivers and canals. From the mouth of the two rivers, ships constructed of river-reeds sailed down the Persian Gulf to Melukkha (the Indus Valley) and the East Arabian ports of Magan (Oman) and Dilmun (Bahrain). From the western-most loop of the Euphrates, a tradesman could reach the Mediterranean Sea over a relatively short distance of 160 miles by donkey caravan. Again, civil administration was necessary to regulate this river traffic and to tax the cargos of the various merchants. Controlling ship traffic had both an economic and military use. So, the kings in every city took special interest in this work.

Trade by river was not some minor pastime by primitive aborigines in reed boats, as some modern readers might assume of the people of those ancient times. It was a well-organized, sophisticated, and hugely lucrative industrial enterprise from its earliest inception. It involved large networks of both wholesale and retail traders and their related suppliers and customers.

As an example of scale, Sumerian reed ships in the third millennium could hold about 25 tons and Babylonian ships in the first millennium about 40 tons of cargo. A cuneiform text mentions 13,000 minas (roughly seven tons) of copper as part of one ship's cargo. This was the goods of just one importer. The metal came in ingots of up to four talents (about 200 pounds) shaped like a cowhide with legs at each of the corners so that it could be lifted and carried by four men.

In the earliest days of Sumeria, the merchants and tradesmen did their business with the temples as the main supplier of both export goods and the recipient of the imported items. But as their wealth increased, the moneylenders and merchants became independent of any religious ties and worked for their own personal profits. Boat captains, away for so long from their home ports, have always had an independent character. So, there were plenty of opportunities for the ships' captains and the river boatmen to form working alliances with the merchants who hired their services. In this way, the merchants and moneylenders always had close relationships with the ship captains.

The principal exports from Sumeria to Dilmun (Bahrain) were garments, grain, and oil provided by private businessmen. Contracts were drawn up, giving the value of the goods in terms of silver, and stating the agreed silver value for Dilmun copper to be brought back by the return trade. But there were some important differences between how the merchants and the moneylenders dealt with one another that depended upon whether transportation was by land or by ship.

In the caravan trade with Capadocia (Central Turkey), the money-lenders who were financing a trade agent were entitled to two-thirds of the total profits, with a guaranteed minimum return of 50 percent on his outlay and no risk to his capital. On the other hand, in the sea trade to Dilmun (Bahrain), the entrepreneur normally received, instead of a share in the profits, a fixed return. If the investor did become a full partner in the venture, he then shared the risks as well as any profits. The more favorable conditions for the sea trader as against the caravan leader are related to the fact that the trade with Dilmun was a "closed shop" enterprise, admission to which was a matter of great difficulty. It required technical skill to undertake the actual voyage and it was necessary for the trader to have personal contacts on the island before he could trade there.

In other words, from the earliest times, those who practiced international sea trade with India, Oman, and Bahrain, did so as a closed cartel of international merchants and moneylenders who had a closer and more trusting relationship with one another than would be found in the more common kinds of business arrangements in Sumeria. The Sumerian merchants and moneylenders formed cartels at a very early time and practiced monopoly finance. Only those who were part of this elite in-group were allowed to trade in the distant ports. It took a great deal of silver to hire a ship, load it with trade goods, and make the voyage. But if one did not belong to the monopoly trade cartel, then when you arrived at the trade center, no one would deal with you. And if you persisted, you would find that after getting thoroughly beaten by hired goons and guards, that your cargo had been robbed. Also, on the long and perilous sea voyages, ships, cargoes, and people disappeared and were never heard from again. No one was allowed to trade who was not a member of the cartel.

With ships, there was a great chance for loss of the cargo that could not be recovered if the ship sank or if a ship did not return because of piracy, or even if the merchant and captain had decided to steal the cargo and immigrate to a foreign land. With a missing ship, there was no way to know what had happened and no way to even know where to start looking for it. So, better terms were given to the merchants who traveled by ship as an incentive for them to return. But if a caravan did not return, there were ways of tracking it down, so heftier profits could be squeezed out of the caravan traders [see Map 7].

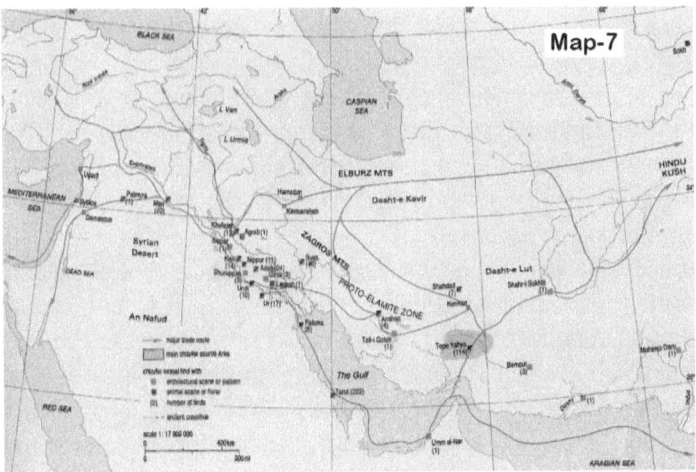

Once the trade goods arrived in Mesopotamia either by ship or by caravan, they were most easily transported throughout the region by the many reed boats that plied the canals and rivers. The large numbers of boats of all sizes can be surmised from a single letter sent to the King of Ur by his governor Ibbi-Sin who had been sent to secure grain for the besieged city of Ur. Ibbi-Sin acquired the necessary grain but sent a letter to Ur asking for 600 boats of 120 gur each, that is, of holding a total capacity of about 186,807 modern barrels. Thus, when thinking about the amounts of goods and wealth that flowed through Mesopotamia, one should not think in terms of a few donkeys with packs but, rather, of huge amounts of wholesale and retail goods, comparable in ratio though on a smaller scale, to the goods flowing through a modern sea port. We are studying here a sophisticated society, not merely an ancient one.

The greed of the moneylenders was just as voracious as it is today but with fewer restrictions. From the very earliest times, the treasonous class had learned how to increase their profits by restricting the flow of goods.

Certainly, they did not like to pay taxes to the kings or to the tribal chiefs through whose lands their caravans had to pass. Taxes meant lower profits and higher prices to their customers. There was only so much their customers were willing to pay, so higher prices reduced sales and ate into their profit margins.

Transportation costs were always a problem since the multitudes of boatmen were free to charge whatever they wanted for shipping. And so, to control these problems, the merchants organized the river traffic into guilds of boatmen who controlled all the shipping fees. This form of monopoly allowed the merchants to further squeeze the small farmers. The boatmen could charge the poor people a higher price to ship their produce than they would charge the bigger merchants who gave them more work though at a lower price per trip.

Through such cartels, the merchants saved money, the boatmen made more money, and the poor peasants were further impoverished. Because poor people always suffer the most from high prices, when the economy became too difficult for the poor, they easily fell into the clutches of the moneylenders who swindled them out of their farms, their families, and their freedom. Thus, the merchants and moneylenders could make greater profits by restricting the availability of goods.

Just as in modern times, through monopoly of wholesale imports and the control over distribution channels, the tamkarum (merchant-moneylenders) learned how to gain more wealth for themselves simply by getting control of the choke points in the trade routes. They perfected Secret Fraud #21:

"As Gatekeepers, control the choke points and master the body; strangle the choke points and kill the body." These Sumerian tamkarum (merchant-moneylenders) learned how to make more money by monopolizing transportation and raising prices as well as by profiting from the ripple effect of a slowly spreading shortage of goods. By the time the Assyrians took control of Mesopotamia, the Sumerian word for "boatman" had become the same as the word for "thief."

Thus, the merchant-moneylenders corrupted the boatmen who were a vital part of civilization.

Trade in Metals

Just as in modern times, the trade in metals was done on an industrial scale. There was no room for the small merchant except as an agent of the big wholesalers or for the small-time peddler of finished goods who would also loan-at-interest a few shekels to the local yokels. Importing of metals was a field open only to the wealthiest of citizens. These citizens were the kings, the temples, and the tamkarum. Because metals were so vital to both the civilian economy and to the military, those who dealt in these commodities could only be the awilum (the Haves).

Because Mesopotamia did not have any metals in the region, everything had to be imported. Of course, all metals are very heavy and whether you import the raw ore and smelt it yourself or import metallic ingots, you need lots of labor in the form of miners, laborers, donkeys, carts, ships, boats, tool and weapons craftsmen, and mid-level retail merchants to get it to market. Thus, the commodity metal dealers were among the wealthiest of the awilum (the Haves). It was a closed society that included among its members the kings, top temple priests, the moneylenders, and the richest merchants. Everyone else were either loyal subalterns, minor partners, or employees who worked for them.

By 2900 BC, copper was in common use as vases, bowls, mirrors, cosmetic pots, fishhooks, chisels, daggers, hoes, and axes. Copper ingots were shipped both overland from the Iranian plateau or by reed ships on the Persian Gulf from Magan (Oman) and Melukhkha (the Indus Valley). Analysis of copper and bronze objects of this period show that in Sumerian times it was the surface ores which were used and not the deeper veins and ledges (which occur as sulfides); thus no deep mining was involved.

Iron of meteoric origin began to be used from 3000 BC onwards, mainly in beads and trinkets because it was too brittle to be useful for much else. It wasn't until after 1500 BC, when the Hittites discovered that iron could be made into steel by the process that we know as carbonizing, which was achieved by the blacksmith who repeatedly hammered the glowing iron that had been heated on a charcoal fire. This new technique gradually spread throughout the Near East and came into use in Mesopotamia from about 1300 BC. But in all of these centuries, the metallic trade was carried out only by the wealthiest merchant-moneylenders who monopolized the wholesale market.

Copper, bronze, zinc, lead, iron, silver, and gold, all had both commercial and military uses. But it was not the hard and useful metals that drove the machinery of commerce and war, it was the soft and useless metals like gold and silver that drove the moneylenders mad. With small amounts of silver and gold, they could buy everything on earth—including the bodies and souls of men. The moneylenders developed Secret Fraud #5 of the Sumerian Swindle: *"The debtor is the slave of the lender."* Therefore, to enslave the world, the moneylenders merely needed to put all of mankind into debt.

PART TWO

Time in History, Warfare, and Money-Lending

CHAPTER 5

SOCIAL CLASSES IN ANCIENT TIMES

Although it was a tradition passed down to the Sumerians that all culture originated in the town of Eridu, it was from the much larger town of Uruk that Mesopotamian culture began to flourish. Uruk is the Sumerian city from which the modern state of Iraq got its name. Uruk is where both the sky god, Anu, and the Goddess of love, Inanna, resided in their great mud-brick temples.

At its height, Uruk probably had 50,000 to 80,000 residents living in 6 square kilometers of walled area—the largest city in the world at its time. Uruk was one of the world's first cities with a dense population. It also saw the rise of the centralized state in Mesopotamia with a full-time bureaucracy, military, and the stratified social classes of the "Haves" and "Have-Nots." Cities that coexisted with Uruk at this time were only about 10 hectares in area, showing that it was a vastly larger and more complex city than any of its contemporaries.

Uruk was an important city because it represented a shift from small, agricultural villages to a larger urban center. And it is from here around 3200 BC to 3000 BC that the crude bookkeeping scratches on clay that the Ubaidians had been using, were turned into the world's first writing by the Sumerians. With this invention, the dawn of written history began. And through the trade routes between Mesopotamia and Egypt, the invention of writing spread west to the land of the pharaohs and east as far as China.

Because the Sumerians bought the land from the Ubaidian money-lenders and so acquired control gradually, they were able to learn the cultural, religious, political, business, and social traditions of the Ubaidians, peacefully without warfare. The greedy Ubaidian moneylenders were eager to sell the swindled properties for silver and to train the new immigrants in the ways of ownership and confiscation. The Ubaidian "Have-Nots" could not prevent the new arrivals from displacing them because they were betrayed by the "Haves" who were, in turn, were protected by the king. So, whether the poor Ubaidians worked in the fields for the Ubaidian moneylenders or for the new owners of the property, the pay was the same.

The new Sumerian owners did not come as conquerors so much as they appeared as the new landlords of the land and all that was on it. All that was on it included slaves, hired hands, and poor farmers who were working the land for subsistence wages. As their numbers increased through the immigration of their relatives, the Sumerians were soon masters of the land. As co-owners and social equals with the Ubaidian awilum (the Haves), the Ubaidian moneylenders taught them everything about Mesopotamian society, inventions, agriculture, urban management, and the most ruthless ways of making money.

Once their children were grown up, within a single generation, the Sumerians had mastered it all and began to add their own ingenuity to the culture. As more Sumerian immigrants bought land and moved their foreign relatives onto the property, all traces of the indigenous Ubaidian culture vanished. A new people speaking a new language became the owners of Mesopotamia. This is always a result of allowing large numbers of foreigners to immigrate into any country. Even though the Ubaidian merchant-moneylenders had betrayed their own people, they made a fortune doing it, so it was all okay. The Sumerians continued with all the cultural traditions that "had always been here": the religion, the social structure, the inventions, and the frauds and swindles of lending-at-interest.

Bronze Age Sumerian Civilization: 3000 BC

As the year 3000 BC dawned, the new invention of writing coincided with many other inventions and discoveries both from Sumerian genius as well as from the peoples living in distant countries. This era was also the approximate beginning of the Bronze Age, where men could set aside their brittle implements of obsidian and flint and their bendable tools of copper and could make use of a stronger and superior alloy. By mixing copper and tin in their furnaces, this new metal alloy gave mankind tough materials for his religious sculptures, corrosion-resistant fittings for his ships, durable plows, sharp tips for his arrows, and cutting edges for his swords and daggers. Bronze enabled civilization to thrive and war to become more deadly.

To again repeat, metals, as well as everything else except for mud, clay, and reeds, had to be imported into Sumeria. Because Sumeria was the bread basket of the ancient Near East, such things as grain, flax, and wool clothing, dates and woven goods, could be used for barter. Because the trade routes were long and hazardous and the volume of goods to be shipped in wholesale lots was large, only the awilum (the Haves) could practice the import-export business. Smaller merchants worked for the wholesalers and, in turn, distributed goods through traveling agents and peddlers to distant villages. Thus, the flow of profits were then, as they are today, always siphoned to the top. The highest profits were in foreign trade, where monopoly of goods was maintained by the big merchants who could distribute through a family network of retail shops and traveling peddlers.

Roads suitable for wagons were few. Long-distance traffic was usually conducted by donkeys carrying packs. Such donkey caravans could follow the most primitive paths and the narrowest mountain trails, which allowed the merchants to penetrate to all of the outlying villages in the deepest mountains and the most distant oasis.

The length of a daily stage of a caravan was between 25 and 30 kilometers. The load of an individual donkey varied from 130 minas (65 kilograms) to 150 minas (75 kilograms). From these recorded data, we can estimate the times, distances, and quantities of goods that the ancient merchants could handle.

Wagons were used for short hauls such as transporting grain to local granaries. Farther north, in Upper Mesopotamia and in Syria, roads were more important than rivers and canals. Wagons were used for loads too bulky and heavy to be carried on donkey back. The ability to carry such heavy and unwieldy loads such as logs of cedar, pine, and cypress over great distances on uneven terrain implied the maintenance of ancient wagon roads. As for building mountain roads for carrying lumber and stone, even greater engineering skill was required.

River traffic in Mesopotamia was always heavy. Cuneiform tablets record the transportation of grain, cattle, fish, milk, vegetables, oil, fruit, wool, stone, bricks, leather, and people over the network of canals, for which clay "canal maps" have been found. As early as the third millennium BC, Mesopotamian seagoing reed ships sailed to distant lands for raw materials. Gold, copper, lapis lazuli, pearls (called "fish eyes"), ivory and ivory objects (such as combs, boxes, figurines, and furniture decorations), dates, and onions were traded. All of this became the business of the Sumerians as they bought up farms and shops from the Ubaidian moneylenders.

Although Uruk was a larger city, drawing its wealth from the agricultural productivity of the soil, the city of Ur became more important for its trade links. Because of the less efficient and rough roads, traders transported large cargos by water routes whenever possible. So, this should be remembered because it is important to the thesis of this history that all river shipping ended at Ur. From there, goods were packed on vessels that were able to navigate the bays and lagoons as far as the islands of Failaka and Bahrain. Thus, the merchants of Ur had a particular advantage over the merchants of all other cities in Mesopotamia. It was from Ur that they were in contact with all the cities of the Fertile Crescent via the rivers and canals as well as those lands reached by ship across the Persian Gulf—Dilmun (Bahrain), Magan (Oman), Melukhkha (the Indus Valley), the Arabian Peninsula and the land of Punt (Somalia). This far-ranging knowledge of distant lands gave the merchants of Ur a very important and unique perspective, not only on trade but also on world events. It was at Ur where the moneylenders had their guild halls and where they prayed at the temple of the Moon God.

By 3000 BC, the route around the Arabian Peninsula and into the Red Sea was navigated. This early familiarity of the awilum (the Haves) with all of those trade routes and all of those distant peoples so early in their history, would be of continuing profit to them throughout the ages. Lengthy journeys were undertaken in the Red Sea, Indian Ocean, and Persian Gulf in the third, second, and first millennia BC. Their ancient ships hugged the coasts and hopped from safe harbor to safe harbor only in the daylight hours. So, trade was naturally controlled by whichever people controlled those harbors. Much of the shipping in the Persian Gulf was controlled by the Elamites who charged a tax for use of their harbors.

As the Bronze Age progressed, the merchants and moneylenders no longer were strictly attached to the temples or to the palace as paid middlemen but they became independent businessmen with their own interests and investments. Of course, both the temple and the palace employed underlings who managed the business of those institutions. But the merchant-moneylenders worked increasingly for their own private profits and not for the benefit of the temples as in earlier times, while ignoring the complaints about them from the priests for not following the "Straight and True Path" demanded by the gods.

*****

Independent businessmen though they were, they could not do business without the king because the king offered protection throughout his territory. The king guaranteed diplomatic prestige and official introductions to foreign courts and to foreign cities outside of his territory. In return, the merchants and moneylenders offered the kings and the temple priests first choice of the best imports of foreign goods, as well as political intelligence about foreign peoples.

"Intelligence" is a polite way of saying, "spy." It should not be underestimated the high value that kings placed on the information that spies brought to them. Spying was not the merchant's primary reason for traveling to distant lands. However, the perfect disguise and alibi for a spy was as a traveling merchant because, in those days, merchants were always welcome in every community.

Not so much in modern times but most certainly in the ancient world, a trader or traveling merchant was always a unique and much-admired visitor to every town both big and small. A caravan of pack-asses was always an instant attraction to the slow and sleepy towns and villages of ancient times. Those strangers from distant lands always had new and unique things to sell or to barter. And if one was lucky enough to share a table with them at a public tavern over a pot of beer, amazing stories of distant places and fantastic goblins and strange creatures were sure to be traded in good fun.

Or even if one was not lucky enough to hear the stories first hand, the tavern keeper or the palace servants were sure to re-tell to their relatives and friends what they had overheard when the merchants were in audience with the king. Gossip was a primary way for information to be passed around in small communities. Who needs a telephone when all of the neighbors talk to one another? The ancient people were more advanced than we modern people in this respect because, in modern communities, neighbors no longer talk to neighbors because they are all indoors watching the Jewish lies on television. Merely by not knowing their neighbors, modern people are less human and more insecure than our own ancient forbearers.

The wealthiest moneylenders who invested in trade expeditions stayed safely at home port, managing their shops, their farms, their servants, and their various manufacturing industries. But their partners, the traveling merchants, did more than just barter and haggle and make profits. They were the eyes and ears of their business partners as well as of the king. The traveling merchants were the premier spies of the ancient Near East. They were spies who worked equally for both sides in politics and in secret for themselves, alone. As merchant-moneylender-spies, they sold goods and information to whomever had the silver, and they used their spy networks to enrich themselves.

This spying function of the ancient merchants has been very much overlooked by modern archeologists and historians. Perhaps the historians think that the kings and armies of the ancient Near East went out blindly to war without scouting out the territory first; or that they would risk thirst and starvation without knowing where the wells and oasis were located; or that entire countries would clash in war spontaneously and without diplomatic reason or without military planning. So, it is a bit odd for the historians and archeologists to overlook this. But no matter. Let's look into this ourselves.

Merchants have always had a unique position among all peoples, most especially among the ancient peoples. They were strangers and foreigners who brought unique and interesting goods from far places. In a time when daily life moved as leisurely as a walking ox and the peaceful silence of the countryside pressed in even to the small cities, there was not very much excitement other than the local festivals, wedding parties, or religious events. And such events were of a well-known nature, having the same songs and prayers performed by the same groups of neighbors, priests, and leaders for as long as anybody could remember "just as it had always been."

Life was slow-paced and tranquil. It was a tranquility unknown by modern people who are surrounded by the noise of automobile traffic, jets flying overhead, and the blare of amplified modern noise that passes for "music." Nature is filled with peacefulness and the ancient peoples lived within the peacefulness of Nature.

But whenever foreign traders rode into town or village with their pack-trains of donkeys in tow, now that was something extraordinary! Who were these dust-covered strangers with their pack donkeys and carts loaded with boxes and bundles, and accompanied by fierce-looking guards armed with spears and swords, maces, bows and arrows? What kinds of rare and delightful goods did they bring with them? What news did they bring? What amazing stories would they tell of their adventures? What stories would they tell to those fortunate ones who could hear them first-hand, stories that would then be repeated countless times from mouth to eager ears to the farthest shepherds in the outback? Yes, the traders were a very welcome change to the dull routine of agrarian life throughout all the ancient lands.

Although these merchants traveled quietly so as to attract the least attention possible from bandits, they were not at all quiet when they entered the vicinity of a town or into the districts of a city-state. Then, they wanted as much attention and business as possible. So, drums and trumpets and horns, tambourines and the loud cries of the carnival barker announced to one and to all—Hurry! Hurry! Hurry!—the merchants have arrived with rare treasures to sell. Aggressive self-promotion was a timeless attribute of the merchants and moneylenders.

But it took another 2,000 years of bragging self-aggrandizement before those merchant-moneylender scoundrels developed what is known as "chutzpah" or insolent audacity as a necessary step towards enshrining themselves as the Greatest Show On Earth, self-glorified as the very apple of God's eye, scampering high up on a pedestal of their own manufacture as the very Children of God. Yet, all of them without exception were hook-nosed vampires without compare!

Even when the trade goods were only obsidian blades and obsidian cores carried laboriously from the northern regions around Lake Van, the traders were always welcomed even during the earliest Stone Age times. They brought new things that could not have been obtained without their efforts or without traveling long distances as a trader, oneself. And they brought news from distant places from over the horizon.

In every sleepy hamlet, the traveling merchants and traders always had a special welcome. But even if they ran into hostile tribes, they were protected by their special merchant's threat—they threatened to never come back with any more trade goods if theirs were stolen or their persons assaulted. Since they also carried special letters and seals of safe passage from the various kings, it was only the most remote and barbaric tribes that they had to fear. And for those, they usually had their own escort troops as well as the troops of the king to protect them as far as the next kingdom's borders.

The merchant-moneylenders have always been a specially protected class in society. They were a class that both the rich and the poor were eager to welcome. They enjoyed and valued, indeed, they demanded and gloried in having such special treatment and special protection because it brought them so much prestige, profits, and personal safety.

When the merchants came riding into town on their donkeys with trumpets blaring and drums pounding, it was with an air of confident bravery and customer-inveigling mystery amid the clamor and noise. Whether striding confidently through a town square beside their pack animals or presenting some rarity before the throne of a king, the tamkarum (merchant-moneylenders) learned the importance of prestige. They were instant celebrities wherever they went, not because of any virtue of their own but because of the trade goods and wondrous stories that they carried. It was this "belief" that these ordinary retailers actually possessed something to be envied or admired that gave them prestige in the eyes of the locals. With high prestige, they could demand higher prices.

Always a quick student in sizing up a customer, the tamkarum (merchant-moneylenders) realized the reverse psychology of this sales technique. By striking certain noble poses and attitudes and by assuming certain authoritative tones of voice, these petty hustlers found that their "prestige" could be raised and their profits increased simply by pretending to be more than they were. It was with this insolent audacity, this chutzpah, of pretending to possess virtues that they did not have that the tamkarum (merchant-moneylenders) developed Secret Fraud #19: "*Prestige is a glittering robe for ennobling treason and blinding fools; the more it is used, the more it profits he who dresses in it.*"

But mainly, it was the wealthier members of society who benefited from the traders and their cargos.

Imported goods were more expensive than local manufactures since they were unobtainable anywhere else and the cost of importing them added to the amount that the traders would ask. So, the average people could not afford them. Since the smaller items often brought the highest prices (such as gems and jewels, spices, incense, perfumed oils, artistically crafted gold and silver items), these could be safely hidden among the more ordinary goods such as fine linen and wool garments, or brass cups and copper pots, or at the bottom of grain sacks.

Merchants always had an audience with the kings and ministers simply because of the goods that they offered. The more costly and rare items, in addition to their high profit margins, were useful as bribes to officials or to tribal leaders or as a means of ingratiating themselves to the kings. The kings and their ministers were always eager to buy expensive luxury goods as gifts for favored wives and as symbols of personal wealth, status, and power. Thus, it was from the palace of kings and ministers that the merchants expected their greatest rewards for the small and expensive items. Even better, because the import items had cost them very little at their places of origin, these deceiving merchants could bribe the kings and ministers cheaply, gaining great business and political influence from grateful administrators and generals with expensive imported gifts that had cost them paltry sums.

The merchants also brought news and gossip. In the taverns they told amazing stories of foreign peoples, tales spiced with awesome adventures and stories of fantastic creatures, ghosts, monsters, and acts of the gods— all, of course, totally unprovable, but since no one could say otherwise, their fabulous stories could not be anything other than true. And like any story told for the satisfaction of seeing the wide eyes and awe-struck faces of their listeners, the merchants were masters of fabricating whatever most pleased themselves and astounded their audience.

Inveterate liars gain a lot of satisfaction from their own lies. It is pleasing to themselves to weave fantasies in their own minds and to watch the astounded faces of their trusting audience accept their fables as reality.

Whether for their own perverse entertainment alone or for manip-ulating the beliefs of their audience so as to persuade trusting fools to buy shoddy goods, the lying merchant-moneylenders were in the perfect business for telling lies simply because the stories that they told were of distant times and places and could neither be verified nor denied. Because no one could prove that the stories were lies, then the lies of the merchants could only be accepted, if not wholeheartedly then at least grudgingly, as the truth.

This is the way of all merchants from the most ancient times. Telling stories was a part of the merchants' craft. Like any salesman from every age, fanciful stories and droll lies helped him to sell his goods in the market. Telling stories also added to his skills for deceit, that is, knowing just how much could be told to be believed, but not saying too much to lose the sale.

The merchants told stories to impress the local fools and to elevate their own heroism and prestige in the eyes of the local populace. They told stories that advertised the rarity of their costly wares and—through giant dust storms, horrible monsters, sheets of lightning, bands of robbers, floods, and earthquakes—the great difficulties they endured in delivering them to such lucky buyers. Such fabricated lies made them greater profits without greater expenses. There were stories for demeaning and lowering the price asked for the trade goods that the locals wanted to sell. And there were stories proving to the seller that the merchant was doing them a favor to buy or trade from them at such low prices. Such stories and prevarications made for them greater profits while costing them nothing more than hot air. Merchants and salesmen have always used plenty of hot air and flapping lips to sell their goods because it has "always been this way."

And there were also stories reserved solely for the king and his councilors—stories that contained information about surrounding armies, the personnel of distant courts, the peaceful or war-like dispositions of those kings, the logistics and locations of food and water supplies in distant kingdoms, and the mapping of walled cities and the relative strength and wealth of those places.

No one could judge the relative wealth of a country as well as could a merchant whose greedy eyes take in such knowledge at a glance. And no one could penetrate the palaces of distant kings as could a merchant whose presence was welcomed and encouraged, and who allegedly had only a commercial reason for being there. Merchants were not suspected of anything other than the buying and selling of goods. Even if they were suspected of spying, it could not be proven. And though the kings could make good use of them for gathering intelligence, they could not force them to divulge this intelligence with other than politeness and bene- volence accompanied by sumptuous banquets and entertainments.

So, the greedy merchants of the ancient Near East became a favored confidant of many kings. With their skills of giving rare presents to court ministers and scribes, with their skills of deceit and bargaining for advantage, with their skills of inventing tales of every description, the merchants and moneylenders were able to gather from each kingdom more than what the king of that kingdom would have wanted them to gather.

Some secrets were for the common peasant. Some secrets were only for the ears of kings. Among themselves, however, the merchants kept their very own secrets of how and where to find the best deals and to sell for the best prices, secrets that they and their sons and their immediate trade partners knew. These were the ordinary secrets that all merchants keep among themselves. But there was more. The merchants discovered that in addition to the Sumerian Swindle, they, and only they, knew more about distant places than anyone else. The tamkarum (merchant-money- lenders) began to realize that through their trade networks, they could foresee events and influence politics from over the horizon.

Most of the people of 3000 BC rarely traveled more than a day's walk from where they were born; and they lived in those confined localities for their entire lives. Most of the kings of the various city-states did not travel much either. Their use of donkeys and ox carts and, later, their use of horses and chariots allowed them to travel around their kingdoms. But travel of more than a few twenties of kilometers for the smaller kingdoms and a hundred kilometers for the larger kingdoms was rare. And even in later times when the Sumerian, Assyrian, Egyptian, and Persian kings extended their kingdoms throughout the Near East, from Mediterranean to Persian Seas, even then, among all of those people from lowly servant to highest king, no one knew more about distant lands than did the merchants and traders. Traveling, bartering, sightseeing, and profiting from the people around them, was all a part of their business.

No matter how big any of the kingdoms that existed in the ancient world were, the trade routes which crisscrossed those kingdoms were far wider and covered a greater area (see Map 7, Chapter 5). From the most distant Paleolithic times, where traders carried obsidian blades and cores along footpaths, up to our modern-day world of giant container ships and jumbo jets carrying millions of tons of goods, the trade routes have always been larger in size than the borders of any country. Thus, the merchants and moneylenders kept a secret belief among themselves. That secret belief was this: "Because we tamkarum (merchant-moneylenders) have knowledge of distant places which is greater than any of the kings and far greater than all of the people, and because we can buy whatever we want, then we tamkarum (merchant-moneylenders) are greater than the kings and we are far greater than the people. We are like gods on this earth."

And with the Sumerian Swindle giving them all the wealth of mankind for free, what else could they be other than the Children of a God who loved them more than he loved any other people? And what kind of a mighty god was this, who loved swindlers, thieves, slave drivers, rapists, liars, deceivers, frauds, and murderers? Certainly, such a god was not part of the Mesopotamia pantheon of gods who urged mankind to follow the "straight and true path." Such a god of the merchant-moneylenders could only be, not a god but a demon.

The Treasonous Class: Merchants and Moneylenders

At first, Sumerian society followed the example set by the earlier Ubaidians and of most other peoples in the world in that they put their gods and their priests at the very top of their social ladder. The priests were the natural leaders of society simply because they looked to higher things than are found in the domains of mortal man. And for dealing with the affairs of their small tribes and villages, the priests were very often the tribal chiefs as well.

But the increasing complexity of the agricultural society that arose in Sumeria made it impossible for the priests to serve the gods and to also lead the worldly affairs of civic administration. Dealing with lawsuits and squabbles over water rights and thousands of petty cases of civil disharmony were not the subjects upon which priests wish to concentrate their time. Also, the priests practiced long periods of fasting, prayer, and meditation that required them to remove themselves farther away from the ordinary people in order that they could grow closer to the gods. It was vitally important to know the will of the gods. The priests could pass along this intelligence to their people—but only if they were closer to their gods and cloistered away from their people.

So, for the day-to-day administration of society, a leader who could concern himself with the ten thousand details on a daily basis, was required. As their villages grew into cities and groups of cities and villages grew into city-states, the priests remained priests while the village chiefs became kings and governors.

At first, the new cities that arose in the fertile plains of Sumeria were dominated both socially and economically by the temples. It was the belief of those people that the purpose of life was to serve the gods. And they did so on a daily basis, both in their humble homes and in the great temples that arose above their mud-brick cities. The temples were not only the center of their religious and social lives but, in the beginning, were the center of their economic lives as well. Temples had their own farms and factories that produced goods for local consumption and for foreign trade. The people whom the priests entrusted to handle these affairs of commerce between cities, were the merchants and traders, that is, specialists in barter, haggling, profits, and logistics.

As early as 4000 BC, before writing was invented, the temples were the hub of the various commercial interests of the desert shepherds, the fishermen, and the farmers because they provided a centralized location for these groups to meet and to trade. By providing factory and craft facilities for pottery making, cloth weaving and spinning, metalworking, beer brewing and other manufacturing, the temples became the center of the entire culture.

By 3500 BC, in big cities like Uruk, the temple ziggurat was built on a raised platform big enough to be seen for miles around. The temples generated writing, government, a judicial system, fine art, architecture, and so on. For the first 500 years of Sumerian history, the temples alone controlled most facets of society and the economy. The priests were the leaders of society during those times. Sumerian society was a god-fearing and moral society.

Large-scale commercial enterprises were at first the sole respon-sibility of the temples. They had the resources to hire the labor, amass the goods, and to sell in wholesale quantities. This was beyond the ability of the ordinary local merchant. In addition, any kind of long-distance trade could only be accomplished on a large-scale basis since the trade routes and sea-lanes were so dangerous.

Even though trade routes had been developed for thousands of years throughout the entire ancient Middle East, there was little traffic on those routes. Traveling was dangerous due to bad weather, drought, dust storms, marauders from the deserts, migrants, runaway slaves, and wild animals such as lions. Only army contingents, foreign ambassadors traveling under military protection, royal messengers, and guarded donkey caravans, carrying loads from city to city, dared to travel those routes. In fact, there were few periods in the history of Mesopotamia when private persons could travel freely and when private letters could be sent from city to city.

Thus, from the earliest times, only those merchants who were employed by the temples or who had military escort or who had enough wealth to organize guarded caravans, could hope to do any business beyond the local level. The merchants and moneylenders arose in an environment where they could only operate under the protection of either the kings or the temples. They could only profit while being protected by a higher power than what they could muster on their own. And even when they had attained great personal wealth and could afford a personal militia of caravan guards and body guards, they still needed the permission and the trade licenses of the kings to travel across state borders. Through military power, the kings controlled the state borders.

Yes, Mesopotamia had fertile soil and the irrigation water necessary for abundant crops; and yes, the country had plenty of sunshine to grow those crops; and yes, it had plenty of dirt and mud to make bricks and pottery; and yes, it had reeds with which to make mats and huts and boats, but that is all that it had—sun, water, mud, reeds, and abundant food. For all other things besides these, the civilizations of Mesopotamia vitally needed to engage in trade with other kingdoms. And for gaining the lowest prices and the best quality, the crafty and cunning skills of the merchant-moneylenders were necessary.

As long as the merchants worked for the temples and served the gods, society prospered. As long as the merchants and moneylenders had the religious feeling of serving their gods first and foremost, society prospered. But once the merchants began to feel the power that came with wealth, and once they began selfishly to do business for their own personal profits, then mankind's long history of suffering, starvation, disease, and warfare began in earnest. Yes, civilization began in Sumeria, but hiding behind this infant civilization and doing their utmost to drain into their counting houses all wealth for themselves, was the secretive Treasonous Class of the merchants and moneylenders.

Because those swindlers at first grew in power rather slowly as civilization advanced, their deleterious effects on society were not noticed, any more than the effects of a tapeworm are noticed by its host. Yes, the businessmen and moneylenders helped society to increase in material wealth but only for their own benefit, never for any altruistic reasons such as might be expected from the kings or priests.

Those of you who are observers of modern society in the 21st century, can see obvious similarities between what the ancient Sumerians had, with what we have today, that is, a society composed of the "Haves" and the "Have-Nots." We should not make the same mistakes that the Sumerians made in believing that this situation is natural just because it "has always been here."

We have more experience with history than the Sumerians had. So, why are we continuing to make the same mistakes of civilization that they made? Because the Treasonous Class profits from those mistakes and does everything that it can to increase their own, private profits by prolonging the sufferings of mankind while concealing its causes. They keep the Sumerian Swindle a secret even in our modern times by hiding and obfuscating an understanding of it because only they profit from it.

In Sumerian society, the awilum (the Haves) alone had the obligation to pay taxes to the state and to perform military duty. And they could bequeath property to their heirs. It was not necessary that they were all super-rich because, again, wealth is relative. The only necessary require-ment for those people to be recognized as belonging to this high social group of "freemen" and "gentlemen" was that they were not in debt to anyone or in servitude to anyone. They were the "Haves." They had. They owned. They collected payments and rents. They bought and sold. They loaned. But they were not in debt. Debt was for the "Have-Nots."

Muskenum (the Have-Nots) is an Amorite term, literally meaning "the one prostrating himself." Whenever the muskenum (the Have-Nots) appeared in relation to the awilum (the Haves, the "freeman" or "citizen") the status of the muskenum (the Have-Nots) was always inferior. The muskenum (the Have-Nots) often served at the palace in exchange for rations or land allotments. Numerous legal provisions may have been necessary to identify the muskenum (the Have-Nots) with the palace because he was not protected by customary law. After 1500 BC, the word muskenum (the Have-Not) appeared in texts with the connotation of "the poor." With this meaning, "muskenum" made its way into Hebrew, Aramaic, and Arabic, and much later, into the Romance languages, namely, French (as mesquin) and Italian (as meschino) or "petty."

So, even though the muskenum (the Have-Nots) were not slaves, they were servants. And to whom were they the servants? To the awilum (the Haves), to whom they paid obeisance and bowed down and offered their loan payments. Perhaps they did not owe money to the awilum (the Haves) but they farmed the land of the awilum as tenant farmers. They plied the boats of the awilum as boatmen and stevedores. They served in the palace and the mansions of the awilum. And they were paid for their services with food and clothing. This payment in food and clothing kept them alive and clothed but was never enough for them to advance themselves into the society of the "Haves." They were the paid servants and the employees of the awilum (the Haves) or they repaid their debts by working for free.

This is why Secret Fraud #5 of the Sumerian Swindle is: "*The debtor is the slave of the lender.*" Those of you who have ever sold some of your valuable and precious possessions in the panic-stricken attempt to raise cash to pay credit card and mortgage bills before they accrued late-payment fees, know from experience how you have been a slave of the moneylenders. But it was worse in Mesopotamia. In those days of 3000 BC, slavery was an ordinary part of life. A poor farmer, fully expecting to make a profit and fully confident that he would be able to pay back the loan and the interest, would place as guarantee of the loan, his wife or his daughters or sons.

But the moneylenders of Sumeria usually charged 50 percent interest compounded. So, getting out of debt was extremely difficult. A farmer would have to work very hard in the hopes of a bumper crop. Because of the Sumerian Swindle, the tamkarum (merchant-moneylenders) were not only parasites but also slave drivers and brothel owners and pimps. They became the owners of the land and even the owners of the very lives and bodies of the people, through no other reason other than that they were swindlers and parasites. They knew the secret of the Sumerian Swindle and kept its criminal nature hidden from their fellow men.

Are you seeing any similar pattern in our modern times, as the rich get richer and everyone else works for them? If so, then in modern times, you are observing the Sumerian Swindle in action, where the rich money-lenders and stock market crooks, swindle everything that they have from the poor. The poor and the middle class accept being defrauded because the Sumerian Swindle "has always been here." But in actuality, it has *not* always been here; it is merely older than anyone can remember when it all began.

Another such Sumerian Swindle is Secret Fraud #10: "*Time benefits the banker and betrays the borrower.*" Over time, every bit of money in society goes to whomever is allowed to charge interest on a loan. Through interest fees, which create on the ledger books the illusion that there is more money required to be paid back than actually exists in circulation, there is always less money available to the individual borrower than what the banker demands to be paid. The banker knows this, so how can the banker (who offers the loan with a smile on his thieving, hypocritical face) expect to ever be repaid? Neither the bankers today nor the moneylenders of 3000 BC would give a loan to anyone without secured collateral. So, if the money could not be paid back, the moneylender would have a way of recuperating his money-plus-the-interest by seizing the collateral.

The average person accepts being swindled by the bankers and credit card companies because they have "always been here." A moneylender seizing property for defaulted loans sounds fair and reasonable if you don't think about it, simply because most people do not understand that the Sumerian Swindle has never ever been an honest or a legitimate business model. The Sumerian Swindle has always been *an actual swindle*. The excuse of the bankers and moneylenders to swindle people' money by offering lies and fake excuses for charging interest-on-a-loan because they claim to be taking a "risk," is as phony as they are. It is all a part of the sham and the fraud of both ancient and modern moneylending. It is nothing but a math trick of demanding something that cannot possibly exist and then foreclosing on real goods and real property which do exist.

Just as the bankers of today swindle the farmers out of their lands, whether in the Mississippi River Valley or the plains of Ontario or the rice patties of Old China, so did the moneylenders of 3000 BC swindle the farmers out of the alluvial soil lands laid down by the Tigris and Euphrates Rivers. Exactly as the bankers of today swindle the entire world out of our goods and money, so too did the ancient moneylenders of Mesopotamia swindle their fellow Sumerians out of their land and goods and wealth. Using Secret Fraud #10, they used Time as their method for stealing a profit: "Time benefits the banker and betrays the borrower."

A moneylender or a banker only has to deal with the unfailing numbers of arithmetic. One plus one always equals two, no matter if the sun is shining brightly or the rains and winds are blowing sheets of water across the fields. Fifty percent times two shekels plus the two shekels on loan always equals three shekels by arithmetic calculation, no matter if the Tigris and Euphrates Rivers dry up and the land is parched; or whether the fields flood and wash away all of creation. The swindles of the money-lender and the banker are not affected by sun and wind, rain and drought, fire, earthquake, flood, pestilence, locusts, blight, disease, or any other act of Nature or act of God that affects other men. The numbers in his ledger book are all exactly the same. One plus one always equals two, no matter the weather. One shekel of silver lent out at 50 percent interest, always returns a shekel and a half at the end of the year. However, the numbers are false no matter how exact they are because it is impossible to create more real money by multiply it with unreal numbers.

Whether the year was one of prosperity or disaster for the people around him, doesn't matter to the moneylender. For the moneylender, the arithmetic never changes. He is immune to change. His profits are a mathematical certainty and not a gamble. His profits are based on trickery and deceit as he swindles those who trust his alleged "honesty." A banker's certainty is not linked with the same fate as the farmer. Rains coming early or late can mean a bad crop. Bugs and blight, too much sun or too little, a low river from too little snow falling in the distant mountains hundreds of miles away, or too much snow melting with rains and bringing floods, can all spell disaster for a farmer. And without a crop that can be bartered or sold, the farmer has little to live on and nothing to sell. A bad year does not usually affect only one farmer but all of the farmers in an entire region or an entire country. So, where can they obtain help, since all of them are left with so little to live on?

But the moneylender has only the slow turning of the wheel of time and the sure calculations of arithmetic with which to contend. He does not gamble. He does not put himself into the hands of Nature or of Fate like his fellow men. His is a unique occupation that is insulated from the real world. The world of the moneylender is a synthetic one, where weather, Nature, and even the Gods cannot change what the moneylender creates.

And this was what the Sumerian moneylenders began to discover about their moneylending scam. They could make a profit not only when times were good but also when times were bad. They discovered, over 5,000 years ago, that charging interest on borrowed goods produced a profit. But they also discovered something else. They found that they could make *even more of a profit when their fellow men were destroyed*. But this profit was only possible if they could keep for themselves the secret of how the destruction of mankind always brought a profit to the moneylenders.

Secret Fraud #10 of the Sumerian Swindle: "Time benefits the banker and betrays the borrower," has ancient roots. But more than the farmers are betrayed by this swindle. Anyone whose monetary income is slowed by bad timing also falls into the moneylenders' snare because time on a ledger book is unlimited and constant, while fate and bad luck will throw all men into the moneylender's clutches. Calculated time marked in a ledger book is regular and predictable. But real time, which wears down the fine schemes of man and upsets his nice schedules and careful expectations, works against man. And so, the farmers and petty merchants and ordinary people of Sumeria found that Time betrayed them to the moneylenders, bad weather betrayed them to the moneylenders, a run of bad luck betrayed them to the moneylenders. The moneylenders profited by the destruction of mankind.

Indeed, the moneylenders knew that to keep the secret of moneylending to themselves was not only a vital means to increase their wealth but also vital to their very lives. If their fellow townsmen learned that the moneylenders, merchants, and bankers were nothing but thieves and swindlers, it would not be long before the swindled goods would be confiscated and the swindlers themselves either hanged or chased out of town. And so, the secrets of moneylending were never written down and were carefully passed along only to reliable sons who were as cunning and avaricious as their fathers. The sons of the moneylenders had to be sly in order to skillfully acquire the criminal methods that their fathers taught them.

In fact, since lending-at-interest is both a trick and a swindle, it is impossible for the lender to be an honest person if he expects to make a profit. So, from earliest times, the moneylenders were both tricky and dishonest. They were even more so once arithmetic and writing became a common tool because, with the use of arithmetic and writing, the moneylenders could calculate larger loans and swindle entire countries; and then "prove" that the money was actually owed to them by the fraudulent numbers in the ledger books. "Numbers don't lie," is an ancient bankers' lie that they perfidiously told their impoverished clients. *But liars who write the numbers, always lie.*

*****

Religiously, the moneylenders were like everyone else in their villages and towns. They believed in the gods and performed their duties to those gods through prayer and temple donations. So, it is useful here to inquire about the actual religious beliefs of the Mesopotamian people.

The gods in Mesopotamia were very much local in nature because they were believed to reside in certain cities and in certain places. Each city had its own god as its primary protective deity. There were both supreme gods and lesser gods, but all of those gods were powerful and worthy of man's devotion.

But regardless of the variety of gods, the Mesopotamians had a common belief in a common origination of both gods and men. Their creation stories began with an abyss or a void from which the waters of the earth and the immensity of the sky were created out of nothing. The two main ways that their religious stories brought mankind into creation was that he was either molded out of clay by a god (the method which the Jews plagiarized for their own creation stories) or a god had decreed that men just sprang out of the ground like weeds.

Regardless of which story was accepted as true, all of the people of Mesopotamia believed that the purpose for the creation of mankind, was for the same reason. Man was created by the gods *to serve the gods*. As servants to the gods, mankind walked a holy path throughout life. After all, when your every act is as a servant of God, what else can one's life be other than a holy life? What sins there were among those people, were mainly sins of omission or trespasses against the gods. Trespasses against the gods were often the main topic in Sumerian religious literature. By the end of the second millennium BC, the priestly text "Surpu" listed 200 acts and omissions as sins, including not speaking one's mind, causing discord in the family, neglecting a naked person, and killing animals without reason. Can you see in these, the great humanity and religious worthiness of those ancient people? Although the gods punished the sinners, they also forgave them. But if the gods refused to forgive the sinner, that person could not be helped.

The list of sins was based upon service to the gods. But since those early people were still inventing civilization, what they considered to be sins against their fellow man, was still in the formative stages. So, there was a lot of leeway for sinning against one's fellows since there were so few religious constraints to prohibit such deeds. What was practiced as religion in Mesopotamia gave the moneylenders the freedom to make full use of their usurious and ruthless proclivities. There was no "hereafter" for the Mesopotamians. When they died, they did not look forward to a paradise in heaven or rebirth in another life. To them, their grave was their only future and any life in the Underworld was not something to look forward to enjoying because, in the gloomy underworld, there was no joy. This belief gave them all of the incentive that they needed to enjoy the life that they had and to make the most of whatever opportunities the gods bequeathed.

Such beliefs, as found in their own literature, prove that the Mesopotamian people had not reached the highest levels of religious knowledge. No matter what levels of material culture that they had devised, they had not discovered the spiritual level of life such as was found at an earlier time by the Stone Age European peoples of Ireland, Britain, Gaul, and Germany.

The Sumerian moneylenders followed the same ideals towards their gods as everybody else. As the priests advised:

Daily, worship your god with offerings, prayers, and appropriate incense. Bend your heart to your god. What befits the

office of a personal god, are prayers, supplication, pressing
(the hand to) the nose (as greeting) shall you offer up every
morning, then your power will be great, and you will,
through the god, have enormous success.

Doing their duty to their god meant offering food and drink to the image
and then going about their daily business. Thus, the moneylenders could
"feel good about themselves" and just as holy as everybody else, as they
offered up prayers to their gods in the morning and dragged a farmer and
his family off of their land in the afternoon. Or if a farmer or petty trader
had put up as collateral his wife and daughters or his sons, the moneylender had no hesitation about dragging them off to the whorehouses or
slave markets after using them for his own sexual pleasures first. From the
very earliest times, the merchants and moneylenders were both slave
traders and pimps. And in this capacity, they had a very deleterious effect
upon society.

After all, in a society where there are men who own slaves and
prostitutes and who want to profit from them, it does not take long before
these men are able to reduce large portions of the population into a
debauched lifestyle. The moneylenders became the foremost slave traders
as well as the foremost sex fiends in Mesopotamia. Through bondage and
slavery, they could realize their every lust. And when their lusts were
satisfied, they could sell their used-up sex slave to someone else or donate
her to a temple or sell her to a whorehouse.

By the second millennium BC, the Sumerian goddess Inanna, who
was of lesser import in the Sumerian pantheon, came to be called Ishtar
and the most widely worshipped Babylonian deity. She was the goddess of
the date storehouse, the goddess of shepherds, the power behind the
thundershowers of spring, and was also the goddess of love and sexuality.
She was the patron goddess of harlots and the alehouse. That Ishtar, the
goddess of whorehouses and booze halls, became the most widely
worshipped deity among the Babylonians was because the moneylenders
had made her so through their enslavement of so many women.

Over the centuries, as the moneylenders acquired wealth and slaves,
they also became the owners of brothels and wine shops. Moneylending,
brothels, and booze, were profit centers that made them ever wealthier and
increased their influence over the people whom they had impoverished and
debauched. After swindling away his farm, his wife, his children, and his
self-respect, the moneylenders could still wring a few grains of silver or
hours of labor out of the drunken farmer who staggered miserably about in

the moneylenders' beer halls, digging ditches for his beer or doing odd jobs for his bread.

But there was also the matter of justice. Because the sun god, Shamash, could see everything in heaven and on earth with his gleaming eye, then Shamash was naturally the god of justice. And with this sun god, all the world could be brought to justice. So, men who had disputes with anyone could bring their disagreements to the town elders or to the king for resolution before the gods. Men who felt cheated by the moneylenders could ask for justice. But in Mesopotamia, justice seemed best served by those who could afford to buy it. This is true in modern times as well, simply because we accept a variety of legal fictions foisted upon us because they "have always been here."

One thing that has always been here, is the injustice of what the moneylenders create. The people could never, ever get justice from the thieving moneylenders. In Sumeria, the god of the tamkarum (merchant-moneylenders) was not the God of Justice, Shamash, the sun god. The god of the moneylenders was the Moon God, Sin, who began his "day" in the evening, after the sun had gone down. "The evening and the morning," is how the tamkarum (merchant-moneylenders) counted their "days" by beginning at night. This is the same way that the Hebrew writers of the Old Testament counted their days.

As the farmers were dispossessed of their lands and the laborers were defrauded of their wives and daughters, the Sumerian religion changed in its philosophy. When righteous men fell into poverty and families were destroyed even as the wicked moneylenders thrived, the simple piety of the people led them to the false conclusion that it was the work of the gods rather than the machinations of evil men. The actual cause of their loss and suffering—the Sumerian Swindle itself—was not recognized for what it was because this simple secret was so carefully concealed by the moneylenders. It was their source of wealth and power, and they were not about to divulge it to anyone other than their trusted sons.

By the second millennium BC, so many people had been defrauded and enslaved and their lives destroyed by the tamkarum (merchant-moneylenders) that the problem of the righteous sufferer became part of the Mesopotamian religious consciousness. Two main works, "The Poem of the Righteous Sufferer" (what the rabbis plagiarized when they wrote their Book of Job) and "The Babylonian Theodicy," considered the workings of divine justice. Both works arrived at the same conclusion: in reality, the wicked often fared better than the righteous.

In the materialistic views of the Mesopotamians, the wicked were the ones who loaned money at interest, foreclosed on farms, debauched and pimped daughters and sons, and profited from wars. But they had been around longer than anyone could remember, so they were accepted as having "always been here." After a thousand years, the tamkarum (merchant-moneylenders) were allowed to continue their depredations without being hanged, simply because no one could remember any time when society was free of those voracious parasites.

Monied Class versus Kingly Class

Both the kings and the tamkarum (merchant-moneylenders) belonged to the same awilum (the Haves) social class. While the kings had the responsibility to protect both the people as well as the merchant-moneylenders, the merchant-moneylenders' only responsibility was to make a profit for themselves from both the kings and the people. Parasitizing and swindling everybody was their specialty.

If you look at a map of the ancient trade routes, you will see that from the very earliest times, this extensive network of roads, paths, and waterways stretched all across the ancient Middle East and beyond (see Map 20). No matter how secluded or how cosmopolitan any of the ancient peoples were, it is an indisputable fact that they knew of their distant neighbors over the horizon. What they knew of those neighbors was transmitted to them not by the mighty kings but by the traders and merchants who traveled those trade routes.

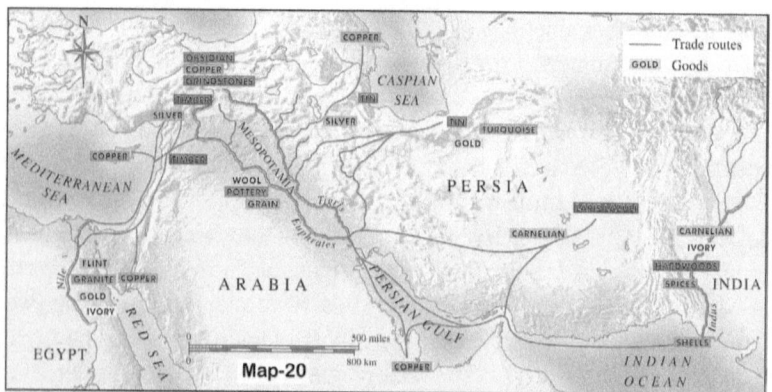

Map-20

The trade routes were all very much longer and larger in extent than any of the ancient kingdoms ever were. Even in the days of Assyria's greatest expansion, the trade routes that ran through Assyria were connected to distant lands and to distant peoples that no Assyrian king had ever seen. But those distant lands were visited by the merchants who traveled the trade routes. It was the merchants and traders who connected the various countries and the various peoples and not the kings. The kings were guarantors of safe-conduct for the merchants within their own kingdoms alone. Although a merchant could travel the dangerous trade routes in caravans and with the protection of the king's troops as well as with his own hired guards and mercenaries, once he had left the country controlled by a particular king, he would have to negotiate protection from the kings and tribal chiefs of the next country that he entered, if such protection had not already been arranged by the treaties between the kings.

Being of a protected class was something that the tamkarum (merchant-moneylenders) very much cherished. It became a demand wherever they went, a demand to be protected by the king while they did their utmost to swindle the subjects of the king.

In their relations with dangerous territorial bandit chiefs, the merchants were protected by the threat that if they were harmed or their goods stolen, their fellow merchants would never again bring goods to those domains and trade would cease. This was an old trick used by even the pre-historic obsidian traders, and it was a powerful and useful argument. The traders and merchant-moneylenders became a protected class of con-artists and carnival barkers who could move their swindles across state lines and national boundaries with the strut and swagger of great men, even though at heart they were all weasels.

Although lies told by one or two merchants can be dismissed as lies, but when the same lies are told by every band of merchants who arrived in town, then they became accepted as the truth. How could it not be the truth when all of the merchants were telling the same lies? Even when different merchants arrived in town at different times and all of them told the same lies but—unknown to the townsmen—they all belonged to the same secret trade guilds, then the people were thoroughly convinced of the truth of their tall tales. The merchant-moneylenders realized that by working in collusion that even the biggest lies can be told and be accepted as fact, as long as there is no proof to the contrary—or if they destroyed any proof to the contrary.

Truth, alone, was their special enemy, just as Truth is the special enemy of those more modern merchant-moneylenders, the Jews. However, with the Jews, no matter how many of them tell the same lies, modern archaeology proves them all to be liars. But for nearly 4,000 years before modern archaeology was developed, people tended to believe the lies of the Jews because, as you will see, they destroyed all proofs to the contrary as they still do today.

Once they were able to break free from being the merchant-servants of the temples, the moneylenders and merchants were able to rival the wealth of the temples. Because of the swindle of moneylending and the profits obtained from the monopoly cartels of international trade, the moneylenders and merchants were able to amass huge fortunes large enough to rival that of the kings. Because the Sumerian Swindle was not recognized as the fraud that it is since it "has always been here," even the kings respected the huge amounts of loot that the merchants and money-lenders were able to gain.

As the moneylenders gained slaves for their sexual pleasures, they became increasingly perverted. When Leonard Wooley excavated the Sumerian city of Ur, he found the grave of a moneylender. His private coffin contained one of the richest finds at Ur. A double axe made of electrum, a gold dagger with silver sheath hanging from a silver belt, and an amazingly beautiful gold helmet, gold bowls, and a gold lamp, each inscribed with his name—Meskalamdug ("hero of the good land"). Outside the coffin were two more gold and silver daggers and vessels of gold, silver, and electrum. Laid to rest among his treasures, this Sumerian moneylender was a homosexual pervert and a cross-dresser who was also buried with his collection of women's jewelry.

A recurring theme throughout history as well as into modern times, can be observed from those ancient days, that is, as the moneylenders and merchants gained wealth and power in society, perversions became in-creasingly commonplace, warfare increased, poverty increased, and civilizations collapsed. This was entirely because those who controlled the wealth and the property of the ancient civilizations, were depraved criminals and lust-filled perverts who brought ruin upon the people around them through their limitless greed. This is observable even today in modern times.

In Sumeria, they were known as tamkarum (merchant-moneylenders). But none of them were Jews because there were no Jews in those ancient days. Even in this claim of their great age, the Jews are liars. They are not the ancient people whom they claim to be, as you shall see. In modern times, those perverted parasites are known as merchants, financiers, and bankers. And in modern times, almost all of them are Jews.

CHAPTER 6

SARGON OF AKKAD

Early Dynastic Period of Akkad: 2900 – 2700 BC

The Sumerians had about 300 years of uncontested development in which to create a culture that was the greatest ever known up until that time. Their writing, their religion, their customs were copied by every country around them. Those Sumerian awilum (the Haves) who were ruthless and greedy enough, found that the profits from the Sumerian Swindle were much to their liking. Although they spread Sumerian culture to other people, among the moneylenders, the one part of their culture that remained their very own secret was the Sumerian Swindle.

Soon after the Sumerians established their agricultural states in the southern part of Mesopotamia, Semites in small numbers began moving in from Arabia in the West (Amurru). They spoke the West Semite dialect from the Amurru (the West) and so they are known to us as the Amorites. Some of the earliest Sumerian inscriptions contain words derived from Semitic speech, which indicates that they were present at an early time. But their Amorite dialect disappeared as they became absorbed into Sumerian culture.

Because only irrigated agriculture with its associated canals and ditches could produce crops in this arid region, no one could live among the Sumerians who did not also participate in the organized labor that such agriculture required. Following the long-established Secret Fraud #11: *"Dispossessing the people brings wealth to the dispossessor, yielding the greatest profit for the bankers when the people are impoverished,"* the Sumerian awilum (the Haves) hired the Amorites as laborers and soldiers. They worked cheaper than did their own people.

This method of swindling their own people out of the land through moneylending and then hiring cheap foreign labor to work the foreclosed properties, was very profitable. The Ubaidian moneylenders had used it to sell the land to the Sumerians. And now the Sumerian moneylenders used the same treason to sell Sumerian land to the Amorites. Secret Fraud #11 was profitable but it inevitably proved to be a weakening influence for the whole country as the numbers of foreigners increased and as the racial characteristics of the Sumerian people became diluted with the Semitic strain.

But there was no dilution of the gene pool in the north, as large numbers of Semites settled into the underdeveloped and unpopulated regions of Babylon and Akkad. The methods of irrigated agriculture became available to any people who could secure land and work the soil. As the older fields in Sumeria had trouble with salt build-up, the Sumerians shifted to barley production, since this grain can grow in saltier soil, while wheat production shifted to the north into Akkad, the land that would one day be known first as Akkadia and then as Assyria.

As the traveling merchants spread word among the scattered tribes of Semites in the West about the richness of crops that could be grown in Sumeria, more Amorites desired those fertile lands. These tamkarum (merchant-moneylenders) instructed the Semitic chiefs where the lands were weakly defended and, acting as agents for the Sumerian landlords, which lands were for sale to the highest bidder. Although the merchants were from the various cities in Sumeria, their allegiance was to their profits and not to their people. Their loyalties were to the lumps of silver and gold in their purses.

Continuing with their system of betrayal and treason, the tamkarum (merchant-moneylenders) sold the foreclosed farms and village houses that they had acquired through their Sumerian Swindles to the Semites from Syria. Beginning around 2900 BC, large numbers of these Amorites settled into the lands around Babylon, its surrounding towns, and around the city of Kish in the region of Akkad. As usual, they adopted the Sumerian culture and lifestyle.

But the Amorites were not fools. They could clearly see the advantages for themselves to occupy the land and the disadvantages to the Sumerian farmers. So, their natural suspicions prompted them to ask, "Why are you selling the land to us? Are you not betraying your own people by doing this?"

The Sumerian moneylenders had been born and raised in Mesopotamia. So, one might think that if they were not filled with a patriotic enthusiasm toward the good of their country, then at least they would have a friendly warmth in their hearts toward their neighbors and fellow citizens. But parasites only recognize their fellow parasites as friends, while all of them recognize their victims as victims. So, the tamkarum impoverished, betrayed, and dispossessed their own people by importing cheap foreign labor and then selling the land to foreigners.

Shrewdly peering through their slit-like, half-closed eyelids as they sized up their questioners, those wily merchant-moneylenders, those "gentlemen" and expert salesmen that they were, always had a ready answer to overcome such an objection.

"What are those people to us? They are not our friends because they hate us and wish to do us harm. We have loaned them silver and helped them to buy goods and to purchase property. As the great god Enlil is our witness, we have done everything that we can to loan them silver and help them buy the best farms and the finest orchards. But still they hate us for our goodness and generosity because they are full of bigotry and hatred. But you are our friends. You can protect us from those who hate us. So, we will give our friends and protectors a good deal in buying whatever goods and properties you want because we own much lands and will make you an excellent bargain. Because of our friendship, we will loan our friends silver in any amount at low interest rates. And to further show our friendship, we have many wonderful daughters who will make fine wives for your sons."

And so, the bargain was made. The Amorites had no reason to hate the Sumerian moneylenders—yet.

They accepted the offers of cheap land. And to prove their friendship and generosity to the new immigrants, those poor Amorites who could not afford the full price, the tamkarum (merchant-moneylenders) let them buy on time at low interest rates. Like blood-sucking fleas, the moneylenders jumped from their old victims who hated them onto their new victims who innocently accepted the moneylenders as their friends and guides and mentors. The ancient snake, once again with soft words and low interest rates, coiled around its prey. Its bite would come later.

But what became of the Sumerian people who had been betrayed and dispossessed by the Sumerian merchant-moneylenders? After all, the land can only support so many people. Outside of the agricultural areas, it was only desert. So, having no way left to them for making a living, most of them were reduced to poverty and starvation as they became the slaves and menial servants of the foreign Amorite aliens who had replaced them. Those whose only avenue for survival was to join the army, were killed off in the battles. As a result, their wives and children were left to starve to death or to sell themselves into slavery to the moneylenders. Little-by-little, as the Sumerians died out as a people, the Sumerian merchant-moneylenders became even wealthier while being protected by their new allies from the wrath of those whom they had swindled, dispossessed, and betrayed. Thus it was that the moneylenders ate their fill while their victims perished.

But the moneylenders did not destroy the people among whom they had been allowed to live by using their own money. Every particle of gold and silver and every square measure of land which the merchant-moneylenders claimed as their own, they had swindled. They had destroyed the people among whom they had been allowed to live by first swindling away their silver and gold, and then using that peoples' very own money against them. Those parasites had sucked away the wealth of the entire nation. But they had not earned it. They had not worked for it. They had gotten it all for free because that is how the Sumerian Swindle operates.

By 2750 BC, those Semitic Amorites had 150 years of increasing their population through birth and immigration and to fully absorb the Sumerian writing and culture. Just as a modern alphabet can be used to write many different languages, so too was the cuneiform characters used by those ancient people to write their own language. They retained their own language, which is called by the name of the region of their greatest power, Akkadian. These Semitic Akkadians, with their high birth-rate and the increase in the immigration of their wandering tribes into Sumeria, became the most dominant people in the region.

Up until that time, the southern lands of Sumeria had never been a unified country. It was a region that had many city-states, each of which controlled their own territories. Those territories had been gradually falling into the hands of the moneylenders and merchants over a period of five hundred years as the Sumerian Swindle worked its relentless fraud. By 2500 BC, most of the land of Sumeria was privately owned while the remainder was owned by the temples and the palace.

These city states were rather small—so small, in fact, that between many of these city-states, from the top of the ziggurat in each city, one could look across the plain to the distant ziggurat of the neighboring city-state. The Early Dynastic inscriptions of Sumeria are full of references to battles between these squabbling city-states. The Sumerians were a people who insisted upon their individual rights and were quick to haul an opponent before a judge in lawsuits concerning the very same issues that modern people also find to be worth the fight: disputes over lands, boundaries, inheritance, rents, loans, marriage and divorce, and every conceivable argument. And what they argued over between individuals was also carried across city boundaries into the bordering city-state.

An example of these squabbles was between the city-states of Lagash and Umma. The city of Lagash was set in the middle of a most fertile region crisscrossed with small irrigation canals fed from two large canals connecting the Tigris and Euphrates Rivers. In antiquity, these big canals ensured to Lagash not only bountiful crops but also a thriving river-borne trade and, in consequence, considerable material prosperity. Such economic and social stability provided conditions in which a dynasty founded there by Ur-Nanshe (~ 2500 BC) was able to rule in unbroken succession for over a century. The city of Umma was the residence of the grain god, Shara, so its own agricultural dependence upon the canal system is obvious.

Umma lay to the north of Lagash and was situated on the same two big canals. The direction of flow of the canals being from north to south, Umma was in a position to interfere with the water supply of Lagash, and this gave rise to conflicts between the two cities on a number of occasions. It is the documents recording the circumstances of such events which provide our first substantial historical narratives, beginning in the period shortly after 2500 BC. The earliest of these are some inscriptions of Eannatum, third ruler of the dynasty of Lagash and grandson of Ur-Nanshe. Notable among these is a stone relief set up to mark his defeat of Umma. The monument is known as the Stele of the Vultures from the gory details shown of carrion birds fighting over the entrails of the slain after the battle in which Eannatum led his city to victory (see Figure 6). A little later, a cone-inscription of Entemena, Eannatum's nephew, gives a history of the conflict between Umma and Lagash for several generations up to his time.

Figure 6. Vulture Stele

Mainly, the fights between city-states began over land and water. In the treeless and unremarkable landscape of Mesopotamia where there was nothing to define boundaries other than dry ditches and water-filled canals marked off with boundary stones, the land boundaries and the water rights were often in dispute. These arguments between city-states led to fist-fights, village brawls, and wars. Wars led to the enthroning and the throwing down of kings.

In prosperous Lagash, "just as it had always been," the tamkarum (merchant-moneylenders) became the dominant property owners in the state after 500 years of practicing the Sumerian Swindle. Very few free men could claim to own their own lands. Under the alternative of starvation, most were required to work the foreclosed properties owned by the moneylenders. Those who fell victim to the Sumerian Swindle were reduced to servitude and slavery. Although the Sumerian Swindle "had always been here," the people accepted its legitimacy even though they hated its results and hated even more those evil monsters who controlled it.

The dispossessed and enslaved people were numerous enough that their voices could be heard. In a dissatisfied and rebellious mood, the people demanded a change. Too many proud and free farmers had been reduced to slavery along with their wives and children through the moneylenders' swindles. Too many daughters and sons had been turned into prostitutes in the moneylender's whorehouses and as the money-lender's sex slaves. Too many old people had been thrown out of their houses to starve and be eaten by dogs and wild pigs.

The rich were very rich, and the poor were not only very poor but were also increasing in numbers.

Of course, the poor prayed to their gods and beseeched the temple priests for aid. The priests, who were following the "straight and true path" to the best of their ability, offered what aid they could to the poor, but the problems caused by the Sumerian Swindle required both religious and political remedies. The priests could not solve the problem alone primarily because the temples had always practiced the Sumerian Swindle and did not recognize it for its intrinsic evil of being a "crooked and false path."

The temples had been practicing the Sumerian Swindle for so long that it was an unquestioned fact of life. Because everyone in Sumeria accepted the legitimacy of the Sumerian Swindle, its methods were never criticized. Although they tried to help their people with charity and shelter, the temples did business as usual because such methods for the past 1,000 years "had always been here" and because the loan contracts between the victims and the moneylenders were written on the clay tablets and sworn before the gods to be agreeable to all parties. So, both the victim and the perpetrator of moneylending had sworn oaths before the gods to abide by the contracts.

And so, Secret Fraud #5, "The debtor is the slave of the lender," was a mechanism that brought both debt slaves and wealth into the temples of the gods where the debt-slaves were safely cared for as employees of the temples. But it was the debt-slaves of the perverted and greedy tamkarum (merchant-moneylenders) who rebelled against their cruel masters.

At that time, some of the temple lands were rented on a share-cropper basis. A rent equivalent to one-third of the crop was paid, one-sixth of it in silver and the rest in kind. With this temple-mandated price, even here, where the poor share-cropper had to pay one-third of his crops to the landlord, the Secret Fraud #4 of using silver as a part of the payment, prolonged the man-years of labor required of the share-cropper. The crops alone would give the landlord a profit but when one-sixth of that payment had to be made in silver, the share-cropper was put in danger of being victimized by Secret Fraud #4 of the Sumerian Swindle: "Loans of silver repaid with goods and not with silver, forfeit the collateral."

If money was tight, that is, if silver was in short supply, such as when the moneylenders purposely hoarded bullion out of circulation, then even if he could pay all of the rent in crops, he would still become enslaved to the moneylenders and landlords if he could not obtain enough silver from other sources. Great wealth and great abuses of the power that wealth can buy, became commonplace in Lagash.

The Good King

In this city-state of Lagash, the dissatisfaction of the poor was championed by a pious leader named Urukagina (~2350 to 2340 BC) who became king with the backing of the temple and the approval of the people. Under his pious leadership, the ancient and natural class system of priest-king-merchant-worker was reestablished among the people of Sumeria who had been reduced to poverty and slavery by a thousand years of moneylending.

No king could become a king in Sumeria without the approval of the gods. The gods expressed their approval through the temple and the priests. The laments of the people had been heard by the gods, the gods gave their approval to the priests, and the priests passed along this approval to Urukagina who "took the hand of the god" in the temple and became king and champion of the people.

Urukagina understood the divine way of life whereby man was created as the servant of the gods and not the servant of the moneylenders. He could see with his own eyes the evil effects that the merchant-moneylenders had on society. He questioned the dictum that just because usury and debt-slavery "had always been here," much longer than anybody could remember, that it should continue to be here. Why should an evil be allowed to continue to exist just because it was an ancient evil? "From their works, you will know them," was advice that Urukagina had never known. However, with his own eyes and his own experience of them, he could see that the merchant-moneylenders were not leading the people along the true and straight path of the gods but rather along the crooked and false path of the demons. But as evil as the Sumerian merchant-moneylenders were and as damaging as they were to all of society, they had not become Jews—yet.

Urukagina was the world's first social reformer. He listened with compassion to the cries and suffering of the people and took positive action. Everything that can be discovered about his changes in society are found in the cuneiform inscriptions that he left. He decreed that "since time immemorial" evil men had been undermining the original "divinely decreed way of life." He wrote that all the leaders of society—priests, administrators, powerful men, and even the ensi ("governor") and their extended families—were not serving the people as the just and good servants of God but were acting solely for their own benefit. As a true servant of god, Urukagina swore to Ningirsu, the god of rain and irrigation and the patron god of Lagash, to bring justice to the land.

Like every good leader—even up to the present day—he could see the *effects* of the Sumerian Swindle but did not identify *the cause* itself. He identified the blatant abuses of power but he did not recognize the secret workings of the Sumerian Swindle that was the driving force behind much of that abuse of power. He noted such abuses of power as the seizure of property and the enslaving of debtors by temple officials and money-lenders, all working in collusion with corrupt judges. He saw that the greed for gain had blinded many people from their duties to God. In his inscriptions from 2350 BC, he stated:

> Since time immemorial, since the seed grain first sprouted forth, the head boatman had the boats in charge for his own benefit, the head shepherd had the asses in charge for his own benefit, the head shepherd had the sheep in charge for his own benefit; the head fisherman had the fishing places in

charge for his own benefit. The incantation-priest measured out the barley rent to his own advantage the [temple] oxen of the gods plowed the gardens of the governor; the gardens and the cucumber fields of the governor were in the best fields of the gods; the asses and oxen of the priests were taken away by the governor. No barley rations of the priests were administered by the men of the governor. In the garden of a muskenum [a Have-Not], a priest could cut a tree or carry away its fruit. When a dead man was placed in the tomb, it was necessary to deliver in his name seven jars of beer and 420 loaves of bread. The priest received one-half gur [about fourteen gallons] of barley, one garment, one turban, and one bed. The priest's assistant received one-fourth gur of barley...

The workingman was forced to beg for his bread; the youth was forced to work in the temple factories for free. The houses of the Governor, the fields of the Governor, the houses of the Governor's wife, the fields of the Governor's wife, the houses of the Governor's children, the fields of the Governor's children—all were joined together side by side. Everywhere from border to border there were the priest-judges... Such were the practices of former days.

What Urukagina was observing was the blatant destruction of society by greedy individuals through their selfish monopoly over resources. By 2350 BC, the greed of the tamkarum (merchant-moneylenders) had thoroughly corrupted Sumerian society. The Sumerian Swindle had reduced the workers to begging for their rations while the workman's children had been forced to work in the factories for free to pay off the debts of their fathers. And above this starvation and poverty stood the awilum (the Haves), taking more than they needed and giving less than they should while growing fat from the labor and the wealth of the poor.

To right these wrongs, Urukagina removed corrupt officials.

He removed the head boatman in charge of the boats. He removed the head shepherd in charge of the asses and sheep. He removed the head fisherman from the fishing places. He removed the head of the storehouse from his responsibility of measuring out the barley ration to the incantation-priests. He removed the palace official in charge of collecting the tax

from the priests... The houses of the Governor and the fields
of the Governor were restored to the god Ningirsu. The
houses of the Governor's wife and the fields of the
Governor's wife were restored to the goddess Bau. The
houses of the Governor's children and the fields of the
Governor's children were restored to the god Shulshaggana...

Everywhere from border to border, no one spoke further
of priest-judges... When a dead man was placed in the tomb,
(only) three jars of beer and eighty loaves of bread were
delivered in his name. The priest received one bed and one
turban. The priest's assistant received one-eighth gur of
barley... The youth was not required to work in the temple
factories for free; the workingman was not forced to beg for
his bread. The priest no longer invaded the garden of a
humble person...

These priest-judges were a type of con artist who claimed to speak for the
gods and to pass judgment upon the people based solely upon their alleged
holiness and special communications with the gods. They would witness
"sins" and "transgressions against the gods" and their particular scam was
to tell their god-fearing victims that the sins could only be extinguished
though special sacrifices and prayers that the priest-judge would make on
their behalf. Of course, the priest-judge treated himself to the sacrificed
foods and enriched himself with the sacrificed goods. Urukagina did away
with their frauds. But as you shall see in *The Monsters of Babylon*, the
priest-judges scam became the favorite swindle of the Jewish rabbis, who
used the same deceits to entangle the Hebrew bandits in their demonic net.

Urukagina decreed that:

If a good ass is born to a muskenum [Have-Not] and his
overseer says to him, 'I will buy it from you,' then if be
wishes to sell it he will say, 'Pay me what pleases me,' but if
he does not wish to sell, the overseer must not force him. If
the house of an awilum [Haves] is next to the house of a
muskenum [Have-Not], and if the awilum says to him, 'I
wish to buy it,' then if he wishes to sell he will say, 'Pay me
in silver as much as suits me,' or 'Reimburse me with an
equivalent amount of barley'. But if he does not wish to sell,
the powerful man must not force him.

After 1,000 years of the Sumerian Swindle being used by the money-lenders to parasitize and betray their own people, Urukagina freed the Sumerian inhabitants of Lagash from usury, burdensome controls, hunger, theft, murder, and seizure of their property and persons. He established freedom. The widow and orphan were no longer at the mercy of the rich and powerful. It was for them that Urukagina made his covenant with the god, Ningirsu. While Urukagina was reforming the temple, he was rebuilding it, as well as the other shrines in Lagash. He is the first ruler in recorded history who tried to established freedom and equality through reforms in society and in government.

But these abuses "had always been here" and the awilum (the Haves) and tamkarum (merchant-moneylenders) who profited from swindling their neighbors and abusing their power also "had always been here." They were not willing to let a religious reformer take away their criminally-obtained loot without a fight.

While good king Urukagina served the gods and the people, the merchant-moneylenders ruthlessly served themselves with a vengeance fueled by greed. They profited from the Sumerian Swindle and the corruption to society that it brought. They did not want good kings and good priests ruling over them because the moneylenders enriched themselves more when the kings and priests were evil and corrupt. This is another standard throughout history—that is, when the merchants and moneylenders gain control over a society, criminality, low morals, and debauchery accompany them like dirt clings to pigs. They benefited immensely from Secret Fraud #6 of the Sumerian Swindle: *"High morals impede profits, so debauching the virtuous destroys their moral superiority and pulls them below the depravity of the moneylender, who thereby masters them and bends them to his will."* Thus, blackmail works when bribes cannot. But the moneylenders could not corrupt the virtuous king Urukagina, a man of god. He had the holy priests and the people on his side, so the tamkarum (merchant-moneylenders) could not oppose him openly and reveal the true depths of their evil souls for fear that the people would discover their truly evil character. Those lying hypocrites wanted the people to believe that they were "gentlemen," "honest businessmen," and "obedient to the gods."

In the city-state of Lagash, the temple was the only owner of large properties, other than the moneylenders and merchants. Without the bless-ing of the temple priests, Urukagina could not have seized power. Ob-viously, within the priesthood, there most certainly were holy men who objected to the abuses practiced by their fellow priests. A true priest is the conduit of Goodness between man and God. They pray the desires of men to the god and relate the desires of the god to men.

That Urukagina, in his piety and gratitude, would bestow gifts and wealth upon the temples probably had something to do with such a temple-backed rebellion because considerations of finance played a big role in all the temples of the ancient Near East. Those temples were great industrial, commercial, agricultural, and cattle-raising establishments in addition to being the center of religious worship.

Cynics may say that considerations of "what the god wanted" were directly tied to considerations of what was most profitable for the temple but, in fact, the temples were also repositories of wisdom and mercy. They were not mere money factories because serving God was the basic philosophy for every religion in Mesopotamia.

Everybody believed in the gods and everybody served their gods. Yet, regardless of any impulses of altruism, the greedy and avaricious tamkarum (merchant-moneylenders) always served themselves first, just as they do in modern times. After all, God doesn't need the money but the greedy moneylenders always do.

The priests could see the great hardships that were being forced upon the people by the ever-increasing wealth and the ever-increasing power of the tamkarum (merchant-moneylenders). And they could see that such abuses were not "the straight and true path" in the eyes of God.

The chief god of Lagash was Ningirsu, both a grain god and a god of war. This god was needed for such a city. For centuries, the city-state of Lagash had battled with the Elamites to the southeast and the tribes from the mountains to the east. They had to enforce their boundaries with the Semite cities to the north in Akkad. The spirit of Lagash can be seen in its coat-of-arms: a lion-headed eagle with wings outspread, grasping a lion in each talon. In those days, there were still lions roaming about the Near East. But regardless of its fierce nature, the fiercest people in Lagash were the moneylenders who had been ruthlessly enslaving and disenfranchising their own people since the Sumerians had first learned the Sumerian Swindle nearly a thousand years previously.

Urukagina was also the first reformer recorded in world history to learn, to his woe, the wrath of the moneylenders. As a pious devotee of the gods, his power came from the temple. He was a reformer more than he was a military general. His devotion was to his god and to his people. He followed the mandate of Heaven in righting wrongs and protecting the weak. Those people who did not have land, he took the land of the moneylenders and returned it to the poor and the disenfranchised. Those people who had been sold into bondage by the moneylenders, he freed them and returned children to their parents and wives to their husbands.

He took away from the moneylenders their debt slaves and much of the property that they had swindled. And he confiscated much of the lands that they had stolen. He returned all of this to the people. And he did all of this with the blessings of the priests and the gods of Lagash. Urukagina was pleasing to his god, pleasing to the priests, pleasing to the people of Lagash, but he was hated by the tamkarum (merchant-moneylenders). So, he would learn to his woe, what happens to even the best of kings who threaten the wealth of the moneylenders.

In Mesopotamia, every city had its own god. The god of Lagash was not the main god of the other cities because the people of the entire ancient Near East believed that the gods had their own territories and resided in their own personal temples located in their own cities.

Passing through all these cities throughout the Near East and across the Mediterranean and Persian Seas, throughout the deserts of Arabia, across the waste lands of the far north and the Iranian plateau to the east, were the far-flung trade routes of the money lenders and merchants. The boundaries of the city-states had limits but the boundaries of the moneylenders and merchants were bigger than all of the city-states combined. The city-states were local and national in scope. The horizon of the moneylenders and merchants was international and stretched far beyond the borders of any state.

The states were wealthier and more powerful than the moneylenders but the city-states were like a powerful insect in the web of a spider. Just as the insect is subdued little by little with entangling threads of silk, so too were the city-states subdued as they depended upon the trade routes for their wealth and power. These routes were controlled by the secretive guilds of the merchants and moneylenders.

So, when Urukagina confiscated the property of the tamkarum and gave it back to the people, he unleashed upon himself an unforeseen wrath by a secretive, cunning, and cruel gang of swindlers.

The tamkarum (merchant-moneylenders) guilds could either be good citizens and kindly neighbors to their people and acquiesce to the con-fiscation and loss of their wealth, or they could resist. By this time, after nearly a thousand years of wealth gained by subterfuge, deceit, and ruthlessness, the moneylenders were not about to be good citizens or good neighbors to anyone other than their own guild members. The tamkarum had never been honest and they had never been good. They had always been greedy, acquisitive, avaricious, ruthless, callous, cruel, secretive, and murderous.

Every occupation in Sumeria had its own professional guilds or social clubs which were open only to members of each particular craft. It is natural for people to congregate around similar interests. A modern-day knitting club or coin club or Model-T Ford club are an identical idea to the clubs and guilds that have been a part of mankind since prehistoric times. Within the club, members can share information and material resources, talk about areas of mutual interest, and share techniques that benefit the group. Such guilds allowed them to sell more efficiently their particular products to outsiders at a profit. Guilds of brewers, smiths, and other trades were organized under an administrator, as part of the palace or temple organization. These guilds were not only very ancient social frameworks, but some of them were very secretive in nature, especially the merchant and moneylender guilds which were strictly closed to outsiders, just as they are today.

As organized institutions, the guilds not only provided capital for investment but also the time and freedom from economic pressures for craftsmen to experiment and produce new inventions. Though crafts were usually taught orally during on-the-job training, cuneiform tablets have been found, such as The Farmer's Instructions, as well as instruction tablets on horse-training, glass making, cooking, and beer brewing. The technical terminology of the craftsmen were recorded on these tablets along with the caution to "Let the initiate show the initiate; the non-initiate shall not see it. It belongs to the tabooed things of the great gods."

If such secrecy was such an important part of the ordinary crafts-man's guilds such as glass making and leather tanning, where secret recipes and techniques gave the guild members an economic advantage over other guilds in other cities and certainly an advantage over private individuals, then secrecy was of even greater importance among the guilds of merchant-moneylenders; there, the methods of the Sumerian Swindle and the cunning skills of the merchant gave them an economic advantage over everybody, both citizens and kings alike.

If such warning was given to members of those guilds which dealt with the ordinary crafts of honest workmen, then the exhortations of the moneylenders' guilds, would certainly have been much more emphatic and dire. In the merchant-moneylenders' guilds, where every sly trick and every dishonest scam was used to filch the wealth of mankind, those who divulged the secrets of making money and swindling mankind might be threatened with violence and assassination. Indeed, such diabolical threats of murder and mayhem have been preserved and practiced in the laws and traditions of the Jews who, even in modern times, murder any Jew who informs the civil authorities about the crimes of his fellow Jews. The moneylenders were (and are today) very ruthless with those who take away their ill-gotten loot, as good king Urukagina would learn.

Murder is one of their methods; revolution and genocide are others.

The merchants had their own guilds of both a general nature as well as specialty guilds for merchants who dealt in particular goods such as copper merchants, spice merchants, wool merchants, grain merchants, boatmen, brick dealers, etc. Trades were passed from father to son, so that family connections tended to concentrate members of the same craft into one part of a city.

But the professional moneylenders did not have to congregate in any one particular place other than where money was to be found, which was *everywhere*. Unlike brickmakers or bakers or boatmen who were tied to places where the convenience of transportation and logistics worked in favor of all, the moneylenders could congregate wherever they chose. So, they could call their meetings secretly anywhere and locate their guild halls in unobtrusive locations.

Of all the guilds in ancient times up to and including the present day, the most secretive and the most difficult to enter was the Guild of the Moneylenders. In the first place, the basic commodity that they dealt with was silver and gold which were both very valuable as trade goods as well as easily concealed and quickly stolen if not guarded. The mud-brick houses and shops of Mesopotamia could be burgled merely by a man digging through the dirt walls with a pick and shovel, or even tossing water on the wall and digging into the next room with a spoon. So, secrecy and the hiding of valuables was very much a part of the moneylenders' methods which were not often shared by individual moneylenders, even among their guild brothers. They might all be in the same guild, but each moneylender and merchant was always most interested in what he could get for himself. So, the "brotherhood" of their guild had its limits.

From the earliest times, the tamkarum (merchant-moneylenders) strove to attain Secret Fraud #7 of the Sumerian Swindle, which is: "*Monopoly gives wealth and power, but monopoly of money gives the greatest wealth and power.*" The moneylenders had learned that if they were to make the biggest profits, then their trade had to be a monopoly. It would not be a lucrative business if one moneylender loaned at interest rates of 50 percent while another loaned at rates of 10 percent. Of course, both interest rates would produce a profit. But moneylending is not the kind of business where competition increased quality of the product and thereby reduced prices to the consumer. Competition between money-lenders tended to chase all of the borrowers to the lowest loan rates. In a competition for customers by lowering rates, could only lead them all into lowering rates to zero-percent interest and thereby returning society to its natural order. The moneylenders were not a part of the Natural Order; they had become a cancerous tumor upon mankind, a blood-sucking parasite.

The moneylenders formed their specialized guilds, and from those guilds they created cartels for the control of interest rates throughout Mesopotamia. There were moneylender guilds in every city in Mesopo-tamia, all interconnected as guild brethren who maintained the same interest rates from city to city. They could compete with one another for customers but they did not profit by competing with one another for the lowest interest rates. Although the tamkarum (merchant-moneylenders) were all citizens of different city-states, they were also secretly in collusion with one another as guild-brethren. Thus, they all offered the same (or nearly the same) rates across all city-state boundaries.

The moneylender guilds were secret societies not only because of the swindles that they conspired but also because of the danger of bandits and thieves and the tax collectors of the king. Outsiders were just that, out-siders. Whether new members were accepted immediately or with a variety of rituals and monetary donations, was determined by the particular city's guild. Their personal bodyguards served the additional tasks of aggressive loan collectors and strong-arm goons who could be used for seizing goods and lands and shackling debt-slaves as forfeited collateral. The money-lenders, themselves, did not have to dirty their hands. They considered themselves to be "gentlemen." They could hire plenty of gangsters from among both the "Haves" and the "Have-Nots" to coerce the debtors.

Every trade guild had its own patron deity. The brickmaker's god was Kulla. The love goddess Inanna (later named Ishtar) was the patron deity of brothels and beer taverns. The patron deity of the moneylenders was the Moon God, Sin. This was not a bright god like Shamash, the Sun God, who was limited to only half the day. The Moon God lived in both the day and the night sky and was mysterious and full of secrets. His "day" began in the evening and he reigned throughout the night, a time when debt-slaves were captured and properties confiscated.

The Moon God was the god of both the city of Ur in Sumeria and the city of Harran in Akkad. Both of these were major guild cities of the moneylenders and important cross-road cities for the merchants. Both Ur and Harran were the central terminals of major trade routes. Ur controlled the river and sea trade routes with the Persian Gulf and India, while Harran controlled the river and overland routes to the Mediterranean Basin. Located at each city, were the major temples for Sin, the Moon God, the god of the merchants and moneylenders.

Once Urukagina began his social and ethical reforms, returned the swindled properties to the people and re-united the enslaved families, the tamkarum (merchant-moneylenders) called upon all of the might of their guild brothers and the blessing of their Moon God, Sin, to avenge their losses. These prayers were backed up, of course, with the monetary power of gold and silver wielded by all of their trade guilds throughout their entire Near Eastern network. As many other kings at many other times would find to their surprise, even though they attempted to curb the wealth and power of the moneylenders in their own city-states, all of the moneylenders in every other kingdom would rise up against them.

As Urukagina began his reforms, guild leaders met in secret places through the region to plan strategy. The moneylenders of Lagash warned their guild brethren from cities far outside of the territories of Lagash that they would see a similar fate occurring to their own wealth if the confiscations by Urukagina were not reversed. Every moneylender made his profits by swindling the poor and the ignorant, and they did not want Urukagina's reforms to become popular with the poor and the ignorant in other city-states, also. None of them made their money from one city-state alone. All of those tamkarum were intertwined in business and marriage ties all along the trade routes.

True, the kings, the priests, and the people had greater *total* power than the moneylenders and merchants. But the merchant-moneylenders knew that although they only had wealth at their command, that this wealth could be used to buy influence over kings and priests anywhere. The kings and priests directly controlled both the people and the state. Wars could be fomented with the money used to corrupt the kings and the priesthood. Secret Fraud #6 again came into play, "High morals impede profits, so debauching the virtuous destroys their moral superiority and pulls them below the depravity of the moneylender who there-by masters them and bends them to his will."

This power of money was international and reached far beyond the borders of any state. The tamkarum (merchant-moneylenders) were finding that their control of wealth gave them control over both kings and people. It was from this time in 2350 BC that Secret Fraud #12 of the Sumerian Swindle was developed: "*All private individuals who control the public's money supply are swindling traitors to both people and country*." But treason was not a character flaw new to the tamkarum because, for the merchants and moneylenders who both controlled private spy networks, treason was not a flaw; rather, it was a business technique.

In Secret Fraud #12, the moneylenders and merchants knew how to betray the people and steal their property. They knew how to make the people work in the fields and give the moneylenders the fruit of their labor. They knew how to turn the daughters and sons of the citizens into slaves to serve them, both menially as servants and sexually as whores. And it was all accomplished with the simple principle of lending out two pieces of money and then asking the impossible—that *three pieces of money* be returned. It was in ancient Mesopotamia that all of our modern bankers, merchants and financiers got their ideas for betraying the people of the world and destroying mankind, all for their own benefit.

A Traitorous Enemy

To begin their conspiracy to regain their confiscated wealth, the tamkarum (merchant-moneylenders) did what most traitors of every country do: they approached the worst enemy of Lagash with their schemes. His name was Lugalzagesi (or Lugal-zage-si), the governor of the city of Umma.

Umma was only 29 kilometers from Lagash. Over the centuries, the two cities had fought many times over land and water rights, and thus Umma was a natural choice in allies for the merchant-moneylenders because of the ancient animosity between the two cities. Nisaba, the goddess of scribes and grain, had her main temple at Umma. Strictly from self-interest, the scribes were aligned with the merchant-moneylenders because they offered the scribes the most employment and the richest rewards. The grain merchants of Umma were also aligned with the merchant-moneylenders of Lagash because they profited so much in mutual businesses.

None of the awilum (the Haves) of Umma wanted to see a general return of confiscated property to the rightful owners as had happened in Lagash. They wanted to keep what they had already swindled. All of them wanted to make sure that the reforming ideas of Urukagina did not spread to their own dispossessed muskenum (the Have-Nots) and slaves. Thus, the merchant-moneylenders of Lagash had plenty of sympathetic allies among the trade guilds of Umma and its surrounding towns.

The awilum (the Haves) of all of the city-states of Sumeria were alarmed by what Urukagina had done for his people. As a unified Treasonous Class, the scribes and the greedy awilum (the Haves) of Umma aligned themselves with the merchant-moneylenders of Lagash.

Citing the past military defeats of Umma to Lugalzagesi, and warning him that the reforming ideas of Urukagina would spread to his own people if something wasn't done to stop it, the moneylenders offered their financial backing if a war against Lagash could be waged. All they asked for, was that their loans to him be repaid—plus interest—from the spoils; and they wanted their confiscated properties in Lagash returned to them.

The ambitious Lugalzagesi of Umma agreed. With the war chest provided by the moneylenders, he was able to pay and equip a large army and to attack Lagash sometime around 2340 BC. Even though the moneylenders already knew of the huge profits that could be made in financing warfare, this is the first time in recorded history that the moneylenders, merchants, and accountants were able to conspire the overthrow of an entire kingdom. They would repeat such treason and war mongering many times through-out history. However, those deceiving bean counters and lying con-artists were not Jews—yet.

While Lugalzagesi harangued the people with histories of how Lagash had defeated them in past battles, the priests of Nisaba, the scribal goddess, stirred up the people with lies and deceits of how Urukagina had broken the ancient laws of land ownership, how he had stolen the temple property from the priests, how he had stolen the slaves away from their owners, and how he had insulted Nisaba, the goddess of scribes, by smashing the legal contracts of the moneylenders and landlords.

Even though Urukagina had freed his people from debt, the deceived and ignorant people of Umma did not know that. So, they were lied to by their leaders as to the true nature of Urukagina's reforms. Their priests and leaders decreed and the people obeyed because, in innocent trust, the people believed that their leaders were telling the truth. The educated and the wealthy led the illiterate and the poor into war. The educated and wealthy sought their happiness in wealth rather than righteousness before God, so they betrayed the illiterate and poor. The corrupt leaders deceived their innocent followers so as to send them to fight and die in a war against the holy and the true. It was all an evil hoax upon his own people that Lugalzagesi perpetrated, backed by the silver and gold of the demonic merchant-moneylenders of Lagash.

With the moneylenders' financing, Lugalzagesi hired the impoverished laborers from the surrounding countryside and the tribes from the Zagros mountains as soldiers in his mercenary army. The rich hired the poor to fight for them in exchange for grain and loot. Grain was cheap pay that the poor would eat and then have nothing. The loot was also cheap pay because it had cost the merchant-moneylenders nothing and they would eventually swindle it away from the poor along with their freedoms.

In Lagash, the reformer Urukagina was a king of the people, not a conquering king intent upon empire. In this, the wily moneylenders, through their slit-like, half-closed eyelids, had read his character quite well. He was interested in freeing his people from oppression and slavery but he was not prepared to fight a war with anyone. As a religious man, Urukagina did not have the ruthless heart to slaughter the people of Umma who were just as disenfranchised as his own people in Lagash had been. He had spent his time as king in rebuilding and refurbishing the temples and re-establishing a religious way of life for his people, where God was the first consideration and the welfare of his people was the first duty of the king, just like in the olden days a thousand years before.

To work so hard to free his people from the slavery of the money-lenders and then to see an army of equally enslaved peasants led by the same moneylenders beating at his gates, was too much for him. He did not have the heart for battle and offered little resistance. The moneylenders made sure that after his capture, Urukagina was executed.

Thus, after only eight years of Urukagina's rule, the army of Umma led by its governor, Lugalzagesi, attacked Lagash, burnt the shrines, and carried off the divine image of Ningirsu. Lugalzagesi burned, plundered, and destroyed practically all of the holy places of Lagash. The temples that Urukagina had rebuilt and furnished with gold and silver, Lugalzagesi seized, stripped its treasures, and destroyed.

It was a rare thing for Sumerians to attack the temples, even of their enemies. But these holy temples and their priests had backed Urukagina and had been behind the uprising against the wealth and criminality of the merchant-moneylenders. The temples were destroyed and looted so that Lugalzagesi could avenge the moneylenders and repay to the money-lenders his war-loans from the plunder. The moneylenders were avenged and their loses were returned to them, plus interest, from the looting of Lagash.

This looted wealth then financed Lugalzagesi's army. He no longer needed merchant-moneylender financing. With the looted wealth, he could buy whatever military goods that he needed from the merchant-money-lenders. With the enthusiasm of his army of impoverished peasants and fierce tribal mercenaries, newly enriched and eager for even more loot, Lugalzagesi went on to conquer the Semite city of Kish in the north, where he killed Ur-Zababa, the king of Kish.

This void left in the leadership of Kish was to prove to be Lugal-zagesi's undoing. But defeating Kish was an important strategy to protect his borders for future campaigns and to keep the king of Kish from taking over the lands that were no longer defended by a defeated Lagash. Then, Lugalzagesi turned south and conquered the rest of Sumeria, unifying it under his kingship and making himself the king of all Sumeria, with his capital city at Uruk.

Uruk (biblical Erech) was the city where the sky-god, Anu, dwelled, the god of heaven, lord of constellations, king of the gods, he who dwelt in the highest heavenly regions. Later, this position was absorbed by Enlil, the main god of Uruk. It was believed that Enlil had the power to judge those who had committed crimes, and that he had created the stars as soldiers to destroy the wicked. The goddess Inanna (Venus or Ishtar) also had her temple in Uruk, where the slave girls who had been seized by the moneylenders were sold in the brothels or dedicated as the temple prosti-tutes of Inanna. And so, Lugalzagesi felt that such a city, filled with debt-slaves and whores, befitted such a great king as himself.

With Kish out of the way, and the cities of Sumeria under his rule, he claimed that all foreign lands were subservient to him, "from the Lower Sea along the Tigris and Euphrates Rivers to the Upper Sea." That is, Lugalzagesi claimed that he had unified Sumeria and controlled the trade routes from the Persian Gulf to the Mediterranean.

But these trade routes which he claimed to control were the very routes that extended far beyond his territory and beyond his power. These routes were traveled by, and best known to, the moneylenders and merchants. He could claim to be the king of a large empire, but his claims were based upon his control of Sumeria while the trade routes that served Sumeria were serviced by a power that he did not possess and did not understand: *the money power* that had financed his war against the good king Urukagina. These trade routes which brought everything that Sumeria needed to exist as a civilized country, were controlled by the merchant-moneylenders.

With Urukagina's reforms smashed, the merchant-moneylenders were free to enlarge the limits of their secret and subterranean power. For the first time, those secretive merchant-moneylender guilds could see the great possibilities and profits that could be realized by manipulating the kings into either waging war or refraining from warfare, all while safely disguising themselves as advisors, financial councilors, and innocent businessmen.

Before the overthrow of Lagash, the tamkarum had busied themselves with *business*. Buying and selling and slave trading and moneylending had proven very profitable to them. But now, with their coffers filled with the loot of conquest and their social prestige raised by the grateful Lugalzagesi who had proclaimed himself king of Uruk and all of Sumeria, they realized a new source of wealth and power for themselves. They began to understand the huge profits that could be made from war, especially from wars in which they did not have to do any of the fighting.

However, Lugalzagesi's "empire" did not long endure. The huge profits realized by the moneylenders of Sumeria did not go unnoticed by the moneylender guilds of the north. The northern trade routes controlled by Sumeria were not tightly held and those that ran through Sumeria were worked by the moneylender guilds and the merchants within Sumeria. Lugalzagesi's so-called "empire" was, from the very beginning, sapped and undermined by the Treasonous Class.

After just two decades of successful rule over all of Sumeria, Lugalzagesi was defeated in battle and brought in a neck-stock to the Ekur gate of Nippur to be reviled by all who passed by. He was reviled not because he was a loser in battle but because he had robbed and desecrated the temples of Lagash. So, as a public humiliation, he was dragged like a dog and tied to the gates of Nippur, the holiest city in Sumeria. His conqueror was a man of considerable importance: Sargon of Kish.

Lugalzagesi's reign (2358 to 2334 BC) marks the end of the Early Dynastic phase in Sumeria. After this time, the balance of power begins to totter and shift away from the Sumerians and toward the Semites of the north, whose capital city was Kish and whose moneylenders were a more ruthless variety. Those moneylenders had no fraternal sentiments toward their fellow moneylenders in Sumeria because, where profits are at stake, blood is thicker than water; the Sumerians were not Semites and it was every man for himself.

The Semitic moneylenders of Kish were not Sumerians. Although they had their own moneylender guilds which were allied with all of the other moneylender guilds in Sumeria and with the rest of the ancient Near East, they had not shared in the looting of Lagash. And much worse, they had lost much in Lugalzagesi's looting of Kish from whence their silver and valuables had been carried off to Sumeria. It was among the Semites of Kish that Secret Fraud #9 of the Sumerian Swindle was perfected, that is, *"Only the most ruthless and greedy moneylenders survive; only the most corrupt bankers triumph."* Only the most ruthless and greedy money-lenders survive because, as time goes by, and the relentlessly increasing sums of the Sumerian Swindle multiply, then the most ruthless and wealthiest moneylenders must destroy the weaker moneylenders and feast upon the remains. Thus, in the moneylending rackets, there is a winnowing process which brings the most ruthlessly greedy monsters into control of the less voracious monsters. Bankers, moneylenders, loan sharks, financial swindlers—name them whatever you like, but they are all monsters, even when dressed in pin-striped suits.

Sargon Gains Control of Sumeria: 2334 BC

The city of Kish has a history that goes back to pre-literate times. Because it was situated away from the more densely populated regions of Sumeria, it was settled by the Semites from the Syrian desert who entered that less inhabited part of Mesopotamia from the north and west around 2900 BC, several hundred years after the Sumerians had arrived in the region. Like all other people who settled in the Fertile Crescent, they absorbed the older Sumerian culture and made it their own. They wrote their Semitic language with Sumerian cuneiform characters and they worshipped the same gods and followed the same cultural patterns that "had always been here."

Because the Semitic Amorites who settled this region built their culture based upon what the Sumerians had already created, nearly everything was Sumerian in origin, but with embellishments of a Semitic style. While Sumeria continued to be a thriving and prosperous culture to the south, the Semites in the area of Babylon and Kish built up their own independent strength and power.

After Umma's governor, Lugalzagesi, overthrew Urukagina of Lagash and killed king Ur-Zababa of Kish, Ur-Zababa's chief minister and cup-bearer took over the kingship of Kish. The cup-bearer's name was Sharrum-kin, known to us as Sargon.

Sargon the Great (2334 to 2279 BC) was the first of the ancient personages who was given a divine beginning which, more than a thousand years later, the Jews plagiarized for their own myths about Moses. According to one tradition, Sargon's father was unknown, which meant that he was of humble birth. One story, as found in "The Legend of Sargon" written around 2300 BC, gives him a peasant origin:

> Sargon, the mighty king of Agade, am I.
> My mother was a lowly; my father I knew not. The brothers
> of my father loved the mountain.

My city is Azupiranu, which is situated on the bank of the
Euphrates.
My lowly mother conceived me, in secret she brought me
forth. She placed me in a basket of reeds, she closed my
entrance with bitumen,
She cast me upon the river, which did not overflow me. The
river carried me, it brought me to Akki, the irrigator.
Akki, the irrigator, in the goodness of his heart lifted me up;
Akki, the irrigator, as his own son. brought me up;
Akki, the irrigator, as his gardener appointed me. When I
was a gardener, the goddess Ishtar loved me, and for four
years I ruled the kingdom....

Other legends of Sargon claim that he was the illegitimate son of a
priestess of Kish. Since the king was the chief representative of God, the
priests and scribes created the necessary divine link in the legend of
Sargon. The legend told that Sargon was the son of a high priestess who
bore him secretly because she was prohibited from having sexual relations
with a man. A high priestess was often of royal lineage and often the
consort or 'wife' of a god.

Although his origins are uncertain, the later histories agree that
Sargon served as the king's cup-bearer. The office of Cup Bearer to the
King was an important political station in the hierarchy of ancient Near
Eastern politics. He who stood by the king and offered him a cup of wine
was also an official taster to ensure that the wine had not been poisoned. In
addition, he would act as a casual bodyguard so that others could not
approach the king too closely. Such a person would be well acquainted
with the entire kitchen staff and the logistics of supplies for the palace.
Also, being present during all official banquets, ceremonies, and receptions
of foreign dignitaries, the cup bearer of the king was privy to the most
intimate secrets of kingly office. He could overhear or be invited to
participate in discussions and entertainments. Such a trusted person would
be asked for his advice by the king.

A cup bearer also met the various merchants who visited the palace.
Such an officer of the court became educated in the far regions of the
surrounding countries and gained an understanding of the strengths and
weaknesses of each. The cunning merchants were always alert for those
who could be of use to them, weighing their characters and ambitions as
carefully as weighing specks of gold.

Luxury items were important for maintaining the prestige of the royal palaces and the temples. Because of the expense and risk involved in obtaining these rare materials, their acquisition remained the business of kings and queens, powerful governors, and temple priests. All of them would deal personally with the merchants and moneylenders. Money lending and import-export were usually amalgamated within the same business families of tamkarum (merchant-moneylenders). The merchant-moneylender families became intimately familiar with many kings and administrators over many generations. Just as they do today, those old scoundrels passed this political and personal information along to their sons; this way, the data base of information about the kings and their families increased and was perpetuated over many generations, while what the kings knew of the moneylenders remained relatively constant.

Over the centuries, both raw materials and finished products were imported to Mesopotamia from every direction, such as lapis lazuli from Afghanistan, reaching both Mesopotamia and Egypt through a complicated network of overland routes. These routes were complicated because over the millennia, the various game trails and foot paths through the mountains and deserts were expanded both to serve outlying villages and to enable caravans to out-maneuver roving tribes of bandits. Flooding rivers, drought through the deserts, and mountain landslides all contributed to re-routing even the oldest trails through the wilderness. Commodities arrived by sea from East Africa, the Arabian Peninsula, Iran, and the Indian subcontinent. Under such conditions, trade could only occur through carefully-organized and well-funded organizations. So, an individual merchant had an almost zero chance of success against the odds of Nature or in competition with the monopolistic and wealthy trade guilds.

Although the palaces, temples, and kings were the main customers for luxury goods, all of those goods without exception, passed through the hands of the merchants and moneylenders who, each and every one, were members of the same trade guilds. There were no independent business-men in those days who were not guild members. Thus, the tamkarum knew as a corporate entity what the private treasures of the palace and temples were, as well as the character and depth of greed of both royalty and priests. This royal inventory of secrets were collected through the generations of merchants within their extended family groups and quietly discussed during guild meetings.

True, the kings knew their own people and something about the surrounding cities and territories. But it was the merchants and money-lenders who knew the surrounding territories better than the kings. This scheming group of merchants and moneylenders made it their business to know everybody else's business and to profit thereby. Through their guilds and marriage connections, the business families controlled information and spy networks that were larger than that of any individual kingdom.

By the time of Sargon, these secret and subterranean guilds of moneylenders began to exercise their power of the purse to control the destiny of the people. Secret Fraud #7 of the Sumerian Swindle gave them an important advantage: "Monopoly gives wealth and power, but monopoly of money gives the greatest wealth and power."

With their skills in accounting and numbers, the tamkarum (merchant-moneylenders) and their scribes could estimate to precise degrees of relative strengths of the various nations and the wealth of their kings. In an age where even the kings were illiterate and dependant upon the scribes for writing and calculating, the scribes became both important sources of information and targets of corruption. Thus, what the merchants actually controlled was not just wealth but also *information* about resources and kingdoms. Besides inventories of the palace treasuries, grain field areas gave them close estimates of grain harvests—valuable knowledge when weighing the strengths and weaknesses of a kingdom. All this information was known by the scribes.

Subverting and bribing the scribes for such data, gave the tamkarum guilds military intelligence about the capabilities of every country. But they could only control the destiny of nations and the fate of mankind if they worked secretly and always pretended to be simple merchants and moneylenders.

To work secretly meant that only verbal orders and agreements could be made between trusted sons and guild members. Even though the vast majority of the people were illiterate, that did not prevent them from hiring a scribe to read the merchant-moneylenders' letters and contracts. By using cylinder seals and stamps impressed upon wet clay, even the illiterate could mark their possessions, seal their packages, and seal the doors of warehouses and safe rooms. (see Figure 7)

Fig-7

With each cylinder seal being a unique stamp, everybody could authenticate a legal document. When pressed into the wet clay, both these impressions and the cuneiform writing, could not be altered once the clay had hardened. Cylindrical seals were rolled on lumps of clay to seal doorways, pottery jars, and packages. Seals that could be carved on stone, bone, metal, or shell were within the budget of everyone who could afford to buy one. The use of these cylinder seals continued throughout Mesopotamian history.

Although the clay tablets and cylinder seals are superior even to modern paper and computer disks in terms of permanence and longevity, they did not have any privacy. Cyphers and secret codes had been used for centuries. The secret meaning of words was a standard part of the scribes' schooling. This need for secrecy brought about a new invention: around the time of Sargon (2334 to 2279 BC), *envelopes* were invented (see Figure 8). These were flattened sheets of clay modeled around the clay tablets. The clay envelopes protected the contents from damage and fraud by safeguarding against someone moistening the clay and changing the writing. They provided a kind of "notary seal" or a "poor man's copyright" that protected the legitimacy of the contents. Sometimes the text was repeated on the envelope so you could read what was sealed inside. In the case of a dispute, the envelope would be opened and the contents examined and compared. Some envelopes opened in modern times have been found with the information written on them different from that of the tablets inside. So, fraud was not unknown.

Figure-8

Lugalzagesi had provided the merchants and moneylenders the means of regaining their property by overthrowing Urukagina, the reformer king of Lagash. But greed is a demon that is never satisfied, just as a fire is never satisfied by adding more fuel. The huge quantities of gold and silver that had been looted from the temples of Lagash gave the moneylenders new ideas for acquiring even more. This vast new source of bullion flowed into their businesses from the soldiers and laborers who had looted this wealth during Lugalzagesi's victories.

For the sacking of the temples—as financiers, conspirators, promoters, military suppliers and catering services—the merchant-moneylenders could plead complete innocence before the gods. "Not Us! We didn't do it." Yet, through their businesses, they had gained all the loot. Silver and gold made available to the people as war booty meant that the people had more silver to buy the grain, the garments, the beer, the prostitutes, gamble at the dice table, and buy the slaves and the luxury items which were the stock-in-trade of the merchants and moneylenders. War was very profitable to the winners. Profit meant power. And the greedy Treasonous Class desired ever more wealth and power without themselves being impious or subject to being cursed by the gods.

So, why not encourage warfare while avoiding any risk to their own persons? Why not arrange for *everybody* to go to war, and then have them bring the booty back to the merchant-moneylenders who could then buy it at a low price?

The tamkarum (merchant-moneylenders) had learned how to seduce the poor into doing all the looting with Secret Fraud #20: *"Champion the Minority in order to dispossess the Majority of their wealth and power, then swindle the Minority out of that wealth and power."* Using this method, it didn't matter whether the merchant-moneylenders, themselves, took possession of a temple's wealth or not, because they ended up with all of it, anyway. They could avoid both risking their own lives in combat as well as avoid the curses of the gods, by letting the poor soldiers loot the temples. Then, they could swindle the loot away from the soldiers with moneylending, with wine, with gambling and with prostitutes. Taking the gold from the gods was a curse, everybody knew that. But the gold was not cursed, only the looters who took it were cursed. The merchants who swindled the gold away from the looters were completely innocent. Oy Gevalt! So innocent! Always so innocent!

Even so, it would be another 800 years before the merchant-moneylenders would figure out how to permanently gain *all* the above benefits and *all* the profits while permanently being able to avoid military service. It would be another 800 years before the merchant-moneylenders would be able to foment wars and profit from wars, all while sitting on the sidelines and watching everybody else maim and murder each other on the blood-drenched battlefields.

However, no matter how rich the merchant-moneylenders were, only among the kings and the priests were power and prestige to be found. Mere merchants and moneylenders were forever spat upon and hated by the people whom they had robbed. Only among themselves did they have prestige, a prestige based upon who among them was the richest. According to Secret Fraud #9 of the Sumerian Swindle, among the moneylenders, bankers, and merchants, "Only the most ruthless and greedy moneylenders survive; only the most corrupt bankers triumph." Thus, the most ruthless and greedy of the merchant-moneylenders were also the most prestigious leaders among them. In every gang, it is the most violently criminal, who is the boss of the gangsters. This also holds true among bankers and financiers.

Semitic Revenge

For the greedy moneylenders of Kish, Lugalzagesi had been a king for too long. His 24-year reign had allowed him to assemble all of the cities of Sumeria into one, single empire. This was the first time in over one thousand years that all of Sumeria had been united. But Lugalzagesi was a Sumerian and he was satisfied with being the king of Sumeria. He had been financed by the moneylenders of Sumeria to destroy Urukagina of Lagash and to eliminate the Semitic king of Kish before turning south and conquering all of Sumeria. He was happy with his victories and was not ambitious for further conquests.

But in Kish, the merchant-moneylenders had lost their treasuries to him. They were Semitic Amorites, not Sumerians. Although they had absorbed the Sumerian Culture, they were of a different race and temperament and language. As merchants and moneylenders, they were adept at perceiving the strengths and weaknesses in men and of taking advantage of their weaknesses while undermining their strengths. They knew of the great wealth their guild brothers in Sumeria had gained through Lugalzagesi's wars. They had lost much of their wealth to the Sumerians. They wanted those war profits for themselves. They wanted their looted treasures returned.

And they wanted their Semitic revenge.

The merchant-moneylenders of Kish found their champion in Sharrum-kin, the cup bearer of the former king of Kish. Like most court officials, Sargon had the manners, charisma, and air of authority to make a natural leader. He knew the subtle ways of politics and court intrigue. He had the drive toward avenging his former master's death at the hands of Lugalzagesi. And with the assurance from the moneylenders of their un-limited financial support in buying weapons and paying for an army, he had the means of attacking Lugalzagesi at Uruk.

What's more, he had the military intelligence supplied by his money-lender informers and merchant-spies. Sargon was apprised of the relative strengths and weaknesses of the many cities under Lugalzagesi's rule. He knew how many men they had, how rich was their treasuries, how full was their granaries, how strong were the walls of the cities, and which of the numerous kings would be willing to fight against him and which would acquiesce to his rule in exchange for liberality. All of this information was with the compliments of the tamkarum (merchant-moneylenders). Vital information, indeed! Information that could only have been supplied by the merchant-moneylenders who did business with all of those cities.

In addition, from the earliest days in pre-literate times, none of the city-states of Mesopotamia had kept standing armies. Their armies consist-ed of the ordinary citizens—farmers, fishermen, brick makers, court officials, and city governors—assembling as a yeoman army whenever there was a threat. Mankind had not reached such large numbers in population that necessitated standing armies as protection against other armies in other countries. When threats of war between cities seemed immanent, it was simply a matter of sending runners to outlying villages and criers throughout the cities to assemble enough farmers and fighters to go to battle. While supplies were drawn in and city gates were shut, the populace secured themselves behind their city walls of mud brick. Although this was "how it had always been," this ancient Sumerian system was about to change.

Sargon kept secret his war preparations. With sufficient financing and access to the tamkarum (merchant-moneylender) trade routes, he did not need to do business with the Sumerian cities in the South for his supplies but could buy directly from the Semitic cities far to the north and west, away from the knowledge of Lugalzagesi.

Directly to the west of him on the Euphrates was the city of Mari, which was a major manufacturer of copper and bronze implements and weapons. After all, this was still the Bronze Age and such weapons could be bought through the merchant-moneylender monopolies at Mari without raising suspicions. Once his army was armed and trained, Sargon struck swiftly, attacking Uruk and dragging away Lugalzagesi like a dog in a neck-stock to be tied to the gates of Nippur.

While Lugalzagesi had fought against each of the Sumerian city states in order to defeat them, Sargon used politics to win most of his victories. First, he demonstrated his military might by defeating Lugalzagesi at Uruk. He then turned to the other cities of Sumeria. To those kings who refused to acquiesce to his rule, he fought against and defeated them in battle. But those kings who agreed to accept his rule, he granted them their kingships intact and their cities as their own, as long as they paid tribute and maintained Sargon's own relatives and trusted friends as resident advisors in the palace.

Sargon the Great was a brilliant military leader as well as an innovative administrator. Sargon was the first king to unite all of Mesopotamia, both the north (Akkad) and the south (Sumer) under one ruler. His Akkadian empire became a prototype for later kings. Sargon's policy was to destroy the walls of cities within his empire, thus depriving potential rebels of strongholds. He also took members of local ruling families to his capital as hostages. If the city governors were willing to shift their allegiance, Sargon kept the old administration in office; otherwise, he filled governorships with his own citizens and appointed only Semites to high administrative positions. In this way, he encouraged the collapse of the old city-state system and moved toward centralized government, backed by reliable garrisons. Sargon installed military garrisons at key positions to manage his vast empire and to ensure the uninterrupted flow of tribute. And he was the first king to have a standing army.

In the scribal records, 34 battles are recorded, with the victorious Sargon gaining control not only of Akkad but of all Sumeria on his way to the Persian Gulf, where he washed his weapons in the sea in a ritual commemoration of his victories. On the way back, he completed his conquest of southern Sumeria. Sargon then turned west and north, traveling along the trade routes of the Euphrates toward the Mediterranean where he conquered the lands of Mari, Yarmuti, and Ebla up to the "Cedar Forest" (Amanus Mountains) and the "Silver Mountain."

Mention of cedar and silver reveals clearly the motivation for this distant campaign. Gaining control of the silver and the wooden building materials meant both wealth and power for himself and his economic backers of the Treasonous Class. Returning to Kish, he then turned east to conquer Elam and neighboring Barakhshi. Later legend adds still further victories, taking him across the sea as far as Anaku, the "Tin Country" (location uncertain) and Kaptara (Old Testament Kaphtor, or Crete).

His victory over two major commercial centers, Mari on the middle Euphrates and Ebla in northern Syria, were important because of their strategic position on trade routes. Ebla was the center of metal trade in the third millennium BC. In these decisions can be seen the work of Sargon's advisors. Wealth acquisition and trade were paramount. The "silver mountain" mines provided Sargon with the wealth to increase State power and to buy influence.

But most importantly, he needed free silver to balance the false accounting books of the tamkarum (merchant-moneylenders). Without an injection of free silver, the debts of the king and the people could never be repaid under the cheating Sumerian Swindle, the accounting tablets of which always claimed to be owed more silver than actually existed in the known world.

By this date in history, silver had become the ultimate commodity with which all other commodities could be bought. This shiny metal that was too soft for anything other than making trinkets, was useful in its rarity as a type of commodity money. Those who owned the sources of this metal could dig it out of the ground at low production costs using war slaves and debt slaves. The silver that was obtained for free as war booty or cheaply from slave-labor mines, actually had a higher buying power than silver obtained through taxes. Taxes only recycled existing silver and left the problem of the phantom and fraudulent moneylender's interest accounts unpayable. However, newly-mined silver increased the existing total by digging it out of the ground to pay off the phantom interest that the Sumerian Swindle had created out of thin air. Silver was a commodity money. So, if the king needed money, all he had to do was capture a mine from some other king, then dig it up and spend it.

Theft was the only way for the moneylenders to balance their books because, in reality, interest-on-a-loan creates more debt than there is money in existence to repay it. Sargon's power was greatly increased by the monopoly over the silver mines which helped to finance his empire. And the wealth of the tamkarum (merchant-moneylenders) was increased as the people used their war booty to pay the moneylenders their fraudulent interest payments.

To judge from the much later legends and chronicles, Sargon's conquests continued to range far and wide; he may even have sent his armies to Egypt, Ethiopia, and India. To control so vast an empire, he stationed military garrisons at various key outposts.

Large armies require large taxes and income in the form of tribute. In Sumeria, itself, where rebellion was chronic, he appointed fellow Semites to the higher administrative posts and garrisoned those cities with all Akkadian troops. For himself and his huge court of officials and soldiers, the archives boast that "5,400 men ate bread daily before him."

He built a resplendent capital city of Agade, not far from Kish. In a brief span of time, Agade became the most prosperous and magnificent of the cities of the ancient world. Gifts and tribute were brought to it from the four corners of Sargon's realm. At its quays, ships docked from far-off Dilmun (Bahrain), Magan (Oman), and Melukhkha (the Indus Valley).

Most of Agade's citizens were no doubt Semites related to Sargon by ties of blood and language, and it is from the name "Agade," or rather from its Biblical counter-part, Akkad (or 'Accad,' Genesis 10:10), that the word "Akkadian" has come to designate today the Mesopotamian Semites in general.

Notice should be taken of the importance of the wharves and quays of Sumerian cities. Water transportation was naturally the most efficient way to move men and materials on the Two Rivers and through the network of interlinking canals and irrigation channels. Of course, international merchant ships from the Persian Gulf moved up river and docked at the wharves and then off-loaded onto smaller boats. So, the commercial value of the wharves was carefully monitored. Because they were a stop for foreign sailors and traders, the wharves also had to function not only as a place of commerce but as a guarded enclave to prevent foreign spies and troublesome sailors from infiltrating into the city proper.

Aside from the walled city with its temples and royal palaces and the suburbs outside of the walls, the average Sumerian city also included a special, official area of wharves. The wharf section functioned not only as a docking facility for ships but also as a center of commercial activity. The wharf had administrative independence and separate legal status for the citizens transacting business there. Foreign traders had stores there, and their needs were met by the *sabitum* (alewife-moneylender) of the wharf. These women tavern-keepers and madams provided the sailors with everything that a boatman would want. So, the problems associated with controlling foreign sailors and sea captains were minimized by keeping them restricted to the wharf area of the cities. And on the quays and wharves, the *tamkarum* (merchant-moneylenders) could keep a close eye on their cargos and bargain for newly-arrived goods.

The close cooperation between Sargon and the *tamkarum* (merchant-moneylenders) can be seen throughout his career. Under his rule, international trade flourished between the Mediterranean coast and the Persian Gulf. Trade goods from as far away as India could be carried into regions of the Mediterranean basin. Even when a local king as far away as Purushkanda in Asia Minor was oppressing a Mesopotamian merchant colony, Sargon sent a military expedition to protect it. Rich inducements were offered to Sargon by the merchants and he marched with his army with great difficulty to Purushkanda where his presence alone brought about a settlement of the merchants' grievances.

Sargon the Great appreciated the power of the moneylenders and merchants because they had helped him to win his empire. And he understood the importance of trade to the general well-being of his administration. Military coercion increased the flow of goods to the imperial center from areas firmly under his control. But the private enterprise of the merchants not under Sargon's rule also engaged in limited trade throughout his empire.

For example, Aratta, a city-state most probably in northwestern Iran near the Caspian Sea, is described in Sumerian myths and epics as the rival of Uruk. Aratta was known for its stone, metals, craftsmen, and artisans. And, of course, Magan and Melukkha were written about in texts from the time of Sargon the Great to the middle of the first millennium BC. Sargon recorded that boats from Magan (Oman), Melukkha (Indus valley), and Dilmun (Bahrain) dropped anchor in his capital, Agade. Melukkha was described as the place of "black men" and its people as "men of the black land" or "black Melukkhaites." "The black land" was described in myths, epics, and economic documents as a prosperous, populous country, full of trees, reeds, bulls, birds, various metals, and carnelian.

There were always foreigners in Mesopotamian cities. The Sumerians and later the Babylonians and Assyrians knew about the geography, economy, political organization, religious beliefs, and customs of foreign countries and their peoples. From archaeological and literary evidence, the world that the Mesopotamians knew about, extended north into Anatolia, the Caucasus, and westerly parts of central Asia; to the south into Arabia; to the east to India; and to the west to the Mediterranean Sea, Cyprus, Crete, and Egypt. Under Sargon the Great, business prospered and great wealth flowed all across the empire. And all of this wealth passed through the hands of the moneylenders and merchants, all of whom extracted a profit for themselves.

By merely being the middlemen in any transaction, wealth was siphoned by the tamkarum (merchant-moneylenders) in handling fees and commissions, in addition to profits from sales. And so developed Secret

Fraud #18 of the Sumerian Swindle: *"When the source of goods is distant from the customers, profits are increased both by import and export."*

The new supplies of silver, the tribute from conquered territories, as well as taxes, gave Sargon the spending power to not only enrich the merchants through an increase in trade and luxury goods but to buy off the priests and laity. Rebuilding temples was not just an act of piety but was a public work where the wealth of the empire could be used to employ the people and to increase political support from the temple priests. The new wealth of the laborers gave the merchants bigger profits also. This new system of centralized government with its bureaucracy of administrators, set standards for all future empires in the Near East.

One of Sargon's innovations was the establishment as a royal sinecure: the office of high priestess to the Moon-God at Ur. This was apparently a deliberate move to ally to his Akkadian administration the loyalty of the 2,500-year-old, once-powerful Sumerian religious centers. His daughter, Enheduanna, was the first holder of this celebrated post. For the next 500 years, until the end of the reign of Rim-Sin of Larsa, this appointment was a royal prerogative which was exercised continually through numerous dynastic changes. This appointment of the priestess provided to Sumeria a unifying link even in periods of apparent disunity.

As well as being the first holder of this office, Enheduanna was the most distinguished in this long line of priestesses. There survive a number of hymns that she herself, a Semitic Akkadian, is said to have composed— in excellent Sumerian! Since the ancients did not usually sign their names to their literary creations, we know Enheduanna as history's first known literary figure. Even her portrait has survived.

But there was another reason that has been overlooked by the archeologists as to why Sargon put his daughter into the high office of the Moon God at Ur. As the king of Akkad and Sumeria, he could have installed his daughter in any temple that he chose. Why not make her priestess in the greatest temple of the highest god in all of Sumeria, the god Enlil in the city of Nippur? Why make her priestess of the Moon God at Ur?

The Moon God was the tutelary deity of the moneylenders of Sumeria. And the city of Ur was the main depot of all international trade from the Persian Gulf. Ur is where the sea-going ships off-loaded their cargo onto shallow-draft river-going, reed boats. Because the Semitic moneylenders of Akkad had helped Sargon to take power, it was important in his control of Sumeria to also control the Moon God's temple in Ur. In this way, Sargon had firmly under his control, both the main temple in which the Sumerian moneylenders prayed as well as administrative control of the main terminal city of the international Persian Gulf trade.

But Sargon had considerable difficulty in controlling his vast empire. Even during his reign, and among the cities of Babylonia, there were never-ending rebellions. The "Sargon Chronicle" tells us that "in his old age, all the countries revolted against him and they besieged him in Agade." Although Sargon crushed these insurrections, his sons and grandsons did not inherit a peaceful empire.

End of an Empire

Sargon's empire lasted just over a century (~2334 to 2150 BC). Its final collapse was prompted by the invasion of a people from the Zagros mountains who disrupted trade and ruined the irrigation system. Although Sargon could defend his empire during his lifetime, his habit of tearing down the walls of the cities under his rule made it difficult for his descendants to protect what he had created. He destroyed the city walls so he could keep rebellion in check. But once again, the limited vision of the kings were not far-ranging enough to see the greater world beyond their domains. With no safe havens, the people of the empire were easily attacked by the barbarian hoards from the mountains. The mountains offered safe haven and protection to the barbarians but the plains of Mesopotamia offered no protection for the people without city walls.

It was not just the mountain tribes who were giving Sargon's empire trouble; the cities of Sumeria were also in constant agitation and rebellion. A thousand years of Sumerian rule had been upset by Sargon. The Sumerians liked things "as they had always been." Even though Sumerian society had its share of inequalities with the awilum (the Haves) swindling the lands and lives of the muskenum (the Have-Nots), at least the people could appeal to the king or to the priests for some relief. In Sumeria, over and above all, were the gods, and it was to them that the people owed their ultimate allegiance.

Yes, Sargon had shown his loyalty to the gods in the traditional way by rebuilding the temples. So, the people could see that their taxes and tribute were being used to serve the gods. Yet, it was *not* the way that things "had always been" because the wealth of Sumeria was being siphoned off to the empire of Sargon while the people were ruled by Semites from the north—Semitic Amorites who had always been regarded by the Sumerians as barbarians, nomads, and lowly paid laborers.

But what was worse, Sargon had given the merchants and money-lenders full rights of exploitation—full rights of exploitation, that is, if you were a Semite of Kish, an Akkadian. As in ancient times, merchants could travel the trade routes through the safe passage guarantees of the king to whom taxes were paid. But it was Sargon's *Amorite* moneylenders who had financed Sargon's empire, not the moneylenders of Sumeria. The Sumerian moneylenders and merchants were given the same access to trade routes but with a higher tax to the king. Losing money like this, did much to align the Sumerian merchants behind the rebellions that were springing up in Sargon's empire.

Nowhere were the Sumerian merchants more opposed to Sargon than in the city of Lagash. Lagash is where the pious king Urukagina had freed his people from the greed of the tamkarum (merchant-moneylenders), so it might seem odd that the merchant-moneylenders of Lagash who had helped to overthrown Urukagina, would want a return to Sumerian rule, especially since they had been guilty of financing the overthrow of Urukagina and installing Lugalzagesi in his stead. But under Sargon, the Amorite moneylenders had been given full authority to practice the Sumer-ian Swindle throughout his empire and their preferential treatment had reduced the Sumerian moneylenders' profits.

What was even worse for the Sumerian merchant-moneylenders, Lagash had been one of the main river ports for trade coming upriver from the Persian Gulf. Once Sargon had built his capital city, this trade by-passed Lagash for the quays and warehouses of Agade, leaving the merchant-moneylenders of Lagash without a wholesale source. Taking away the money of a merchant-moneylender is like taking away a bone from a dog—you will get bitten every time. And these were *Sumerian* moneylenders, not the vengeance-crazed Semites of Akkad.

Sargon ruled for 56 years and died at a very old age. But his son Rimush, on his accession, found the empire torn by revolts and rebellions. The Sumerian people longed for those holy times when the people served the gods rather than serving the kings and their moneylenders. In bitter battles involving tens of thousands of troops, Rimush reconquered the cities of Ur, Umma, Adab, Lagash, Der, and Kazallu, as well as the countries of Elam and Barahshi. To be a king meant to also be a warrior.

A fragment of a vase bearing his name was found at Tell Brak in northeastern Syria and, like his father, he claims to have held "for Enlil" the entire country from the Mediterranean to the Persian Gulf, together with all of the mountains. Rimush was killed in a palace conspiracy, assassinated by certain of his courtiers, possibly even including his elder brother Manishtushu who succeeded him, and whose name, meaning "who is with him," perhaps indicates that they were twins. Rimush reigned only nine years and Manishtushu followed him as king.

Manishtushu (2276 to 2261 BC), like his father Sargon, carried his victorious armies to far-distant lands, or at least so it might seem from a passage in one of his inscriptions which reads: "When he (Manishtushu) had crossed the Lower Sea [the Persian Gulf] in ships, 32 kings gathered against him, but he defeated them and smote their cities and prostrated their lords and destroyed the whole countryside as far as the silver mines."

Again, the ancient records name the primary goal and chief prize of those wars: *silver*, which could be seized rather than paid for; silver, which could be mined by the debt-slaves and the war-slaves for the cheap pay of a bowl of barley porridge; silver, which could be dug out of the mountains and given to the moneylenders to pay the interest on their loans to the king; silver, mined to balance the phantom interest created by the Sumerian Swindle.

Manishtushu brought back "black stone" from the mountains beyond the sea, shipping it directly to the quays of Agade; this was almost certainly the beautifully grained diorite in which his surviving statues are carved in a naturalistic style, striking in its contrast with the stylized conventions of the Early Dynastic period. That Manishtushu held Assyria is clear from a votive inscription dedicated to him at Assur and from a later text of king Shamshi-Adad who, while restoring the Ishtar temple at Nineveh, found a number of statues and stele recording the Akkadian king's founding of that temple. Manishtushu reigned fifteen years and was followed by his son Naram-Sin.

Naram-Sin was the grandson of Sargon. He controlled an empire from Central Asia Minor to the southern end of the Persian Gulf. Ultimately, the empire collapsed under the pressures of the peoples from the mountains of the north and east. Those people were known as Gutians. This is what most historians will tell you, but there were other factors at play pushing the events beyond what people can control.

Temple of Enlil

Only the merchants and moneylenders belonged to a guild which was devoted solely to buying and selling all things and lending-at-interest both grain and silver. So, the merchants and moneylenders found their greatest profits by promoting rebellion and fomenting warfare, just as long as they could be the military suppliers while avoiding battle, themselves. That was the tricky part: being able to profit from war while avoiding any actual combat, themselves. They were completely happy to let everybody else fight and die, just as long as they could live to count the profits.

Naram-Sin's own inscriptions mention a general rebellion of the principal cities of Sumeria and Akkad, including Kish, Uruk, and Sippar. While the tradition mentions that the goddess Innin decided to abandon the capital, Agade, the immediate cause of the withdrawal of divine favor is now known, thanks to the modern archaeologists.

A Sumerian text, put together from a number of fragments in various museums, describes in the opening lines the early splendor and wealth of Agade, to which people came from all quarters of the world bearing their tribute. But an impious deed of Naram-Sin brought this to an end, for he had allowed his troops to desecrate, sack, and loot the Ekur, the great temple of the highest god, Enlil, in the holiest of Sumerian cities, Nippur.

The religions of Sumeria, all without exception, were based upon the belief that mankind was created to serve the gods. Once Sargon and his sons and grandsons had gained the kingship of Sumer and replaced the Sumerian governors and kings with their relatives and subalterns; once the taxes and tribute and labor of the Sumerian people began to be siphoned off toward the construction and embellishment of Sargon's capital city of Agade rather than being used toward a pious and prosperous life of the Sumerian people; and once Sargon had allowed the Sumerian Swindle to again ravage the people through his Akkadian moneylenders, the priests declared the displeasure of the god, Enlil. And so they helped to promote rebellion. After the rebellion was quashed, when Naram-Sin again took control of Nippur, he punished the priests of the Ekur temple by allowing his troops to loot it.

The importance of Nippur is reflected even today in the great size of its mud-brick ziggurat mound of Enlil's temple located between Baghdad and Basra in southern Iraq (see Figure 7). Nippur was one of the longest-lived Sumerian sites, beginning in the prehistoric Ubaid period (5000 BC) and lasting until about 800 AD.

From earliest recorded times, Nippur was a sacred city, not a political capital. It was this holy character which had allowed Nippur to survive numerous wars and the fall of dynasties which had brought destruction to other cities. Although it was not a capital city, Nippur had an important role to play in politics. Kings, on ascending the throne in cities such as Kish, Ur, and Isin, sought recognition at Ekur, the temple of Enlil, the chief god of the Mesopotamian pantheon.

Figure 7.

In exchange for such legitimization, the kings lavished gifts of land, precious metals, and stone, and other commodities on the temples and on the city as a whole. At the end of successful wars, rulers would present booty, including captives, to Enlil and the other gods at Nippur. In an effort to win the blessings of the gods and the goodwill of the priests and the people of Nippur, successful kings carried out expensive construction and restoration of the temples, public administrative buildings, fortification walls, and the canals of Nippur.

Under the protection of the mighty gods, the temples of Mesopotamia were used by the moneylenders and merchants as safe havens to store their hoards of gold and silver. So, when Naram-Sin allowed his troops to loot the Ekur temple, he was destroying the wealth of the very ones who had been fomenting rebellion—not a good way to make friends among people who already hated him.

The literary tradition that later attached itself so strongly to Sargon and Naram-Sin saw them not only as two of the most illustrious figures in the ancient world but also as rulers whose disastrous final years implied some stigma of ill-fate.

Sargon, following the usual public-relations ploy of rebuilding Sumerian temples, had provided all of the cities of Sumeria, including Nippur's Ekur temple, with renovation work and treasures for the god. All of his sons followed in this ancient Sumerian tradition. But during the Akkadian reign, Nippur was among the rebellious cities who chaffed at Semitic rule. The priests of Nippur were not so foolish as to believe that the gifts of Sargon had been anything but a bribe to the gods offered by a foreign king.

The Sumerian people wanted to be free of the Semites and the rapacious moneylenders who stood behind the throne. The priests of Nippur wanted to serve the gods and protect their people. And the moneylenders and merchants of Sumeria wanted the wealth that was being siphoned away from them by the Dynasty of Sargon. So, the priests and the Sumerian merchant-moneylenders put their wealth and influence behind whatever anti-Akkadian alliances arose.

We know from contemporary inscriptions that Naram-Sin had refurbished the Ekur temple and had dedicated statues there celebrating his victories. Like his grandfather, Sargon, he had given the temple even more wealth. But when rebellion broke out, Naram-Sin did not forget his grandfather's generosity or his own gifts toward what appeared to him as ungrateful temple priests at Nippur. Knowing from his spies that the Sumerian moneylenders were involved in those rebellions and tribal uprisings, he decided to take the silver and gold that was helping to finance those revolutions.

Naram-Sin sacked Nippur as well as the Ekur temple. His ships docked at the quay by the temple in order to load and carry off the loot to Agade. Once again, the moneylenders and merchants had lost their wealth to the confiscations of a king, even though it was stored in the holiest temple of the greatest god in the holiest city in Mesopotamia. Oy Gevalt! How can this be!? Is there no god who protects the wealth of the moneylenders? Oh, cruel fate!

Pillaging a temple was not something that was usually done in Sumeria since the armies on both sides feared all the gods equally. Very few individuals would dare to risk the curse of a god for doing so. Sargon respected this, and his humility before the gods can be seen in his kingly titles, which were comparatively modest and reflected little more than the titulary used by the Early Dynastic kings. But under his grandson, Naram-Sin, a major change in kingly attitude had taken place which was so startling that it proved in the long run unacceptable to the people.

Naram-Sin could dare to pillage Nippur's temples because he considered himself a mighty king who was *as strong as a god!* He adopted a naming style that was previously the exclusive prerogative of the gods. On his own inscriptions his name appears preceded by the determinative for "divinity," that is, the cuneiform sign "god" normally written before the name of a god. The language in texts dedicated to him was even less reserved, and in these, his servants address him not merely as divine but literally as "the god of Agade."

This divine form of name was adopted by Naram-Sin's son, Shar-kali-sharri, and the later kings of Ur and Isin. Although there is evidence to suggest a widespread cult of the divine king under the succeeding dynasty at Ur, the principle of a divine kingship was never wholeheartedly adopted in Mesopotamia. Certainly, the deified Mesopotamian king was in no way comparable with the divine and absolute Pharaoh in Egypt because even divine Mesopotamian kings, along with their people, remained at all times subject to the will of the gods.

With their network of spies as a foundation, Sargon and his sons, Rimush and Manishtushu, and his grandson Naram-Sin, were adept at squashing rebellion. So, the uncoordinated uprisings of drunken hooligans and hired goons scattered around the Akkadian Empire were efficiently suppressed. Remember, Sargon had torn down the walls of the Sumerian cities precisely as a preventative to such rebellion. Without safe refuge and with Akkadian troops stationed in all cities, successful rebellion was difficult. And the king was supported in all of his actions by his own Amorite moneylenders, priests, and merchants.

But because the Sumerian people, who had Akkadian troops stationed around their various cities, could not raise an army strong enough to defeat the Akkadians, the moneylenders and city governors devised a plan to induce the wild tribes of the mountains to attack.

Far up in the mountains, away from the prying eyes of Akkadian spies, through gifts, bribes, supply of weapons and promises of future wealth, the moneylenders hired an army of wild tribesmen to attack Akkad on many fronts. Remember, the moneylenders had vast fortunes which they had swindled for free. So, they could well afford to liberally spend large amounts of silver with promises of plunder as an added incentive. This would be a recurring technique used throughout history, where private persons with large fortunes and evil intent could upset entire nations with their crooked money as the lever. With the Sumerian Swindle, whatever the moneylenders spent for creating war and havoc, would all come back to them as they sold goods, loaned silver, peddled wine and beer, operated crooked gambling dens, provided numerous prostitutes, bought war plunder and swindled away the possessions of the soldiers.

This would be a recurring technique throughout history; Secret Fraud #15 of the Sumerian Swindle, *"Loans to friends are power; loans to enemies are weapons."* By making loans to friends at low interest rates and easy terms, the moneylenders gained the goodwill and cooperation of people who acquiesced to becoming their friends, following their advice and buying their goods. The profits are low but the power is great.

By making loans to enemies, regardless of the loan rates, the money-lenders give enemies strength. In this case, the Sumerian moneylenders gave gifts of grain and silver and sold to the Gutian tribes shiny new bronze weapons and encouraged them to attack and loot the cities of Akkad. To hide the Sumerian sources of Gutian financial backing, the merchant-moneylenders blamed the god, Enlil, for bringing the attacks upon the Akkadians.

According to the priests at Nippur, it was their furious god, Enlil, who had brought down from the mountains the barbarous race of Gutians. These savages disrupted communications and trade, upset and ruined the irrigation system—which always required careful, constant, and centralized control—and this produced famine and death throughout the land. To turn aside Enlil's wrath from Sumeria and Akkad as a whole, the priests claimed that eight of the senior gods decided that Agade should itself be destroyed in reprisal for Naram- Sin's violation of Nippur. This is a way of saying that as representatives for their own gods, the chief priests from eight of the temples in Sumeria had made this decision.

With famine and desolation rampant, so the tablets written by the priests continue, eight of the major gods decided that for the good of Sumeria, Enlil's rage must be assuaged. The priests then vow to Enlil the total destruction of Agade and pronounce upon that city a lengthy curse:

> May your groves be heaped up like dust....
> May your clay [bricks] return to the depths of the earth...
> May your palace built with joyful heart, be turned into a depressing ruin...
> Over the place where your rites and rituals were conducted, may the fox who haunts the ruined mounds glide his tail...
> May no human being walk because of snakes, vermin, and scorpions.

The poet-historian who wrote of the fall of the Akkadian Empire concludes that such, indeed, was the case. Thereafter, Agade remained desolate and uninhabited. The site of Agade remains unidentified today though it is almost certainly to be found in the vicinity of Kish or Babylon. It is possible that the city was situated somewhere within the later city boundaries of Babylon itself or even buried today in the ancient dust beneath streets and buildings of modern Baghdad. It may even have been washed away by the meandering Euphrates. No one knows.

CHAPTER 7

THE THIRD DYNASTY OF UR AND UR-NAMMU

The Dynasty founded by Sargon the Great, though it endured for little more than a century, left a permanent imprint on Mesopotamian history. Sargon's administrative skills proved that many cities could be consolidated into a single empire, all with the central administrative city of Agade at its core.

Sargon's empire, which had been financed by the Semitic money-lenders of Kish, flourished through its monopoly of the trade routes and its control of the silver mines. With silver as the international medium of exchange, political power and material goods could be purchased across international boundaries with the cheap silver that Sargon's empire dug out of the Taurus Mountains. A shekel of silver that could buy a large quantity of grain, gained in its buying power when it was seized for free as war booty or mined from the Silver Mountains by slaves. Circulation of that free silver from mining, war booty, tribute, taxes, and loot, allowed the people to pay their debts with real metal—real metal that the phantom numbers of the moneylenders' account tablets claimed as interest due. With their Sumerian Swindle paid off and with balanced account ledgers, the Sumerian merchant-moneylenders were ready to increase their investments.

With a larger empire, the moneylenders and merchants realized the enormous wealth that could be swindled more efficiently from larger numbers of people when the volume of business increased through international trade and taxes. The government could be sustained with taxes, war booty, and tribute while the merchant-moneylenders could be enriched with a monopoly over a larger market and by swindling the war booty away from the soldiers.

Unlike modern times, the moneylenders did not have an international, interlocking monopoly over all finances in every country, like they do today. In 2200 BC, civilization was still young. The moneylenders still worked in extended family groups, in clans, in city-wide cartels, and in city-states where the guilds of several cities controlled prices.

Armed with the best bronze weapons and fed with Sumerian grain, the Gutian tribes rushed out of the Zagros Mountains and attacked Akkad on a broad front. As Sargon's empire fell, the brunt of the Gutian attacks was directed against his great-grandson's capital at Agade and toward the other cities of Akkad. Because the war material, food, and financing for the

Gutian tribes came from the Sumerian moneylenders of Lagash, Nippur, and other cities of Sumeria, the Gutians avoided those cities and directed their attacks at the center of Akkadian might to the north of Sumeria, that is, the cities of Agade, Kish, Babylon, and surrounding areas.

However, controlling wild barbarians once unleashed has never been a simple matter. Although the Gutians' allies were the Sumerians, some of the northern Sumerian cities inevitably suffered from the Gutian attacks.

Since their defensive city walls had been torn down by Sargon, they were easy targets. But whether they were allies or not, the Gutians were like the 800-pound gorilla invited to dinner—friendly, as long as he is fed, but not at all easy to un-invite.

The defeat of Sargon's great grand-son, Shar-kali-sharri, at the hands of the Gutians, brought political confusion and anarchy to Mesopotamia as the Sumerians threw off the foreign domination and began to reestablish their society "just as it had always been"—that is, devoted to serving the gods and living the peaceful life of an agrarian society under Sumerian governors speaking the Sumerian language.

Although "just as it has always been" was a good slogan for attracting the common people to fight in the battle, it also meant that the Sumerian moneylenders could practice the Sumerian Swindle "just as it had always been." The Twenty-One Secret Frauds of the Sumerian Swindle were fully operational during the Akkadian occupation. So, the people were glad to be offered a relief from the mounting debts and confiscations of the Semitic moneylenders of Akkad. The Gutian destruction of the Akkadian Empire canceled all debts and tribute that the Sumerians had paid to their Semitic overlords. As the empire of Sargon and Naram-Sin fell, the Akkadian temples were plundered and neither women nor children were spared by the Gutians. The Akkadian moneylenders who had placed their trust in the protection of the gods by putting their silver on deposit in the temples of Akkad, lost everything.

While the impact of the Gutians was felt most severely in Akkad, in Sumeria only a few of the old city-states suffered some minor material damage in the first wave of barbarian invasion. However, all of the Sumerian cities and, most importantly, the wealth of the Sumerian merchant-moneylenders, remained virtually autonomous.

The Gutians knew who their friends and benefactors were. Even though the Sumerian cities had no defensive walls, the Gutians spared both the Sumerian cities and the wealth of their "friends" the Sumerian merchant-moneylenders. This would become a recurring theme throughout history, where attacking tribes and political parties which ravaged a nation, avoided harming the moneylenders who had financed the violence.

Even though it was geographically close to the battles in Kish and Agade, one of the cities which suffered the least was Lagash. This city had been rebuilt during the prosperous days of the Agade dynasty, and immediately regained much of its old importance as a river-port. Once the Akkadians were defeated and the Gutian troubles had subsided, Lagash was able to recover much of its past splendor. Lagash once again controlled the Tigris River trade from Melukkha (India), Magan (Oman), and Dilmun (Bahrain).

Even though they did not have an army at their command, the merchant-moneylenders of Sumeria were able to destroy their rivals, the Semitic merchant-moneylenders of Akkad. Their use of outside military might was ingenious. Without actually leading or controlling the Gutian hoards, but merely through financing them, arming them, and providing them with military intelligence and direction, they were able to have their enemies destroyed and the Sumerian lands of their ancestry unencumbered.

But they still did not have a free hand in swindling the people because it was the priests of the temples and the governors living in the city palaces who actually managed society, not the moneylenders. Both kings and priests served the gods and thereby could stand between the moneylenders and the peoples' wealth which the moneylenders wanted to swindle. These dangerous kings and pesky priests were a constant impediment to the unrestrained, voracious, acquisitive greed of the merchant-moneylenders. It was a great puzzle as to how the kings and priests could be removed so that the merchant-moneylenders could stand in their place. It was a very great puzzle which required careful consideration.

Although the Gutian rulers became the dominant political element throughout the seven or eight decades following the death of Shar-kali-sharri, they were ignorant and illiterate tribesmen who ruled through military domination. The Gutians were too primitive to understand the Sumerian Swindle and were perfectly happy with taxes and tribute alone. They were illiterate tribal barbarians who were unfamiliar with the complexities of civilization. They did not have the knowledge or skills to control large populations or to operate complex societies. Besides, their homes were in the mountains. They had conquered the Akkadians for the loot, not for the land. For actually administering the cities and controlling the canals and the grain-growing operations and businesses, the Gutians, content with tribute, appointed Sumerian governors.

A list of 21 so-called "kings" of the Gutian period is given in the Sumerian King List, but in view of their extremely short reigns (only one exceeded seven years and about half of them were three years or less) it seems likely that they were chiefs appointed for a limited term of office.

Later tradition emphasized the barbarity of the Gutians, and if their social organization was primitive, it is likely that kingship as a developed and permanent institution had not yet arisen among them. Some of the later names in the list of Gutian rulers are Semitic, which indicates that assimilation of the barbarians was taking place. A few dedication inscriptions show that, as was the custom of people living among resident gods, that they had adopted the religious cults of the land. The Gutian period, which may be taken as beginning at about 2250 BC, was certainly at an end by 2120 BC. In later days, the civilized peoples of Babylonia remembered the period of Gutian domination with abhorrence, as a time of barbarism. But it was also a time of profits for the Sumerian merchant-moneylenders.

The Gutians favored Lagash because their richest Sumerian allies lived there and because its Tigris River traffic and trade advantages brought supplies close to the overland routes into their Zagros Mountain homeland. Lagash became the dominant city in southern Sumeria, controlling at times Ur, Umma, and Uruk. As their strength returned under the leadership of the governors of Lagash, the Sumerian people began to throw off, but not to completely eliminate, the Gutian barbarians.

The founder of the new Lagash dynasty of governors was Ur-Bau, who has left several dedicatory inscriptions recording his reconstruction of numerous temples in Lagash. He was also in control of Ur. He was influential enough to have his daughter installed as high priestess of the Moon God, Ur's tutelary deity. Note once again the importance that a king placed on having his daughter installed as high priestess of the guild deity of the merchant-moneylenders. As governor, he controlled through his daughter, both the guild city of Ur and the temple of the Moon God where the moneylenders worshipped. Ur-Bau had three sons-in-law, Gudea, Urgar, and Namhani, each of whom became governor of Lagash.

Gudea was the best-known of these. As governor, Gudea's authority extended well beyond Lagash—he claimed to be suzerain to Nippur and Uruk and even undertook a campaign to loot the Elamite city of Anshan. But according to his inscriptions, he was principally concerned with religion and in the building or restoration of temples and the fulfillment of his duties to the gods. The ancient ways as they "have always been" had returned to Sumeria. The kings, priests, and people served the gods with piety and happiness. And "just as it has always been," the Treasonous Class of Sumerian merchants and moneylenders served themselves with usury, fraud, and deceit without the Akkadian merchant-moneylenders siphoning away their profits. The moneylenders were happy to have gotten rid of their Akkadian competitors but under the Sumerian governors of Lagash, the old reforms of Urukagina were again instituted to limit their ruthless application of the Sumerian Swindle. Once again, the kings and priests stood between the moneylenders and their victims, the people.

Gudea's peaceful face, reflecting his blissful piety, have become familiar to the modern student from the numerous statues of him that have been recovered (see Figure 8). Some of these carry long inscriptions recording his religious activities in connection with the building and rebuilding of Lagash's more important temples. From them we learn that, in spite of Gutian domination, Gudea had trade contacts with practically the entire civilized world of those days. He obtained gold from Anatolia, silver from the Taurus mountains, cedars from the Amanus mountains, copper from the Zagros mountains, diorite and gold from Egypt, carnelian from Ethiopia, and timber from Dilmun (Bahrain).

Figure 8.

Nor did he seem to find any difficulty in obtaining craftsmen from Susa and Elam for the decoration of his temples:

Cedar beams from the Cedar-mountain (Lebanon) He
had landed on the quayside ... ;
Gudea had ... bitumen and gypsum brought in ... ships
from the hills of Madga (Kirkuk) ....
Gold dust was brought to the city-ruler from the Gold-
land (Armenia)....
Shining precious metal came to Gudea from abroad,
Bright carnelian came from Melukha (the Indus valley).

And all of this was purchased with grain from the fertile soil of Sumeria,
from manufactured trade goods, and from taxes. Regardless of the Gutian
victories over the Akkadians, the Sumerian people demanded that their
leaders fulfill their promises to make Sumeria like "it had always been."
Both the Sumerian leaders and the Sumerian people believed that the
Akkadian domination of them was a result of neglecting their service to the
gods. So they were happy to rebuild temples and dedicate pious works.
Taxes were repaid to the people through wages for labor in the rebuilding
operations. Thus, the Sumerian government spent the tax money on infra-
structure improvement, building temples, city walls and wharves, and
maintaining the canals while paying the people to do the work.

The governor of Lagash re-instituted Urukagina's reforms of 120 years
earlier. Society once again operated in the ancient and natural way with the
people serving the gods while sustaining the government; and the governors serving the gods while protecting the people. It was a prosperous and
happy time for everybody, with plenty of food, beer, and useful work for
fair wages.

Gudea was followed by his son, Ur-Ningirsu, and his grandson, Ug-
me, who between them ruled less than a decade. They were succeeded by
Urgar, another of Ur-Bau's sons-in-law, whose rule, however, was ephem-
eral. There then followed the third of Ur-Bau's sons-in-law, Nam-hani,
who was probably governor of Umma as well as of Lagash. The power of
the Gutians in Sumerian society is reflected in a Sumerian year date under
Namhani, who dates one of his inscriptions to the days when "Yarlagan
was king of Gutium." Sumerian society had once again attained the Ancient Way, but the Gutian barbarians were still there, collecting tribute.

Politics being what it is, alliances rise and fall as easily as taking off
one cloak and putting on another. The Gutians were very useful to the
Sumerians for helping to rid them of Akkadian domination. Unlettered and
barbaric as they were, the Gutians recognized the advantage of cooperating
with the civilized moneylenders and governors of Sumeria. As barbarians

standing in awe of civilization, they allowed Sumerian culture to continue very much as "it had always been." They even accepted the Sumerian religion and culture and became more civilized, themselves. The rich harvests of Mesopotamia provided the Gutians with plenty of food, while wealth through tribute and taxes provided them with the silver and trade goods of the merchants which they could not glean from their mountain strongholds.

But the Sumerians, who had been managing their society for a thousand years, were not happy with the Gutian barbarians lording over them. The tamkarum (merchant-moneylenders), as well as the people, were losing money through the taxes and tribute required to support both the Sumerian government and the Gutian occupiers. So, the Sumerian people were ready to support whatever Sumerian leaders could rid them of this burden. They found their hero in Utuhegal of Uruk. Utuhegal led his people out from the barbaric, though benign, rule of the Gutians—and into the grasping claws of the merchant-moneylenders.

Warring against armed invaders requires both armaments and food. And these cost lots of silver. Who else had lots of silver other than the moneylenders who only loaned it for a price? The price that the moneylenders asked of Utuhegal was a return to "the way it has always been"—but not with the debt-easing reforms of Urukagina that the governors of Lagash were practicing under Gutian protection. What the tamkarum (merchant-moneylenders) wanted was the "way it has always been" with the merchant-moneylenders practicing the Sumerian Swindle without restraints. With the backing of the moneylenders and the patriotism and blood of the people, Utuhegal of Uruk arose to break the Gutian yoke and to bring back the kingship to Sumeria.

The Rise of Ur-Nammu

Utuhegal of Uruk (2120 to 2114 BC) drove out the last of the Gutians and was duly recognized at Nippur as "King of the Four Regions" (a title first employed by Naram-Sin). Utuhegal was included in the Sumerian King List. This marks the reemergence of the system of centralized government employed by Naram-Sin; subordinate city-states were ruled through governors who recognized Utuhegal as overlord.

However, a popular uprising against the Gutian rule was only one-half of a successful revolution because good leadership of the post-war empire was also necessary. Although Utuhegal of Uruk could free the country of barbarians, he did not understand the basic threat to the well-being of the people and to the strength of the country which was caused by the invisible and pervasive tamkarum (merchant-moneylender) class of conspirators. In exchange for the support of the merchant-moneylenders, he had agreed to do away with Urukagina's reforms.

For Utuhegal, returning Sumeria to the way that "it had always been" meant allowing the moneylenders and merchants to swindle the people just as they had always done. So, high prices, false weights and measures from the thieving merchants, loansharking, foreclosures, debt-slavery from the greedy moneylenders, and extortionate transportation costs from the boatmen, were once again allowed to increase under his rule. Utuhegal freed his people from the barbarian Gutians but he then turned them over to the ruthless swindles of the merchant-moneylenders, "just as it had always been."

In spite of his resounding victory in ridding the country of the Gutian barbarians, Utuhegal did not long hold power over Sumeria. He had the military strength but he lacked the moral strength to hold together a religious people. Under Utuhegal's rule, the people were being once again defrauded and swindled by the tamkarum (merchant-moneylenders). They cried out to their priests for relief. After some seven years of corrupt rule, Utuhegal's throne was usurped by Ur-Nammu (2112 to 2095 BC), one of his more ambitious governors, who succeeded in founding the last important Sumerian dynasty, commonly known as the *Third Dynasty of Ur*.

The Third Dynasty of Ur (2112 to 2004 BC) was a time of revival for all things Sumerian. The people glorified their ancient past, the Sumerian language was spoken once again, and the entire Sumerian culture was revived "just as it had always been." Ur-Nammu, who reigned for sixteen years, proved to be a capable military leader, a great builder, and an outstanding administrator. He promulgated the first law code in man's recorded history [see Figures 10 and 11].

Figure-11 Fragment of a limestone stela set up by Ur-Nammu of Ur. The king is pouring overflowing waters on the tree of life while the god Nannar offers to the king the measuring rod and cord so the king can make laws leading to the "straight and true path." [University Museum, Philadelphia, height 46 cm.]

Notice in this bas-relief (Fig. 11), the "hat" worn by the god on the right. The archaeologists call it a "horned helmet," but this clay sculpture (Fig. 10) proves them to be wrong. Most of the gods are sculpted with the "helmet" sitting square on the head. Ur-Nammu's bas-relief proves that these were not "horned helmets"; they represent the holy spirit of both Man and the Gods.

At this point, I want to emphasize something regarding laws. Laws are not usually made for no reason at all. When a need arises in society, laws are made to address that need. Just laws are made to protect both the people and society from those who would do harm. Unjust laws are made to protect the corrupt from justice or retribution. Merely because a law is created, does not mean that such a law is necessarily a Just Law. Some laws are created by corrupt officials which are unjust and designed to benefit only certain classes of people while causing injustice and harm to the rest of society. Modern society is filled with examples of this. So, again, I caution not to consider the ancient people to be inferior to us modern people, especially because they have proven to be superior to us in many ways. But in those early days when mankind was exploring and testing various ways for perpetuating society and advancing civilization, they used both Just Laws and Unjust Laws in the same ways that our Jewish-lawyer-corrupted societies do today. Their only real superiority to us in this regard is that they had no Jews to corrupt them, so they had to learn how to do that, themselves.

Ur-Nammu is the first leader in history to not only see the injustices in his society but to try to correct them in an enduring way with written laws. In the previous 3,000 years, society had experienced the usual tyranny of the strong over the weak, and the rich over the poor. Although everyone could see the injustice in this, the problem had never before been addressed other than with the uneven and patched-together opinions over the millennia of the priests and kings and governors who were, themselves, not bound to any established reference of Justice other than the opinions of their own minds and the urging of their own hearts. Up until the time of Ur-Nammu, what laws there had been, were oral laws which the king would declare orally but which were quickly forgotten. Oral laws did not survive the king who decreed them. Thus, civilization tended to follow a bumpy trail of ups and downs and detours without a steady and consistent map of useful rules and laws to follow through the ages.

According to Sumerian belief, mankind was created by the gods to serve the gods. All that was necessary in life was to do one's duty toward one's god. One's "duty" was very much as each man saw such a duty, combined with daily prayer and offerings. Other than the teachings of the priests for mankind to follow the "straight and true path," there were no hard-and-fast rules of conduct for men except for the traditional mores involved in marriage, theft, or murder. Marriage was handled in a tribal way between kin. Theft required a double replacement of the goods, and murder required execution or banishment. These were all obvious social and legal situations that could be recognized by everyone ever since the most ancient times.

But even as society grew and evolved, the more subtle crimes of usury and its related corruptions of poverty, confiscation, foreclosure, slavery, cruelty, debauchery, prostitution, and warfare, were not understood as being interrelated phenomenon. Nor were the tamkarum (merchant-moneylenders) and the Sumerian Swindle recognized as the prime cause for all those crimes.

But Ur-Nammu could witness with his own eyes the evils that had resulted from those who practiced moneylending and grand larceny under the protection of king Utuhegel. So, he put a stop to those abuses of the moneylenders and he made written laws to restrict them. With written laws, the power of both the king's decree and the power of the written contract were combined to give the common man a solid point of reference. With written laws, Ur-Nammu made *a contract with the people*. This contract was composed of laws that the king decreed and the punishments to be meted out to those who broke the law, all ensconced within the unchangeable and eternal words written on the clay tablets for all to see. Thus, the laws of the king did not become invalid after the king who made them, died. The written laws of the king now transcended time. The laws became valid across as many centuries as the clay tablets existed. In the case of the clay tablets which were baked into bricks or the laws which were written in stone, such laws lasted forever.

Among the many and varied documents of the Third Dynasty of Ur, a special group, largely from Lagash, reveal the structure and operation of an elaborate judicial system. Although the royal proclamation of social reforms and remission of debts was already known under two earlier governors of Lagash—Entemena and Urukagina—it is Ur-Nammu who is especially remembered as the promulgator of the world's first-known law code.

Court procedure is clearly shown in court records known as *ditilla*, literally "case closed," the phrase with which these tablets end. Proceedings were heard occasionally before the king himself, but more often by his governors or his judges. Cases involved such subjects as breach of contract and disputed inheritance of property. From documents dealing with marriage law, it is clear that the legal position of Sumerian women was equal to that of men. This equality should be noted because, over the centuries, as the merchant-moneylenders gained wealth and power, the position of women deteriorated. Also, penalties were financial, not corporal. Because they were not Semites, *lex talionis* (an eye-for-an-eye) was unknown, or is at least unrecorded by the Sumerians at this period.

Even in modern times, Ur-Nammu's justice, piety, and humanity shines brightly from his words written on those 4,000-year-old tablets of clay. Again note, laws are generally made to address a social problem. Studying his words gives us insight into his solutions for the problems of his times. In the Laws of Ur-Nammu:

> The mighty warrior, king of the city of Ur, of the lands of Sumer and Akkad ... he established 21,600 silas (liters) of barley, 30 sheep, 30 silas (liters) of butter per month as regular offerings in the land.

In this way, in his piety, he insured that the temples and priests were provided with food offerings while limiting to a set number of supplies what they could take from the people. After all, it was the eternal gods whom they were serving, not an ever-growing crowd of priestly families.

> I, Ur-Nammu, mighty warrior, lord of the city of Ur, king of the lands of Sumer and Akkad, by the might of the Moon God, Nanna, my lord, by the true command of the Sun God, Utu, I established justice in the land.

He promoted Namhani to be the governor of the city of Lagash. He reestablished the trade between Magan (Oman) and Ur. This re-routed the Persian Gulf trade from Lagash to the quays of Ur, just as it had always been.

At that time, the tamkarum (merchant-moneylenders) had swindled the fields away from the people. These fields, Ur-Nammu returned to the rightful owners. The practice of the moneylenders of taking away the livelihood of the people by confiscating their sheep and oxen was done away with. He righted whatever wrongs the people brought before him.

Pirates (sea captains) were also a problem in the Persian Gulf. He established

> freedom for the Akkadians and foreigners in the lands of Sumer and Akkad, for those conducting foreign maritime

trade free from the sea-captains, for the herdsmen free from
those [rustlers, thieves, and moneylenders] who appropriate
oxen, sheep, and donkeys.

He waged war against Anshan and freed the cities of Akshak, Marad,
Girkal, Kazallu, Usarum and their settlements from oppression by the
Gutians and the ravenous moneylenders. He freed the people from the
thefts and frauds of the merchants by standardizing the weights and
measures. No longer could the merchants buy a farmer's produce using
large measures and heavy weights and then re-sell the produce using small
measures and light weights.

The river boatmen were also monopolizing the traffic and raising
their prices for transporting goods and passengers. Ur-Nammu put a stop to
this and regulated the traffic, requiring inspection of goods and standard-
ization of transportation charges. Along with the river traffic, he made the
roads safe for travel.

Like most modern-day leaders and politicians, Ur-Nammu did not
actually understand the moneylenders' fraud of the Sumerian Swindle. But
he could see with his own eyes and feel with his own heart the wrongness
that was the result. So, he forbade the enslaving of people for debt. Unlike
our craven modern politicians who allow the bankers and credit-card
swindlers to defraud our wealth and to impoverish our modern nations in
their entirety, Ur-Nammu did not allow the rich and powerful to take
advantage or defraud the poor and the weak. The widow could no longer be
enslaved for the debts of her dead husband. The orphan could no longer
be enslaved for the debts of his dead parents. Ur-Nammu did not allow the
moneylenders to seize and enslave people for debt. If they did so, they
would be imprisoned and pay 15 shekels of silver to their victim. Slavery
was still an accepted social position in those ancient times, so Ur-Nammu
made just laws to protect both the slaves and the masters.

Ur-Nammu put a stop to the excesses of the moneylenders. But, like
so many leaders who followed him, he did not put a stop to lending-at-
interest simply because "it has always been here." Dishonest swindle that it
is, he overlooked its criminality because it was practiced long before he
was born. So, he accepted lending-at-interest as an ordinary business
model. In the Laws of Ur-Nammu, he stated:

I did not deliver the orphan to the rich, I did not deliver the
widow to the mighty. I did not deliver the man with but one

shekel to the man with 60 shekels. I did not deliver the man
with but one sheep to the man with one ox.

He did not place his own relatives over the citizens of the various towns, as
had been done by most previous kings and governors, but he settled them in
their own lands and did not allow them to tell him how to run the empire.
"I did not impose orders, I eliminated enmity, violence, and cries for
justice. I established justice in the land."

Unlike the modern Jewish lawyers and communists who tear down
society by promoting murder and crime while they protect criminals from
justice, Ur-Nammu used his god-given common sense in his Laws. "If a
man commits a homicide, they shall kill that man."

What is unusual about this law is that it protected the poor from being
murdered by the rich as well as the rich being murdered by the poor. In
those early days of somewhat lawless societies, if a rich moneylender
could not collect the principal and interest on a loan, he could enslave and
beat the debtor. If he killed him, there was not anything except personal
vendetta that the poor could do. Likewise, after a moneylender had seized
a farm or enslaved a beloved daughter, the poor might retaliate with a
physical attack. Walking in the marketplace or in the countryside became
dangerous pastimes for a moneylender if his vengeful victims could hide in
wait on some dark night and beat or kill him. With Ur-Nammu's Laws,
both the rich and the poor were equally punished for murder.

In disputes, where the judges could not make a determination of truth,
the Divine River Ordeal was used to determine truth from falsehood. There
was none of the *lex talionis* "eye-for-an-eye" cruelty of the Semites in the
Laws of Ur-Nammu. If a man brought physical injury to another, the law
merely prescribed a payment in silver, not the reprisal of an equal injury
committed upon him.

It is not merely as a law-giver that Ur-Nammu's memory should be
cherished. He was also an example of a true leader in the Natural Way of
Life, a king who served God by also serving his people. Ur-Nammu was a
rarity among men. So rare, in fact, that it is difficult to find anyone else
like him in either ancient or modern times.

It was also rare for a king to die in battle. Ur-Nammu—to judge from
the statement that "he was abandoned in the battlefield like a crushed vessel"
—probably died in battle with the Gutians, who, in spite of Utuhegal's
great victory, continued to trouble Sumeria throughout the period of the
Third Dynasty of Ur.

Ur-Nammu was succeeded by his son, Shulgi, who ruled 48 years and ushered in a period of relative peace and prosperity for Sumeria. It was a time when the people served god, the king protected the people, and the merchants and moneylenders were restrained in their greed. And all was well.

Enter the Amorites

The Third Dynasty of Ur was Sumerian civilization in its most fully-developed form [see Map 8]. Tablets in vast numbers have been excavated from the period of the Third Dynasty of Ur—perhaps 15,000 legal, administrative, and economic documents already translated and published, and perhaps 100,000 or more still untranslated and unpublished.

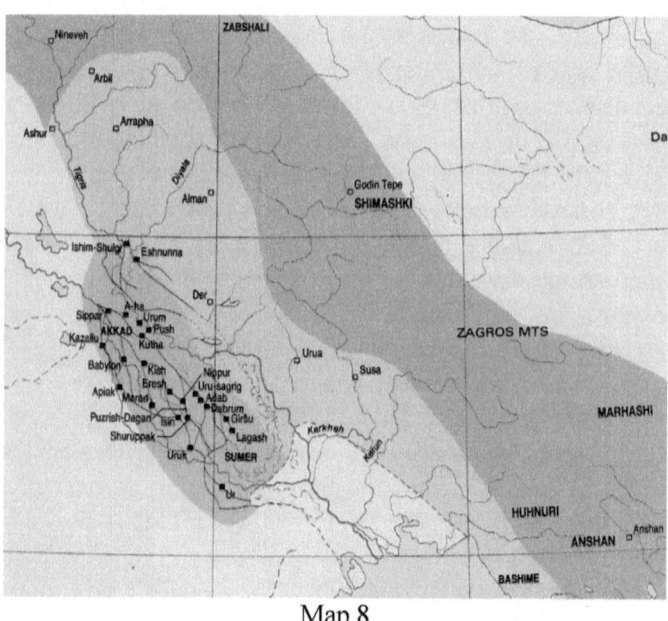

Map 8

Texts from Umma also provide an extraordinary picture of day-to-day administration. The daily numbers of men working in the fields, digging canals, harvesting, loading, and towing canal boats, were recorded. The amount of work completed was noted, and rates of work and pay minutely calculated. Female workers were tabulated cutting reeds, draining fields, harvesting, and as weavers. Ration texts detail the issue of "pay" in the form of beer, bread, oil, onions, seeds for seasoning, and fish.

Beer was a basic commodity and its quality was carefully controlled. According to one text, inspections were often carried out by a royal princess, and in another, by a constable of the king. "Ordinary," "royal," "strong," and "weak" beers were brewed.

Closely associated with the control of state herds, was a profitable industry in wool and leather. Merchants were only allowed to operate by royal warrant. They imported a great variety of goods by land and sea: exotic foods, aromatic woods, fruits and herbs, raw materials for industries such as tanning and metal-working, timber for roof beams and ship-building. Such items were paid for largely with agricultural products such as wool, barley, wheat, dates, fish oil, dried fish, and skins.

Silver had become a standard of value. At this early time, silver served as a medium of account, thus already fulfilling all the classical functions of money. Long lists of commodities valued in silver provide the earliest price index for the staples of Mesopotamian life. These price lists not only established prices but also indexed the various goods in relation to silver so that they could be used directly in barter. Again, silver was a commodity money, not a True Money. The ancient Near East was a barter economy but everything could be bought and sold through weighed amounts of silver bullion or weighed pieces cut from silver jewelry.

At Ur, the quays too were rebuilt, and a year-name early in Ur-Nammu's reign records "the return of the ships of Magan [Oman] and Meluhka [India] into the hands of Nanna [the Moon God]." Ur-Nammu's devotion to the ancient shrines, particularly at Nippur, brought him recognition there by Enlil's priesthood. Early in his reign, he adopted a new title, "King of Sumer and Akkad," which was to assume great importance in the succeeding centuries. His coronation at Nippur was commemorated in a new literary genre, the so-called royal hymn, which was addressed not to the gods but to the king himself "as a god."

The exalted position of the kings of Ur is even more evident during the reign of Shulgi, who not only continued his father's administrative, architectural, and literary interests, but went one step further in emulating the later Agade kings. Sometime early in his reign, he assumed divine status. Shrines were erected for him. Local manifestations of the royal god were worshipped and more royal hymns composed in his honor than are known for any other Mesopotamian king.

Like Sargon and Naram-Sin, Shulgi became in later times a favorite literary figure. Both of the great scribal schools at Nippur and at Ur traced their foundation to him. He was a devoted patron of Sumerian literature and culture, even claiming to have been trained in his youth as a scribe.

Such education was as rare for a Mesopotamian king as it was for most members of society. Besides the temple priests, only the merchant-moneylenders and the scribes had a high literacy rate, since written contracts and calculations for silver amounts were their business.

Direct archaeological evidence witnesses to a considerable material prosperity at this time, in that traces of building activity are discernible almost everywhere. Ur-Nammu built or rebuilt temples in many of the ancient cities, including Uruk, Lagash, Nippur and Eridu, but his most striking work was at his capital, Ur. Here he rebuilt, in honor of the Moon-God, Nanna (Sin), the ziggurat, a great rectangular-stepped tower in three stages—about 200 feet by 150 at the base and perhaps 70 feet high with a shrine on top. This gigantic stack of mud bricks, restored by later kings, still stands today as a monument to the piety of Ur-Nammu [partially rebuilt in the 1980s; for before-and-after images, see Figure 9].

Figure 9.

But the Third Dynasty of Ur collapsed after about a century, leaving Sumer and Akkad in temporary chaos. The main factor in the collapse was a fresh movement of Semitic peoples, this time the group called the Amurru.

"Amurru" in Sumerian means "west." As noted, these people from the West became known to us as Amurru or Amorites.

It was difficult to keep these people out of Mesopotamia; the land was relatively flat and lacked any natural defenses other than the mud-brick walls of the cities, the military skills of the governors, and the fighting spirit of the people. In all of these categories, it is always the fighting spirit and morale of the people that is the paramount and most vital element. When this spirit is weakened or subverted or diluted in any way, all other factors cannot fill the breech. The Third Dynasty of Ur was strong and prosperous but it could not withstand the subterranean and corrosive influence of the moneylenders and merchants. Once again, the Treasonous Class and the merchant-moneylenders worked diligently to enrich themselves at the expense of and the very existence of their own people.

The Sumerian merchant-moneylenders had prospered during the Third Dynasty of Ur. Indeed, all of the people had prospered when they served God. The greed of the merchants was kept in check by the king because they were only allowed to do business under a royal warrant or license. With oversight by the king's agents, profits were reduced because false weights and measures, excessive interest rates, illegal seizures of debt-slaves and property and other of their criminal tricks were not allowed. And yet, the Sumerian Swindle was still their secret method for eventually overcoming such obstacles.

Just "as it had always been," the moneylenders and landlords of Mesopotamia had been renting and selling the land to foreigners and hiring cheap immigrant labor to enrich themselves throughout the entire history of Sumeria. By mixing foreigners into the native population, they diluted the patriotism, the morale, and the spirit of the people, creating mixed loyalties, all while stuffing their counting houses with silver and their barns with grain.

Once again, immigrants gave the merchant-moneylenders cheaper labor to farm their foreclosed fields and orchards and to undermine and displace the native labor of the Sumerian workers. Because the Sumerian workers had to lower their own wages in order to compete with the cheaper immigrant labor, the people were reduced to a lower economic level and robbed of the income necessary to pay their debts to the moneylenders. Thus, the property which they owned, fell into foreclosure and dispossession by the moneylenders. This robbery was accomplished simply by importing cheaper immigrant labor from the West, leaving the merchant-money-lenders "completely innocent" of any crime that they could be accused of. Thus, immigrant labor enriched the moneylenders but it brought poverty and enslavement to the people.

As before, the Amorite immigrants displaced the Sumerian workers, unemployed Sumerian workers were hired by the kings and city governors as soldiers to defend the ever-increasing wealth of the awilum (the Haves). Although the Laws of Ur-Nammu ameliorated the rapacity of the money-lenders over the people, his laws did not prevent their subversion of the entire State. Subversion of the State and impoverishment of the people are the inevitable results of the Sumerian Swindle by allowing private moneylenders to acquire wealth that is greater than that of the State. When that happens, private moneylenders can overthrow the State, as was continually shown throughout history.

The Laws of Ur-Nammu had put the moneylenders on alert. Their swindles were not understood by the people, the priests, or by the kings because the Sumerian Swindle was accepted from ancient times just "as it had always been." Lending-at-interest and its related frauds and swindles, were simple, like a lever and fulcrum. As simple as a lever is, its power can move mountains. The methods of the Sumerian Swindle are also simple— so simple that it is easy to overlook the workings of its diabolical power.

The people of Sumeria respected the ancient ways that they had followed for thousands of years. Yet the unjustness of the resulting poverty and enslavement that moneylending led to, was obvious to all. As society prospered, the various family groups could avoid borrowing-at-interest from the moneylenders merely by following the ancient way of loaning to one another within the family. This could avoid interest payments while simultaneously strengthening family bonds and family wealth. It was most efficiently practiced within large families and always practiced among the moneylender and merchant families. They were all in the business of robbing all of mankind from whom they had obtained their wealth in the first place; they did not want to use the Sumerian Swindle to rob each other.

The large and conspiring moneylender families and guilds wanted to prevent interest-free lending from being practiced among their victims because it reduced their profits. Their greatest profits came from ignorant and illiterate people who could not read written contracts or understand either simple or compound interest rates.

So, the moneylenders' solution to the problem of too many Sumerian people understanding the moneylenders' swindle and lending to one another interest-free and without a professional moneylender as the middle-man, was to eliminate the more intelligent Sumerians and to replace them with ignorant victims. Thus, both war and immigration became major tools in the moneylenders' techniques at a very early time.

War was used to kill off the best, the most intelligent, and the most patriotic of the people; while immigration was used to substitute less intelligent people to take the Sumerian peoples' place on the debt-slavery treadmill. In this way, Secret Fraud #11 of the Sumerian Swindle was perfected: "Dispossessing the people brings wealth to the dispossessor, yielding the greatest profit for the bankers when the people are impoverished."

No matter what king ruled or what god resided in the temples, all of society ran smoothly with the invention of silver as a means of exchange for goods and services. Silver was not a true money. It was a type of commodity money. It was an ingenious method for helping society function smoothly, like oil lubricating a machine. Silver was a good and natural invention for commercial exchange as long as commercial exchange was its sole function, as long as silver was used in the buying and selling of goods and services. But when silver was used to generate profits through the swindle of interest and usury charged on the silver, itself, it became an unnatural apparition controlled by evil and unnatural creatures known as merchant-moneylenders. That is, this guild of vampires was composed of merchants who bought and sold people and goods, and they lent money; as well as moneylenders who lent money and bought and sold people and goods.

Those who understood money were the only ones who profited from money, while all others became the slaves of the moneylenders—all others included kings, governors, priests, and people. Everybody became slaves except the moneylenders who controlled the slave chains made of silver and gold. Although the tamkarum (merchant-moneylender) guilds had slyly and surreptitiously colluded to enslave the people, they were not the masters of the people; they were the betrayers of the people.

For those criminal merchant-moneylenders, their only concern was in obtaining more wealth so as to buy more power and then to use that power to gain more wealth. And they devised a variety of stratagems for their successful acquisitions of both. As previously explained, the "illegal aliens" of Mesopotamia—the immigrants, the Amorite shepherds and goat herders, the cheap foreign laborers from other countries whom the Treasonous Class had imported—became a prime method for the moneylenders to enrich themselves and undermine the nation. Most, but not all, of those immigrant laborers were Semitic Amorites from the Arabian deserts to the west and the Syrian plains to the northwest.

Other non-Semitic peoples were also in evidence at this time, in particular the Hurrians, who became of high importance later in the middle of the second millennium. There were already Hurrian workers at Nippur during Sargon's Dynasty (~2334 to 2150 BC). They were employed in manufacturing garments and were probably prisoners-of-war taken in the Zagros mountains. A coalition of peoples in the west also came into military conflict with Naram-Sin, inflicting upon him a severe defeat. So there were a variety of different peoples with different language groups who were eager to acquire for themselves the fertile plains and advanced culture of Mesopotamia. By far the largest group of these people were the Semitic Amorites, whose many wives produced children "countless as the sands of the sea."

References to the Amorites become more and more frequent during the Third Dynasty of Ur (~2112 to 2004 BC). One passage shows the contempt of the city-dwelling Sumerians for those savage desert-dwellers and bandits, who are described as "the Amurru, ... who eats raw meat, who has no house in his lifetime, and after he dies, lies unburied." Quickly, however, those Amorites ceased to be despised desert savages and became a despised threat to the security and the very existence of the Third Dynasty of Ur. Some of the rulers of that dynasty built fortifications against those people. Such measures did not, however, succeed in holding back the mounting pressure. The ancient cities gradually fell under the domination of the Amorites—but it was a domination through subversion rather than through warfare. These foreigners had "friends" behind the city walls, "friends" who were eager to sell them land and make them loans of silver and grain. During the empire of the Third Dynasty of Ur, there was a considerable amount of peaceful penetration into Babylonia by the Amorites, as the presence of West Semitic names in lists of temple personnel clearly shows.

The merchant-moneylenders once again used the subversive trick that had worked so well for them during the previous 25 centuries. They sold the foreclosed properties that they had acquired to foreigners. With their contacts and business associates stationed along the trade routes of the ancient Near East, the tamkarum (merchant-moneylenders) had become an international organization devoted solely to making money for themselves and their fellow guild members. If money could be made by betraying and subverting their own people, then why not, since they were already deceiving and swindling their own people?

The tamkarum became a secret menace that continued its subversive existence while its members went about their lives as respected members of society, buying and selling and making loans just as "it had always been." The merchant-moneylenders sold the vast tracts of foreclosed farms in their very own country and the bankrupted businesses within their very own cities to foreigners.

With their high birth rate as a result of many wives and hired wet nurses, the expansion of Semitic people continued for about two centuries and left a lasting mark on the culture of the area in its political, religious, and social aspects. These immigrants (referred to by modern authorities variously as East Canaanites, West Semites, or Amorites) settled in a number of ancient centers where they formed kingdoms which showed some important differences from the earlier Sumerian temple-states. They were different, too, from the last independent Sumerian political unit, the Third Dynasty of Ur.

One of the main differences was in the Semitic ideas of *land tenure*. In the original pattern of Sumerian society, the city's land belonged to the local god, while the Semitic notion was that land could be owned by the clan, the king, or the private citizen. It was this Semitic conception of private property that the land-owning and slave-owning Sumerian money-lenders desired to perpetuate for themselves because this covetous Semitic concept was a much better match with their own grasping greed. They wanted to maintain ownership and permanent possession of their swindled loot by claiming that "property rights" were superior to either "the rights of the kings" or "the rights of the gods" or "the rights of the city" or "the rights of the state" or "the rights of the people." They wanted to be landlords over all and to forever charge all of mankind rental fees for a place to live.

Thus, it was from ancient Sumeria where the modern Crime of Corporate Acquisitiveness arose. This Crime of Corporate Acquisitiveness is the false idea that modern corporations and bankers, simply by amassing huge fortunes, have greater rights than the governments of the nations in which they reside—and even greater rights over the entire populace of the nations in which they practice their financial crimes and monopolistic frauds.

They base this false assumption only on the fact that their various frauds, swindles, and thefts of public trust have resulted in a corporately- and privately-owned big pile of money, which they claim gives them greater rights as a corporation than all of mankind. It's a false assertion, and just another merchant-moneylender hoax by modern frauds wearing three-piece suits.

The rights of the moneylenders to own all property and to enslave all of mankind, were the only rights that the Sumerian tamkarum (merchant-moneylenders) were interested in promoting. Even at this early date, their scribes had proven with their arithmetic calculations, and the merchant-moneylenders had fully realized as a proven fact, the full implications of the Twenty-One Secret Frauds of the Sumerian Swindle which are encapsulated by Fraud #14: "Anyone who is allowed to lend-at-interest eventually owns the entire world."

This was the great promise of their god of the accounting tablet, that they—lowly merchants, clerks, and loan sharks—could become the ultimate masters of all of mankind and the ultimate landlords of the entire world! They could become supreme kings over all of mankind, veritable gods of the Earth, merely by adding and multiplying their sums on a clay tablet and standing in august splendor in their goat-hair garments on a wagon pulled by under-fed donkeys. It was a bean counter's epiphany!

If the moneylenders were to be the kings of the Earth, then they could not wait for that happy day in the far future. By grasping in their avaricious claws and practicing every low trick and subversive plot, they immediately began assuming in their daily lives that they were *already* owners of the world and masters of an enslaved mankind. They began to do everything necessary to bring into reality the arithmetic "promise" written in their books made of clay. It was but one conspiracy of the tamkarum (merchant-moneylender) guilds to use immigrant labor and foreign kings to promote their schemes through subversion, treason, and warfare. After all, their trade routes "embraced" all countries, so they were already greater than all kings in that regard. Even the kings bowed their heads to the moneylenders when they wanted a loan. So, how could the moneylenders show the kings and all of the people who their real masters were—without getting their heads chopped off?

The Third Dynasty of Ur finally crumbled under the pressure of Amorite immigrants who had weaseled their way into positions of authority with the backing of their sponsors, the merchant-moneylenders. Once these Semitic foreigners were in positions of authority in sufficient numbers, they betrayed the Sumerians.

At first, as the subversion of the merchant-moneylenders spread, city after city ceased to acknowledge the sovereignty of Ur. The internal integrity of the state was undermined by the tamkarum traitors spreading slanders in the taverns and by the foreign Semites whom they had promoted into positions of authority. The final overthrow of the Third Dynasty of Ur was, however, not actually the work of the Amorites, but of the Elamites from southern Persia. Using the military intelligence provided by the Sumerian merchant-moneylenders who had taken the precaution of moving their bullion and families to Babylon, the Elamites seized the opportunity offered by tamkarum betrayal to sack and occupy Ur, slaughtering the inhabitants, and carrying away the king.

This stunning blow, marking the final overthrow of the Sumerians as a political power, shows clear evidence in the relics of destruction found when Ur was excavated. This disastrous event was long remembered through the cuneiform writings of Babylonia. The fall of Ur marks the beginning of what archeologists have named the Old Babylonian Period (2000 to 1750 BC), a time of contentious Amorite city-states.

The Old Babylonian Period

This destruction of the Third Dynasty of Ur was brought about not just by the treason of the merchant-moneylenders. It was also brought about by the reliance of those people on their gods. The fear that the Sumerians had of their gods created much superstition. In fact, the fear that all people in the ancient world had for their gods was remarkable.

Omens and predictions based upon such things as the markings in the liver of a sheep could determine the choices that men and women made in their lives. Which way a certain kind of bird flew in the morning, the direction smoke traveled, dust-devils on the desert, whether a dog howled in the night, the meaning of one's dreams, and thousands of other omens were looked for and accepted as messages from the gods for a man's daily choices in life. Important decisions, such as whether or not to go to war, were made solely on the divination over a sheep's liver.

One example of this was the last king of the Third Dynasty of Ur, who thought that he had been cursed by the markings on a sheep's liver. Modern archeologists have heaped much destain upon the unfortunate Ibbi-Sin for his weakness in defending his Sumerian empire. His cuneiform letters are full of begging and fearful pleading to his subordinates as he attempted to hold the crumbling empire together. But he had inherited an empire that his own father, Shu-Sin, had cursed by believing the omens found on a sheep's liver.

Shu-Sin's inscriptions predicted the disasters that would befall his son and successor, Ibbi-Sin (2028 to 2004 BC). And Ibbi-Sin believed that those predictions would come to pass. So, regardless of his own intelligence, he was a victim of superstitious prediction that—avoid it though he tried—came to fruition through his acceptance of its inevitability. His surviving letters attest to his pitiful pleas for help from treacherous allies.

Ibbi-Sin succeeded in holding on as ruler of Sumeria for 24 years. But throughout his reign, his situation was insecure and even pathetic. Much of the time he was confined to the city of Ur itself, which often suffered from hunger and famine. As a result of the incursions of the Amorites and the attacks of the Elamites, his empire finally tottered and crumbled while the governors of the more important cities of Sumeria found it advisable to abandon their king and to fend for themselves. We learn of this piteous situation primarily from Ibbi-Sin's correspondence with his provincial governors, which provides a graphic picture of the rather confused and pathetic Ibbi-Sin and of his scheming, ambitious, and double-dealing functionaries.

One such was an Amorite governor by the name of Ishbi-Erra, who was in charge of the city of Isin. The text of three letters belonging to this royal correspondence contains a report sent to Ibbi-Sin by the scheming Semite, Ishbi-Erra, on the results of a grain-buying expedition with which Ibbi-Sin had entrusted him. The letter sheds considerable light on the incursions of the Amorites into western Sumeria as well as on the difficulties the Elamites were making for Ibbi-Sin.

Ishbi-Erra begins his report with the statement that he had succeeded in buying 72,000 gur of grain at the normal price of one shekel per gur. (1 gur = 300 liters). So, grain was very cheap even during wartime. This scheming Amorite heard that tribes of his Semitic relatives had entered Sumeria and had "seized the great fortresses one after the other." So, he shipped the grain not to Ur, the capital where it was desperately needed, but to his own city of Isin, from where he sent an artful letter to the besieged Ibbi-Sin. "If the king would now send me 600 boats of 120 gur each," his letters say, "I will deliver the grain to the various cities of Sumeria." However, he continues, "I should be put in charge of the places where the boats are to be moored." In other words, he had been taught Secret Fraud #21, "As Gatekeepers, control the choke points and master the body; strangle the choke points and kill the body." Ishbi-Erra was asking the king to give him authority over all territories where he could moor a grain boat.

The letter closes with a hypocritical plea to Ibbi-Sin not to give in to the Elamites, "because I have enough grain to satisfy the hunger of the Palace and its cities for 15 years." This was a very strong form of black-mail to make to the starving king of Ur. In any case, he pleads, the king must put him in charge of both Isin and the holy city of Nippur.

The scheming Ishbi-Erra was also in charge of the king's northern troops. Since he was able to carry the grain to Isin by boat, he had both the troops and the transportation to deliver the grain to Ibbi-Sin at Ur. He had all of the advantages and he used them to wrest control of Sumeria from Ibbi-Sin. So, he pressed his advantages and, in mock loyalty, pleaded with the king to declare him to be governor of both Isin and Nippur.

That Ibbi-Sin actually did entrust Nippur and Isin to him we learn from his letter of reply. Unfortunately for king Ibbi-Sin, Ishbi-Erra was as disloyal as he was capable and competent. With plenty of grain and troops, he was successful not only in defending Isin and Nippur but in usurping his master's throne as well. This we learn, not from Ishbi-Erra's correspondence with Ibbi-Sin but from a letter written to the king by Puzur-Numushda, a governor of the city Kazallu, along with king Ibbi-Sin's reply.

According to Puzur-Numushda's letter, the treasonous Ishbi-Erra had become firmly established as the ruler of Isin, which he had turned into his royal residence. He had, moreover, subdued Nippur and extended his sway all along the Tigris and Euphrates from Hamazi in the north and east to the Persian Gulf. He had taken prisoner those of king Ibbi-Sin's governors who had remained loyal, and returned to office those who had been dismissed by king Ibbi-Sin because of their disloyalty. Ibbi-Sin's pathetic impotence and pitiable vacillation are revealed in his answer to Puzur-Numushda.

Ibbi-Sin realized full well that the latter was on the point of betraying him because Puzur-Numushda had actually failed to march to the help of Ibbi-Sin's loyal governors, although a select body of troops had been put at his disposal for that purpose. But he could do nothing more than plead with him to stay loyal. Ibbi-Sin believed desperately that somehow the Semite, Ishbi-Erra, "who is not of Sumerian seed," would fail in his ambition to become master of Sumeria and that the Elamites would be defeated. Ibbi-Sin wrote that "Enlil has stirred up the Amorites out of their land, and they will strike down the Elamites and capture Ishbi-Erra." But king Ibbi-Sin was referring to the very Semitic Amorites who had been plaguing Sumeria from the days of his father, the same Semitic Amorites that the tamkarum (merchant-moneylenders) had been immigrating in large numbers as farm workers; the same Semitic Amorites to whom the moneylenders had sold the foreclosed farms; the same Semitic Amorites of whom the treasonous Semite Ishbi-Erra was one.

With the growth of Ishbi-Erra's independence and power, Sumeria found itself under the rule of two kings: Ibbi-Sin, whose dominion was limited to his capital at Ur, and Ishbi-Erra, who controlled most of the other cities of Sumeria from his capital at Isin.

In the 25th year of Ibbi-Sin's reign, the Elamites besieged Ur, but they could not capture it. As a result of the siege, severe famine overtook Ur's defenders. In desperation, they unlocked the city gate. The Elamites brutally slaughtered everybody and ransacked homes and temples. The poetic "Lamentation over the Destruction of Ur" recorded this tragedy:

> Dead men, not potsherds, covered the approaches;
> The walls were gaping, the high gates, the roads, were piled
> with dead. In the side streets, where feasting crowds would
> gather,
> Scattered they lay.
> In all the streets and roadways, bodies lay.
> In open fields that used to fill with dancers, they lay in heaps.
> The country's blood now filled its holes, like metal in a mold;
> Bodies dissolved—like fat left in the sun.

The Elamites carried off king Ibbi-Sin a prisoner, leaving a garrison in control of the city. Several years later, Ishbi-Erra attacked this garrison and drove it out of Ur, thus becoming king of all Sumeria, with Isin as his capital.

The treasonous Ishbi-Erra founded a dynasty at Isin which endured for over two centuries, although its later rulers were not his direct descendants. This is known as the Isin-Larsa Period (2006 to 1884 BC).

Theoretically, the city-state of Isin laid claim to the suzerainty of all Sumeria and Akkad. Actually, however, the land was divided into a number of city-states under separate rulers because there was no longer a centralized empire. For nearly a century, Isin remained the most powerful of these states. It controlled Ur, the old imperial capital and the shipping terminal for the Persian Gulf trade, as well as Nippur, which continued as Sumeria's spiritual and intellectual center throughout this period. (See Map 9, the shifting boundaries of the Isin-Larsa city-states.)

The fourth ruler of the Isin dynasty, Ishme-Dagan, boasts in his archives of restoring Nippur to its former glory. So, even while the Sumerians were then being ruled by the Semitic Amorites, the traditional Sumerian religious values were being maintained. Prior to his reign, Isin seems to have suffered a severe attack at the hands of an enemy; perhaps the Assyrians who were gaining power in the north. His son and successor, Lipit-Ishtar (1934 to 1924 BC), claimed control over the major cities of Sumeria and took the proud title "King of Sumer and Akkad."

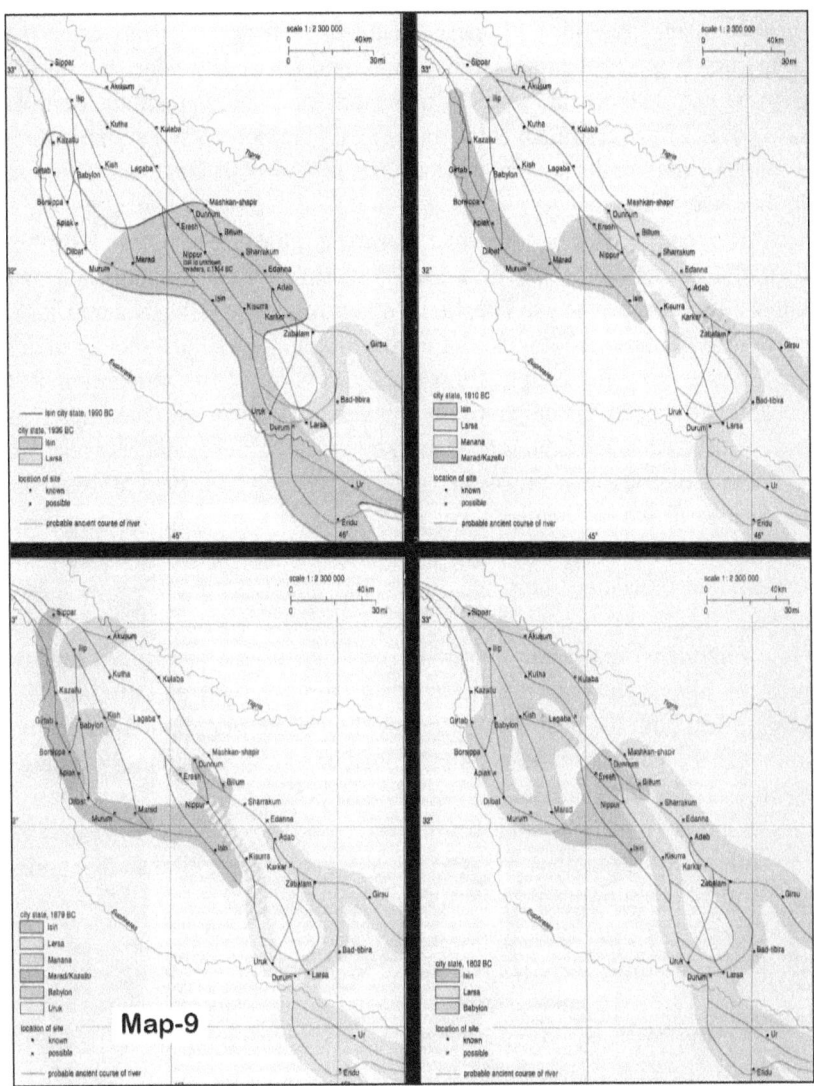

Map-9

The Good Shepherd

But Lipit-Ishtar was not the sort of king who was popular with the tamkarum (merchant-moneylenders) because he had the ancient idea that the leaders of society should serve and protect the people rather than the merchants and moneylenders. Early in his reign, Lipit-Ishtar promulgated a new Sumerian law code, which was later the model for the renowned Law Code of Hammurabi (circa 1750 BC). The Laws of Lipit-Ishtar were written in the traditional Sumerian language about 160 years after the Sumerian king Ur-Nammu's Law Code, and about 140 years before the Semitic king Hammurabi's Law Code. Both the Sumerian and the Semitic law codes show a similar concern for maintaining peace by eliminating arguments among the people, but they are, as you shall see, much different in their social intent.

The Third Dynasty of Ur had marked a return of Sumerian kingship over the Sumerian people in a Sumerian Renaissance of language and culture and moral values. The Laws of Urukagina and Ur-Nammu, also written in Sumerian, both show a desire to maintain a holy society under God and to free the people from the oppression of the tamkarum. But because the moneylenders and wily merchants had "always been here," it never occurred to the Sumerians that the merchant-moneylenders were not legitimate businessmen but were, in fact, criminals. So, laws were never made specifically to penalize them for their crimes. Instead, the laws were made merely to soften the results of their crimes while they were allowed to continue practicing their businesses and grand larceny "just as it has always been."

Although Lipit-Ishtar wrote his laws in Sumerian and even though most of his subjects were Sumerians, he, himself, was an Amorite. His laws reflect both the necessity of freeing the people from oppression while allowing the tamkarum the continued practice of the Sumerian Swindle to betray and defraud everybody in society except themselves.

Semitic king Lipit-Ishtar begins his Laws by extolling the greatest of the Sumerian gods such as An, the Sky god and father of all the other gods, and Enlil, the god of the air. Lipit-Ishtar wrote:

> At that time, the gods An and Enlil called Lipit-Ishtar to be prince of the land—Litpit-Ishtar, the wise Shepherd, whose name has been pronounced by the god Nunamnir—in order to establish justice in the land, to eliminate cries for justice, to eradicate enmity and armed violence, to bring well-being to the lands of Sumer and Akkad.
>
> At that time, I, Lipit-Ishtar, the pious Shepherd of the city of Nippur, the faithful husbandman of the city of Ur, he who does not forsake the city of Eridu, the befitting lord of the city of Uruk, the king of the city of Isin, king of the lands of Sumer and Akkad, the heart's desire of the goddess Inanna, by the command of the god Enlil, I established justice in the lands of Sumer and Akkad.

He goes on to say that "at that time I liberated the sons and daughters" of the cities of Ur, Isin, Sumer, and Akkad who had been enslaved by the yoke of the moneylenders. But the debauchery that the moneylenders had brought to the land through their use of alcohol and gambling and whoring and warfare, had also produced orphans and illegitimate children who had been abandoned by their parents. Because of the loose morals brought on by war and usury, the family bonds between fathers and sons and daughters and mothers were broken, so that the children were not taking care of their parents in old age. Lipit-Ishtar, the good king, decreed that they mend their ways. The Good Shepherd took care of his people.

He obligated public works for the repair and weeding of the canals. Military service was an obligation of each household depending upon whether the household was composed of the wealthy or of the poor laborers. The wealthier households were required to do public works for 70 days per year, while the laborers were required ten days per month. Once again, the rich were required to work less. After all, the awilum (the Haves) were the leaders of Society and part of their work was found in that leadership. And yet, even they were required to do 70 days of manual labor per year.

Striking a woman so that she lost her baby cost the aggressor 30 shekels of silver. The same crime to a slave woman cost 5 shekels of silver. If the woman died, it was a capital offense. Thus, drunken husbands and moneylenders were dissuaded from violently causing abortion in their wives and sex slaves.

As a characteristic of Semitic rule, ownership of property was given a much higher status than the laborer who farmed the property. Lipit-Ishtar's Law stated: "If he leases an orchard to a gardener in an orchard lease, the gardener shall plant for the owner of the orchard and the gardener shall have the use of the dates from one-tenth of the palm trees."

Thus, the landlord got his orchard farmed for a cost to him of only ten percent of the produce. And following the more humane Sumerian custom, thieves were not tortured or imprisoned but were required to pay a fine: "If a man enters the orchard of another man and is seized there for thievery, he shall weigh and deliver ten shekels of silver."

Again, following the humane Sumerian customs, property damage was also fined: "If a man cuts down a tree in another man's orchard, he shall weigh and deliver twenty shekels of silver."

And yet, the moneylenders were allowed a double profit, but no more than a double profit, from their debt-slaves. (Remember, those slaves were Mediterranean, Caucasian, Semites, and Indo-European people but none of them were Negroes.) "If a man's slave contests his slave status against his master, and it is proven that his master has been compensated for his slavery two-fold, that slave shall be freed."

Thus, the moneylender doubled his money on what a debt-slave owed him in addition to whatever he had already collected on the original debt. But debt-slaves who did not challenge their status could be enslaved for life. And debt-slaves were not entirely restricted. They had freedom of movement in their free-time: "If a debt-slave goes into service to a man of his own free will, that man will not restrict him but that debt-slave may go wherever he wishes."

Slaves were also sex slaves of the masters. But for a master to make his slave pregnant meant that she was released from slavery. This prevented a ruthless slave master from increasing the number of his slaves merely by making them pregnant or to use them without cost to himself. Illegitimate slave children would also cause social disharmony as the children fought over inheritance. For the slave women to be forced to bear children without also being cared for, was prohibited in this way: "If a man marries a wife and she bears him a child and the child lives and a slave woman also bears a child for her master, the father shall free the slave woman and her child; the children of the slave woman will not divide the estate with the children of the master."

And in this way: "If his first-ranking wife dies and after his wife's death he marries the slave woman (who had borne him children), the child of his first-ranking wife shall be his (primary) heir; the child whom the slave woman bore to her master is considered equal to a native free-born son and they shall make good his (share of the) estate."

And in this way: "If a man's wife does not bear him a child but a prostitute from the street does bear him a child, he shall provide grain, oil, and clothing rations for the prostitute, and the child whom the prostitute bore him shall be his heir. As long as his wife is alive, the prostitute shall not reside in the house with his first-ranking wife."

And in this way: "If a man's first-ranking wife loses her attractiveness or becomes a paralytic, she will not be evicted from the house; however, her husband may marry a healthy wife, and the second wife shall support the first-ranking wife."

To protect the thieving merchant-moneylenders, false testimony and slander were also dealt with: "If a man, without grounds, accuses another man of a matter of which he has no knowledge, and that man does not prove it, he shall bear the penalty of the matter for which he made the accusation."

Moneylenders were in the habit of paying the delinquent taxes on property and then claiming ownership of the property merely for the price of its tax. But this was prohibited in a fair way like this: "If the master or mistress of an estate defaults on the taxes due from the estate and an outsider assumes the taxes, he (the master) will not be evicted for three years; (but after three years defaulting on the taxes) the man who has assumed the tax burden shall take possession of the estate and the (original) master of the estate will not make any claims."

And so, Lipit-Ishtar was a Good Shepherd for his people. Although he, himself, was a Semitic Amorite, most of his people were Sumerians and he ruled them with Sumerian ethics. He protected women with humane Sumerian ethics and protected the people with the justice of a "straight and true path."

He claimed: "In accordance with the true word of the god Utu, I made the lands of Sumer and Akkad hold fair judicial procedure. In accordance with the utterance of the god Enlil, I, Lipit-Ishtar, son of Enlil, eradicated enmity and violence. I made weeping, lamentation, shouts for justice and suits taboo. I made right and truth shine forth, and I brought well-being to the lands of Sumer and Akkad." In this way, Lipit-Ishtar shows the moral uprightness and spiritual goodness of the Sumerian people as well as how the earliest Amorites followed in their footsteps.

But the tamkarum (merchant-moneylenders) had already had experience with kings of high morals and feelings of civic duty. In their experience, kings who served the country and protected the people were bad for business. Kings who were honest, virtuous, or religious were not as easy to manipulate as kings who were corrupt and perverse. Secret Fraud #6 of the Sumerian Swindle was their guide in such matters: "High morals impede profits, so debauching the virtuous destroys their moral superiority and pulls them below the depravity of the moneylender who there-by masters them and bends them to his will." When neither bribes nor blackmail could sway a king, then the well-tested basic characteristic of the merchant-moneylenders—treason and subversion—worked just as well.

In the third year of Lipit-Ishtar's reign, an ambitious Semitic ruler named Gungunum (1932 to 1906 BC) came to the throne of Larsa, a city to the southeast of Isin [see Map 10]. With the financial backing of the tamkarum (merchant-moneylenders), he began to build up the political strength of the city with a series of military successes in the region of Elam and Anshan. It was from the east (Elam) that the greatest threat to their businesses would come. So, the tamkarum needed a king who would defend their profits with pre-emptive strikes.

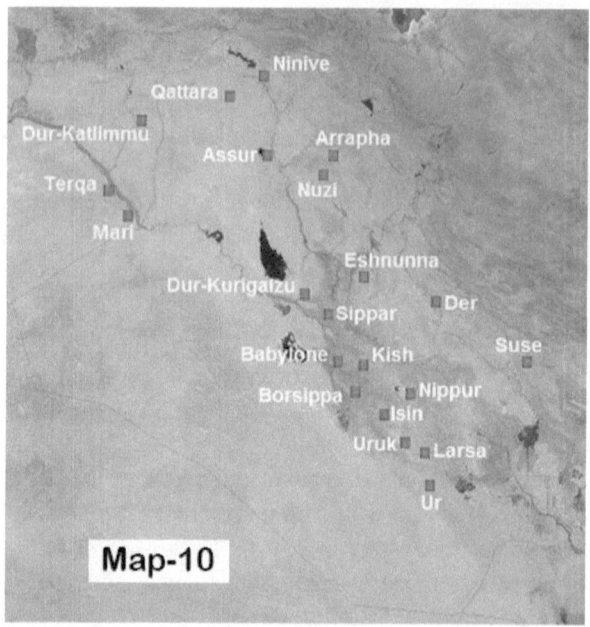

A few years later, in a "friendly" occupation, this same Gungunum gained control of Ur, the old imperial capital and sea-trade terminal. This added to Larsa's prestige and commercial power. Ur was thus threatened by a new invasion of even more Amorites. Gungunum demonstrated that he and not Lipit-Ishtar was the protector of the merchant-moneylender's home port and their temple of the Moon God at Ur.

From then on, King Lipit-Ishtar and his moral laws ceased to be a significant political force. Moral laws which protected the people from the swindles of the merchant-moneylenders and brought justice to mankind, were always opposed by the merchant-moneylenders. They made their highest profits when mankind was enslaved and corrupted because they did the enslaving and corrupting. They were an evil influence upon these earliest civilizations of mankind, but they were not Jews—yet.

Isin held on to some of its former claims for another century or more but Larsa was now on the ascent. The reign of Gungunum at Larsa marked the beginning of the first Semitic Amorite dynasty in the south. After Gungunum had occupied the old capital city of Ur, a group of Amorite-controlled city-states competed for dominance throughout Mesopotamia. All of them were Semites but none of them were Jews—yet.

Following the moneylenders' and merchants' strategy of offering their most sincere "loyalty" as advisors to the kings, the Amorites consolidated their power first in the commercial centers such as Larsa, Eshnunna, and Babylon. But at first, they avoided the prestigious Sumerian cities like Kish, Ur, and Uruk, where the richest tamkarum (merchant-moneylender) guilds had long been firmly established.

As the urbanized Amorites rose to prominent positions in Mesopotamia, including kingship in independent states, the Sumerian language was no longer spoken. Akkadian became the language of daily life. Thus, through the treason of the merchant-moneylenders, the Sumerian language and the Sumerian people were replaced by foreigners. Like fleas on a dog, the merchant-moneylenders had jumped onto their new Semitic host, offering loans of silver and their most "sincere" advice on how to make money "just as it had always been."

With the Amorite Gungunum (1932 to 1906 BC), the fortunes of Larsa improved. Notable among his achievements was the annexation of Ur by taking it away from Isin. This gave Larsa control of the valuable Persian Gulf trade which had apparently languished since the fall of Ur. Under the protection of Gungunum, the merchant-moneylender guilds of Ur had no fear of losing property or silver to the moral leadership of a good king such as Lipit-Ishtar of Isin. Once Lipit-Ishtar had lost the financial backing of the merchant-moneylender guilds and the prestige of controlling many cities and their tax revenues, he became powerless and replaceable.

That there was no open conflict between the two cities, however, can be seen in the traditions of the office of high priestess of the Moon God at Ur. Both the daughters of Ishme-Dagan and of Lipit-Ishtar of Isin had been made high priestesses of the Moon God. Both of them continued in office under Gungunum, even after a usurper to the throne of Isin made dedications at Ur while that city was under the hegemony of Larsa. So, obviously worship of the gods transcended the politics of the Sumerian city-states even when they were ruled by Amorites.

Gungunum claimed the titles both of "King of Sumer and Akkad" and "King of Ur." He and his successors did much to improve the political and economic standing of Larsa, along with the economic standing of the merchant-moneylenders.

Transition to a New Era

The two key dates for Sumerian chronology are the end of the Third Dynasty of Ur, when the Sumerians lost their predominant political position in Mesopotamia (2000 BC), and the beginning of the reign of

Hammurabi of Babylon (1792 BC), when the Sumerians ceased to exist as a political, ethnic, and linguistic entity.

This period of squabbling city-states and shifting alliances, where the last of the Sumerian civilization began to disappear and the Semitic Babylonian state began to rule the region, is known as the Old Babylonian Period (2000 to 1750 BC) because it is the beginnings of the rise of Babylon into world history.

Strategically, as will be seen again and again throughout history, the driving force of political power is, namely, *physical occupation*. Political power comes from physical occupation: not historical rights, not title deeds, not moral rights—only occupation. Physical bodies of people need to be standing on the land, itself, in large numbers to push out the previous inhabitants regardless of all other "rights of ownership." The perfidious moneylenders knew this from long experience of throwing people out of their homes and moving in new renters and selling to new owners. They merely extended such small-scale tactics into nationwide strategies of ethnic genocide.

This was how the merchant-moneylenders of the early Ubaid culture had betrayed their own people by selling the land for occupation by the Sumerians—and then hopping onto those new people like blood-sucking fleas. This was how the Sumerian merchant-moneylenders had betrayed their own people by selling the foreclosed properties to the Semitic nomads for occupation by the Akkadians—and then hopping onto those new people like blood-sucking fleas.

In modern times, this is how the Jewish merchant-moneylenders betrayed the white Europeans and Americans, by selling the foreclosed properties to foreign Mexicans, Asian Indians, and Chinese, while protecting their newly-arrived victims with Sumerian Swindle #20: "Champion the Minority in order to dispossess the Majority of their wealth and power, then swindle the Minority out of that wealth and power."

Without warfare but by using treasonous subterfuge and diabolical cunning, a country can be overrun and taken away from the native population through the simple process of occupation by immigration. By replacing the population with foreigners, the parasitic tamkarum raised up a new nation of victims, a fresh nation of workers with young blood to suck, an inexperienced people who had not learned to hate the merchant-moneylenders—yet.

The Sumerians trusted their gods and their leaders to protect them because this was the ancient and the moral way of high civilization, living lives devoted to the "true and straight path." But the kings and priests could not protect the people because secretly, and behind everyone's backs, while making deals with everyone's enemies, debauching families, and stealing the wealth of the nation, were the merchant-moneylenders conspiring in their secret guild halls for swindling profits from the people among whom they were allowed to live.

Using cheap immigrant labor to undermine and under-employ the people and then defrauding them of their possessions while stirring up foreign armies against them, the moneylenders and merchants reaped huge profits while the civilized Sumerians were destroyed.

However, this time, instead of rising again and continuing their ancient culture, the Sumerian people were dispossessed of their lands entirely. Their way of life was taken over by the Semitic Amorites. The Sumerians were dispossessed and impoverished, becoming muskenum (Have-Nots) in the lands which they had once ruled. As Sumeria and the Sumerian people fell, the parasitic tamkarum jumped like blood-sucking fleas onto a fresh and unsuspecting host.

CHAPTER 8

BABYLON AND HAMMURABI:
2000 TO 1750 BC

As we begin to study Babylonia, we find ourselves somewhere at the mid-point in the history of ancient Mesopotamia—not just a changing history in regard to kings and dates and places but a changing history in regard to the moral, spiritual, and intellectual life of mankind. And the change was quite diabolical because those changes in the history of mankind were not directed by human beings, rather they were directed by the parasites who prey upon human beings.

Under non-Semitic Sumerian genius, the region had grown to the highest level of civilization yet known in the world. For over a thousand years, the Sumerians created a society that worked so effectively that very little change took place in all that time. Except for Egypt, all the people in the surrounding countries emulated and copied what the Sumerians had developed.

This mid-point in the history of Mesopotamia begins to include the earliest timeframe for certain groups of wandering goat-rustlers and bandits who would later play a crucial and corrosive part in world history. So, it is from this timeframe that we begin to unravel from world history the earliest known tendrils of this diseased Semitic aberration of the parasitic, organized criminal conspiracy which is known today as *Judaism*. This Jewish fungus later developed a malignant Semitic tumor which branched off to form what is known as Islam. But let's first continue our story from the previous chapter.

Counting the Ubaidian prehistory, Mesopotamian society had functioned smoothly for well over 3,000 years of planting and harvesting, canal digging, city and temple building, raising their families, and praying to their gods. Change was not necessary since Sumerian civilization provided everything that the Sumerian people could ever want. Their reed huts and mud houses provided adequate shelter. And since the reeds and mud were free for the taking, all that was required to own a house was their own labor to build it. Their herds provided meat, milk, and wool. Fish were in the rivers and ponds; grain was in the fields; fruit was in the orchards. There was plenty of food.

A workman's pay was about 10 liters (2.5 gallons) of barley per day. This was enough to feed him and a large family, with enough left over to barter for vegetables, fish, garments, and beer. And with barley selling for about 300 liters per shekel of silver, a workman could sell his surplus barley for silver and, within a few years, save enough to buy some farm land. With his own farm, he was automatically counted among the awilum (the Haves) and his higher social status became an additional benefit of working hard and saving much. This is how Natural Living allowed the Sumerians to thrive and to prosper. Through their protective kings, their wise priests, and service to their gods, they had created a society filled with plenty of everything for everyone.

But independent farmers did not benefit the ruthless and greedy moneylenders who parasitically lived on the wealth which they had sucked away from the unfortunate and from the distressed. Independent farmers, who were wealthy enough to never need a loan, did not give the money-lenders the profits they desired. It was only from those farmers who fell into difficulties and whose only hope of escaping starvation was to borrow from the moneylenders, could a profit be made.

And so, as the centuries progressed, the moneylenders learned that their profits increased in direct proportion to an increase in the suffering of mankind. Secret Fraud #11 became their strategy for moneylender success: *"Dispossessing the people brings wealth to the dispossessor, yielding the greatest profit for the bankers when the people are impoverished."*

The moneylenders, fat in their bellies and broad in their butts, wearing the best in finely-woven garments, drinking the best in wines and beers and enjoying perverted debauchery among their sex slaves, sought only to bring the highest profits to themselves. Since there were both Sumerian as well as Semitic Amorite moneylenders, it only required advantageous marriages between the two ethnic groups to cement their families into a single conspiring organism which spanned the borders of the city-states and connected their guild halls stretching from the Mediterranean through Mesopotamia, and onward to Oman and India. The common rallying cry among all of them, was not so much a rallying cry as it was a rallying whisper and they all whispered among themselves very quietly, "How can we get what mankind has?"

Doing no work, themselves; producing no products with their own soft hands, themselves; but using the fake arithmetic calculations on tablets of wet clay which swindled away the wealth and the labor from all of mankind, those cruel swindlers, smugglers, slave mongers, war mongers, liars, and deceivers, produced nothing but suffering, hardship, poverty, and death for mankind. All the while, they did not consider themselves to be the criminal parasites that they are, but rather to be "gentlemen" and "businessmen" who sucked off the silver, gold, and property of mankind using lies, deceit, and the Sumerian Swindle.

Besides the daily question of "How can we get what mankind has?" which was taught to them by their parents since babyhood, they had a specific question: "How can the people be brought to the most suffering in a way where they are eager to borrow from us moneylenders?" This might seem like an odd question, but as the moneylenders had learned to their great loss and woe, the people hated them. And that hatred always got in the way of their profits and it put them into personal danger. But when that hatred for being cheated and swindled was overcome by a fearful desperation, when the impoverished borrower is frantic from starvation or fearful of losing his farm from foreclosure or losing his children as debt-slaves; then such a borrower smiles, bows his head with subservient respect, and treats the moneylenders with reverence and feigned happiness while paying his debts.

Thus, the scheming merchant-moneylenders found that although the people would never love them, at least the moneylenders could get the gratitude and respect which they craved, if the people feared them. Even when the people hated them with burning fury, the moneylenders learned that they could demand gratitude and respect, just so long as the people needed them. With this in mind, the moneylenders conspired to always create conditions of need. Secret Fraud #11 of the Sumerian Swindle gave the moneylenders profits from the extreme neediness of the people as they took advantage of the poor by causing them to lose whatever property that they had. What the poor lost, the rich gained. The Sumerian Swindle allowed no other inevitability.

In this way, the guilds of merchant-moneylenders conspired to create hunger, poverty, and suffering among the people of the world so that the people, in extreme desperation, would then turn in gratitude to them to relieve that suffering through loans-at-interest guaranteed by personal property and real estate. And in times of want, who else could give loans other than the moneylenders, who had amassed the wealth of mankind in their temple strong-rooms? Thus, through purposeful and ruthless impoverishment on the one hand and hypocritical offers of loans-at-interest on the other hand, the merchant-moneylenders gained the fruits of Secret Fraud #14 of the Sumerian Swindle: "Anyone who is allowed to lend-at-interest eventually owns the entire world."

However—and this was absolutely and vitally important—whatever sufferings that the people were caused, could not also be seen as coming *from the moneylenders*, whose services the people must be coaxed into accepting. The purposely-engineered food shortages, dispossessions, and wars resulting from the Sumerian Swindle had to be accomplished in secret and without any apparent cause pointing to the conspiring money-lenders and merchants. Otherwise, they would not get away with their crimes and would also be killed for their evils.

Society can operate quite smoothly without interest-bearing loans. But for the moneylenders, 'no loans' equal 'no profits.' So, keeping the people poor, ignorant, and in distress created wealth for the moneylenders in those ancient times, just as it does for the bankers in modern times. But such social manipulation can only be successful with the most secret of plans and the tightest security because if the people ever learned of the real source of their miserable poverty and the betrayal of their countries, they would rise up and kill all of the bankers and financiers; or, at the very least, beat them and take back the stolen properties.

Even though the various cities and lands of ancient Mesopotamia were ruled by kings of city-states and tribal chiefs of villages scattered between the Mediterranean Sea and across the Persian Gulf to India, all those kings and people did business with *silver* as the basic unit of measure. Barter was the basic method of commerce among both rich and poor, and silver was the basic measure of value. All goods and services were valued in relation to a weighed amount of silver. Silver, in barleycorn weights or grains (~0.05 grams) or shekel weights (~8 grams) or mina weights (~500 grams) or talent weights (~30 kilograms), could be traded across the ancient Near East for any product or any service. If two merchants did not have silver, they could still barter their goods by first valuing each trade good at its worth in silver and then making a trade of their goods in ratio to those silver valuations. From the Persian Gulf to the Mediterranean Sea, from Arabia to the Mountains of Cappadocia, the shekel-weight of silver was the standard in monetary transactions that spanned all languages and cultures for over 3,000 years, right up to the days of Jesus.

The moneylenders and their meticulous scribes could calculate the relative wealth and strength of all the countries around them, down to the tiniest barleycorn-weight in silver. They could calculate on their moist-clay accounting tablets the value and the manpower of every city. With this secret money-power, the moneylenders were in the position of knowing which kings were strong and which kings were weak, who could afford the best armaments, and who needed loans to get them.

In this Bronze Age, the armaments industry was not complicated. Yet, it was as controlled and as carefully guarded as the weapons industry is today. A bronze dagger can kill an enemy just as dead as can an atomic bomb. So, the manufacture of bronze weapons was a state monopoly, controlled by the kings and the merchant-moneylender guilds.

Although melting the copper and zinc alloy to make bronze and then pouring it into molds to make swords and arrowheads might seem like a simple affair, it did require the skill and knowledge of the metal workers guilds who knew the secrets of smelting and alloy, which they did not share with anyone not of their trade guild. Thus, weapons manufacture was a state-controlled monopoly, just as it is today. The king wanted military control through weapons manufacture. But the tamkarum wanted the profits from arms sales, from copper and tin import sales, and from war, itself. Although anyone who could afford one, could buy a sword, the really big profit was in arming entire armies.

End of a Dynasty

As the Third Dynasty of Ur fell, circa 2000 BC, and with it the Sumerian peoples' reliance upon the gods, the tribes of Semitic Amorites whom the moneylenders had invited into the country as cheap immigrant labor and to whom they had sold Sumerian lands, all rose up and dispossessed the Sumerians of their lands and usurped political control of their cities. Such ethnic changes in society which occurred are still being engineered in our modern world today by similar merchant-moneylender guilds, more than 4,000 years later.

Unlike the Sumerians who preferred the "straight and true path," the Semitic peoples cherished the use of craftiness and deceit as a basis of tribal success. The Semitic cultures valued the telling of lies if such gave an advantage over other men. The better man in Semitic cultures, was he who could deceive his fellows most thoroughly and thereby gain an advantage. Thus, materialistic, acquisitive greed began to increase in power as spiritual knowledge decreased. The Sumerian ideas of social harmony through a godly life, began to give way to the Semitic ideas of social control through property ownership. Under the Amorites, the awilum (the Haves) increased their wealth and gained State-enforced protection while the muskenum (the Have-Nots) became ever more impoverished and enslaved.

As the Semitic tribes took over Sumerian society, the true knowledge of the gods and of spiritual well-being began to disappear. First, because the Semitic races have always sought material goods through banditry and murder, these were the major desires of those wandering goat-rustlers and thieves. Lies and deceit have always been highly developed among the Semites and much celebrated, either when trading goats and sheep or in talking a stupid fool out of his property. Such people could never find religious Truth because dishonesty and lies were the foundation of their bandit societies. Lies put shanks of mutton, pitchers of beer, and silver shekels on the table. The Amorite Semites even had a word for their cultural deceits: *Abracadabra*, which means "I create as I speak" (see *The Monsters of Babylon*).

For the Semites, the gods were worshipped as a means of pleading for rain or good pastures or piles of loot during a planned raid on their neighbors. When they purchased the lands of Sumeria from the money-lenders, there was nothing of a good or godly nature that such liars and deceivers could add to the already robust Sumerian religious lore. So, they mimicked what religions were already established. The Mesopotamian gods watched over specific cities and local regions so, like everybody else, the immigrant Semitic tribes began worshipping whichever local gods resided in whatever city.

Secondly, as the Sumerian people were gradually being dispossessed and betrayed by the merchant-moneylenders, the Sumerian people no longer served the gods as their primary goal in life. They were forced to serve the moneylenders and kings in a desperate bid to sustain their in-creasingly poor and hungry families.

Every day, working from dawn to dusk in the very fields which they had once themselves owned, they earned just enough grain to feed their starving families. The dispossessed Sumerians had little time to devote to the contemplation and adoration of the gods in the temples. They were being pushed out of their own country by the large numbers of foreigners immigrated into the country by the merchant-moneylenders. The Sumerian people had been thoroughly betrayed by the Semitic moneylenders. Such events would be repeated many times throughout history into the 21st century AD in Europe and the USA, all perpetrated by the same criminals.

With over a thousand years of a relatively peaceful existence, the Sumerians had first-hand experience with such things as the realization of God-consciousness in their temple meditation cells. Their religious art works testify to this. While their spiritual attainments were level with or superior to anything attained by the modern people of the 20th and 21st centuries AD, very few of the Mesopotamians or the Egyptians ever reached the high levels of spiritual power and knowledge that had been attained by the Celtic Europeans over two thousand years previously, in the centuries before 3500 BC.

This is obvious from the dearth of art works depicting their experience of the living holy spirit as a surrounding and protective aura. This holy spirit radiates as halos and beams of light emanating from their high priests, priestesses, kings, and mighty warriors. This knowledge, because of its rarity among them, was not taught by the priests to the Semitic Amorite interlopers. Wealth and political power were all that the materialistic Semites were interested in having, not spiritual knowledge. It was what the gods could do for them and give to them, that was most important, not what Man could do for the gods, such as being honest and true.

The Amorites learned the material and obvious elements of Sumerian society such as reading and writing, administration, farming, and general culture. And they learned the outer manifestations of religion, such as servicing the idols and celebrating the festivals. But the secret religious and spiritual knowledge that was only passed along by the priests to trusted disciples, they did not learn. So, it began to disappear. Their knowledge of the swastika power, for example, was almost unknown to them, even though they practiced the swastika sitting meditation in their temples and palaces [see Figure 9]. Knowledge of the spiritual power represented by the swastika and by the Maltese Cross completely disappeared as the Semites took over Sumeria and the empires of Babylonia and Assyria began to arise. Those Semitic empires, backed by the moneylenders, were based on commerce and warfare; they were not based upon serving the gods and finding bliss, as had been practiced by the Sumerians.

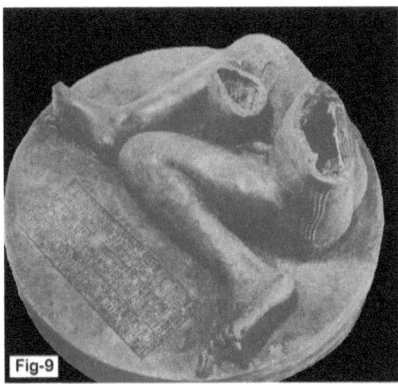

A loss in the knowledge of the "horned helmet" can also be seen in the religious art work of the Babylonians and the later Assyrians. Most arche-ologists assume that this "helmet," as seen being worn by the various Sumerian gods in their carvings and cylinder seals, was merely a "symbol" of a god since it is worn in all drawings and carvings of the Sumerian deities, as if the god had the strength of many bulls.

Although this assumption of its symbolic quality is basically true on an elementary level, the so-called horned helmet was actually a represent-tation of the internal spiritual levels of those wearing it. The helmet was not a "helmet" worn on the head. That is, it was not a piece of head gear. It was a symbolic representation of the power of the holy spirit as it rises through the muscles and fascia in the crown of the head and circulates upward from a straight neck to a point above the crown. It was the Sumerian way of indicating the holy spirit above the heads of every holy man (or holy woman). This was later represented in Christian art as a halo.

The horned helmet, the swastika, the "Maltese" cross, the sun disk, as well as the caduceus serpent-and-staff representing the spiritual knowledge of the physician, all disappeared. (See *Monsters of Babylon* for an explanation of these symbols.) Although these symbols represented the spiritual knowledge of the Sumerians, the actual knowledge was not passed along to the Semitic culture which followed them.

Of what use were the secrets of Sumerian religion to the money-lenders? As long as they donated to the temples and made a show of serving the gods, they were free to swindle the people and to reap the profits. The moneylenders had learned how to solidify their grip on society while hiding behind the kings and ministers. They had learned how to create war in order to profit from other people's losses. And they had learned how to use foreign troops as their enforcers. Foreign mercenaries do not have the brotherly empathy for the people whom they police and against whom they are willing to commit any atrocity. And they are willing to follow any order given by those who pay their salaries.

*****

Two symbols that are falsely claimed by the lying Jews to be Jewish symbols can be traced back to the religious art of ancient Mesopotamia. These are the menorah, or ritual lamp, and what the Jews call the Star of David or the Seal of Solomon. Both of these occur together on an Old Assyrian seal of the early second millennium BC, long before there were any Jews in the world to lie to us about how ancient they claim to be [see also Figure 11].

Figure 11: Tree of Life (pre-3000 BC)

Modern, so-called "feminists" should take note of the following. As the tamkarum gained power, the status of women began to break down. Sumerian women had basic rights and a high social status on equality with men in most cases. But under the power of the Semitic merchant-money-lenders, women became personal property, trade goods, and whores. Doing business "just as it had always been," the merchant-moneylenders would seize the wives and daughters of debtors as payment for debts. The merchant-moneylenders then abused, beat, raped, and reduced them to prostitution and servitude.

As mere chattel goods, the status of women and the respect which they had enjoyed among the Sumerians, disappeared. Women became the Semitic merchant-moneylenders' most profitable inventory item. Taverns, which were the monopoly of the *sabitum* (the alewife-moneylender-madams), advertised the additional services that their bar maids provided with clay plaques, such as the following three examples. Note the comfortable, air-cooled, woven-reed bed in this example.

In early Sumerian religion, a prominent position had been occupied by many goddesses who were consorts to particular gods. But as the Semitic merchant-moneylenders became owners of more and more women as their personal slave property; and as the Semites gained control of the lands while the Sumerians were disenfranchised, all of the Sumerian goddesses disappeared—except for the Semitic goddess Ishtar, the goddess of love, of beer taverns, of prostitutes, and of warfare. The last three occupations were the private business monopolies of the moneylenders.

The Sumerian underworld, itself, was originally under the sole rule of a goddess. A myth explains how she came to take a consort; and goddesses played a part in the divine decision-making "Assembly of the Gods" in the

Sumerian myths. There is even a strong suggestion that polyandry may at one time have been practiced because the Sumerian reforms of Urukagina refer to women who had taken more than one husband. But in general, as the wealth and power of the merchant-moneylenders increased, the poverty and degradation of women also increased because they became slaves, commodities, and the play things for drunks in the taverns. Defrauded by the moneylenders of their lands, of their husbands, and of their children, they became drunken prostitutes, trading tricks for a bowl of barley gruel and a sipping straw to drink from a beer vat [see Figures 13a, 13b, 13c]. Cheap pay, indeed! Under the Semites, it was a long fall for women — from equality with men to whores and slaves. But the merchant-moneylenders made money, so it was all okay.

Fig-13a   Fig-13c

As previously stated, the Third Dynasty of Ur was destroyed and Sumerian control dwindled. Amorite dynasties arose in other cities, the two most prominent initially being Isin and Larsa. For this reason, the century or so after the overthrow of Ur is known as the Isin-Larsa period (2006 to 1894 BC). The Larsa dynasty gradually increased its influence at the expense of Isin, but was finally itself overthrown in 1763 BC by the sixth ruler of the Dynasty of Babylon, the great king Hammurabi (1792 to 1750 BC).

From that time onward, none of the new rulers in the Sumerian cities were Sumerians. They were the Semitic Amorite sons of the wandering goat-herders and sheep-rustlers who had been infiltrating Mesopotamia ever since the Sumerian merchant-moneylenders had first hired them to replace the swindled and dispossessed Sumerian farmers. Similar to the modern-day illegal aliens and foreign workers who infest Europe, America, and Australia, within a single generation, their sons and daughters spoke perfect Sumerian as well as Amorite. With such unaccented language skills, they could talk their way into being allowed into Sumerian society and to gain positions of influence and power for themselves while at the same time pushing out the Sumerians.

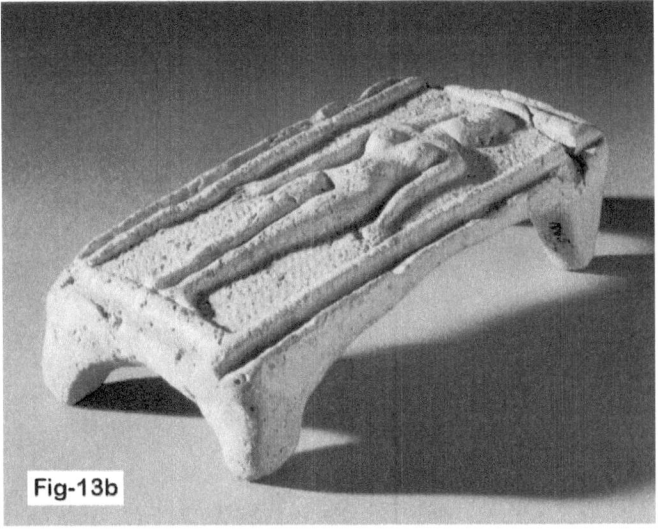

Fig-13b

With the always-eager treason of the merchant-moneylenders, they learned how to take over everything that the Sumerians had built—everything except the spiritual knowledge of True Religion, something for which the merchant-moneylenders had no use, since they had not learned how to make religion produce a profit for themselves—yet.

Indeed, the greedy moneylenders were, in general, opposed to all religions because in every temple, the priests preached mercy and generosity for ones' own people, especially toward ones' fellow members of the temple. And that always meant that they were expected to give liberal donations and forgiveness of debts, freeing those they had enslaved and letting impoverished widows and orphans to continue living in their foreclosed homes. All of these were a bothersome loss of silver for the moneylenders. As the wealthiest members of every temple, the money-lenders not only had to suffer through priestly sermons about mercy and forgiveness of debts but they were also constantly bothered with their poor victims either cursing them or begging for alms at their feet. It was so embarrassing to be a rich moneylender! But turning a blind eye and hardening a hard heart was just part of the business.

Although they were ruthlessly avaricious in daily life, during temple services, the moneylenders found themselves under the persuasion of the priests and the implied threats of an angered god. They were constantly annoyed by requests to donate and give away money which they wanted to keep for themselves. The tamkarum had not yet figured out how to avoid such inconveniences while still remaining respected members of society. These problems were privately complained about in their guild halls, but a solution to such irritations would not be devised for another 400 years.

First Amorite Dynasty of Babylon

Finally, in 1894 BC, bringing to an end the Isin-Larsa Period, an Amorite dynasty was founded at Babylon which was to bring that city to a preeminence that it maintained, psychologically if not politically, for an additional 2,000 years. Up to this time, the rather small city of Babylon had made no mark on Mesopotamian history. Yet in a little over 100 more years, this city ruled all of Mesopotamia, albeit briefly, and subsequently it was to give its name, Babylonia, to the entire region of Sumer and Akkad.

The language written on the cuneiform tablets of this time, and presumably spoken by the majority of the population, is known to modern scholars as Babylonian, or more specifically, Old Babylonian—to distinguish it from later dialects. Archaeologists refer to the period from the fall of Ur (~2000 BC) to the Hittite sack of Babylon in 1595 BC as the Old Babylonian period. Babylonian was not a new language but simply a later form of Semitic Akkadian. That dialect from the time of Sargon and the Agade kings, is specifically designated 'Old Akkadian' to differentiate it from later Babylonian forms. It was spoken by the same Amorite goatrustlers speaking two different dialects of the same Semitic language.

The existence of the town of Babylon, itself, can be traced back to the latter part of the Early Dynastic period. By the time of the Agade king, Shar-kali-sharri (~2150 BC), this small town of Babylon boasted at least two temples. Later, under the kings of Ur, Babylon was of sufficient importance to be the seat of a local governor. The name, Babylon, was first found in the Akkadian form, Babilim and later in the biblical form, Babel or Bab-El, meaning the "gate of god," and much later—through Greek transliteration—as Babylon.

Please take note of the use of the name, "El." In this example, the ancient Semitic name of God, "El," was in use at this early time, long before there were any Jews to utter it with their guttural "H" sound.

The First Dynasty of Babylon (1894 to 1595 BC) is rightly thought of, particularly during the reign of Hammurabi, as one of the highlights of ancient civilization. It was an age of material prosperity, and it is also one of the periods about which we are best informed. There exist not only many thousands of business documents and letters from Babylon and other cities, but we also have the collection of laws promulgated by Hammurabi himself. Together, these documents make it clear that the preeminence of Hammurabi among his contemporaries, which enabled him to raise Babylon to a cultural supremacy which it was never to lose, was not due solely to his military ability. His success also owed much to his political insight and aptitude for diplomacy, and to his administrative ability and concern for social justice throughout his land.

However, it would be a mistake to think of Babylon as the only city-state of significance at this period. Farther north there was the kingdom of Assyria, where another prince of Amorite origin, Shamshi-Adad I, an older contemporary of Hammurabi, established himself as king in 1814 BC. He exerted considerable influence upon the regions to the south and south-west.

In the early part of his reign, Hammurabi also had another powerful contemporary in the King of Eshnunna, who controlled the cities along the Diyala River and in the neighborhood of modern Baghdad. There were also Amorite centers of power in North Syria. The situation is summed up in a cuneiform letter from this period which says:

> There is no king who of himself alone is strongest. Ten or fifteen kings follow Hammurabi of Babylon, the same number follow Rim-Sin of Larsa, the same number follow Ibal-pi-El of Eshnunna, the same number follow Amut-pi-El of Qatanurn [in Syria], and 20 kings follow Yarim-Lim of Yamkhad [Aleppo in North Syria].

First of all, note should be taken here that these kings were all Semitic Amorites and not Sumerians. Also note once again that the names of God were often part of the personal names of the people and of the various kings, not only of Sumeria but of the later dynasties throughout the ancient Near East as well. Once again remember, all the ancient people believed in the gods and often named their children with a name of god as a part of their personal names. This was both a dedication of a child by a parent to a god as well as a God-Name-protection of the child by both parent and god. These two kings, Ibal-pi-El and Amut-pi-El, were using the Semitic names of the god, El, more than 1,300 years before there were any Jews in existence.

In addition, please note that even before there were any Jews, the Amorite tribe of Binu-Yamina (Benjamin) was a well-known ally to some of the moneylenders of Mesopotamia. In other words, more than a thousand years before there were any Jews in existence, the tribe of Benjamin was serving the moneylenders of Babylonia. We know this from the fire-baked cuneiform tablets of those people, dug up and translated by the archaeologists. The lies of the Jews will only become significant in later centuries—after the lying Jews come into existence.

The Genealogical Swindle

As Semites, all the kings of Mesopotamia were all related to one another through their tribal affiliations. It is very much overlooked by modern historians and archeologists that those people could call upon their tribal and family relationships as a means of bonding distant tribes through their bloodlines to give them a method for infiltrating other peoples while keeping a cohesive unity among themselves. Thus, among these Semitic goat-rustlers, the kings were related to those whom they ruled through genealogy. So, it is of benefit to take a quick look at this "Genealogy Swindle of the Semites."

The wandering Semitic tribes of goat-rustlers, not having specific cities or a specific place to give them social cohesion, developed the genealogy of their bloodlines as a basis of social stability. The wandering Amorite bandits and goat-herders in those days, like the Bedouins of modern times, did not place a great emphasis on the individual. After all, they worked in bandit gangs and tribes, so the group took precedence over the individuals within that group. This is standard gang mentality. Blood ties serve to link people to their past and to bind them together in the present. Members of those early desert tribes could trace their lineage back in time with genealogy. The blood-ties with long-dead ancestors formed an important part of their personal identity, at least in their own minds.

Knowing who their fathers were, was even more important among those wandering goat-herders because, like their billy goats, polygamy was the rule and not the exception. While the Sumerians usually were mono-gamous, the Semitic Amorites were polygamous. A wealthy Sumerian might take a second wife but a wandering Amorite could have any number of wives depending upon the size of his herds of goats and sheep to sustain them. Numerous wives produced numerous children and so the Semite population increased "like the sands of the sea" in comparison to the generally monogamous Sumerians. Significantly, the Sumerians practiced a kind of natural birth control by nursing their babies for two or three years. Women do not ovulate and are relatively infertile while nursing a child. So, children can be born at two-year intervals while the mother can still maintain an enthusiastic sex life with her husband without becoming pregnant until after the child is weaned.

The Amorites with their many wives and numerous children quickly became the dominant population wherever they settled. Numerous children was one method that they used for dispossessing the Sumerians simply by out-breeding them. Like the modern day promiscuous Mexicans, Pakistanis, Chinese Black Africans, and Asian Indians who are encouraged by the modern-day Jewish bankers to settle in a birth-controlled America and Europe, the promiscuous Semites of the ancient Near East quickly over-ran the original population of Sumeria—both by sheer numbers, as well as by their Semitic proclivities for telling lies and deceiving the naïve Sumerians, whose gods encouraged them to speak the truth and walk the "straight and truth path."

When people tell each other the truth, great strides are made in civilization and in the arts and sciences, as is witnessed in the achievements of the Caucasian race in Europe and the United States of America. But societies which value lies, deceits, and subterfuge such as the Jews, Muslims, and Mexicans, never advance beyond a primitive level of gross superstition and idiocy, sustaining themselves by stealing from other cultures what they are incapable of attaining, themselves. Their own histories and cultures prove this.

Remember, occupation of the land is the driving force of political power. The Amorites did not need large armies to overrun Mesopotamia. All that was required was as many children as possible and the treasonous moneylenders inviting them all in. That, and the ability to amalgamate dispersed tribes into large forces through genealogical allegiances, gave the Amorites the ability to launch quick raids with relatively large forces and then run away to the desert and hide in a guerilla warfare-style dispersal of their forces into scattered bands.

For these reasons, from the safety of their city walls, the Amorite Dynasties which first took control of the Mesopotamian cities, kept a wary eye on the roving gangs of goat-rustlers. They knew the tricks of the Semites simply because they were all from the same Semitic tribal stock.

They had won those city walls because they knew how to infiltrate, deceive, out-breed, and take over an honest agrarian society. They didn't want the wandering Semitic tribes to use the same tactics on them. So, they guarded their city walls and defended their farms from their relatives, the voracious goat-rustlers of the ancient Near East who, like their sheep and goats, ate everything.

The ancient peoples did not suffer from the modern, Jewish-Marxist concepts of "politicized genetics" as a way of confusing and down-breeding themselves into extinction. They had common sense and could see with their own eyes the effects of breeding and of bloodlines. Breed a black goat and a white goat, and the offspring will be spotted goats and shades of gray. They knew of the same general principles when applied to the marriage of daughters and sons. They were careful to choose wisely in their marriage mates by taking into consideration the health, intelligence, character, social standing, and wealth of prospective marriage partners for their children. After all, they wanted intelligent and heroic sons and strong, wholesome daughters, not half-wits and weaklings like the modern Jews encourage all people—except themselves—to birth and nurture. So, unlike modern people who stupidly follow evil Jewish encouragements, the Amorites prided themselves in their good breeding. There were no Jews in existence anywhere in the world in 1814 BC, only demonic tamkarum (merchant-moneylenders). And they had not become Jews—yet.

The Amorites and other Semitic goat-rustlers observed that intelligence, health, beauty, strength, and a variety of other physical traits are passed down through breeding. But oddly enough, they believed that a "special something" other than genetics was also passed along in their genealogies. That "special something" is actually, upon inspection, quite ridiculous. Certainly, they were wrong about the Earth being flat. They were equally wrong about a certain aspect of genealogy, the hoax of which is still being perpetuated today into modern times by the perfidious Jews, all of whom claim to have a "special something."

Through this ancient delusion, the Semitic goat-rustlers and donkey-molesters achieved a miracle! Time travel! By identifying the past with a genealogical connection, they could transform themselves into the exact bodies of their ancient ancestors! Time no longer had any power over them. No longer did they speak of an ancient ancestor in the past tense. What a relative did a thousand years ago was the same as if the story-teller did it, himself, just yesterday. And it was all accomplished through genealogical transmogrification!

Goat-rustlers! Dreaming dreams of greatness while grinning content-edly at the thought that they were every bit as wonderful as their myth-ological ancestors whose fairy-tales they bragged about around a campfire made of cattle dung! Or in modern times, telling the Passover Fable over candle flames and matzo balls.

In the tribal gangs, each individual in a tribe is related to every other member through careful memorization and discussion of their genealogy. If there were great leaders or heroes in one's own genealogy, then that was claimed to be a glory to one's own self. So, a lot of pride was taken by the goat-herders and camel drivers of the Middle East in their genealogies. Anyone living in those societies who could not recite a genealogy, implied that he had a lesser moral worth. And this moral worth, like the colors of the goats that they bred, was accepted as reflecting down through the ages to everyone in that bloodline.

In the same way, individuals of an inferior bloodline who were recognized as having noble qualities and moral qualities associated with their ancestry, then their character was always explained away as having some bloodline from a superior family line—perhaps from a maternal uncle or grandfather. Among the Semites, morality and character were believed to be an inheritable part of one's genealogy.

This idea that great glories and moral attributes of an ancestor were passed down to one's own individual self, became an important part of Semitic mythology. Sitting proudly on their glorious foundation, even the cruelest, greediest, most rapacious Semitic moneylender could claim moral superiority over all of his victims, merely by alleging the existence of a long dead ancestor who had a reputation for virtue. He was a rotten bastard in his daily life, but a good one! His distant relative from a thousand years ago made him into a good person, regardless of his thefts, rapes, and murders! Present loathsomeness and psychopathic evil could be instantly erased by calling up alleged ancient virtues from long-dead ancestors. In this manner, by using only their ancestry as "proof," modern Jews are experts at such deceit and self-delusion, forgiving themselves for in-credible crimes and atrocities under the cover of an alleged virtue by a Moses or Abraham.

There is one more thing to know about the false ideas preserved in goat-herder imaginations and genealogies. A genealogy is as rigid a frame-work and as fixed and final a grouping as can be imagined. From their young boys to their old men, the modern-day wandering Bedouins are expert genealogists; and the names of ancestors, for one reason or another, are never far from their lips. Names are kept alive by constant use, since all references to inter-group relationships must be in terms of those names. More than this, the Bedouins are proud to the point of boastfulness of their genealogical knowledge.

But their memories tend to become vague and foggy at about the third generation. By the fifth generation, their genealogies get lost and become vague. In other words, the genealogy of the wandering goat-herders is only useful to them as far back as the fifth generation—at which point their memories fail and the trackless, timeless deserts give any farther remembrance of distant relatives a futility not worth the mention.

But among some of the goat-rustler tribes, the technology of writing gave their genealogies longer branches and pathways into the foggy and mythical past. Not only were the fables connected through genealogy to living relatives, but both the remembered genealogies and the mythological lies were written down in unchanging ink on real, one-hundred percent, genuine goat skins. So, of course, that made their fairy tales just as real as the goat skins!

The more the goat-rustlers told their ancient myths about long dead relatives, using fact and fiction and theatrical talent around a cheerfully flickering campfire of cow pies, the greater their personal prestige became—at least in their own minds. Because the most incredible ancient tales could never be refuted by anyone living, then even the most impossible stories could be told, embellished, and retold until they became even better than what actually had happened. Even if the stories never happened at all, they just had to be true because they were passed down from a long line of lying goat-rustlers.

Once the genealogy was accepted as true, then the myths and fables were also accepted as true, because they were connected to a guaranteed genealogy which led from the distant past right up to the very tribesman who held the genealogy scrolls in his hands and read the ancient lies as if he had actually been there, himself. And if there was any doubt about the truth of the stories, then a few lines could be added to the genealogy tables with the names of ancient ancestors who had never existed attesting to their truth! There is nothing more convincing to the truth of an ancient fable than the real names of famous people who never existed, all claiming to have witnessed the entire fraud with their own eyes.

As the Semitic goat-rustlers became civilized members of the emerging Amorite kingdoms, and as they learned how to read and write, they began to record their genealogies stretching back farther than the mere five generations usually allowed by human memory. This is odd because, how could they record a genealogy stretching back hundreds of generations and thousands of years if they had only just now learned to write and so could remember only five generations back? But such questions are easily deflected by the ancient Jewish logic, which is: "If it is difficult to believe and impossible to have occurred, then it really happened because it was a miracle!"

Through their crude sophistry of claiming that great merit and wondrous virtue are passed down from distant relatives to even the most flea-bitten member of the tribe, the Semitic goat-rustlers began to assume a ridiculously overbearing pride in the storied virtue of those ancestors. Using the concept of ancestry, the goat-rustlers could claim great deeds and virtues as personal attributes, identical to those of fabled and mythical ancestors. With a famous and dead ancestor in their genealogy, every thieving knave could claim to actually be as virtuous as a saint through the simple process of genealogical osmosis!

Because the kings who had taken over leadership of the Sumerian culture were all Semitic Amorites, they were all related to the various tribes which infested those dry and desolate lands. On the one hand, the various kings—the alleged servants of the gods—had the political baggage derived from a humble origin to overcome. They were descended from goat-rustlers and bandits instead of from noble kings and servants of the gods. And everybody, both Amorite and Sumerian, knew it. On the other hand, once the Amorites began to insinuate themselves into kingship, some tribes of bandits and goat-herders thus acquired an Amorite king in their own genealogy with whom they could take pride and bask in his glory as it was passed down to them through their genealogical fantasies.

While picking fleas out of their shaggy beards, swatting at the flies buzzing around their grimy heads soiled with goat dung while bragging about the glories of their mythical ancestors, those Semitic goat-rustlers and wandering Amorite bandits, swooning in the heat of a desert mirage, invented prestigious fantasies and considered themselves the better for it. After all, a dirty goat-rustler riding into town on his donkey might just find a better bench at the tavern and maybe a free beer if he made it known that he was related to some famous king or pious saint through no-matter-how-long-and-complicated a genealogical recitation from his furious memory. And if his ancient relative was *God, Himself,* then the possibilities for free beer and stolen loot were endless.

From Sumerian to Semite

Most histories regard the lives of the kings and their accomplishments to be of utmost importance. But for this history, it is the *consequences* that these kings had upon their subjects and upon the surrounding peoples that are the most important. After all, a king is but one man. But this one man affects the lives of many. So, let's take just a short look at the kings, while being more concerned with what they wrought.

The first few years of King Hammurabi (1792-1750 BC) cannot have been encouraging because he was surrounded with powerful kings in the major cities. The powerful king Rim-Sin (1822-1763 BC) dominated the south. The kingdom of Eshnunna controlled the region just to the north of Babylon as far as the Euphrates. In the far north, Assyria under the astute Shamshi-Adad was a growing power already in control of vast territories.

Rim-Sin's family is of some interest: his elder brother Warad-Sin (1834-1823 BC) was maneuvered to the throne of Larsa by their father, Kudur-mabuk, a clever tribal sheikh. Kudur-mabuk's name and that of his father are Elamite, yet Kudur-mabuk bore the titles "Shaikh of the Amurrum [Amorites] and of Yamutbal." Yamutbal was an area east of the Tigris settled by Amorites at the time of the Third Dynasty of Ur. So, he was an Amorite whose family had at some time entered the service of the king of Elam. His sons' names, however, are pure Semitic Akkadian.

Rim-Sin's daughter was consecrated high priestess of Sin, the Moon God at Ur, under the Sumerian name Enanedu. Indeed we see here the best-documented example of the path from goat-rustling nomad to Mesopotamian monarch. All accomplished within two generations! Note once again, the importance of Sin, the Moon God of Ur; he was the god of the moneylenders in the city where the sea trade routes and river trade routes converged.

Like the Isin and Ur kings, Rim-Sin was worshipped with divine honors. His rival, Hammurabi, never assumed the title of divinity in any form. And all subsequent kings were to follow Babylon in this respect, as the very numerous Semitic Amorites completely infiltrated, subverted, and overran all of Sumer and Akkad.

Hammurabi's first few years seem to have been devoted to matters of internal administration. In his second year he "established justice in the land," a reference to the inauguration of reforms that culminated in the promulgation of his famous code of laws. After all, with the Sumerian Swindle of the moneylenders being allowed to rob the people of their wealth, it was a popular political move for the kings to free the people from indebtedness and slavery by "establishing justice in the land." That is, it was popular with everyone except the moneylenders.

During Hammurabi's first 30 years, only three of his year-names record military campaigns. It was not until the latter part of his reign that

Babylon became a major power. Undoubtedly the dominant personality of the age was Shamshi-Adad (1813-1781 BC), king of the region to the north of Babylon that would become the future Assyria.

Shamshi-Adad was a ruler of great military and administrative ability. His forceful personality is intimately revealed in letters found among some 13,000 cuneiform documents recovered from the royal palace at Mari. The city of Mari, as you might recall, was an important way station since ancient times for Sumerian caravan and boat traffic along the Euphrates. And it was a major manufacturing center for copper and bronze implements and weapons. In 1796 BC, Shamshi-Adad, taking advantage of a palace revolution in Mari, placed his simple-minded son Yasmakh-Adad on the throne of Mari as his sub-king and representative.

Although Shamshi-Adad was a Semitic Amorite, like the other Amorites who had begun buying land from the moneylenders and taking over the Sumerian cities and Sumerian culture, he prayed to the Sumerian gods. It was the habit of all people who moved from one part of Mesopo-tamia to another, to leave their gods behind in the city which they had moved from and to pray to the god of the city in which they had taken up a new residence. In one inscription, he boasts: "When I built the temple of my Lord Enlil, the prices in my city of Ashur were two gur of grain for a shekel of silver (about 600 liters of grain for a shekel of silver), fifteen minas of wool for a shekel of silver." Thus, he is stating that under his rule, prices were cheap and the people were well-fed, fully-clothed, and prosperous.

An older and more capable son, Ishme-Dagan, was placed as governor at Ekallatum, an administrative center east of the Tigris River above Ashur. Shamshi-Adad, himself, ruled from two capitals, Ashur and Shubat-Enlil in northeastern Syria, where an administrative archive from his time has been found. The Mari archive covers the period from about 1810 to 1760 BC, and provides a day-to-day view of contemporary events unequalled elsewhere in the ancient world. The family correspondence of Shamshi-Adad and his sons is particularly revealing of the politics of the time and includes some of the most touchingly human documents re-covered from the ancient world.

From his capital at Shubat-Enlil, Shamshi-Adad could rule the Khabur valley while watching his sons. Thus, the whole area between the middle Tigris and the middle Euphrates and northward into the mountains was consolidated under a single Amorite family by about 1800 BC. Just as the tamkarum (merchant-moneylender) families controlled large business enterprises, it should be reemphasized that this rather huge territory of

Mesopotamia was controlled by a single Amorite family, the family of Shamshi-Adad and his sons.

The Semitic kings and crown princes, working as family groups, would most certainly have also assigned their variety of kith and kin to the various political positions below them, not just sons but uncles, nephews, and trusted members of the extended family. Their genealogical tribal and family relationships gave them a covert chain-of-command alongside of and within any overt political hierarchy.

Also working in family and tribal gangs were the Semitic money-lenders and merchants who controlled the trade routes, markets, and guilds. The business of being the rulers of a country was a family project, just as the trade guilds were dominated by individual families and tribes. Like the subterranean mycelia of a fungus branching out in all directions, this genealogical and covert chain-of-command is found to this very day among the Jews who infest the seats of power in the governments of the modern world. A single mushroom cap that pops above the forest floor is what you see, but it is supported by a vast network of mycelia hidden underground.

The Sumerian leaders also had assigned their relatives to positions of trust. But the Sumerians saw themselves as members of city-states with loyalty to the god of that city as their supreme devotion. As the shiftless, wandering, promiscuous, desert-dwelling, Semitic goat-rustlers took over Mesopotamia, their genealogical connections which were based on patri-archal hierarchies, replaced loyalty to the gods who resided in each particular city with loyalty to the top tribal goat-rustler who controlled the tribes both inside and outside of the city. The propensity for the king of the goat-rustlers to claim to be a god was something new that the Semites introduced into Mesopotamia.

But these Semitic kings claim to godhead was not based upon spiritu-al knowledge like the pharaohs of Egypt or the priests of the temples. The Semitic claim to godhead was based upon the coercive dictatorship of a king who could do whatever he wanted and could have whatever he want-ed. These Semites were gods of the material world and bosses of men. As they profited from the Sumerian Swindle, the Amorite kings, who were backed by shekels of silver, tossed spirituality into the trash heap as detri-mental to making money and gaining political power.

Although surrounded by so many able kings, Hammurabi remains the symbol of his age. His modern reputation as great king and legal innovator owes much to the early discovery of cuneiform documents from his reign. His cuneiform letters reveal Hammurabi was an efficient administrator supervising even the most mundane matters and also as a just and humane ruler who genuinely made the welfare of his subjects his personal care.

But one fact alone will ensure Hammurabi's lasting fame: his role as the most successful king of the dynasty that made Babylon thereafter the leading city in Western Asia. Never again did any southern city of Sumeria rule Mesopotamia, and indeed the sociological pattern imposed on the country in his time continued to be felt until the end of its history nearly two thousand years later.

This being so, what were these sociological patterns imposed by Hammurabi? First, it must be understood that the Sumerian people had not completely vanished. They were being disenfranchised and replaced by the Amorites who thereby became the majority population. They had been swindled and foreclosed and dispossessed by the moneylenders. And they were being assimilated by language into the dominant Akkadian-speaking society. At the same time, however, the Amorites accepted the higher Sumerian culture as their own and began to follow the ancient Sumerian ways. Those ancient ways were represented by worshipping the Sumerian gods and practicing the Sumerian culture, with all of its inventions. It was only slowly that the Amorites began renaming the old Sumerian gods with their own Akkadian names. But this process took centuries.

Of a more immediate need, Hammurabi found himself as an Amorite leader of territories that included the original Sumerian people as well as increasing numbers of his own Amorite people. To lead this mixed racial society required political skill and wisdom. His was not a very big kingdom compared with many others, but it was very prosperous since it controlled the trade routes along the two rivers. Under the leadership of his sons, Babylonia greatly expanded its territory. [see Map 12]

Hammurabi followed a vigorous policy of canal-building, to increase agri-cultural prosperity in his land. He welded into one kingdom the many city-states of Sumer and Akkad, and gave the whole land one language for ad-ministration and business and a unified legal system. But reflecting their debt to and respect for Sumerian culture, they continued to use the ancient Sumerian language liturgically in the temples for as long as Babylonia endured.

Cuneiform texts from the reign of Hammurabi, documents from Larsa at the time of Rim-Sin, contemporary letters from Shemshara in northeastern Iraq, and archives from Mari and Sippar provide social and economic data far greater than exist for many later periods in history, even in western Europe. And most certainly, this historical data exists in greater extent than those stories found in the Hebrew Bible, the Old Testament.

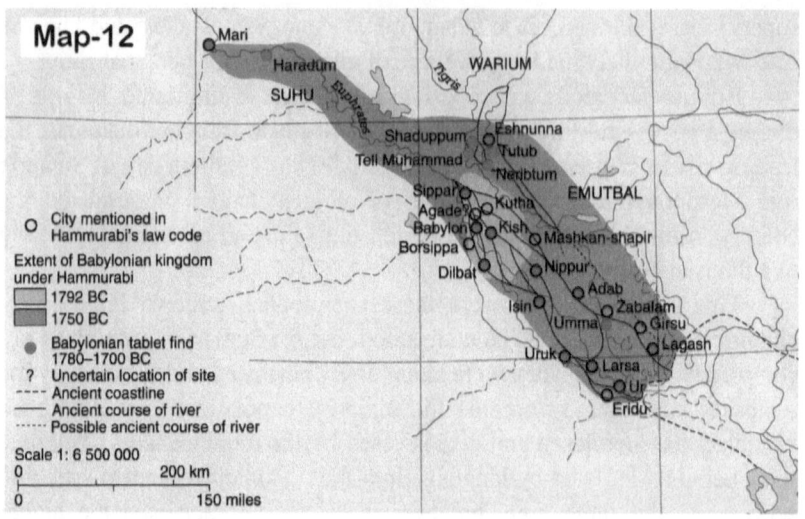

But these cuneiform documents were only discovered beneath the rubble of millennia during the past 150 years of modern archeology. Therefore, the persistent lies and myths of the rabbis, repeated for over 2,500 years, have had a longer influence on Western culture than the long-buried and recently-translated cuneiform documents of the ancient Near East. I repeat: The lies of the Jews have worked to the detriment of mankind for 2,500 years while the truths of archaeology have had a mere 150 years to correct those Semitic deceits. The present study aims to correct the Jewish lies and hoaxes of the world's most horrible monsters.

*****

The sociological pattern imposed upon the land by Hammurabi continued to be felt until the end of Babylonian history. His military achievements, however, did not long survive Hammurabi himself. Racial movements caused by the stirring of the Indo-European tribes beyond the Caucasus and the effects of the southward migration of the mighty Aryan peoples now began to be felt.

During this Old Babylonian phase of Mesopotamian history, new ideas began to form about how a society should be led and why a society exists. The Semitic Amorites were quite different from the Sumerians in their ideas about what makes an honest and true society.

The Semitic Akkadians and Semitic Amorites were an entirely different strain of people than the Sumerians who had founded civilization more than 1,500 years previously. Basically, they were more deceitful, ruthless, and cruel. They did not have behind them thousands of years of the mellowing effects of reliable crops and full stomachs. They were more imbued with a scrubby existence with their herds of goats and sheep as they roamed from one watering hole to the next. Though they absorbed Sumerian culture and made it their own, the Semites did not value honesty and the "straight and true path" as much as they valued clever craftiness. Even in modern times, those traits persist among today's Semitic peoples where they believe that the worthiness of a man is found in his ability to deceive his fellows and to gain an advantage through trickery and lies. This is how "it has always been" among those people, and 6,000 years has not been long enough to erase this cultural and genetic trait, even in today's modern world of lying Jews and deceitful Muslims.

Herding goats and sheep, dwelling in tents, living the nomadic life in the semi-arid and desert regions of Arabia, Palestine, and Syria, those crude and barbarous people were in awe of the great cities and ingenious ways of the agrarian Sumerians. When they could leave their stinking, goat-hair tents and half-starved existence on the deserts in exchange for the clean labor and full stomachs of a farming life; or when those bandits could exchange military service for land ownership, they did so.

The moneylenders of Sumeria had been hiring cheap labor from the surrounding barbarians for over 2,000 years, treasonably replacing the Sumerian native sons with foreign workers. Also, the Sumerian kings had been hiring foreign mercenaries in exchange for farm lands, army rations, and loot. In this way, between the greedy moneylenders and the ambitious kings, the Sumerian people were gradually disenfranchised from their own lands and replaced with foreigners. They were not dispossessed by a military invasion; they were betrayed by the Treasonous Class from among the "Haves." The wealthy awilum (the "Haves") sold their lands out from under the very feet of their own people and sold the lands to foreigners.

But the kings and moneylenders did not disenfranchise or replace themselves. Of course not! They became the Ruling Elite over the new immigrants. The kings and merchants and moneylenders were the awilum (the Haves), the Treasonous Class who were willing to betray their own people just as long as they could continue to be the Ruling Elite, with the "Have-Nots" bowing at their feet. And if their own people demanded fair pay for their labor, even just enough to barely live on and did not bow down low enough, then this Treasonous Class replaced them with foreign muskenum (Have-Nots) who would accept being the footstool for the feet of the "Haves" in exchange for a bowl of barley gruel.

To repeat once again, just as in ancient times so it is today, the driving force of political power is *physical occupation*. Political power comes from physical occupation, not historical rights, not title deeds, not moral rights—only occupation. Historical rights, title deeds, and moral rights come later, to bolster the power of occupation by the interlopers. The moneylenders and merchants claimed title and ownership to all properties which they had swindled from the Sumerians. Then, they occupied those lands with their own hired gangs of alien labor to whom they sold the dispossessed properties. All the while that the moneylenders were betraying their own people, the "good deals" and the "generous loan arrangements" which they had made to the alien and foreign immigrants, made them the "best friends" of these new "owners" of the land.

This Secret Fraud #15 of the Sumerian Swindle was developed by the moneylenders at an early date: "*Loans to friends are power; loans to enemies are weapons.*" The moneylenders of Sumeria had used loans at high interest rates as a weapon against their own people so as to betray, impoverish, dispossess, and enslave them. And then, to sell off the foreclosed properties and to enslave the previous owners, they gave loans at low interest rates to the foreigners, thus entrapping the new immigrants into the Sumerian Swindle. They did not sell the property to foreigners for less than the current market value; they merely sold it at a lower interest rate.

The treasonous merchant-moneylenders began their long series of swindles throughout world history by destroying their own people while befriending the enemies of their people. And why not? They made a profit both ways. Once the immigrants were locked into paying low interest rates with the Sumerian Swindle "just as it had always been," then the tamkarum raised the rates on their next loans and eventually they swindled their new "best friends" out of the property. The moneylenders rarely lost money; they merely manipulated the people and the market so that sometimes they made more profit and sometimes they made less profit. But they always profited from the Sumerian Swindle.

Historically, the Semitic Amorites (2200-2000 BC) were followed by the Semitic Aramaeans (1200-1000 BC) who, in turn, were followed by the Semitic Arabs (800 BC). But they all had in common their Semitic language dialects and nomadic lifestyle that was not tied to a single geographical area. Because they had no permanent territorial claims, those wandering groups identified themselves not by city or country but by tribes and by the ties of their genealogical bloodlines. Not being associated with a geographical area, descent from a common ancestor was of great importance in tribal affiliation. As they all moved about in search of grazing lands and water, tribal affiliations changed, tribes constantly absorbed other tribes or split up and individuals even changed their tribal status.

So, their connections to one another through genealogy became an important part of their personal identity. Though this genealogical identity could be altered merely by lying about it, it was still an important part of the tribal hierarchy and the social prestige between tribes and between individual members of tribes. The relationship of the Semites to one another transcended any affiliation or loyalty to any particular city or country because they were racially and genetically related. They were all a single nation connected genealogically. At least, that is what both the ancient and the modern gangs of Jews claim, even though it is just another Semitic lie.

The incursion and settlement of nomadic groups was, and remains today, a complex process of interaction between settled societies and the tribal societies which has often been misunderstood. Certainly these bandit tribes at various times preyed upon the people of the settled lands. A Sumerian story describes the Amorites as "hovering over the walls of Uruk like flocks of birds," but in general their incursions took the form of raids, not invasions. Economic distress caused by drought or too many children often persuaded nomadic peoples to seek employment as laborers on the land, or—and this is frequently attested in the cuneiform tablets—as hired mercenaries. Other immigrants appear deliberately to have chosen the mercenary role because their pay included grants of land as well as loot from the campaigns on which they served. By such means, groups of pastoralists, indeed sometimes whole tribes, acquired not only the settled ways of their hosts but their language and culture as well.

Exactly like the Mexicans in modern-day America, or the Muslims in modern-day Europe, they were an undermining and subversive element to society who were brought in by the moneylenders as dispossessors of the people in order to create poverty among the citizens, who thereby required loans from the bankers to survive the influx. It is an ancient moneylender scam.

There is certainly no direct route from the role of true Bedouin to that of head of state. The groups that became true city-dwellers had passed some time in the intermediate stage of dependence upon their settled agricultural neighbors. As can be seen in modern societies, within a single generation of children, such immigrants as Mexicans, Pakistanis, or Chinese can become fully functional in a European or American country, learning to read and write and speak the language without inflection. So much the better to undermine and dispossess the citizens.

Such cultural subversion by the immigrants was actually faster than in modern countries because the many professional scribes reduced the need for anyone to learn to read and write. And in the time frames of one or two hundred years, the social climbing from goat-rustlers to city governor became increasingly common. Just as in modern America or England, where such an oddity as a turban-wearing, English-speaking Sikh in the space of one generation becomes elected to city councils, it was no different than in the ancient times. And the manipulators and betrayers behind the scenes were the exact same greedy fiends as are found today.

One Hundred Percent Interest!

One of the aspects of Babylonian business practices that seems to have been overlooked by the archeologists is how these kinds of interest rates could have endured for so long. The Laws of Hammurabi were not declared by him simply to right wrongs, or to protect the people, or to prohibit excesses, or to fix commercial rates, or to set limits on the price of goods—although they did all of these things—but also to protect the monopoly of the merchant-moneylenders.

And why? Because in a truly free-market system, it is impossible for moneylenders to make a profit of 100% or more on a loan! In a free-market system, where anyone can loan money at any interest rate they please, the best way to make a profit on loans is to offer loans at a rate of interest below that of the other moneylenders and thus attract more borrowers. Also, in a free-market system, the biggest moneylenders can actually afford to offer loans below the rates of the less wealthy money-lenders. And the less wealthy moneylenders can increase their profits by undercutting the competition from the richer moneylenders. Both situations arise in a free market system.

But as was earlier shown, this did not happen. It did not happen because throughout Mesopotamia, money lending rates were standardized by the tamkarum guilds. Moneylending even in 2000 BC, was a cartel monopoly that extended beyond the borders of any one state.

This monopoly over moneylending is still jealously possessed and viciously guarded by the Jews to this very day, with all of the same abuses to society as in ancient times. It is a monopoly that, secretly and covertly, has "always been here," even though it should not be here at all. (My use of the term "free market" should not be confused with the modern term, "free trade.")

The Laws of Hammurabi show that Babylonia did not have a free-enterprise or a free-market system because it was a system that was regulated so that the merchants could not take total control of prices and thus drive the people completely into poverty. It was a system where the interest rates were officially fixed so that such high moneylender rates were legitimatized and legalized by the king, himself.

Although King Hammurabi did not know it, this was an application of the merchant-moneylenders' Secret Fraud #17 of the Sumerian Swindle: *"Kings are required to legitimatize a swindle, but once the fraud is legalized, those very kings may be assassinated or betrayed."* The king, who was a representative of the gods, legitimatized the swindles of the moneylenders by writing a law declaring their frauds to be "legal" but within the boundaries established by the laws of the king. The money-lenders were allowed to be voracious parasites because that is "how it had always been." But the laws of the king put a limit on their greed. Hammurabi called it, "bringing justice to the land." But I call it, "legalizing a criminal swindle."

Even more than this, Hammurabi's Laws show that this merchant-moneylender class of swindlers and crooks, over the centuries, through their guilds and cartels and through their financial bribery of the various kings and dynasties, had ingratiated themselves so much with the kings that they had achieved actual laws which protected their businesses from competition!

By Babylonian times, business could not be practiced either on a local or an international scale without both permission of the kings and permission of the trade guilds. Thus, by 1750 BC, although the money-lenders had a huge opportunity for enormous profits, they were still limited by the laws of the kings and by the censure of the priests. Yet, even between those two ameliorating forces of palace and temple, they were still able to position themselves as a money power which could influence both the palace and the temple in the increasingly hostile political environment of the ancient Near East.

Excessive rates of interest were frowned upon, so the laws of Hammurabi provide that a tamkarum who charged more than the legal rate would forfeit his capital. Still, these legal rates were extremely high and they guaranteed huge profits and power over the people who fell into the moneylender's snare. Hammurabi did, however, prohibit the ancient Sumerian Swindle from stealing a man's property or enslaving him if he did not have silver but did have grain or goods of equal value to the silver with which to repay the debt. Secret Fraud #4 of the Sumerian Swindle is:

"Loans of silver repaid with goods and not with silver, forfeit the collateral." But under Hammurabi, this part of the Sumerian Swindle was recognized as a swindle and declared illegal. Yet, neither Hammurabi nor any other king, recognized the entire Sumerian Swindle for the larceny that it was (and is), simply because it "has always been here."

Hammurabi's Laws decreed that:

> If a man who has acquired a debt has no silver to return but has grain, then the tamkarum shall take the interest on it in grain, but if the tamkarum raises the interest on it above 100 qa of grain per gur [33 percent] he has delivered (on loan), he shall forfeit whatever loan that he made.

Thus, the moneylenders could be assured of high profits, but a limit of 33% was the law. With their interest rates being written into law, they could claim to an illiterate peasant that such high rates were not only "routine" but were also decreed by the king. Under the authority of the king, the people could thus be swindled legally.

This was very important to the moneylenders to legitimatize their frauds under protections of the king and his soldiers. But woe to the king who did not know Secret Fraud #17 of the Sumerian Swindle: "Kings are required to legitimatize a swindle but once the fraud is legalized, those very kings may be assassinated or betrayed."

CHAPTER 9

THE MESOPOTAMIAN MAFIA
AND THE GUILD WARS

As I stated in the beginning of this history, the Jews are no different than any other sort of organized criminal conspirators. If there is any slight difference at all, it is simply that they have been unusually successful at hiding their perfidious evils. How they have managed to do this, will be found in the following chapters, as well as in *The Monsters of Babylon*.

But for now, you and I, standing in the middle of Babylonia in the year 1750 BC—with 2000 years of history behind us—you and I can stand on the highest ziggurats of baked clay, those mighty temple mounds of mud bricks in the Old Babylonian Dynasty of King Hammurabi. From the broiling sun, we can shade our squinting eyes with our protecting palms pressed against our sweaty brows and gaze out across the entire known world!

From our lofty view from atop such ancient temple skyscrapers, which soared a dizzy 80 feet into the heavens, we can look outward across time and space. We can gaze up the Euphrates River or down the Tigris River, peer into the distant reaches of the Persian Gulf at Bahrain, Oman and distant India, strain our eyes to see into the wiggling mirages of the Syrian Desert, or west into Canaan, or northwest into Anatolia, or southwest into Egypt or Arabia, or across the Mediterranean Sea to Crete. But no matter where we look—now, at this point in world history, over 2000 years after civilization began—there are absolutely no Jews to be found anywhere. Oy! It's such a miracle!

No matter where we look in this time period of 1750 BC—from the reed swamps of the south where Sumerian civilization was born, to the northern plains of Assyria where much of history was soon to begin, across the deserts to the west where dwelt the Canaanites and Egyptians or toward the Eastern Iranian plateau where the Elamites and Persians would soon begin their own mighty steps into the historical record—no matter where we look in the entire world, there are no Jews anywhere to be found. None. Zero. Not one. It was a world without Jews. And mankind was relatively happy. But how was this marvel possible?

Today's Jews hold aloft what they swear to be their "holy scriptures" wherein they claim to be the original and the very first and most favored people to be descended from the original couple, even naming their prehistoric ancestors as Adam and Eve! In those days, there was no need for surnames such as Adam Goldstein or Eve Horowitz, since there were only two of them and everybody knew who they were.

Those hoary old "scriptures" of the Jews even includes detailed genealogies spanning several thousand years while microscopically listing and bragging about hundreds of generations of their alleged ancestors in lists longer than any human brain could ever possibly have remembered without writing it down. But they could remember all of this before writing was even invented! Such amazing memories from a people who could remember the first 2,000 years of their history, during which time they did not even exist! What a miracle! Everybody else in the world did exist, except for the Jews, who are here to tell us all about the time when they didn't exist.

And since they were nowhere to be found, they decided to fill in the blanks of 2,000 years of history with what they could remember about it! It was truly a miracle! After 2,000 years, nobody had ever heard of a Jew, but when the first Jews appeared, they claimed to know everything there was to know about everybody else! My, oh my! Such lying scoundrels!

Four or five generations is all that it takes for most people to forget their ancestors. You, Dear Reader, may even remember from your childhood, seeing your great-grandmother or great-grandfather. Some may even remember a great-great grandparent. But after four or five generations, no one has ever met any of their relatives older than that. The life spans of people are too short and memories are too dim after four or five generations to even think beyond such time frames. But the Jews have hundreds of generations worth of characters listed in their fables, who they claim had lived thousands of years before writing was invented. That's what miraculous memories the Jews have! But the greatest miracle of all the miracles from the miraculous Jews, is that they can keep such serious looks upon their lying faces while pushing forward such flimsy affirmations of authenticity.

The lies which the Jews tell, do not match up with what history and the science of archaeology says about them. It is now 1750 BC in Babylonia. Civilization has been thrashing around for over 2,000 years without a single Jew making an appearance. In addition, the archeological record shows people living on the Earth during the Stone Age for millions of years previous to the appearance of these miracle mongers. When the Stone Age had a respite from the Ice Age, farming and civilization began in the flood plains of Mesopotamia and followed soon thereafter in the

Nile River valley with the beginnings of the Egyptian civilization. Agriculture then spread to Europe and Ireland by 4000 BC. But in all of this time, there were no Jews to be found anywhere, under rocks, beneath trees, anywhere on the entire Earth nor found anyplace under the vast sky.

Although there were no Jews for all of those long periods of time, there were, however, some rather well-connected, rich, ruthless, greedy people working in the background who were *very similar* to Jews. Rich, ruthless, avaricious, and interconnected they were, but they were not Jews —yet. They were *tamkarum* (merchant-moneylenders); they were *naditum* (priestess-moneylenders); they were *sabitum* (alewife-moneylenders). Along with their relatives who helped them oversee their vast land holdings, monopoly business enterprises, and stables of slaves, they all belonged to the same social upper class of the awilum (the Haves). None of them were Jews because Jews and Judaism had not been invented—yet.

In the ancient days, sons were expected to follow the occupation of their fathers; while daughters were expected to accept a good match and to marry into mutually beneficial families. Families worked as extended-family groups and there was very little room in society for individuals making their own way without help. Our modern concepts of the "rugged individual" was unknown because such "rugged individuals" all perished in all of the ancient societies.

In those days, everyone lived communally with the help of their family, friends, and neighbors. Without such a social safety net, the lone individual had little chance of survival. So, the son of a farmer became a farmer. The son of a tamkarum either became a merchant-moneylender or he managed one of the family businesses. Thus, the family enterprises prospered without interruption.

All of those merchant-moneylender businesses were extended-family operations. Large families of wealthy men—who would perhaps also have a second wife and several concubines along with all of their children, plus the many relatives attached to each wife—would always have many mouths to feed and many jobs to fill. More children meant that more jobs were needed to satisfy the increasing size of the family and to perpetuate and increase family wealth. Thus, as family sizes grew, the tamkarum patriarchs sought greater control of existing markets along with expansion into foreign markets, as well as greater control over their extended families, relatives, and tribal relations.

Somewhat like a cancerous tumor, the merchant-moneylender families grew in size, sucking the wealth out of society while ruthlessly practicing Secret Fraud #8: "Large crime families are more successful than lone criminals or gangs; international crime families are the most successful of all."

A moneylender could teach his most trusted sons the secrets of the Sumerian Swindle, but by its very criminal nature it had to remain a secret among a select few. The Sumerian Swindle was simple, but it was a secret nonetheless. The Swindle was not something that was shared among every member of the moneylender families for fear that the actual criminal nature of the Swindle would become generally known. Not all sons were taught unless they were directly working in the racket. Much like modern day Mafia, Yakusa, Triad, and Banker crime families do today, they employed numerous relatives in legal businesses, while only a very few of the inner circle were entrusted with the secret, illegal side of the operations. Lending silver and grain at interest had "always been here," so why would anyone question it?

Like the "trickle down" economy of the Mafia crime families, the profits were shared with the entire extended family and clan, leaving no one out. Whether they worked in any of the businesses or not, everyone benefited.

All of them were not equally guilty of committing crimes, but all of them were beneficiaries of those crimes that their patriarchs and tribe members had committed. The source of their wealth was never discussed with anyone not of their family and tribe. Telling the secrets of the family business was taboo. Because they all benefited in the profits, they all benefited by keeping their mouths shut, doing what they were asked to do, and protecting their clans from outsiders.

The promiscuous Semitic goat rustlers of Mesopotamia always had very large families. Because of their genealogical organization, everyone knew the hierarchical position of everyone else. Order and discipline was maintained both because the father or patriarch, was head of the family and head of the clan; but also because the patriarch had control of the family businesses and portioned out the shares in the form of high wages to family members, and low wages to the strangers who served the family members.

Silence about their dealings was foremost. The Sumerian Swindle was the basis of their power, but *how* this secret money-making engine could be used to enhance all other aspects of their operations was on a need-to-know basis only. With the shekels of silver gained through money-lending, the loan-sharking side of their operations required that they also have under their employ a variety of enforcers to help them extract payments from those who were unable or unwilling to pay. These strong-arm goons did not have to be members of the family. They only needed to do what they were told, such as dragging a screaming child away from his parents or a wailing daughter away from an indebted father who drank too much or gambled too much in the tavern of the sabitum. Debt-slavery was an accepted social disability in Hammurabi's Babylonia because "it had always been here." But it could not exist without the moneylenders insisting that it exist. The moneylenders were parasites who lived and prospered under the protection of the king, just as they do today under the protection of the laws in every country they infest.

And so, the tamkarum class was not just wealthy businessmen who dealt in the usual goods of commerce and industry. They were not just the rich and respected members of the wealthy awilum class (the Haves) whose members included the kings and court officials and the priests and priestesses of the temples. The tamkarum class was also something quite worse: overtly honest businessmen but covertly they were, each and every one of them, crooks.

Of course, they had money and property gained through their numerous commercial businesses. But their wealth was also guaranteed to be continuously resupplied from the secret dealings of loan-sharking, alcohol debauchery, gambling, prostitution, smuggling, weapons sales to enemies of the state, and slavery. All of these were part of the Old Babylonian moneylenders' scams of 1750 BC, just as they are a part of the hidden business mix of our own modern-day banking dynasties. As criminals, all of them had their own collection agents in the person of soldiers (police) and hired gangsters. But there is more.

The moneylenders first gained their wealth through the Sumerian Swindle by taking advantage of both the rich and the poor through lending-at-interest. But their greatest victims were the poor, who not only lost everything that they had, but their very freedom into slavery as well. The moneylenders ruthlessly took advantage of the poor because they have always been deceivers and betrayers of trust. Pretending to be honest businessmen, they took advantage of the people's good faith through Secret Fraud #2: "Loans rely on the honesty of the borrower but not the honesty of the lender." Those who borrowed from them believed that the stated percentages were simple interest, even while the covert compound interest drove them into servitude.

The moneylenders of Babylon were also seducers of the innocent in that they debauched the girls and boys and young women whom they had wrested from their parents and husbands through debt-slavery, and then used them for their own perverted desires. The merchant-moneylenders were rapists and pimps who prostituted those abused youths to the brothels and taverns under their control. Some of them were homosexual perverts who raped the boys whom they had seized and seduced their male slaves under threats of death or castration. Cruel perverters of the downtrodden were they. And they became traitors to the gods.

Those Bothersome Gods

As the various tamkarum families vied with one another for profits and political leverage, they found that their gods were getting in the way. The Sumerian-Babylonian religions were composed of many gods, each of whom lived in different cities and who had their own geographical regions of power separate from all other gods. Those ancient cities, whose temples had monopolized the worship of the most powerful gods, prospered the most. Nippur was still the holiest city in Babylonia as it had been for the previous 3,000 years of Ubaidian and Sumerian Culture. The Sumerian gods were the same gods worshipped by both the Babylonians and Assyrians. But the Semitic-speaking Akkadians, Babylonians and Assyrians changed the names of the gods as the political influence of the temples began to shift away from Sumeria and toward Babylonia and Assyria.

Inanna, the Sumerian goddess of love, became identified with the Semitic name of Ishtar, whose visible form was the planet Venus, the morning and evening star. She absorbed many attributes which originally had belonged to a number of other Sumerian goddesses, but her major aspects were those of goddess of love and of war. Cults of a sexual nature were practiced in her honor in many places. Those cults required a steady supply of sex slaves to serve the goddess and to bring income to the temple from the men who came to "worship" her via the temple prostitutes. Ishtar was also a goddess of war because war brought more slaves into the power of the merchant-moneylenders—slaves who could be used both for personal sexual gratification and as whorehouse profits of their masters.

Ishtar, as the planet Venus, is often thought of in a group with Sin, the Moon-god, and Shamash, the Sun-god. Because the Sun-god saw everything in his daily course above the Earth, Shamash was the god of justice. There was a strong moral element in the cult of Shamash who was an unsparing enemy of the wrongdoer and who was a friend of the just and of the oppressed. A god often associated with Shamash was Adad, a storm-god who was originally of West Semitic origin as the storm-god, Baal.

Even with the changes of the names of the gods from Sumerian to the Semitic Old Babylonian language, the gods were still the same gods, teaching the same lessons as had been taught for over 3,000 years. Truth, integrity, uprightness, honesty, and the benevolent justice of the gods was taught within the temples. Thus, the moneylenders were always at odds with the gods because by the very nature of the Sumerian Swindle, they could never do business and be honest both at the same time. Over the millennia, as their methods of making profits became more intertwined with a variety of socially-corrosive occupations and criminal enterprises, not only did the moneylenders fall under the restrictive laws of the kings and the religious censure of the priests, but the moneylenders became absolutely the most hated people in all of Mesopotamia. So, to save their lives from the wrath of the people, they demanded extra protection under the laws of the king.

To repeat, laws do not arise in a vacuum; they are promulgated as needed to meet the requirements of society or they are created to further the schemes of those who want to control society. The laws are made by the rich and powerful and never by the poor and powerless, except in cases where the poor and powerless rise up and destroy the rich and powerful. *Only then*, do the poor make the laws. But such events have been short-lived rarities throughout history.

Of course, the crass impulses of the people must be regulated so that everyone in society understands that deeds such as theft, rape, assault, murder, etc., are anti-social and socially destructive. Such acts cannot be tolerated in society and are thus declared to be crimes. And yet, the Sumerian Swindle, itself, was never declared to be a crime simply because "it has always been here." The laws were written by the awilum (the Haves), the very people who profited from it. So, they had no intention of making the Sumerian Swindle illegal.

But laws also were developed to control the more subtle, but no less crass, deeds of the awilum (the Haves) so that their greed and deceit did not bring unbearable harm or suffering to the victims of their schemes and frauds. Certainly, the awilum (the Haves) cannot be trusted to fairly create true justice in their laws because it is by their very nature, as members of the awilum class, not only to have wealth but greedily to desire more. Conversely, the poor among the people cannot be trusted to fairly create laws because it is by their very nature to ignorantly not know what is best but rather to choose what fulfills their immediate and venal needs.

Thus, it was recognized by all members of the ancient societies that only the king, under tutelage of the priests and the guidance of the gods, would have the best interest of all the people at heart—both for the "Haves" and for the "Have-Nots." After all, the king was the servant of the gods and stood between the gods and the people, so it was his responsibility to "bring justice to the land." With the gods giving him authority, the king was an even more imposing figure when he was backed by his soldiers.

Another Look at the Laws of Hammurabi

Among all of the kings of the ancient Near East, Hammurabi was the most famous. Hammurabi, as we saw, was the sixth ruler of the First Dynasty of Babylon, circa 1750. So, he had plenty of help from previous kings in understanding how to best rule the region around Babylon which he had inherited. The prologue to Hammurabi's Law Code stresses that because of his piety, the gods appointed him as ruler of the people to perform the role of guardian and protector of the weak and powerless.

The types of cases dealt with in the Laws of Hammurabi include judicial procedure, theft and robbery, slave sales and matters affecting slaves, agricultural and irrigation work and offences, pledges, debts, deposits and loans, real estate sales and rentals; marriage, matrimonial property and sexual offenses; inheritance, adoption and foster care; assault and bodily injuries; rates of hire for equipment, laborers and craftsmen; failure to complete contracted tasks; renters' and shepherds' liabilities; and goring oxen. But for our present study, I shall mainly direct the reader to an inspection of the laws which indicate the growing menace and power of the tamkarum class as it arose in Babylonia.

As did the previous two thousand years of Mesopotamian culture, the Laws of Hammurabi distinguished three classes of people: the *awilum* (the Haves), the *muskenum* (the Have-Nots), and the *wardum* (the slaves). So, nothing had changed in the social structure of Mesopotamia in two thousand years. The people were still accepting their ancient culture as being the same "as it had always been." However, the power and wealth of the moneylenders had increased tremendously in those two millennia, while the poverty and suffering of the people had deteriorated in like ratio.

Through the centuries, successive generations of the people were so gradually impoverished that the actual methods for causing their poverty went unnoticed. The great difference between the "Haves" and the "Have-Nots" was, of course, noticed by everybody. But the gradual impoverishment that had made it so, was not recognized as a growing financial cancer because it was accepted as "always having been here." Only the merchant-moneylenders knew that Secret Fraud #14 was the reason for their supremacy above the common man, that is, "Anyone who is allowed to lend-at-interest eventually owns the entire world."

Through their illiteracy, the people had no way of knowing that they were slowly being swindled and enslaved to the "Haves" as lifetime servants of the fraudulent money power of debt, usury, controlled wages, and warfare. This was not some accident of history and finance nor the results of some uncontrollable, Darwinian natural selection process because the moneylenders kept the account books and knew with precise craftiness how to squeeze the people for every shekel of silver and every man-hour of labor. The awilum (the Haves) left nothing to chance; they planned and schemed with vicious avarice. They knew how to swindle wealth. It was no accident of mindless evolution, but was a precise and willful application of intransigent greed and demonic cunning which was fueled with the astronomical profits of the Sumerian Swindle.

Dozens of duplicates and extracts of Hammurabi's laws have been recovered from a variety of sites in Mesopotamia as well as commentaries, references to his laws in a first millennium catalog, and a bilingual Sumerian-Akkadian manuscript. Some of the manuscripts date to Hammurabi's immediate successors in the first Dynasty of Babylon, while others are copies from a thousand years later. This wide and varied evidence attests to the enduring popularity of the Laws of Hammurabi, which was both an influence on and a reflection of contemporary literary, political, and legal thought. As a "great law giver," whose laws circulated throughout the ancient Near East for so many centuries, Hammurabi was undoubtedly the model upon which the Semitic goat-rustlers and Babylonian moneylenders would later base their own heroic myths in the fable of Moses. But more about that later.

Hammurabi directed the political expansion of his empire, and he organized a complex, sophisticated government and military bureaucracy to administer it. He defeated powerful rival kingdoms and extended his political and diplomatic influence throughout the ancient Near East in an expansion rivaled only by that achieved by his early contemporary to the north, Shamshi-Adad of Assyria. To give us a wider perspective of those people, it is from this same time frame that we have the Laws of Eshnunna to also consider.

Eshnunna was an Amorite-controlled kingdom in the Dayala River region east of Babylon which flourished for about 250 years between the fall of the Third Dynasty of Ur (about 2000 BC) and the rise of Hammurabi's Babylonian Empire (1750 BC). Hammurabi incorporated that kingdom into his own empire and no doubt had read their laws before writing his own. It is the differences between the three major law codes of Ur-Nammu (Sumerian), Eshnunna (Sumerian-Semite), and Hammurabi (Semitic) that will give us vital clues to the changes that were taking place among the people who wrote those laws and the people who suffered under them.

The Stele of Hammurabi, now in the Louvre, stands seven feet six inches high. On the top of the monument is a carved bas-relief of the Sun-god, Shamash (the God of Justice), receiving the homage of King Hammurabi. Beneath this carving is engraved the cuneiform text of the Laws. The laws themselves are sandwiched between a prologue and an epilogue [see Figure 14].

Figure 14

The prologue at the top of the stele begins with a claim that the gods called upon Hammurabi "to make justice visible in the land, to destroy the wicked person and the evil-doer, that the strong might not injure the weak." The prologue contains a series of titles in which Hammurabi boasts of his piety toward the gods and his care for their cities and shrines.

The epilogue at the bottom of the stele speaks of the purpose for writing down the laws, which is "to set right the orphan and widow ... and wronged person," and it goes on to recommend that succeeding rulers pay heed to Hammurabi's words, on pain of incurring the curses of the gods upon whom Hammurabi calls. The laws themselves consisted originally of about 280 sections, of which some 35 were erased from the stele in antiquity, presumably by the Elamite conqueror who took the monument to Susa. Fortunately, about half of the missing text can now be restored, partly from some diorite fragments which must have come from another monument of the same kind, and partly from clay tablets of various periods containing parts of Hammurabi's laws. These missing parts give a valuable indication of what the Elamite moneylenders disliked about Hammurabi's Laws.

The modern translation and publication of the Laws of Hammurabi in 1948 AD, stirred up a violent controversy among the Jews and the Bible-believing Christians, as well as the atheists. The Jews were violently opposed to anything that shook their monopoly over the history of the ancient Near East. They had spent the previous 3,000 years stamping into dust the clay tablets and burning the history books of all other people, and to have actual archaeological evidence which revealed their lies, has always been a good enough reason for the Jews to riot. They rioted when Jesus told the truth about them, too. So, modern-day examples of how they try to muffle the Truth with tears and loud screaming, is not something new for the Jews and this, their well-practiced ruse.

Since the establishment of the science of Assyriology in 1812, the boasts and grandiose claims of the Jews have slowly been whittled away by the discoveries of archeology. What the Jews were claiming in their own Old Testament as true stories of a wonderful gang of mighty Jewish kings and miracle-performing priests dwelling in their mountain fortress of Jerusalem, became, under archeological scrutiny, increasingly the story of a bunch of petty tribal goat-rustlers and lice-infested Hebrew bandits riding donkeys and hiding from their enemies in the rocky wilderness around Jerusalem. The famous "Holy Word of the Children of God" was proving to be the word of demonic liars.

So, of course, the Jews become violent whenever the truth is told about them because they have learned over the centuries that screaming at the tops of their lungs, tearing their shirts, yanking out their hair, jumping up and down, and crying rivers of crocodile tears, tends to draw peoples' attention away from the accusations against them and to concentrate on how "offended" the poor, innocent Jews were that anyone would doubt the word of these self-proclaimed "Children of God." Although they opposed all new discoveries which showed them to be liars, their ruse didn't work because their very opposition to the Truth, proved that they were frauds and charlatans and not at all truthful people.

Although modern Christians did not have the major investment in myths and historical hoaxes as did the Jews, some of them tended to oppose any new discoveries of archeology if those discoveries shook their basic beliefs in the "infallibility of the word of God" as found in the Bible. This so-called infallible "word of God," proved to be nothing other than a very fallible and false "word of the Jews," which only seemed true because it had been around longer than anybody could remember. And because the Jews had been destroying any annulling evidence for the previous 3,000 years, their lies in the Old Testament just had to be true because there were no ancient records to refute them—that is, until modern archaeology began to dig up and translate the original cuneiform archives from across the Near East.

But, in general, the Christians welcomed new archaeological discoveries as leading them to a better understanding of the Bible. Christians tended to look to archeology as a means of proving the Biblical stories. But the Jews tended to smear the archeologists as frauds and their discoveries as forgeries. This is a very different reaction of two Bible-based religions to the same archaeological discoveries. Why there was such a vast difference between the Christians seeking Truth and the hate-filled Jews seeking to perpetuate their lies, will become clearer in later chapters.

Without any doubt, the Laws of Hammurabi had been in existence many centuries before the period in which Moses allegedly had lived. Also without any doubt, the laws of Hammurabi frequently legislated for the same kind of circumstances, sometimes in almost identical terms, as those laws, supposedly of divine origin, which were associated with the name of Moses. Direct borrowing is indicated. Orthodox Jewish theologians, mentally wriggling in embarrassment, sought to lie about it and to claim that, where similarities could not be denied, the Hebrew laws showed a "higher ethical content." Apparently, the Jewish Orthodox theologians' "holiness" gave them a special ability to see "a higher ethical content" that was neither a fact nor in evidence.

The atheists and other opponents of religion gleefully argued that the Hebrew lawgiver (whether Moses or some later legislator using that name) had simply plagiarized, in the name of his God, as much of the existing Babylonian laws as suited him, adapting it to the more primitive society of the Hebrew goat-rustlers. One such writer stated dogmatically: "if there be any relationship between the Hebrew and the Babylonian legislations, there is only one possible conclusion, and that is that the Hebrew was borrowed from the earlier Babylonian." But the Hebrews did a lot more than just "borrow"—the Hebrews were the foremost thieves of the entire ancient Near East, as you shall see.

Forgeries in antiquity were by no means uncommon. But a forgery is not made from documents which do not exist; it is made from previously existing documents in order to qualify as a forgery. With each new archeological discovery, the screaming rabbis, with enraged spittle frothing around their beards, were shouting, "Fake!" However, they were more worried about some archeological discovery that would prove that their own "scriptures" were the actual fakes. Hammurabi's Laws were written in stone and dug out of 30 meters of solid dirt that had been in place for a thousand years before the Jewish "scriptures" were written. Laws written in stone are unchanging and survive throughout eternity. But the so-called "laws of Moses" were written on rotting goat skins and edited as required.

One of the greatest points of interest in the Laws of Hammurabi is that they show that the mild Sumerian laws had been superseded by the more barbaric Semitic principle of *lex talionis*, or the principle of "an eye for an eye." This thoroughly barbaric Semitic principle, basic to the laws of Babylonia and the laws of Assyria, is the same unmodified laws of the modern Jews. Why those rather fair and benign laws of the Sumerians were replaced by the cruel and more repressive laws of the Semites, will become clearer as we compare them one with another. It is unnecessary and overly tedious to compare each of the various laws of Babylonia item by item. We only need to inspect the ones that show most clearly the awilum (the Haves) using those Laws to protect and to enrich themselves. And what a coincidence! Just like the modern Jews do today!

It is from this juncture in our history that most of our modern-day catastrophes and tribulations arise, where the laws are used to manipulate mankind for the benefit of the moneylending parasites.

The Sealand Dynasty

Hammurabi, the great king and servant of the gods, was too powerful for the schemes of the merchant-moneylenders to succeed during his lifetime. After Hammurabi died, his son, Samsu-iluna (1749-1712 BC), was initially successful in emulating his father's policies. But soon the south was in revolt. The remaining Sumerians (the Southerners) had grown weary of Amorite greed and ruthlessness. In 1738 BC, the south fell to Iliman (Iluma-ilum), founder of the Sealand dynasty, who ruled the Babylonian lands as far north as Nippur. The Sealanders had begun to move into the area shortly after Hammurabi's death.

This new Sealand Dynasty, under the influence of the Sumerian priests, appears to have taken on the mantle of the earlier rulers of Isin as an attempt was made to bring back civilization "as it had always been" where the people served the gods and the kings protected the people.

This Sealand Dynasty provided refuge for the Sumerian priests who moved away from the Amorites of Babylon and set up their Sumerian centers of culture and learning in the south, once again at the ancient Sumerian holy city of Nippur. Not only did the Sealanders encroach on the immediate territory of Babylon in the years after Hammurabi's death, but in the early 16th century BC, they appear to have succeeded, at least briefly, to the Babylonian throne. This we infer from the King List which includes the Sealand Dynasty "of Urukug," a city otherwise unknown.

But the Sealanders were not Babylon's only enemies. Samsu-iluna's ninth year-name mentions *the Kassite army*. This is the first reference to the Kassites who, some 150 years later, would inherit the hegemony of Babylon. Where did the Kassites come from?

The Kassites were cheap labor imported from the mountains to the east into the agricultural region of western Babylonia on the Euphrates. The Kassites arrived as cheap labor and as buyers of the foreclosed farms that were being sold by the merchant-moneylenders. But the Kassites were not fools. They could clearly see the advantages for themselves to occupy the land and the disadvantages to the Babylonian farmers. So, their natural suspicions prompted them to ask, "Why are you selling the land to us? Are you not betraying your own people by doing this?"

The Babylonian moneylenders had been born and raised in Babylonia. So, one might think that if they were not filled with a patriotic enthusiasm toward the good of their country, then at least they would have a friendly warmth in their hearts toward their neighbors and fellow citizens. But parasites only recognize their fellow parasites as friends, while all of them recognize their victims as victims. So, the tamkarum impoverished, betrayed, and dispossessed their own people by importing cheap foreign labor and selling the land to foreigners.

Shrewdly peering through their slit-like, half-closed eyelids as they sized up their questioners. Those wily merchant-moneylenders, those "gentlemen" and expert salesmen that they were, always had a ready answer to overcome such an objection:

"What are those people to us? They are not our friends because they hate us and wish to do us harm. We have loaned them silver and helped them to buy goods and to purchase property. As the great god Marduk is our witness, we have done everything that we can to loan them silver and help them buy the best farms and the finest orchards. But still they hate us for our goodness and generosity because they are full of bigotry and hatred. But you are our friends. You can protect us from those who hate us. So, we will give our friends and protectors a good deal in buying whatever goods and properties you want because we own much lands and will make you an excellent bargain. Because of our friendship, we will loan our friends silver in any amount at low interest rates. And to further show our friendship, we have many wonderful daughters who will make fine wives for your sons."

And so, the bargain was made. The Kassites had no reason to hate the Babylonian moneylenders—yet. They accepted the offers of cheap land. And to prove their friendship and generosity to the new immigrants, those poor Kassites who could not afford the full price, the tamkarum let them buy on time at low, low interest rates. Like blood-sucking fleas, the moneylenders jumped from their old victims who hated them onto their new victims, who innocently accepted the moneylenders as their friends and guides and mentors. The ancient snake, once again with soft words and low interest rates, coiled around its prey. Its bite would come later.

But the moneylenders did not destroy the people among whom they had been allowed to live by using their own money. Every particle of gold and silver and every square measure of land which the merchant-money-lenders claimed as their own, they had swindled. They had destroyed the people among whom they had been allowed to live by first swindling away their silver and gold, and then using that peoples' very own money against them. Those parasites had sucked away the wealth of the entire nation. But they had not earned it. They had not worked for it. They had gotten it all for free because that is how the Sumerian Swindle operates. Thus it was, that the moneylenders ate their fill while their victims perished.

Yet again, the moneylenders had betrayed their own people. Yet again, their immigration of foreigners as cheap labor undermined the social and ethnic integrity of the nation. Yet again, the moneylenders were able to impoverish their own people by lowering wages by hiring foreign labor and selling foreclosed farmland to foreigners. Yet again, the immigrants took over the lands wherein they previously had been guest workers. This change in the social fabric was gradual, taking place over a century. Again repeating the pattern, once the Kassites had reached a large enough proportion of the population, they took over the country. And their "friends," the Babylonian merchant-moneylenders, helped them to do it.

Political Upheaval

The period of the 17th to 16th centuries BC was a time of great political change in Western Asia, and the Kassites were but one of a number of non-Semitic peoples—the Hurrians and Hittites are others whom we shall meet shortly—who began to exert pressure from the north on the weakening kingdom of Babylonia. The linguistic affinities of the Kassite language have yet to be established, but some features of their religion suggest descent from Aryan Indo-European peoples.

As their numbers increased and as the merchant-moneylenders sold the foreclosed properties and farms to these foreigners, Kassite personal names began to appear with increasing frequency on Babylonian business documents. Like all of the other foreigners who had taken over the lands into which they had been invited by the merchant-moneylenders, the Kassites began their steady influx into the country peacefully as hired workers and land buyers. By the end of the 1700s BC, Kassite settlers had obtained real estate even within the city of Babylon itself. Yet, it is clear that, beginning with the reign of Samsu-iluna (1749-1712 BC) onwards, the Kassites were also a military threat because Kassite tradition implied the founding of an independent state at this time somewhere on the borders of Babylonia on the middle Euphrates.

Remember, political power comes from occupation of the land. Not land deeds, not national boundaries, not ethnic majority, not claims of ownership, not claims of historical precedence but occupation alone gives ownership and power; and this occupation is not necessarily achieved by military means.

Once the foreigners had been settled on the land by the treasonous moneylenders, and once their numbers had increased to a near-majority, instead of being the smiling and friendly guest workers and hired laborers who were striving to ingratiate themselves and fit into the dominant society, their attitudes changed into the less-friendly demeanor of land-owners and usurpers. They did not have to pretend to be friendly in order to be accepted by the Babylonians. Once these alien laborers and petty land owners had occupied the land, they could do as they pleased to control it.

Samsu-iluna maintained some control to the northwest, but the middle Euphrates was certainly lost to Babylonia by the time of his son, Abi-eshuh (1711–1684 BC), whose reign is notable for little more than his failure to catch the Sealand ruler Iliman by "damming the Tigris."

Although there appears to have been no serious challenge to their authority from the other cities of Sumer and Akkad, the last kings of Babylon's First Dynasty clearly presided over a kingdom that was dwindling steadily in both territory and prestige. The Sealanders were trying to reestablish a revival of Sumerian culture in the south, and the Kassites were buying up land all around Babylonia. The power of Hammurabi's Dynasty was weakening.

However, literary and economic documents preserved from this period continue to reflect an apparently prosperous society in which the arts flourished. For example, the scribe who copied the only known Old Babylonian epic cycle of the Flood Legend, known as "Atrahasis," worked in Sippar at this time. Even though there were still no Jews anywhere to be found on the entire planet, the early Biblical stories as found in the Old Testament—such as the Flood, Noah and the Ark, the Laws of Moses (Hammurabi), Sampson (Gilgamesh), the Garden of Eden, Genesis, Adam and Eve, and Job, were already being written by the Babylonians—and certainly not by the lying Jews. At that time, there were no Jews anywhere on the entire planet, but there were plenty of treasonous merchant-moneylenders.

The national state that Hammurabi established did not long endure after his death. But by defeating the major city-states of Babylonia and uniting the country, if only briefly under the hegemony of Babylon, he achieved a political result which was to affect the history of Mesopotamia for the next two millennia. No longer was there a Sumeria, but the entire region from the Southern Sea (Persian Gulf) to the borders of Assyria became known as Babylonia. Babylon became the established seat of kingship, a position she was to maintain unchallenged until the Greeks built Seleucia 1500 years later. As a religious center for the many gods, Babylon survived until the 1st century AD, while the mystique surrounding its name remains with us today. Much of Babylon's religious hold over the country involved the Semitic cult of Marduk, which replaced the Sumerian god Enlil of Nippur as the bestowal of legitimate kingship. But this religious transformation did not take place until long after Hammurabi's reign.

Hammurabi's son and successor, Samsu-iluna (~1749-1712 BC), tried to follow his father's policies. But the moneylenders were not pleased with the Law Code of Hammurabi and sought to establish more of a "free market" where they could practice the Sumerian Swindle and its related frauds unrestricted. Within ten years, Samsu-iluna gave up most of the new empire. In 1738 BC the south fell to Iliman, founder of the Sealand dynasty, who ruled Babylonia as far north as Nippur. The so-called "Dynasty of the Sealands" continued to control a region approximately the size of ancient Sumeria for more than two hundred more years, outliving, indeed, Hammurabi's First Dynasty of Babylon. The political history of Samsu-iluna's successors, Abi-Eshuh (~1711-1684 BC), Ammi-ditana (~1683-1647 BC), and Ammi-saduqa (~1646-1626 BC), was largely a matter of small-scale border campaigns and work on defensive walls, perhaps indicating an awareness of the possibility of attack.

Even with the Sealanders taking control of the southern lands and the Kassites increasing their land ownership throughout Babylonia, there was no hint of impending doom to Hammurabi's Dynasty. The fatal blow, when it fell, came not from the troublesome Sealanders or the Kassites but from far to the north in Asia Minor, where the Hittites, an Indo-European Aryan people, had created a rapidly growing kingdom. From its capital of Hattusha, a king named *Murshili* (~1620-1595 BC), a contemporary of Samsu-ditana of Babylon, attacked northwestern Syria and then swept down the Euphrates toward Babylon without opposition. Murshili must have appeared to the unprepared Samsu-ditana like a thunder clap.

Surprisingly, it was not just the wealth of Babylon that Murshili coveted, but also the fabulous wealth of Egypt which was being carried to Babylon by the Babylonian merchant-moneylenders. At the time of king Murshili's attack, the merchant-moneylenders of Babylonia had been plundering Egypt for the previous 35 years. The huge amounts of gold from the temples of Egypt had been melted down and shipped to the temples of Babylon for safe keeping. Such a fabulously wealthy temptation was more than King Murshili could resist—both the *gold of Babylon* and the *gold of Egypt* all in one place, stored in the Babylonian mud-brick temples and under the terrifying protection of Marduk, the god of thunder. But Murshili had his own Indo-European gods and he wasn't afraid of thunder. Let's turn now to the story of how the Babylonians plundered Egypt.

CHAPTER 10

THE HYKSOS TAKE CONTROL OF EGYPT: 1630 TO 1523 BC

Before considering the Assyrian Empire which was growing stronger on the northern borders of Babylonia, let's have a look to the west, across the Syrian desert at a slightly different population of those Semitic goat-rustlers. It is not the Semitic Amorites, who had created the Babylonian and Assyrian empires that we shall consider, but their flea-bitten cousins and uncles who were riding their donkeys around Northern Arabia and Palestine as small tribes of bandits and sheep stealers. Historically, they have been called the Hyksos, but they were a very different kind of people than what has been assumed of them by the historians and archeologists.

Simultaneously, with the beginning of the history of Assyria but within the geographical area of Canaan and Palestine, also begins the history of a Semitic people who have never been any more than a fly speck on the tail of a donkey. With Semitic craftiness and deceit, those people have claimed to be among the most ancient—indeed, the very most ancient—of all people on Earth. Little by little, I will weave the background of those deceivers into the present history. But first, let's review who those people were.

If you inspect a map of the distribution of the goat- and sheep-raising areas with a map of the grain-growing areas of the ancient Near East, you will see that the land where goats and sheep can forage is much more extensive and rugged than the lands where grain can be grown (recall Map 4, Chapter 2). Goats, especially, are famous for being able to eat anything. Whether succulent green sprouts in a field of spring greens or the spines of a cactus, goats get by on just about any plant that grows. Sheep, too, can forage even barren areas where plants grow in mere clumps separated by barren dirt but, of course, they thrive in fields of wild grasses. However, to grow crops of grain and vegetables, you need reasonably level soil, sufficient water, sun, and labor. But even the rockiest hills can support goats and sheep without the labor of digging in the rocky soil.

So, the roaming bands of shepherds who ranged the arid hills and mountains of the ancient Near East did so both inside and outside of the boundaries of settled areas of farms and villages. The wild areas where the footsteps of man were seldom found was their abode. As long as they could scare away the lions and jackals with their slings and arrows, then their goats and sheep provided them with plenty of milk and meat, wool and goat hair for weaving, bone and horn for implements and decorations. Living in goat-hair and woolen tents and traveling by donkey and on foot, they spent their days roaming about the ancient Near East in search of water and food. They did not know how to farm. But even if they had wanted to settle into a farming life, by this time in the history of the ancient Near East of 1700 BC, the best farming areas had already been settled by other people.

Over the previous two thousand years, robust civilizations based on agriculture had grown up within the grain-growing regions. The peoples of Sumeria and Babylonia, Assyria, Ugarit, Hattiland, Canaan, and Egypt had long held the territories that gave them sustenance.

Because the Fertile Crescent, the breadbasket of the ancient Near East, had for so long been inhabited by farmers, the goat herders were mainly restricted to the wilderness. And that was okay with them since their herds provided everything that they needed. Or if there was anything that they wanted in the villages and cities, they could trade their goats and sheep for grain and salt; they got trinkets and copper cooking pots for the wives; and bronze daggers and swords for the young men. Or they would steal what they could not afford to buy.

Relying on the hidden paths and difficult terrain of the wilderness for protection, those roaming bands of Amorite goat-rustlers, as has been previously stated, were a constant source of anxiety to the villages and cities. Surprise raids followed by quick retreat into the trackless wastelands, or stealthy stealing into a farm or a village at night to burglarize and run away before discovery, were the favorite methods used by the Amorite shepherds. The farming peoples were wary of them but, at the same time, wanted to be on the friendliest of terms with them so as to avoid enmity.

In times of drought, where watering holes dried up and the land was too parched even for goats, these roaming Semitic shepherds would beg for a place to graze their flocks near the well-watered farming communities. Not so much out of compassion, but more from self-serving politics, those shepherds were usually granted permission. This, so as to keep them as docile, peaceable, and as friendly as possible but also as to not drive them, through hunger and thirst, into a desperation leading to banditry and warfare. Between the farmers and the nomads, there was always an uneasy truce broken with sporadic banditry and sudden raids followed by punishing expeditions by the king's troops or the local militia, chasing the shepherds back into the wilderness.

Birth-control through extended nursing of the children had kept Sumerian populations within the natural bounds and the natural needs of a farming people. The mothers of Sumeria practiced natural birth control by suckling their children for two years and thus producing families of well-spaced children while saving themselves from the exhaustions of child-bearing. The mothers of Egypt nursed their children for three years, which also kept the sizes of their families small and produced a slow increase in population.

But the Semitic Amorites practiced polygamy as promiscuous as their billy goats. Through their increase in numbers from their many wives, they quickly became more numerous than the city dwellers. High birth-rates, celebrated with the exhortations from their lice-covered priests to "go forth and multiply like the sands of the sea" became standard operating procedure for the goat-herding nomads who wanted to displace the farmers from their land and to make it their own. The wandering Semitic goat-rustlers celebrated the mothers who produced eight or ten or twelve children, just as the Orthodox Jews and Hasidics do in modern times, and for the very same reasons: to out-breed and out-number the people whom they wanted to dispossess—even resorting to genocide to reduce the populations of those whose property they coveted.

In addition to their large families, the interpersonal and inter-tribal relations of their patriarchal genealogies gave those wandering tribes the political ability to merge with other tribes into larger alliances for war and banditry with a minimum of haggling. When combined, the genealogically-related tribes gave them sufficient numbers to usually pose a unified threat to the towns and civilized lands.

Women who married into other tribes, brought with them the stories and genealogies of their own tribes, in addition to bride gifts. Thus, the clever stratagems and thefts that were famous among their own people, became part of the common lore of the tribes into which those women married. This sly sorcery was only true because these fly-speckled goat-thieves all believed that it was true. So, they parasitically increased their numbers by claiming that the children of their daughters who had married into tribe-B were actually the children of the tribe-A. And why? Because they had all magically inherited the same ancestry.

But I am getting ahead of this history because, in 1700 BC, there were no Jews in existence in the entire world—yet.

City Cousins, Country Cousins

As the Semitic Amorites became civilized by buying into and subverting the Sumerian cities, their sheep-stealing cousins who were still living in tents, learned of the methods in which those usurpers had been able to take over the properties of other people. And they wanted to do that, too.

Stories of their clever stratagems of banditry, burglary, and armed raids upon the farmers, became common traditions, as those nomadic shepherds majestically galloped forth upon their donkeys while herding their sheep and goats across the hot, dusty grasslands and deserts of the ancient Near East.

By 1700 BC, Assyria had not yet grown into its full power. While Babylonia was thriving under Hammurabi's Dynasty, the merchant-moneylenders were already undermining the country with the immigrant labor of the Kassites.

The Babylonian merchant-moneylenders knew from vast experience that the internal weaknesses caused by an immigrant population would set the country on the path to destruction. They knew this from their long and successful application of Secret Fraud #11 of the Sumerian Swindle: "Dispossessing the people brings wealth to the dispossessor, yielding the greatest profit for the bankers when the people are impoverished." Impoverishing the people always brought the merchant-moneylenders great profits from the good deals in lands and heirlooms sold cheaply by desperate victims. The moneylenders always had plenty of silver to take advantage of desperate and starving people. Also, they did not need to work for that silver because the Sumerian Swindle gave it to them for free. As the people labored and sweated, the Babylonian moneylenders enjoyed iced drinks while sitting in the shade and being fanned by their slaves.

Passed down to their sons from over a thousand years of experience, the moneylenders and merchants knew that the people among whom they were allowed to live without being hanged, were always destroyed and dispossessed by the Sumerian Swindle. The allegiance of the merchant-moneylenders has always been to their own personal profits, their own personal safety and to their own crime families and to no one else. The Sumerian Swindle had placed them at the pinnacle of wealth and they stayed at that apex only through its ruthless application married with deceit. And what is the child which comes forth from ruthlessness and deceit? Some "thing" that is very bad for all of mankind.

The Sumerian Swindle had allowed all of the merchant-moneylender guilds to profit from treason, basically because they had supplied weapons, provisions, and money to both sides in every war—at high prices and high interest rates, of course, They had swindled away the wealth from every man, woman, and child, enchaining many of them into slavery while betraying all of them. Although they had assumed for themselves the "prestige" of great wealth, they were hated by everyone.

However, even with all of their wealth and power over the people and the kings, the merchant-moneylenders had one, very great weakness. That weakness was *the actual, physical weight, volume, and burden* of their great piles of silver and gold which had to be concealed, guarded, and protected. During times of crises, it was very difficult to run away with a silver and gold treasure weighing fifty tons. Even a kilo of silver was not easy to conceal by swallowing it. But as long as they could keep their bullion hidden, no one would know how very much wealth that they had. Hidden from sight, the vast amounts would not engender surprised outrage from their many victims, who would never see how very much the moneylenders had been robbing them. But how could they guard their piles of gold and silver without attracting attention to the huge quantities? It was a great worry for them that every building in Mesopotamia was made out of mud bricks and was as easy to break into as digging a hole in a wall with a pick and shovel. Also, how could they trust the guards not to pilfer or steal?

Only the temples offered an answer to their fervent prayers to the Moon God. The temples were the most secure places to keep valuables because the temples were used as the banks. They were the safest places for the merchant-moneylenders to deposit their treasures. The temples were safe from theft, handy of access, and the silver and gold on deposit could be withdrawn on demand as good investments and good deals appeared.

In business, the merchant-moneylenders were merciless and cruel. But in hiding their silver, they were studiously humble and publicly pious, making loud prayers before the idols of the gods in whichever temple protected their bullion. It was difficult to find a more sincerely devout devotee to his god than a moneylender, kneeling before the idol of his god and beseeching the god to protect his gold.

For these reasons, the merchant-moneylenders always sought the protection of the temple treasuries, guarded by both the priests, who charged a deposit fee, and by the mighty gods who would strike with lightning bolt, earthquake, and dread diseases anyone who pilfered the holy silver and gold from within their holy sanctuaries. At least, that was what the people in those days believed. The moneylenders believed it, too. But their faith in the gods was always weakened whenever a king from an attacking army would steal everything that they had.

Stealing is the basic prestidigitation art and pseudo-science of the Sumerian Swindle. Beneath their phony veneer of fancy clothes and expensive jewelry, the moneylenders, themselves, are thieves. So, they are always looking for what else they can steal besides your money and property. The very numbers in the merchant-moneylenders' fraudulent accounting tablets generate huge sums that in reality do not even exist because they are mere numbers, but not actual bullion.

When the accounting ledgers of Babylonia claimed that the moneylenders were owed a billion shekels of silver but only half a million actually existed in the entire kingdom, it was impossible for the moneylenders to get that billion shekels, unless the people of the entire kingdom could find another source of silver and gold outside of the kingdom with which to pay them.

This is where the thievery of *international banking* comes into play. This is where one kingdom must actually rob another kingdom of their gold and silver so that the robbers can pay it to the moneylenders. The merchant-moneylenders did not have to do the actual robbery, themselves, as long as they could inveigle others to do go to war and do the dirty work for them. Whatever gold and silver was looted, would eventually come into the hands of the merchant-moneylenders anyway, through commerce and the payment of debts to them. Only then, could the accounting numbers on the clay tablets be manipulated into "balanced books" whereby the phantom numbers are replaced by real silver and real gold "magically" appearing in the moneylenders' strong rooms from the piles of stolen loot carried to Babylon from the temples of whichever country had been successfully attacked.

Babylonia, although wealthy and powerful, was not a very large kingdom (recall Map 12, Chapter 9). So, the merchant-moneylenders easily owned and controlled all of the silver and gold in Babylonia. That is, they either had physical possession of it or it was out-on-loan and owed to them. And that was a problem. There were never enough physical shekels of gold and silver to repay the imaginary shekels indicated on the accounting tablets.

The colossal amounts of gold and silver imaginarily "owed" to the merchant-moneylenders could never be repaid unless another source for gold and silver could be imported from outside of Babylonia to replace the empty and fantastic numbers. In the ancient near East, the only huge source of such wealth was the ancient land of Egypt, a land that had never known foreign conquest and which had been accumulating gold in its temples, palaces, and tombs for nearly two thousand years.

But stealing from distant Egypt was more difficult than stealing from neighboring kingdoms. Although Babylonia was at the height of its wealth, power and influence during the years of Hammurabi and his sons, Egypt was too far away for a military campaign. Babylon was simply not capable of a successful military assault. Neither could the Babylonian people be inveigled into going to war in such a distant country for no other reason than to steal gold from its temples and thereby stir up the wrath of the mighty gods of Egypt. So, seizing the wealth of Egypt could not be accomplished with Babylonian military might.

But there was a way to take that wealth by using the cunning stratagems of the moneylenders and their network of greedy merchants. Even better, such an assault could be done much more cheaply than by using the Babylonian army.

Although Egypt had an even drier desert climate than Mesopotamia and depended upon the Nile River to sustain its agriculture, any other similarity to Mesopotamia ended there. Mesopotamia had the Euphrates and Tigris Rivers and their many tributaries as well as a relatively easy access by many tribes from surrounding areas. But Egypt had just the Nile River. It was surrounded by thousands of miles of waterless deserts as well as the barriers of the Mediterranean and Red Seas, all of which protected it from all other peoples during several thousands of years. Thus, Egypt developed a unique civilization uninfluenced by, and unlike, any other.

What was even more unique about Egypt—and extremely irritating to the moneylenders of Babylon—was that Egypt had reached a high level of civilization *without using any money*. Unlike the Mesopotamian empires, Egypt did not need, nor did it use, silver or gold for commercial trade. Neither did it have any guilds of moneylenders parasitizing the wealth and sucking it into their own, personal coffers or sending it away to distant lands. Most of Egypt's gold and gemstones were still in the country in huge hoards, derived from over two thousand years of mining, jewelry making, sculptures, gold sheeting, and art works. Of course, the Egyptians traded their gold, copper, ivory, linen garments, and wheat to other countries for such vital commodities as lumber; but within the entire country, itself, they had no use for money of any kind.

Egypt was a theocracy similar to the earliest God-conscious civilization of Sumeria, basing its culture upon knowledge of and service to the gods. Egyptian sculptures, bas-reliefs, and writings indicate that Egypt had a higher knowledge of God and of the spiritual power of mankind than did the Mesopotamians. But it still had not achieved those highest of all spiritual levels which the Stone Age Irish of Newgrange and the Celtic Europeans of Gavrinis, France, had achieved by 3500 BC—five hundred years before the first pyramids had been built.

In 1700 BC, Egypt's theocratic structure and kingly administration had never been subjected to the intrigues and wars caused by merchant-moneylenders and private financiers, such as had been conspired in Mesopotamia. When the Egyptians fought other peoples, it was never conflicts about money or wealth, as was so often the case in Mesopotamia. They fought to defend their country from foreign raiders and to keep their borders secure.

Modern archeologists know that ancient Egypt was a land where nothing was more important to the Egyptian people than the gods of their religion and the fructifying waters of the Nile. The entire Egyptian culture revolved around the gods and the regular flooding of the Nile. The people lived because the gods gave them life, and they expressed their religious resolve and piety in every moment of every day with prayer and joy.

This religious consciousness was extended even to their kings, who were believed to be not just a representative of god on earth, but actually a living god incarnate. With their Pharaoh as a god, whose duty it was to protect and administer his people, Egypt prospered and the people enjoyed a great spiritual power, expressed in their architecture, sculptures, bas-reliefs, paintings, and literature.

The name, "Pharaoh," means "Great House." Thus, the Pharaoh was the Great House in which his people lived. When a new king arose, he made a royal procession to all of the ancient shrines and assured the various religious orders that he would respect their privileges and increase them.

As a part of this ancient tradition, in the first or second year of his reign, Pharaoh would set out to raid some near-by lands in order to show that he was a mighty warrior as well as a god. He fought in person, and the custom demanded that he should slay a number of prisoners with his own hand. Representatives of the vanquished peoples or tribes were made to kneel before him with their arms tied together behind their backs at the elbows, and the pharaoh smashed in their skulls with a stone-headed or a copper-headed mace, or he cut off their heads with a bronze or copper scimitar. These events were celebrated on temple walls in huge bas reliefs showing the pharaoh accomplishing these public feats. But these military campaigns were mainly a demonstration of military power as a sort of religious ceremony and a show-of-strength to frighten away would-be aggressors and to maintain the longer peace.

The history of Egypt shows clearly that the Egyptians, as a nation, were wholly lacking in military spirit and that they abhorred war. Whenever it was necessary to do so, they were ready to fight in a primitive fashion for their fields and canals and homes. But for the defense of their long, narrow country as a whole, they were by nature and by temperament more interested in the religious life and their peaceful meditations upon eternity.

Egyptian nationalism had never developed among them because no one had ever attacked them with anything more than a few outlying raids by desert bandit tribes. So, they had very little of a spirit of nationalism under their Old Kingdom (~2700–2200 BC) or their Middle Kingdom (~2130–1640 BC). The principal object of all of their wars was never for the acquisition of booty and slaves but for the maintaining of Egyptian borders. However, after they had been attacked by the Hyksos, this ancient attitude changed with the beginning of the New Kingdom (~1550–1085 BC). In all of their thousands of years of history, Egypt never possessed anything that could be called a "standing army" until the beginning of the New Kingdom after the Hyksos had been expelled.

Although the Nile River is 3,473 miles long, that portion of the Nile Valley which is Egypt, lays along only the northern 600 miles of the river. Egyptian territory on both sides of the Nile is often so narrow that one can stand on the dry desert edge where the green plants cannot grow, look across the green fields down to the river's edge, then look across the river to the greenery on the other side, and across those green fields see the beginnings of the desert beyond that. Farmland was so precious that the Egyptians built their famous pyramids and temples on the waterless desert away from those yearly Nile floods which brought fresh soil to the river margins where farming was possible in an otherwise harsh desert environment.

Egyptian territory lay open on both sides of the Nile to the attacks of the war-like bandits of the deserts. But this rarely occurred because there were so few desert tribes which could live in such a harsh environment as the Sahara Desert. Invasion from the north and south was always easy for a determined foe since natural geographic barriers from those directions were few. But there were no determined foes until quite late in their history to take advantage of these weaknesses of terrain. Aside from occasional attacks by bandit tribes, Egypt was protected by its deserts from attacking armies of the distant kingdoms for most of its history. So, it was able to peacefully build its unique civilization.

From the earliest days, Egyptians lived in mud-brick houses but their temples were built of stone. Modern people can learn a lot from the ancient peoples even in this respect. Everyone who has lived for any length of time in either Egypt or Mesopotamia will admit that, provided that the walls are thick enough, mud-brick houses are preferable to those built according to the European model. And they are completely eco-friendly and recyclable mud, unlike the synthetic trash which is the construction materials of a modern house.

Every year about the middle of June, the heavy rains that fall in Sudan and Abyssinia cause the Nile to rise and to crest in Egypt sometime in October, after which the planting season begins. The principal crops were wheat, barley, beans, lentils, millet, vetches, lupin, clover, flax, cotton, cucumbers, melons, leeks, onions, dates, pomegranate, carobs, figs and papyrus. In all periods, the Egyptians were primarily vegetarians in diet though, of course, various large and small cattle, fish, ducks, and geese were also eaten.

The average Egyptian was by nature a cheerful, joyous person, fond of amusement and pleasure, and his greatest desire was to "make a good day," to eat, drink, and be merry. They loved to assemble in the "house of beer" and gossip with their friends. But unlike in Mesopotamia, these were not taverns owned by the moneylenders because Egypt did not have a need for money. As a joyous and religious people, they bartered in good faith with one another. Workers were paid in rations such as was common in Sumeria before the moneylenders had betrayed the people with the Sumerian Swindle.

But as much as they enjoyed life and as much as they liked to party and rejoice, they were, after all, a religious people whose main preoccupation in life was to attain a happy hereafter in the immortal realm of the gods.

The moneylenders of Babylonia also shared this philosophy about enjoying life, except for the last part; they did not believe in an everlasting life because for them, the hereafter was a world of gloom. So, whatever evils that they did in this life for their own pleasure and however many people they destroyed for their own benefit, didn't matter to them as long as they got what they wanted. The Babylonian merchant-moneylenders were a much different people—ruthless, materialistic Semites who envied the gold of the god-conscious, *Caucasian* Egyptians. Yes, in addition to the evidence that one's own eyes can see from the paintings, bas-reliefs, and sculptures that the Egyptians created as portrayals of themselves, modern DNA evidence also proves that Egypt was a Caucasian civilization.

Throughout Egyptian history, the individual Egyptian was both by nature and by habit a moral and religious person. But he was also extremely practical because the aim of all of his moral and religious efforts was to secure for himself ease, comfort, and prosperity in this world and a life of everlasting joy and happiness in the next world. Can the modern Christians, Buddhists, or Hindus ask for any more from their own religions?

Gods Everywhere

Like the beliefs of most of the ancient peoples throughout the world at that time, Egyptians believed that every locality had its own resident gods. These gods could be flattered, cajoled, begged, and wheedled into granting requests and bribed with offerings. Offerings became a principal act of worship at all periods of Egyptian history. With offerings, the temples thereby became wealthy. Offerings and donations are a reflection of the piety of the people throughout the ancient times up to the present. They are a result of simple religious devotion common to all religions and to all people. A material offering is a giving-up of material goods and an acceptance of the rewards of a spiritual life. Making offerings to God is an act of pious contrition and devoted love. It is a necessary act of worship.

To help them understand their duties to the gods, an extensive religious system had evolved in Egypt. As one example, the employees of just one temple, the Temple of Amon in the reign of Rameses III, numbered 62,626 persons. This shows that the cult was in actuality a social and family system that supported not only the temple staff but the families of the priests and all employees as well. A detailed list of the offerings that Rameses III made to the temples of Thebes, Abydos, and Heliopolis and the amount of food and gifts was truly huge.

The Egyptian priests were genuine devotees and not mere loafers and parasites of society. Not only did they offer their people solace and wisdom, but the priests of Egypt had some very real mental and spiritual powers aside from the reputed magical powers for which they were famous throughout the Near East. The Egyptian texts make it quite clear that the priests possessed spiritual, occult, and psychological powers of a remarkable character. These powers are common to anyone who can spend long hours in prayer and meditation. But spiritual powers are not common in modern times because modern people have been seduced and deceived by the machinations of the world's biggest liars.

For the ordinary Egyptian—just as in Mesopotamia—the road to success and prosperity could only be traversed by knowing how to read and write. Thus, extraordinary respect was given to the profession of scribe and to the scribe, himself.

But what the scribes wrote about their priests was not always reliable. For example, one of the priests of Egypt was supposed to have had the power "of dividing the water in a lake into two parts and making one part to stand on the other." You, Dear Reader, will also be familiar with a trick that the Egyptian sorcerers could do by changing a rod into a snake. By pressing a part of the neck of a cobra, it could be made to straighten itself like a rod, and when the pressure was removed, the creature assumed its normal form once again. Now you know from where such stories originally came. But they did not come from the Jews.

The Egyptian religion was not just a collection of conjuror's tricks to impress the country bumpkins. It contained a very high knowledge of the spiritual powers of mankind. The religious texts carved upon the walls of tombs, temples, sarcophagi, and surviving papyri show that the Egyptians throughout their long history worshipped everything from birds to beasts. These facts, to the benighted blindness of the atheistic modern scientists, has led them to the false assumption that the ancient Egyptians were idolatrous fools. After all, what modern person in their right mind would worship a hawk or a cat?

However, it is not wise for modern people to scoff at the ancient religions because many of the ancient people had secret knowledge and special powers that modern people are lacking. The key to such knowledge is most easily understood by we modern people who know our own Life Force or "Qi" (pronounced "chee," and also spelled "Chi"). This spiritual power is fully discussed in *The Monsters of Babylon*. It is an esoteric power that has been alluded to in the art works of many ancient cultures, all using the artistic conventions unique to each culture.

Modern scientists are unaware of their own Qi. That is the reason that none of the archeologists have ever been able to understand the real secrets of ancient Egypt—nor of any other ancient civilization. Modern scientists lack the fundamental, human, spiritual skills necessary, simply because they do not look into themselves to see what is there. They look outward at ancient cultures and artifacts, wondering what they are. But they do not look inward at themselves as living Beings in order to find the basis of all human cultures and the reasons the artifacts were created as they were. They do not seek, so they do not find.

Although modern people and modern scientists are completely blind to them, Egypt's high spiritual attainments were quite obvious to the people of the ancient Near East. They beheld the noble and upright Egyptians with high regard and awe. Their spiritual power was evident to everyone who met them. Their noble spirits and peaceful contentment were always with them, wherever they traveled. But, in general, Egyptians did not travel much. Protected by their deserts and nurtured by the Nile, they had just about everything that they needed. And because Upper Egypt also had gold deposits, the Egyptians had, along with abundant grain harvests, the wealth to trade for anything that they needed, such as wooden planks and beams from Lebanon.

Life Without Money

But with all of Egypt's great wealth and the religious attainments and contentment of its people, there was one thing that Egypt did not have, even though all of the other civilizations had this thing in great quantities. After its first two thousand years of high civilization, Egypt did not have, nor did it use, any money.

This is not to say that the Egyptians were poor. To modern people, poverty is equated with "not having any money." But this false concept is promoted by the moneylenders, bankers, and financiers who steal the wealth of entire nations both by using the ancient Sumerian Swindle and by manipulating the False Money which they control. (Gold, silver, and bankers' notes are all types of False Money. For a discussion of True Money, see *Monsters of Babylon*.)

Poverty is not a lack of money; poverty is a lack of the Eight Essentials of Life—Air, Water, Food, Clothing, Shelter, Spouse, Children, and God. Knowing this, the modern demon moneylenders try to control the Eight Essentials of Life through their control of money. If they can control the Eight Essentials of Life, they can completely enslave mankind to their greed and lust. But they can only do this if they control the money.

The Sumerian Swindle and the use of silver as a means of commercial exchange, impoverished both the people and the kings of the entire ancient Near East for the previous 2,000 years. But in the dry deserts and silent vastness of Egypt, the monumental temples and architectural wonders of those great people were all built without using money.

Instead of money, the Egyptian people were paid for their work with rations of grain. With grain as their take-home pay, they could barter for whatever else that they wanted. This was almost the same system used to pay the laborers of early Sumeria but with one important difference: In Sumeria, the land had originally been owned by the temples but eventually it came to be owned by the individual moneylenders. In Egypt, the divine pharaoh owned all of the land while the people worked for the pharaoh.

The grain was kept in central storehouses and paid out to the people as wages or as relief aid during times of drought. The Egyptian people were always fully employed by the pharaohs. All of the great architectural wonders and art masterpieces which are still evident today—over three thousand years later—were all created by the Egyptian people under the pharaohs' employment. All of the temples, statues, bas-reliefs, paintings, canals, palaces, wharves and everything else in Egypt was paid for in wages of grain, gifts of linen clothing, and with regular religious feast days and partying with plenty of beer, all of which were sponsored by the pharaoh. None of it was built with slave labor because the Egyptian people worked for the glory of their gods. Making slaves do the holy work of giving glory to the gods, gave the blessing of the gods *to the slaves*. So, the Egyptian people built the wonders of Egypt, not the slaves who were merely war captives and relatively few in number.

And absolutely none of Egypt's great marvels were built by the Jews. There were no Jews in Egypt or anywhere else in the world at that time. This is one of the early proofs that today's Jews are all liars. For nearly two thousand years, as Egypt arose with all of its glories, it had no money-lenders to impoverish its people or to suck away the wealth of the country. Egypt was a god-conscious land with no Jews existing anywhere on Earth, so the people were happy.

Although Babylonia had nothing that Egypt needed, there was one, most vitally important item that Egypt had, which the Babylonians very much needed: Gold! Without sources of silver and/or gold from outside of Babylonia, the clay accounting tablets of the moneylenders could never be brought into balance. Without extra bullion traded, plundered, looted, or stolen from outside sources, the criminal swindle of their entire money-lending operations would be revealed as their debtors stopped all loan payments simply from a shortage of enough silver or gold to pay the impossible numbers on the account ledgers.

In such an event, the entire, carefully concealed and phony structure of the unpayable debts of the Sumerian Swindle, would come crashing down upon the moneylenders. Their entire economic system based on impoverishing mankind with never-ending debts, would squeak to a halt. This was always a dangerous situation for every moneylender and banker, having to explain to an entire country full of impoverished and dis-possessed people how it is that the people own nothing, the bankers owns everything, and yet the people still owe the bankers even more money!

Babylonia had oil and tar seeps from its underground deposits. And they had plenty of chickens and ducks. Yet, the Babylonians had never figured out how to tar and feather the moneylenders. But the moneylenders had figured it out and they were always frantic to keep that as one of their own, special secrets, too.

Egypt obtained its gold from the Upper Nile, along with exotic goods like ebony wood and elephant tusks from Nubia—that is, from black Africa. The Sinai Peninsula, which was annexed during the Old Kingdom (~2700-2200 BC), provided copper mines. The only import Egypt really needed was the trade in wood which was a necessity for the building of temples, ships, furniture, etc. Wood was of inferior quality and in short supply in the desert lands of Egypt, so, during the Old Kingdom, Egypt began a special relationship with Byblos on the Lebanese coast. Byblos became one of its closest allies for almost two millennia. The imported wood of Lebanon was critical to the development of a navy capable of defending the country and for the boats that plied the Nile.

Arabia likewise had overland and Red Sea connections with Egypt. The reed ships of Babylonia navigated around the Arabian Peninsula to trade with Punt and with Egypt. The Babylonian merchants also took the overland route through Palestine and into the Nile Delta, off-loading their donkeys onto Egyptian boats for trading voyages up the Nile. The Babylonian merchants were very knowledgeable of the architectural wonders, riches, and the trade goods available in that desert land.

No city in Babylonia was better situated to trade with Egypt, Arabia, India, and Africa than was the river city of Ur, where all ship traffic from the Persian Gulf was off-loaded onto river craft and where the temple of the Moon God, Sin, was located—the main temple-bank of the merchant-moneylenders.

However, it was not trade goods that primarily attracted the Babylonian merchant-moneylenders to Egypt. It was *the gold* of Egypt that they most desired. But how could they get their hands on it, was the big question. There was very little that Babylonia had which Egypt needed. So, getting all of that gold through commerce, alone, would require centuries-worth of trade expeditions; and the total quantity would still be very small. The Egyptians valued gold not for its use as money but for the beauty it gave to their temples and the honoring of their gods. Such gold was not for sale or trade. And the temples had so much of it!

The Babylonian merchants who had been allowed entry into Egypt were even more amazed than modern tourists are amazed, because in those days, all of the wealth of Egypt was still dazzlingly in place, not stripped away and stolen over the following three thousand years into modern times. The mud-brick temples and palaces of Babylonia were nothing but piles of mud that had to be rebuilt every few scores of years, in comparison with Egypt's eternal architecture built of stone.

In 1700 BC, the three Great Pyramids of the 4th Dynasty (2575–2465 BC), which were constructed more than 700 years previously, were still covered by their original outer casings of smooth white limestone. Today's tourists see only the stripped-away inner cores of those great structures. Each pyramid in modern times is about 30 feet shorter than the original structures because they were robbed of their outer casings in antiquity for use as building materials. Today, the pyramids are no longer covered with the original white limestone blocks angled into perfect pyramids with smoothly fitting seams. Each perfectly shaped pyramid brilliantly reflected a dazzling white in the sunlight; and at night, they shone silvery white in reflected moonlight under a Milky Way galaxy glittering with stars, which were undimmed by the sky glow of electric lights from the modern-day, smoggy Egyptian cities.

Today's modern tourist only sees the tawny and buff colors of Egyptian stonework unembellished. But the Babylonian merchants saw Egypt when all of the stone temples were still lovingly swept clean, painted, and maintained. In 1770 BC, the gargantuan statues of the pharaohs, their serene stone faces gazing into Eternity with smiling lips, were still painted with bright colors decorating their stone clothing.

The monuments and temples carved out of solid rock or built of huge blocks of granite or limestone, were very unlike the adobe temples and mud-brick palaces of Mesopotamia. The long rows of huge stone pillars that today are open to the sky beneath a blast furnace of a sun, were still spanned by huge wooden beams, wooden roofs, and linen awnings, providing cool and shady interiors. And within, the Egyptian temples were solid stone and sheeted with gold. Statues of the deities were often made of solid gold with large jewels for eyes. Exquisite wonders were to be seen every day and everywhere throughout the 600-mile length of ancient Egypt.

Because the Babylonian merchants were all members of the same trade guilds, what they saw in Egypt, they personally reported during the well-attended guild meetings in Babylon and Ur. Stories of distant countries were always avidly desired by everyone, especially by the international merchant-moneylenders, who would listen to such stories just as they listen today, shrewdly peering through their slit-like, half-closed eyelids and paying close attention with a calculating greed.

As international merchants bearing gifts and greetings from Babylonian kings, they were granted audience with the highest Egyptian officials, including the pharaoh. So, they had seen with their own eyes the huge amounts of gold possessed by the Egyptians. Over many years, this information was carefully cross-referenced with the reports from every trade expedition and used for calculating the value of the temples and palaces throughout all of Egypt, stretched out along both sides of the Nile. All estimates were equated into shekels of silver and enumerated upon the clay tablets by the scribes. Careful note was made of distances by boat along the Nile and how long it took such trade expeditions to travel those distances. Estimates of population sizes and distribution of military troops were always carefully noted by those merchant-spies. After more than a thousand years of hoarding, Egypt had incalculable amounts of the gold that the Babylonian merchant-moneylenders so desperately needed to balance their fraudulent accounts and to enrich themselves. But getting their hands on it was a very big problem.

Ripe for the Taking

To their unending dismay, the merchant-moneylenders of Babylonia knew that Egypt's gold could neither be obtained through the Sumerian Swindle (since Egypt did not use money), nor by trade (since there was nothing that Egypt needed that the Babylonian merchants had). But there was another way to bring Egyptian gold into the Babylonian temple treasuries—a method that could bring all of the treasures of Egypt into Babylonia within a just few years instead of a few centuries. And that method was through their well-tested mechanism of war.

Experienced as they were in secrecy and subversion, for the first time, the moneylenders of Ur began their quest for the loot of Egypt without the protective influence of the kings. In all previous wars in Mesopotamia, they had stationed themselves safely behind the kings, giving loans and selling war material and providing military intelligence from their network of spies. But for now, both the kings of Babylonia and the kings of Assyria were too busy with their own empires to look for conflicts beyond their own borders. They had enough affairs to keep them busy closer to home.

But there was an opportunity in Egypt that could not await the Babylonian kings. Plus, there was a crisis of not enough silver and gold in circulation to pay the moneylenders all that they claimed was owed to them. More gold and silver were needed to be infused into the Babylonian economy so that it could then be paid to the merchant-moneylenders by their large number of debtors.

Time was of the essence; the opportunity would not last indefinitely. The merchant-spies in the caravans had carefully informed the Babylonian guild patriarchs of the situation in Egypt, a country rich with gold, its people happy with their knowledge of the Gods and unheeding of any external threats to their contemplations of immortality and eternity.

Indeed, Egypt had no external threats. The Negroes of Nubia and the Libyans were properly awed and subdued by Egyptian might. Assyria and Babylonia were too far away and too preoccupied with their own problems. Why would Egypt fear anyone? Why would Egypt fear attack from any of its neighbors? Thus, Egypt was ripe for the plucking, a perfect victim for the ruthless moneylenders whose god protected the wealth of the moneylenders' shekels of silver and talents of gold, securely guarded in the temple of Sin, their Moon God.

The moneylenders had the wealth of Babylonia in their strong rooms, on deposit in the various temples, and invested in interest-bearing loans. They were enormously wealthy. If they could not manufacture weapons in their own foundries scattered around the Near East, then they could buy the very best of whatever weapons they needed from other guild members. They could hire and inveigle any number of mercenaries. They could rally vast numbers of their genealogically-connected tribal groups into war alliances. Their spies in Egypt were stationed at every trading post between the Delta and Kush. They could persuade and bribe the Negroes of Nubia to join them. They already knew where Egypt was strong and where she was weak. So, the patriarchs of the merchant-moneylender guild of the city of Ur, decided to subvert and attack Egypt themselves, while ignoring any help from the kings, and by using their own resources to seize the throne of Pharaoh for themselves. They had no need of the military power of the kings because they could hire mercenaries.

By organizing small armies scattered in the countryside between the various cities of Canaan and Syria, they could secretly train mercenary soldiers without arousing the interest or suspicion of the great kings of Babylonia or Assyria. Such small, scattered, tribal troops were outside of the territory of the great dynasties of Mesopotamia, and each individual tribe was too small to offer any potential threat that would arouse a pre-emptive military conflict from the great powers. And Egypt, in rapt contemplation of Eternity, was oblivious to any such preparations and any such danger arising among the scruffy goat-herders and scaly sheep-herding tribes of Palestine.

The guild patriarchs had already collected all available military and economic intelligence, calculated the approximate costs, predicted the profits, and devised a plan of action among themselves. Moving men and material takes a lot of time but the logistics of such an undertaking was all part of their skills as import-export merchants. Training, arming, and organizing troops also takes a lot of time, and for this, their mercenary generals and military underlings, hired for good wages, would be adept.

The first step in putting their plan into action was to find Babylonian generals and military men who could be trusted to keep their plans secret from the Babylonian king and to assume the responsibility to organize the required army in distant Palestine. A successful campaign would bring in enormous loot. So, without spending very much money, the proposed loot could be offered as an inducement. The Babylonian moneylenders needed generals and their entire sub-commanders of a military organization to lead and direct the secret army of foot soldiers which they wanted to assemble.

These Babylonian generals and their military subordinates were not difficult to find because they were already peacefully farming their estates in Babylonia. The guild patriarchs began by inquiring of one or two of the most well-respected generals who were owners of *ilkum* (military land grants) if their services were for hire. Innocent-sounding but probing questions over pots of beer and fine foods, served by pretty slave girls, was an easy entry into such a delicate subject with nothing to pique anyone's curiosity in particular.

When the right general was found and apprised of the plan, he in turn recommended other Babylonian military men of like mind who might also be interested in such an expedition. With such nonchalant probing and questioning, the guild patriarchs very soon had assembled the top-down military structure they needed as the foundation for an army. But it all had to be accomplished with the utmost secrecy if the plan was to be successful. Even in ancient times, news traveled fast. If the Egyptians found out about the planned surprise attack, all would be lost.

The actual commanders to lead their mercenary army, required less than 50 honest men in Babylonia who already owned an *ilkum* (military land grant) and had experience with warfare. These could be hired from under the nose of the Babylonian authorities and transported out of Babylonia disguised as extra "security guards" on trade expeditions to Palestine while their families were provided with enough silver to keep them happy and uncomplaining for as long as their men were absent. As more such mercenary commanders could be found by the guild agents, they, too, could be sent to the training grounds in Syria and Palestine.

After finding the right generals and officers, next they needed the foot soldiers to follow the orders of that military structure.

The moneylenders of Babylonia had established their trade guilds in every commercial city, town, and port in the ancient Near East. Those guild halls and taverns were not just places of business but they also provided their members with food and living accommodations for weary travelers. Such enterprises were well-staffed with numerous relatives, hirelings and slaves. The bribed local officials in their pay kept good contact with the local king and the temple priests, so the merchant-moneylender guild always knew the political climate and the latest local gossip and news in every city and large town.

For the plan to be successful, it could not be trusted to the king and his talkative administration. Nor could it be entrusted to the main guild in Babylon because they would want to run the operation and take all of the loot for themselves. The plan had to be carried out with the utmost precision. So, their agents looked for capable men far away from Babylonia in Syria among the tradesmen whom they already knew who were managing their trade depots. The entire operation would require central warehouses and supply depots, all of them already established as trade centers with trustworthy men operating them and concealing the large supplies of armaments.

It was to these towns that the supply clerks and the Babylonian military mercenaries were sent. All phases of the operation were already in place within the already-operating commercial enterprises of the merchants. From these towns, local guides were hired to lead them into the countryside on trade missions to the roving bands of goat-rustlers. Their job was to make contact with the various Semitic shepherds in every area as far as Canaan. They were to hire those shepherds as soldiers and train them in military discipline and tactics. All of this could be hidden-in-plain-site within the day-to-day operations of the trade guild warehouse and trade route operations. The key was trustworthy men who could do their jobs and keep their mouths shut.

As the actual foot soldiers were found and enlisted, those illiterate shepherds were paid with plenty of grain, gifts of woven cloth, and expensive trade goods such as copper pots and pans. All they had to do was to continue to herd their goats and sheep, obey the military discipline that the commanders taught them, and to spend time daily in practicing with the new and shiny brass swords, spears, and compound bows provided for free to every man who enlisted in a tribal militia.

Thus, small bands of soldiers were trained in the wild lands far away from the towns. Bounties were paid to every man who brought in a relative to enlist from neighboring tribes. These small squads, battalions and scatter-ed tribes would later be combined at the appropriate time into a large army.

The cunning members of the merchant-moneylender guilds were not more numerous than a king's army nor were they more powerful than the kings. But through their control of the trade routes, they had a financial power and a commercial control that was greater in size than any individual kingdom. They could out-maneuver the armies of all nations because their trade territories both surrounded, penetrated, and embraced every kingdom. Plus, their great wealth gave them the funds usually to be able to corrupt the top officials in every royal palace, gaining strategic information on the amount of bullion in every royal treasury, the actual size and strength of every king's army, and often learning of the plans of the king, himself. And it was all accomplished through sly persuasion, bribery, and the giving of expensive gifts to key personnel. There was nothing at all mysterious or complicated in this, but necessarily accomplished with utmost cunning and secrecy.

Enlisting the Nubians

Also, the merchant-moneylenders had the advantage of pretending to be nothing other than harmless, individual merchants who traveled about only in quest of personal profits. But they were all organized into the same Babylonian trade guild of seditious and subversive merchants who traded with both sides in every war, while keeping their mutual membership in the same trade guild as a secret among themselves. For all of these reasons, for seizing of the wealth of Egypt, they wanted very much to trade with the Negro tribes of Nubia.

In the traditional manner after reaching the trade center at the second cataract, the Babylonian merchants offered fine gifts to the Negro chiefs of those tribes and ingratiated themselves to their utmost. As a standard way of doing business, they availed themselves of the hospitality in the homes and huts of the Nubian traders, where private conversations could be conspired out of the sight and hearing of the Egyptian officials. Their hired Semitic Ma'adi relatives were always at their side as translators, so they had fluency in both Egyptian as well as the Nubian languages. There was never any question left open to misunderstanding during those private conversations.

The vast wealth which they had gotten for free from moneylending swindles plus their monopoly trade connections, gave the Babylonian merchant-moneylenders access to the advanced weapons that could give them victory in a war with Egypt—the compound bow, the chariot, horse cavalry, and vast supplies of bronze swords and daggers which could chop through the copper swords of the Egyptian armies. They could hire any number of mercenaries merely for grain, a few shekels of silver, free weapons, and the promise of the looting of Egypt.

The Babylonian merchant-moneylenders guild had its headquarters at the city of Ur, from where large shipments of arms could be transported on reed ships with a false destination to Oman or India and then carried instead to Africa and the Sinai, with neither the Babylonian kings nor the Egyptian kings being alerted. By using the Babylonian calendar, the merchant-moneylenders organized the timing of their conspiracy over the necessary three years. The trade winds for their ships, the distances along the trade routes, the timing of troop and material transport, and the costs, could all be calculated.

A Two-Pronged Attack

The assault upon Egypt was staged as a two-pronged attack. First, through their teams of traveling peddlers and merchants, the tamkarum (merchant-moneylenders) made secret agreements and alliances with the Amorite tribes of roaming shepherds throughout Sinai and Canaan. They carried bronze swords, daggers, and arrowheads as part of their trade goods of copper pots and woven cloth, arming the bands of shepherds as they made alliances.

Advance teams were paid and directed to begin leaving their tribes and visiting their relatives around Ma'adi during the final month before the scheduled attack. This fifth column within Egypt, the Semites of Ma'adi, agreed to rise up in revolt at the appointed time.

The Negro tribes of Kush had fought against the Egyptians for centuries. Usually, the Egyptians won, taking slaves and gold and leaving with unequal treaties involving the payment of tribute. Kush was rich in gold, as well as being a market center for animal skins and ivory. Once the chiefs of these primitive Negro tribes had agreed to attack Egypt on a certain date, numbered by the sun and moon cycles, the first prong of the attack was set.

It was a simple operation. Even though hundreds and thousands of miles separated the participants, all of them could be administered through their genealogical ties and coordinated through the Babylonian calendar, counting down the solar years, the moon phases, and the exact day.

When the agreed upon moon cycle rolled around, two things happened. First, and on schedule, the wild tribes of Nubia and Kush "spontaneously" rose up against Egypt, attacking the southern Egyptian outposts, looting and killing. This caused the pharaoh to order his troops and all available manpower throughout Egypt to sail southward to fight the Nubian insurgency. The Semites who were stationed with their relatives at Ma'adi, then left Egypt and entered Palestine with the news. The attack far to the south was in progress.

The approximate time that it took for such a movement of Egyptian men and boats up-river, was already known by the moneylenders. For example, the distance between the Delta and Thebes could be covered by boat in about 16 days. And an army of shepherds could be marched across the deserts of Canaan under the best conditions, about 200 kilometers, in nine days. Such rates of travel were known factors. Using these approx.-imations, the entire time it would take for the pharaoh's army to reach Nubia could be calculated. Once that time had passed, the Babylonian conspirators knew that Lower Egypt and the Delta would be emptied of fighting men and defenders.

By timing each scattered platoon of shepherds and each tribe to the pre-arranged moon cycle and by the known number of days it would take them to reach Egypt, their Babylonian commanders began moving the tribes, beginning with the farthest tribes first, so that they all arrived in the Delta region within the same day or two.

Thus, stage two, the second prong of the attack was initiated. From Palestine to the Sinai, the small groups of dispersed tribes of mercenaries under their commanders and generals began converging upon Egypt and coalescing into a single, large army of well-armed shepherds and tribes of bandits.

It was during that second moon-cycle when they knew that the entire Egyptian army was in faraway Nubia, that the mercenary generals had their orders to enter and attack Egypt with these armed tribes of shepherds and goat-rustlers. At the same time, they would give arms to the Ma'adian Semites who already had begun pillaging the defenseless old men and women who had stayed in Lower Egypt, while the entire fighting force of fighting men had joined the pharaoh and taken ship south to fight the Nubian rebellion.

Although those wild and rampaging Negro Nubians were primitive stone age tribesmen who had been used as pawns by the conspirators, we should not assume that they were merely uncouth and crazed savages, because they were just as modern, in many ways, as the Negroes are today. But instead rioting and stealing color TV sets and designer jeans, they stole everything else that they could get their hands on. While the Nubians were being pushed back by Pharaoh's army in the south, Egypt in the north was quickly being overrun by the armed shepherds who only had defenseless old people and temple priests to fight.

The weapons that the Mesopotamian moneylenders had provided were the very latest and best and too expensive for poor shepherds to buy. Weapons that the Egyptians had never seen before were brought into action against them, such as the bronze swords and battle axes provided to every shepherd. The powerful compound bows with bronze arrowheads gave the shepherds and soldiers a much greater killing range and penetration power than the simple bows of the Egyptians. But most terrifying of all were the expensive horses and chariots, which could carry bowmen and spearmen swiftly into the fray to trample the screaming old Egyptian farmers' wives and their grandchildren into the dust. The shepherds did not have to fight seasoned soldiers in their attack because those had been lured far to the south to fight in Nubia. Only the old men, women, and children remained unguarded. Without their fighting men to protect them, the Egyptians were swiftly subdued by 1630 BC, mainly without a fight.

With the Pharaoh and his army drawn away to Kush, the Semitic tribes of shepherds and their tamkarum generals merely filled in and occupied the Nile valley behind him with their troops. With such an easy victory, more shepherds came running to join in the looting. The Egyptians were not subdued by a ragtag bunch of poor shepherds but rather by numerous tribes of poor shepherds armed with the latest and most advanced weapons of the age, and backed by professional soldiers and experts in military tactics.

Simple shepherds alone did not build the forts with the advanced fortification techniques that were introduced into Egypt. They had some very sophisticated help. It required money, patience, planning, engineering skills, and scheming ruthlessness, all of which the moneylenders of Babylonia had in abundance.

As the Egyptian historian, Manetho (~300 BC), wrote, as quoted by Josephus:

> Under a king of ours named Tutimaeus, God became angry with us, I know not how; and there came, after a surprising manner, men of obscure birth from the east, and had the temerity to invade our country, and easily conquered it by force, as we did not do battle against them. After they had subdued our rulers, they burnt down our cities, and destroyed the temples of the gods, and treated the inhabitants most

cruelly—killing some and enslaving their wives and their children.

Then they made one of their own king. His name was Salatis; he lived at Memphis, and both the upper and lower regions had to pay tribute to him. He installed garrisons in places that were the most suited for them. His main aim was to make the eastern parts safe, expecting the Assyrians, at the height of their power, to covet his kingdom, and invade it.

In the Saite Nome, there was a city very proper for this purpose, by the Bubastic arm of the Nile. With regard to a certain theological notion, it was called *Avaris*. He rebuilt and strengthened this city by surrounding it with walls and by stationing a large garrison of 240,000 armed men there. Salitis came there in the summer, to gather grain in order to pay his soldiers, and to exercise his men, and thus to terrify foreigners.

After a reign of thirteen years, he was followed by one whose name was Beon, who ruled for 44 years. After him reigned Apachnas for 36 years and seven months. After him Apophis was king for 61 years, followed by Janins for 50 years and one month. After all of these, Assis reigned during 49 years and two months. These six were their first kings. They all along waged war against the Egyptians, and wanted to destroy them to the very roots. (*Against Apion*, I.14)

These invaders, Manetho called 'Hyksos' or Shepherd Kings. But it was not against the growing power of Assyria that the Hyksos had built walls nor was it against the strong but relatively small dynasty of Babylonia far across the Syrian Desert. It was for the protection of their loot that they built the fortified city of Avaris on the eastern Delta. Located on the Bubastic eastern arm of the Nile Delta, it offered both river transportation throughout Egypt as well as shipping to the Mediterranean Sea, and it occupied a strategic location on the caravan routes leading out of Egypt.

Whether the Babylonian generals and moneylenders moved their loot out of Egypt by ship or by donkey caravan, both methods were dependent upon the season and the weather. Ships could only sail with the prevailing winds, and caravans could only travel when it was not too hot or too cold. Both methods linked with the trade routes leading to the Euphrates River and thus to Babylonia.

Although the conspirators were looting Egypt all year round, they needed a central depot where the sculptures, jewelry, and gold sheeting peeled from walls and furniture, could be melted down into the more convenient gold bullion to await transportation at the proper season. That is mainly why Avaris was built: to store and protect the gold looted from Egypt. And, of course, it also provided a strong defensive position to protect that gold.

Until the takeover of Lower Egypt by the Hyksos, most conflicts that the Egyptians had fought had been civil wars. These were mainly armies of conscripted peasants and artisans led by Egyptian noblemen opposed to each other. Or they had exercised relatively short raids and skirmishes in their campaigns south into Nubia to extend the southern borders of the realm. Or they had campaigned toward the east and west into the desert regions toward Libya. Large scale battles, where the entire country was at stake, was a concept new to the Egyptians. They had never fought such a war. However, for the moneylenders of Babylonia, who were experts at turning one king against another so as to subvert and seize entire countries, war was big business and business-as-usual.

Hyksos = Apiru = Hebrew

Although the Egyptian historian Manetho translated the Greek word "Hyksos" as "king-shepherds" or "shepherd kings," he was describing the obvious majority of the foot-soldiers of those people who were simple goat rustlers and sheep herders. Today the term "Hyksos" has come to refer to the whole of those people who ruled Egypt during the Second Intermediate Period of Egypt's ancient history.

But the word conceals the two basic divisions within this group, that is, the rulers and the ruled. Manetho was not describing their leaders who, true to form, remained a minority hidden behind those whom they ruled. He was describing mainly the stinking goat-rustlers and sheep-herders.

The Egyptian term "Aamu" was used to distinguish the Hyksos from the Egyptians. Egyptologists conventionally translate "aamu" as "asiatics." But the Egyptians called them "hikau khausut," which meant "rulers of foreign countries"—a term which originally had only referred to the Babylonian military rulers of the shepherds.

This is what the Egyptians had called them, but what did those invaders call themselves? The Hyksos called themselves by the Hebrew word "Am" or "people," which is why they were called "Aamu" by the Egyptians. But there was another word which they were later called by the

Egyptians. It is a word that you will soon begin to recognize. This word was "Apiru," which was applied by the Egyptians to the Egyptian class of peasant laborers and slaves. Remember the name "Apiru," because you will see it again.

In addition, most of the Hyksos' names were Semitic. Both the troop leaders and the ordinary shepherds had Canaanite names which, according to the custom throughout the ancient Near East, contained the names of their gods—in this case, Semitic deities such as Anath or Baal. Or they had ordinary Semitic names like Sheshi, Maatibra, Ineni and Yaakov-her (that is, "Yakov" or "Jacob"). The Hyksos even named one of the towns that they established as the Aamu city of El-Yehudiya, another Hebrew name.

The actual population of the Hyksos was predominately Canaanite goat-rustlers and Amorite sheep-thieves who were led and financed by their distant relatives, the Amorite moneylenders of Babylonia. *They were all Semites*; they all had only one object in mind, the looting of Egypt. This was followed by a complete financial and commercial subjugation of all trade and industry within the country as well as the monopoly of all trade outside of the country. They were as single-minded in their greed as are the modern-day Hyksos who are presently looting and pillaging the nations of the world from New York, London, Moscow, Tel Aviv, and the other financial capitals of the modern world!

Only with advanced planning, financing and military strategy could Egypt have been defeated. Such help came from the moneylender guilds of Babylonia who had organized and led the tribes of Amorite goat rustlers. Then, these "Hyksos" leaders, these Babylonian conspirators and money-lenders, sat their own fat asses down upon the throne of Pharaoh—but not to rule. They were in Egypt to plunder.

The Hyksos were all Amorites, Canaanites, and other assorted Semites from the east of Egypt. None of them were Jews, because no Jews yet existed at that time in history. Their chief deity was the Egyptian storm and desert god, Seth, whom they identified with the Semitic storm god, Baal. From Avaris they ruled most of Lower Egypt, and Upper Egypt to Hermopolis and south to Cusae, and briefly even beyond. They ruled through Egyptian vassals and Egyptian puppet administrators who could get more work out of the defeated Egyptian people than could Babylonian overseers.

The merchant-moneylender guilds of Mesopotamia well knew how to employ even the kings to do their bidding. By working as a single, conspiring guild with guild-halls "embracing" every city in the Fertile Crescent, the moneylenders and merchants each individually appeared to be independent businessmen, whose loyalty was falsely assumed by the kings as well as by the people among whom they were allowed to live, to be unquestionably loyal to the city in which they resided.

The Babylonian moneylenders were adept at riding on the backs of both kings and peoples while coaxing both into wars from which the moneylenders and merchants, alone, actually profited. They were parasites who hitched a ride safely upon the backs of both kings and peoples—while standing safely behind the royal thrones of their hosts in all conflicts. But their carefully planned attack upon Egypt was the first time in the history of the world that the merchants and moneylenders had actually organized, financed, and provisioned their own private army specifically to attack a major empire. They had always been content to stand behind the kings as advisors and financiers, where it was both safe and profitable for them. But this was the first time that they had actually taken a throne for themselves by using their own financing, their own army, and their own strategy.

But regardless of the monetary investment and careful planning, all of their efforts were based upon deceit. Deceiving the Babylonian king's customs agents as to where the arms shipments were actually destined; deceiving the shepherds as to the actual reason for all of their training in swordplay and military marching; deceiving the Negro Nubians about why they were required to attack Egypt at one, particular, prearranged day; and, of course, deceiving the Egyptians into sailing 600 miles upriver and leaving the entire lower kingdom empty of fighting men.

It was from this date around 1650 BC that the Babylonian merchant-moneylenders began teaching their sons how they, too, could make immense profits by using similar methods. They taught this with a simple-to-remember little saying: "With deceit, thou shalt wage war." By using this same advice, the Babylonian moneylenders' sons and distant great-grandsons were able to cause endless suffering and death among mankind, right up into the 21st century AD. But they all made plenty of money, so it was all okay.

The Plunder Begins

After deceiving and usurping Egypt, the Babylonian merchant-money-lenders lost no time in profiting from their investment. Once the initial looting and pillaging had subsided and the country was secured with armed camps and fortified cities, the Babylonian merchant-moneylenders chose one of their own as pharaoh.

Thus began the 15th and 16th dynasties of Egypt (~1630–1523 BC) with a Semitic non-Egyptian king ruling from the city of Avaris. At the same time, the Egyptians, who had been tricked into moving their army south to fight the sham rebellion of the Nubians, set up the 17th dynasty (~1630–1540 BC) ruling from Thebes. These methods for placing the dynasties in a logical sequence are a modern method for archaeological understanding. The Egyptians, however, certainly did not consider the Hyksos as worthy of being included in the Egyptian dynastic king lists since they were foreign invaders. They rightly considered that the actual pharaohs of Egypt had simply moved south to continue Egyptian culture uninterrupted at Thebes, while they gathered their forces for the counter-attack.

It should be enlightening to Bible students to know that this 108-year-rule over Egypt by the so-called shepherd kings, was the time when the Old Testament stories about Joseph of Egypt occurred. When you understand that both the pharaoh and the mythical Joseph were Hyksos, then you can better understand those stories so carefully forged in the Hebrew Bible —see Genesis 37 to 50.

Although the story of Joseph was carried out of Egypt when the Hyksos were finally defeated, it should be noted that the final form of the story of Joseph in Egypt was written in Babylonia nearly a thousand years later. During that time, there had certainly been some considerable creative editing by the scribes and rabbis so as to always make those scoundrels look better on the hand-lettered goat skins than they actually were in real life (see *The Monsters of Babylon*).

During the Hyksos occupation of Egypt, the Babylonian merchant-moneylenders needed to communicate their written orders to the Egyptians. So, their scribes began to use the simplified Egyptian hieratic script to write on papyrus and to broadcast their decrees through the use of town criers reading their demands in every town, village, and palace throughout the land.

Egyptian hieratic script had been used in parallel with the traditional Egyptian hieroglyphics since the most ancient times. It was an alphabetic system written and read by all educated Egyptians. Gradually, this simplified script began to be used for communicating between the Hyksos merchants and their mercenaries with a writing system that was suited to the Canaanite language. This is known by the archaeologists as the proto-Canaanite alphabet.

This proto-Canaanite alphabet later developed into the Phoenician alphabet consisting of 22 letters, none of which indicate vowel sounds. The names of the letters of the Phoenician alphabet are the same as those used in Hebrew because Hebrew is a Canaanite language, and the Hebrew alphabet is derived from the Phoenician alphabet. This should be remembered in later chapters, when the relationship between the Semitic Phoenicians, the Semitic Carthaginians, and the Semitic Hebrews, is discussed.

Because the lineage of the Hebrew alphabet is so easily traced from Egyptian hieratic script to the Phoenician alphabet to the later Hebrew alphabet, this archaeological proof reveals yet another of the many lies of the lying rabbis. Those rabbinical frauds claim that Hebrew is the original language of God and of mankind, beginning in the mythological "Garden of Eden." Therefore, because the lying rabbis say so, its lisping faggotry and guttural grunts, instantly make Hebrew into a "divine" language, only fit to be spoken by the world's most genetically-inbred frauds and thieving midgets.

Modern physicists and astrophysicists will be astounded to learn from the wise and holy rabbis that the Jewish demon-god magically used the Hebrew alphabet to create the entire universe! Who needs atomic particle accelerators or laser beams when everything can be created from the Hebrew alphabet mumbled from the fishy garlic breath of a rabbi? Their god constructed the entire universe out of the holy Hebrew letters which were filched from the Phoenicians, who grabbed them away from the Hyksos, who stole them from the Egyptians!

Thus, the Jews even stole the alphabet in which they wrote the lies which they use in modern times claiming that their god gave Palestine as well as the entire world to the Jews. Every letter of their own words cry out, "Lie!"

Anyway, the story of Joseph in Egypt took place during the Hyksos occupation. The pharaoh and all of the administrators including Joseph were all Hyksos. Joseph was most likely a Hyksos official who was in charge of enslaving and looting the Egyptians. His relatives kept his story alive in their genealogies by writing it in proto-Canaanite on papyrus and later writing it on parchment. Joseph's story was later rewritten by the scribes of Babylon a thousand years later when they assembled the various parchment scrolls of the Torah for the nefarious purposes which you will soon discover.

During the greater part of the Hyksos period, the major trade routes were reopened. But all trade was monopolized by the Hyksos. Agriculture was promoted as a means for the Egyptian people to pay tribute to the Hyksos overlords. Since Egyptian grain was used by the Hyksos to buy the trade goods of other countries, the more that the Egyptian farmers could be forced to produce, the more the Hyksos could profit.

However, leaving the Egyptians with enough to eat after their tribute grain had been paid, meant that the Egyptians could also keep hidden all of their gold and silver jewelry and precious stones and golden statues of the gods buried in the sand and under the floors of Egyptian houses. It may very well be that the story of Joseph in Egypt masks the time when the Hyksos army *purposely* took so much grain away from the Egyptians as to cause a seven years famine. In this way, they could force the Egyptians to dig up any of the hidden treasures that they had buried in order to buy grain from the Hyksos Pharaoh and Joseph, the Hyksos grain minister. Joseph and the Hyksos Pharaoh forced the Egyptians to dig up their hidden gold in exchange for food. And to whom else could the starving Egyptians sell their children, other than to the international slave traders who were based in Babylonia and who sat on the throne of Pharaoh?

This was a situation where an overseer of grain production such as Joseph, would have been a very important official in the Hyksos pharaoh's trade policies. Because the Egyptians were not Semites, whatever cruelties were visited upon them in the name of profits, were not ameliorated by any brotherly feelings of kindness or mercy. After all, the Semitic leaders of the Hyksos were the cruel merchant-moneylenders of Babylonia who thought nothing of enslaving even little children for unpaid debts of the parents.

A Cruel Reign

Modern Jewish archeologists are lying when they claim that Hyksos rule was benign and beneficial for the Egyptians. We must listen to what the Egyptians, themselves, had to say about those times to get a truer picture of the situation. As Manetho, the Egyptian historian, wrote:

> After the Hyksos had subdued our rulers, they burnt down our cities, and destroyed the temples of the gods, and treated the inhabitants most cruelly; killing some and enslaving their wives and their children.... They all along waged war against the Egyptians, and wanted to destroy them to the very roots. (*Against Apion*, I.14)

Again, for those who study the Bible, this vicious Semitic practice of genocide can also be recognized throughout the Old Testament as a standard operating procedure of the Jews, who consistently murdered everybody whenever they could. But more about this in *The Monsters of Babylon.*

Manetho's reference to a carnival of destruction is confirmed by the inscription of Queen Hatshepsut of the Eighteenth Dynasty, who declared:

> I have restored what was cast down. I have built up what was uncompleted since the Asiatics were in Avaris of the north land and the vagabonds were among them, destroying buildings while they governed, not knowing Ra.

But whether you believe the Egyptians themselves, or the modern Jewish liars, one thing is clear: trade and the looting of wealth was the major goal of the Hyksos. Destroying the temples of all gods other than their own, was an early tactic of these "vagabonds."

Egypt had plenty of grain, beer, bricks, flax and hemp, lamp oil from kikki seeds and later from olives, hippopotamus and elephant ivory, ostrich feathers and eggs, leopard and lion skins, dates, precious stones, artifacts such as sarcophagi and statues, amulets, rings and scarabs, beads made from faience, weapons, jewelry, mirrors, linen, fine veils; mats, ox-hides, ropes, lentils, dried fish, papyrus paper, silver and (from the Nubian mines and alluvial deposits) large quantities of gold. These trade goods, plus the over 2,000-years accumulation of gold and precious stones in the temples and tombs of Egypt, gave the Babylonian merchant-moneylenders plenty of loot in their 108-year rape and exploitation of Egypt. And once the Egyptians had been starved for a long enough time, the Babylonian merchants got the additional gold dug up from their buried hoards. And finally, the Babylonian merchant-moneylenders got the Egyptian children, sold to them in exchange for bread.

But where did all of the wealth of Egypt go? Rather than as bulky statues and art objects, it could be transported most easily when melted into bullion and transferred to their relatives and business partners in Babylonia. It did not go to the kings of Mesopotamia, since the Hyksos invasion was a *private, corporate enterprise*. It went to the trade guilds and tamkarum partners in Babylonia and Ur. Whatever gold and silver that was carried away as booty by the shepherds wound up in the hands of the merchants in exchange for their trade goods, such as woven cloth, copper cookware, needles, and buttons.

Much wealth also flowed into the coffers of the Semitic moneylender guilds within the cities of Canaan such as Sidon, Kadesh, Acre, Byblos, Arwad, and Tyre. These were sea ports. Once the Hyksos were finally expelled from Egypt, it was to these seaports controlled by their Semitic relatives and by the tamkarum guilds that many of them fled.

Revenge

Finally, around 1525 BC, after more than a hundred years of reorganizing and arming themselves, the Egyptians were ready to counterattack from their holy city of Thebes. Under Pharaohs Seqenenre and Kamose, the Theban army set forth.

The Hyksos pharaoh Auserre Apopi tried unsuccessfully to make an alliance with Kush but it was too late. The Negro Kushites had had enough of the Babylonia Hyksos thieves. Originally, the Negros of Kush had been inveigled to join forces with the Hyksos in order to draw the Egyptian armies south into Upper Egypt so that the Hyksos invasion could enter from the north. And then afterward, they were abandoned by their disloyal Babylonian allies. Their king and their warriors were deceived and swindled, and they resented it.

And so, after more than a hundred years of being swindled of their trade goods by the greedy Babylonian merchants, after being dispossessed of their wealth and property with loans-at-interest, and after experiencing the greed of the moneylenders first-hand, rather than join forces with the Hyksos, the Negro Nubians preferred to join forces with the Egyptians to chase the Hyksos out of Egypt. Yes, the moneylenders have always been hated, but not because of any so-called "bigotry" or "prejudice" against them, but because of the evils which they inflict upon all whom they touch.

The modern Jewish historians might consider this as a blatant case of bigotry and anti-Semitism on the part of the Negroes—except for the fact that, although the Nubians hated the Babylonian merchant-moneylenders, there still were no Jews to be found anywhere in the world, even as late as 1525 BC. The only Semites who even vaguely resembled Jews were the greedy, lying, covetous, swindling, thieving, betrayers known as the Babylonian merchant-moneylenders. They were Semites, but they were not Jews—yet.

Once the Negroes of Kush understood what lying and greedy betrayers the Hyksos merchant-moneylenders were, they joined forces with the Egyptians. Large numbers, but not all, of the Nubian bowmen bravely fought the Hyksos under the command of Kamose. Although the Nubians hated the Babylonian merchant-moneylenders, they still feared Egypt and most of them refused to fight.

This time, the Egyptians did not have the disadvantage of inferior weapons. When they counterattacked the Hyksos, they did so armed with their own chariots and horses, their own composite bows, and their own bronze swords, spears, maces, and arrowheads. But where did they get them? The bronze and copper swords, axes, and maces they could manufacture themselves by recycling the metals already in their possession as well as from the copper deposits that were within reach of their trade routes through Upper Egypt to the Red Sea. Of course, because of the vastness of the deserts, none of the trade routes except those which were guarded by the Hyksos at the Delta could be effectively patrolled. So, the Hyksos patrols were outnumbered and outflanked in this regard, and the Egyptians could smuggle whatever they needed. They had the gold to pay for whatever they wanted.

The chariots were of their own manufacture. The Egyptians took the basic design of the Hyksos chariot and improved upon it. They moved the axel from the center to the back of the platform for better balance, speed, and maneuverability. The platform floor, they made out of leather for lightness and less work for the horses and as a shock absorber so the archer was more stable. They replaced the Hyksos four-spoked wheel with a stronger, six-spoked wheel. And they designed a U-joint between tongue and chariot for greater maneuverability and less drag on the horses. With archer and driver, this much-improved Egyptian chariot could attain speeds of twelve miles per hour.

The composite bows, they could also make for themselves once they had the design secrets. These secrets were obtained both by reverse engineering and buying them from the Babylonian traders who had sailed their reed ships from Babylon, around Arabia, and into the Red Sea ports on the African Coast. Anything that they needed, including horses and the knowledge of horse-breeding, they could buy from one or more of the tamkarum families of Babylonia and pay for it with Egyptian gold.

Although it took the Egyptians 108 years before they could expel the Hyksos, within those 108 years, they bought and bred enough horses and traded for and manufactured all the weapons and chariots that they needed.

When they were armed and ready, Thebes counter-attacked the Hyksos. The Theban revolt spread northward under Pharaoh Kamose, and about 1525 BC, Avaris fell to his successor, the Egyptian Pharaoh Ahmose (1550-1523 BC), founder of the 18th Dynasty, thereby ending 108 years of Hyksos rule over Egypt.

Avaris, the stronghold city of the Hyksos, located on the east side of the Delta, was heavily fortified. The site of the city covered about two square kilometers, plenty of area for the thousands of Hyksos who sought refuge there. Modern archeological excavations reveal that it had a Canaanite-style temple, Palestinian-type burials, including horse burials, Palestinian types of pottery, and quantities of bronze weapons. It was a well-developed, international center of trade. Artifacts included goods which were produced from all over the Mediterranean world including a temple with Minoan-like wall paintings similar to those found on Crete at the Palace of Knossos. All of this indicates that the looting of Egypt had attracted people from the entire eastern Mediterranean Basin.

Pharaoh Ahmose led his army in a water-borne attack. Powerful as the city was, it could not withstand a protracted siege. The battering ram had not yet been invented; it would be another 700 years before the Assyrians would use that instrument against city walls. Because the Hyksos were surrounded and trapped, it would be a simple tactic to starve them out and kill them all. But Pharaoh Ahmose had all of Egypt plus Kush and Nubia to pacify and did not want to be entangled with a prolonged siege in the Delta. To do so, would keep his army laying siege in the north, leaving the Negroes of Nubia free to pillage Egypt in the south.

As Manetho wrote,

> The shepherds had built a wall surrounding this city, which was large and strong, in order to keep all their possessions and plunder in a place of strength. Ahmose attempted to take the city by force and by siege with 480,000 men surrounding it. But he despaired of taking the place by siege, and concluded a treaty with the Hyksos, that they should leave Egypt, and go, without any harm coming to them, wherever they wished. After the conclusion of the treaty, they left with their families and chattels, not fewer than 240,000 people, and crossed the desert into Syria. (*Ap.* I.14)

This 240,000 Hyksos is less than half of the number that was claimed in the Book of Exodus as having escaped from Egypt ("about 600,000 men on foot, besides women and children"—Ex 12:37). But whatever the number, they divided into *four unequal groups* and went their separate ways.

CHAPTER 11
THE BEGINNINGS OF JUDAISM

This date of 1525 with the fall of Avaris, is the earliest date which can be applied to what can be named as "Judaism." Some of the Hyksos were circumcised and some of them were normal. None of them were Jews, but the circumcised ones were in the process of becoming Jews, because the patriarchs of their merchant-moneylender guild were formulating and developing answers to the questions arising from "The Fifteen Secret Problems Which Prevent the Babylonian Merchant-Moneylenders from Owning the Entire World"—more on this to come. Answering those fifteen problems, is what developed into the demonic cult which came to be called by the two most odious and cursed names in the history of mankind: "Jews" and "Judaism."

Thus, the Shepherd Kings of Avaris—these "Aamu," these "Apiru," these "Hyksos"—were able to escape Egypt and, according to the terms of the surrender, they were allowed to take all of their loot with them. With whatever silver and gold that they could carry away, some very few of the Hyksos escaped into Moab and Sinai, returning to the previous occupations of their forefathers as sheep herders and goat rustlers. Some very few of the Hyksos turned southeast towards Arabia and there they wandered about in the wilderness of Sinai for 40 years with their goats and sheep for company because they got lost and didn't know which way was north.

A large number of the Hyksos, speaking their Canaanite dialect and writing on parchment with their Egyptian-derived, Canaanite alphabet, moved back to the cities of their ancestors, the coastal cities and towns in Canaan. There, they used their loot and their family connections to begin the seafaring businesses as a people who have become known to us as the *Phoenicians*. What the Phoenicians called themselves in their own Semitic language appears to have been *Kena'ani* (Akkadian: Kinahna) or "Canaanites." In Hebrew, the word *kena'ani* has the secondary meaning of "merchant."

A very few of the Ma'adian Semites who were captured in the Delta region got enslaved. The Egyptians had allowed them to live on the best grazing lands in the Delta for a thousand years. They were welcome to sail up the Nile to trade with the Nubians as they pleased. They had a good life living in Egypt. But the moment that they could betray Egypt to their fellow Semites from Babylonia and Palestine and join in the looting, they did not hesitate. So, they were kept in bondage in Egypt even while those Hyksos who had been besieged at Avaris were allowed to leave. As slaves, they were called by the Egyptian name of *Apiru* or "bandits." But this name would take on a very different meaning later.

The scribes of the merchant-moneylenders who took the desert trade routes through Syria or the sea routes around Arabia and thus back to Babylon, took with them collections of papyrus and parchment copies from the temple libraries of Egypt. many of those Egyptian masterpieces had already been carried off to Babylonia during their 108 years of looting. Before the fall of Avaris, both the original as well as copies of the literary treasures of Egypt had already been deposited in the private libraries of Babylonia, there to be studied and plagiarized by the tamkarum scribes. Besides the wisdom literature of Egypt, these included the records of Joseph, the Hyksos minister of the granary.

A Most Unusual Souvenir

It is a habit of modern tourists, who visit interesting places, to buy souvenirs to remind themselves of their adventures in those distant lands far from home. Very often they buy a T-shirt commemorating the fact that they had actually been to the famous place advertized by the T-shirt design. Perhaps they go to Paris and buy a T-shirt silk-screened with a sketch of the Eiffel Tower and bearing a caption that reads: "I went to Paris and all I got was this stupid T-shirt." Or a tourist might go to modern Egypt and buy a souvenir T-shirt with a picture of the Great Pyramids on it, bearing a caption that reads: "I was there!" In this way, without appearing to be a braggart, he could be admired by one and by all, and even strike up interesting conversations with strangers who question him about his successful and adventurous vacation.

The Babylonian merchant-moneylenders were no different than modern people in this regard. They, too, desired to take back home to Babylonia, a memento of their adventures. Like modern people, they also wanted some sort of souvenir as a reminder to themselves and a proclamation to all of their friends, family and business associates in Ur and Babylon that they, personally, had been a member of the gang who had outwitted the pharaoh, defeated his army, and plundered the great country of Egypt of its gold and gemstones. However, they could not return to Babylonia wearing an Egyptian T-shirt of the Great Pyramids because of the very great scarcity of souvenir T-shirts for sale in Egypt in 1550 BC. So, the Babylonian merchant-moneylenders did the next best thing to prove that they had been to Egypt: they had themselves circumcised.

At that time, among all other peoples, only the Egyptian men were circumcised. In the hot weather of Egypt, nakedness, and wearing the skimpiest see-through clothing, was common among both men and women. So, even when the Hyksos began wearing traditional Egyptian clothing and shaving off their beards, everybody knew at first glance who were the real Egyptians and who were the fake uncircumcised Hyksos invaders. Besides having big, hooked noses, brown and black eyes, and kinky hair, the Hyksos had natural, uncircumcised penises.

In Egypt, boys were circumcised at the age of puberty, between ten and twelve years old. As a religious rite, the sharp pain that circumcision caused them was used as a lesson by the priests to teach those boys just entering manhood to be careful with their little thingy because it could give them not only a lot of fun with the ladies but could also give them a lot of sorrow and hard work if they became too promiscuous. It takes a lot of work to raise a child, and the more children, the more hard work required to properly raise them to adulthood. So, unlike the Semites, the Egyptian boys and girls were taught virtuous self-control at the very beginning of adulthood.

Egyptian women practiced natural birth control by breast feeding their children for two or even three years. For this reason, both husband and wife could enjoy an enthusiastic sex-life without a new baby every year to stress both mother and father. Over-population was never a problem in ancient Egypt.

However, the tribes of Semites always strived for the maximum number of children from their many wives so as to out-breed the people around them. In this way, the Semitic tribes could use their superior numbers to eventually push out other people and outnumber them in battle. Soon after a child was born to Semitic parents, wet nurses were hired to suckle the baby while the wife was impregnated yet again. Thus, the Semite women were always pregnant and very tired, while their children were always very numerous.

Limiting their own population as was practiced in Sumeria and Egypt, was not something that the Semites wanted, especially the Babylonian merchant-moneylenders who were at the top of the economic ladder in Babylonia. They wanted, and could afford, many wives and many children as part of their social "prestige" and proof of their great potency and wealth. The best in mud-brick houses, the finest furniture, the best foods, the best barley beer and grape wines, sumptuous feasting and parties, many wives and many concubines from among their slave girls, all of the luxuries available in the ancient world, were available to them. They wanted numerous sons to manage their many foreclosed properties; and they wanted many daughters to marry into other rich families so as to increase their wealth even more.

So, when these Babylonian merchant-moneylenders questioned the Egyptian priests, wondering why all of the Egyptian young men and adults were circumcised, they learned that the Egyptians circumcised their teenage boys to teach them how to be virtuous and self-controlled. That did not interest the merchants and moneylenders at all. Not at all! The Babylonian moneylenders preferred debauchery; and the more, the better.

However, what "perked them up" were the ominous warnings offered by the Egyptian priests, dire warning that once they had been circumcised, they would be horny all of the time. (The physiological reasons for this are explained in *Monsters of Babylon*.)

The Babylonian merchant-moneylenders were already sex-fiends. As long as depravity did not interfere with making money, then degeneracy was always acceptable in their elite society. As with sex fiends every-where, much of their leisure time was spent over wine or pots of beer bragging about and reveling one another with tales of their many sexual depravities. With their many wives, concubines, slave women and en-slaved little boys to service their lusts, being horny all of the time sounded like a blessing from the goddess Ishtar.

The Egyptian priests had emphatically warned them that if they did not follow the virtues of matrimony and the self-control of a moral man, then being horny all of the time would lead to a hellish existence of manic masturbation, effeminate loss of manhood, sexual perversions of every sort, possible insanity, and much suffering in the Afterlife. Without practicing honest and moral decency, then their over-stimulated penises would point them down the pathways into Hellfire, with their bodies and souls following promptly.

But the Babylonian merchant-moneylenders had never been moral or decent because they have always been swindlers, thieves, rapists, and murderers who worshipped the goddess, Ishtar, the goddess of warfare and sexual lust. Every member of the Babylonian merchant-moneylender guilds practiced the Sumerian Swindle Secret Fraud #6: "High morals impede profits, so debauching the virtuous destroys their moral superiority and pulls them below the depravity of the moneylender who thereby masters them and bends them to his will."

Like the modern-day sex-fiends, they enthusiastically gloried in their libertine life-style of sexual promiscuity and drunken debauchery, just as long as it did not interfere with their profits. Much wealth bought them much pleasures in life. There were no religions of Mesopotamia which promised anything beyond the grave other than gloom. So, while listening to the sermons of the holy Egyptian priests on the importance of moral behavior, the only words that the merchant-moneylenders heard was "horny all of the time." Circumcision was enthusiastically welcomed by the sex-fiends among the Babylonian moneylenders. However, by not wrapping themselves in moral virtue, circumcision became an Egyptian curse upon them for their attack and looting of a country devoted to the worship of the gods.

Circumcision had played no part in the religion of the Sumerians, Babylonians or Assyrians, and the practice seems to have been exclusive to the Egyptians. However, a stone model of a phallus, evidently used in some cult, found at Tepe Gawra (near Nineveh) in a stratum datable as contemporary with the Proto-literate period, is circumcised. This may be the result of early West Semitic influence at Tepe Gawra, and certainly proves that circumcision as a religious practice in the ancient Near East predated by several thousand years its use by the Jews. Those West Semitic goat-rustlers may have been direct relatives of the West Semitic Ma'adians who later betrayed the Egyptians by joining in the Hyksos invasion. Not schooled by the Egyptian priests, they had merely copied what they had seen among the advanced society of Egypt and then carried the practice with them to the east without the moral teachings which had been an important part of the Egyptian cult. The Semites have always been as promiscuous as their billy goats, so being "horny all the time," appealed to these merchant-moneylender looters of Egypt.

But among the Hyksos, circumcision was adopted only by that small group of Babylonian schemers who were returning to Babylonia after getting themselves circumcised in Egypt. But they did not do it because there were no tourist T-shirts for sale with a picture of the Pyramids on them. They had themselves circumcised as a souvenir of their raiding days in Egypt, to set themselves apart from among all of the other merchant-moneylenders in Babylonia, and because circumcision made them "horny all the time."

How today's Jews became the world's foremost masturbators and sex maniacs can be traced to this earliest beginnings of their many perversions, starting sometime before 1550 BC during their 108-year looting of Egypt, when the ancestors of the Jews got themselves circumcised.

Circumcision was something much older than Judaism. It was incorporated into the Semitic cultures of the Hyksos and their Babylonian merchant-moneylender financiers because it made them "horny all the time" and was therefore much desired by the pimps and sex fiends of Babylonia. Instead of a colorful T-shirt proclaiming that they had been to Egypt and returned, the merchant-moneylenders all sported their circumcised penises which proclaimed the same message at the public baths. After all, where else could one get a circumcised penis except in Egypt? Because circumcision was not practiced among any of the cultures of Mesopotamia, it provided them with a way to indelibly mark themselves as members of the same secretive, family-based tamkarum trade guilds who had cooperated in their successful looting of Egypt while keeping their raid concealed from the Mesopotamian kings.

But once their successful raid became common knowledge, it was an accomplished feat which was merely claimed to be "business as usual." Among the Babylonian merchant-moneylender families, circumcision became the mark of those who could secretly conspire scams among themselves without the kings or the spies of the kings or even other guild members who were not circumcised, ever discovering their plans.

Circumcision was not like a tattoo or some other distinguishing mark that could be used by a spy to infiltrate their trade organizations. It was permanent. It was something not readily acceptable to an adult, so very few would willingly do it. And it could be kept hidden unless necessary for trade guild identification. Instead of presenting their membership cards in their hands, these delightful people presented their circumcised cocks.

From the very first, circumcision became a distinguishing mark of that secret fraternity of Egypt-plunderers which placed them apart from competing *un*circumcised moneylenders in the same guild. As the Babylonian circumcised sex fiends and bandits sat around drinking beer in their guild halls and swapping stories of their glory days of rape and thievery, those original swindlers realized that they had become a closed fraternity which excluded all others, even within the same merchant-moneylender guild. The ordinary guild members who were not circumcised and who had not participated in the looting of Egypt, were automatically excluded from their cliques and discussion groups. These circumcised merchant-moneylenders had succeeded in the greatest armed robbery in the history of the ancient world. They did it by working together, each coordinating with every other member of the conspiracy. They trusted each other. They lent money to one another without interest, without collateral or a contract, with just a handshake and a promise. All of them had become fabulously wealthy from swindling other people but not each other. And they knew that by working within that closed fraternity of circumcised thieves, that they could rob other nations if the opportunity arose.

This particular clique of circumcised Babylonian merchant-moneylenders had become *proto-Jews*. But they were not Jews, yet, because they had not solved the "Fifteen Secret Problems Which Prevented the Babylonian Merchant-Moneylenders from Owning the Entire World." This was a huge problem that had been vexing the entire Babylonian merchant-moneylender guild as a sort of puzzle to be solved.

But they were no longer young. All they wanted was to enjoy their immense wealth and pass it on to their sons. For this reason, circumcision was performed on all of their boy babies, thus proclaiming those boys to be descendants of the merchant-moneylenders who had plundered Egypt and had returned to tell about it. They wanted to mark their sons as inheritors by having their little baby gargoyles circumcised eight days after being born. Thus, all of their boys would grow up as manic masturbators and sex fiends, but that was okay with the Babylonian merchant-moneylenders because they had the enormous wealth to pander their boys and let them rape as many of their enslaved little girls as they wanted. Like father, like son.

By being circumcised as babies, those future little merchants, moneylenders, and swindlers could "prove" that they were descended from the original Hyksos robbers. And if none of the other boys believed the incredible stories fabricated from the lying lips of their forefathers, all they had to do was pull out their circumcised cocks and exclaim, "See, here's the proof. My ancestors got one of these in Egypt instead of a lousy T-shirt. Does any of you or your ancestors have anything to compare with this?" Boys will be boys.

Circumcision automatically kept their sons within this secretive inner circle of guild members. In this way, over the centuries, the merchant-moneylender guilds throughout Babylonia began to coalesce into two internal groups: the *uncircumcised* who depended upon the entire guild for their trade concessions and gave in return concessions to all of their guild brothers equally; and the *circumcised* who used the entire guild for their trade concessions and gave in return concessions primarily to their own circumcised guild members and for the benefit of themselves, alone.

Thus, within the parasitic tamkarum trade guilds of merchants and moneylenders, an even bigger parasite arose which drained the wealth away from its uncircumcised guild brothers. These 'parasites upon the parasites' looked exactly like any of the other Babylonian merchants and moneylenders except that they were horny all of the time—very horny, all of the time. Unlike in Egypt where morality was practiced throughout society from pharaoh to commoner, in Babylonia, the lusts of those circumcised sex fiends was allowed its fullest expression and deepest debauchery.

The Pharaoh Reasserts Control

Back in Egypt, after the Hyksos had been allowed to leave, taking with them Egyptian silver and gold ornaments and treasures, the Egyptians razed Avaris to the ground. Pharaoh Ahmose then led his army south by boat to settle the score with the Nubians, those Negros whose wild rioting and looting had initiated the pulling down and destruction of Egypt by the Hyksos. From Thebes, the Egyptian army began to penetrate Nubia and mounted a full invasion of the region.

Thus, Pharaoh Ahmose restored Theban rule over the whole of Egypt and successfully reasserted Egyptian power in its formerly subject territories. He then reorganized the administration of the country, reopened quarries, mines and trade routes and began massive construction projects of a type that had not been undertaken since the time of the Middle Kingdom. This building program culminated in the construction of the last pyramid built by native Egyptian rulers.

Pharaoh Ahmose laid the foundations for the New Kingdom, under which Egyptian power reached its peak. His reign is usually dated to about 1550–1525 BC. But almost all dates from ancient times are not exact and always open to re-calibration from new archaeological discoveries.

Later, Pharaoh Amenhotep I (1514–1493 BC) conquered Karmah and destroyed the kingdom of Cush. Nubia was colonized, and the viceroy of Cush became its chief Egyptian imperial official. Pharaoh Thutmose I extended Egyptian control to Kanisa-Kurgis, upstream from the fourth cataract of the Nile. Gold was the main resource exploited by the Egyptians. Cush produced significant amounts of this metal.

It was a ripple effect. The Babylonian merchant-moneylenders had stolen Egypt's gold to balance the fake numbers in their accounting tablets. They had stripped the temples of gold plating and gold images of the gods. Now, the Egyptians had to obtain a thousand years worth of accumulated gold in a short time by stealing it from the Nubians while punishing them for siding with the Hyksos. However, the Egyptians also needed gold in large quantities for the first time in their history as a means of buying the materials necessary to rebuild their country after the destruction wrought by the Hyksos. Egypt needed to enter the international trade of the other nations in order to buy wooden beams and lumber, tin for making bronze, lapis lazuli, carnelian, all of which had to be paid for with gold. The Hyksos invasion had forced Egypt to confront the realities of Middle East politics and the powers of foreign kings.

Even with this new era in Egyptian history, money was still not used and the un-Egyptian concepts of interest-on-a-loan and debt-slavery were still unknown in the New Kingdom. The entire Old Egyptian civilization which has always been, and is today, a wonder of the world, was developed without the use of money. So, after the Hyksos had been chased away, the Egyptians still bartered among one another and lived life to please the gods with prayer and humility. The ancient way in Egypt was reestablished!

But even with the huge profits from their Egyptian investments, the moneylenders of Babylonia had another problem. Vast though their wealth was, they only owned a very small portion of the entire world. The fortunes that they had accumulated were too easily lost through wars not of their own making and through the attrition by business partners taking shares from the total fortune and afterwards becoming their competitors. Once the Hyksos goat-rustlers had been scattered, instead of gathering the entire wealth of Egypt into their own treasury as they had planned, much of the total fortune had been carried off into the wilderness. Most of it had been safely carried back to the investors in Babylonia, but much of it was carted off to the Canaanite cities and used by competing tamkarum guilds to finance the Phoenician Empire. Although the moneylenders of Ur and Babylon had made vast fortunes, they had seen equally great fortunes slip from their greedy, grasping fingers.

Now that the tribes of Hyksos goat rustlers had been scattered into the deserts, now that the troops of mercenaries had been disbanded and had returned to their Canaanite towns, now that the leaders of this rabble had moved their wealth to the coastal cities and hilly country of Canaan, now that everybody had taken what they could carry away from Egypt and had set up their own domiciles and petty kingdoms—what was left for the Babylonian moneylenders? True, they had gained the greatest fortunes but in their limitless greed and demonic cunning, they had also seen huge fortunes go to others, fortunes which they considered their own rightful property simply because they had planned to get all of it for themselves. But they only ended up getting most of the gold of Egypt and that was not enough for them. Greed is a burning fire which grows bigger as it is fed with more and more and more. And when more is not enough, madness fills the space between the flames.

While it has been said that the Semitic nations—Amorite, Hebrew, and Arab—never invented anything but had assembled all the elements of their cultures from the genius of other people, this is not quite true. The clever skills of money-manipulation and the enslavement of mankind through the power of money and deceit, was a fine art and science that had a wholly Semitic source. True, it was based upon the non-Semitic Sumerian Swindle which they had not invented, but all of the clever stratagems of money manipulation, subtle methods of theft and grand larceny resulting from the Sumerian Swindle, was entirely a Semitic invention. The Semites never invented anything useful to mankind, but they fine-tuned the Sumerian Swindle to be useful only to themselves. How could it be otherwise? For the gold and silver and real properties to be "owned" by the scheming Babylonian merchant-moneylenders, that "ownership" first had to be taken away from mankind because the money-lenders could not become wealthy unless mankind became impoverished. The moneylenders make their fortunes by swindling it away from mankind. In their manipulation of money, nothing is created other than a debt whereby all payments are made to them.

Although their skills with lies, secrecy, and subterfuge were great, the moneylenders of Babylon and Ur had observed a flaw in their schemes. They knew how to enslave mankind through usury and finance. They knew how to use their swindled wealth as a lever for blackmailing kings and administrators. They knew how to use wine and women and homosexual filth and gambling for debauching the virtuous and cheating the people.

They knew how to remain safely in the background while pulling the money-levers which controlled society. They knew all of those things. But instead of a steady rise in their fortunes, they had time and again seen their careful planning dashed to pieces through no fault of their own. Enemy kings fighting wars for supremacy, and the competition from opposing merchant-moneylender guilds had time and again destroyed their fortunes and their properties. The patriarchs of the tamkarum guilds could see these impediments, but finding a solution to those problems was difficult.

In addition, even the members of their very own families had divided loyalties through their devotion to a variety of gods. Sons and daughters and other close relatives of their extended business families, who should have been working for the enrichment of the entire tamkarum family and guild, often gave away their share of the fortune to the temples of Marduk or Sin or Nabu or Ishtar. Thus, from religious devotion, the wealth of the merchant-moneylenders was too often diverted and siphoned away to the temples and to the priesthoods.

In fits of religious piety, trusted relatives and business partners, whose eyes were upon the eternal gods rather than upon the infernal accounting tablets, gave away huge fortunes to the temples, fortunes which diminished the total family wealth, fortunes which could have been loaned out at interest or invested in other profitable conspiracies.

It was because of this loophole in their schemes that much of the wealth of the tamkarum guilds of Babylonia had been diverted into the private fortunes of selfish relatives and business associates or even worse, given away to the temples, never to return. The leverage of great wealth and its industrial economy-of-scale had thereby been dissipated, creating a weakness in comparison with the other tamkarum guild families, families who would ruthlessly and instantly seize upon any financial difficulty.

Too often, the moneylenders' total corporate power had been diminished simply because greedy partners and stupid relatives had cashed out and had taken their silver with them, thereby reducing the total buying power of the family businesses. Such relatives as these, drained away finances and made a large and successful merchant-moneylender family into a less powerful and a poorer one. Such relatives and partners as these, broke two rules of the Secret Frauds of the Sumerian Swindle. Secret Fraud #8, "Large crime families are more successful than lone criminals or gangs; international crime families are the most successful of all." And Secret Fraud #9, "Only the most ruthless and greedy moneylenders survive; only the most corrupt bankers triumph."

In addition, there was the ever-present threat of confiscation of their treasures by the kings. Kings were always in need of money, which gave huge profits to the moneylenders as long as the king borrowed it at interest instead of robbing it from them. How could the merchant-moneylenders keep their bullion out of the hands of the kings and safely stockpiled in their own private treasuries?

Their own scribes had proven to them—and they had rechecked the calculations, themselves—that those who lend money at interest are arithmetically destined to own the entire world and to enslave all of mankind as servants to the moneylenders. Yes, the Sumerian Swindle was certainly a swindle, but as long as mankind did not know that we are being swindled by the bankers, then the moneylenders would continue to enjoy our wealth which they had stolen without being hanged for it.

The Sumerian Swindle had given them such huge quantities of silver and gold and so many thousands of foreclosed properties and tens of thousands of debt-slaves paying them interest on loans, that being able to manage it all had become an ever-growing problem. No matter how carefully they filched, cheated, stole, defrauded, hoarded, betrayed and murdered their competitors, because of all of the above-mentioned flaws, their silver and gold was leaking away and reducing the vast profits which they had so carefully accumulated. Such a leakage of silver had to be stopped if they were actually to own everything on Earth.

The profits were huge and their real estate holdings were vast. So, they needed a system whereby they could own more than just a single country. They wanted a system where they could own the entire world and all of its people and get away with their crimes, a system that was so cleverly sneaky that they could practice the Sumerian Swindle upon all of mankind and steal all wealth for themselves. Their accounting tablets proved that it was possible.

But for their own safety, such a system had to be such a subtle, snaky, sly, stealthy, sneaky stratagem as to be a smoke screen before the keenest eyes of even the most astute observers. Above all considerations, the system that they wanted had to be so clever as to protect them from their violently outraged victims, at least until the very moment where they could slither up to them even in broad daylight and snap the slave collars around their necks.

Those diabolical parasites needed a system where family members as well as business partners remained more loyal to themselves than they were loyal to the gods. Or better yet, they needed a system where the gods were just as greedy for gold as were the moneylenders and merchants, themselves. As experienced master criminals with the limitless riches which the Sumerian Swindle had provided them, the guild patriarchs knew that they could only trust relatives and fellow guild brothers. The question was, how could they keep their relatives and their guild brothers loyal to their own secret ambitions without actually telling them the secret?

Above all, how could they keep the profits of their swindles away from the eyes of the common people and out of the hands of the kings? If the kings understood that the merchant-moneylenders were all conspiring con artists and crooks and not by any definition "honest" businessmen, they would confiscate their wealth and execute them all for grand larceny and treason. If the people saw how very wealthy the moneylenders were in comparison to their own poverty, they would stop paying their debts and demand a refund. So, the guild patriarchs needed to amend their system and repair all of the above-mentioned flaws so as to make the Sumerian Swindle perfect. The Sumerian Swindle gave them limitless wealth for free but that is all; it did not guarantee that they could keep that wealth. They needed something more.

The Kassite Dynasty in Babylon: 1595 to 1150 BC

But for now, let's leave the Babylonian tamkarum counting their loot and scheming their schemes in Babylon and Ur. And also let's leave the Hyksos rustling each others' sheep and goats while practicing banditry in the coastal towns and hill country of ancient Palestine of 1550 BC.

Pharaoh Ahmose had allowed the Hyksos to escape from Egypt along with all of their loot as a means of getting rid of them. He wanted to save time and to avoid more bloodshed which would have inevitably resulted if the siege of Avaris had been prolonged. So, at this juncture we shall leave those Hyksos scuttling around Canaan and turn back the clock by about 45 years to where we left Babylonia in 1595 BC at the very beginning of its fall from glory when the shipments of Egyptian gold were overflowing the temple storerooms.

While the Babylonian moneylender-controlled Hyksos were still in the process of looting Egypt, the Hittite king Murshili learned from his spies the destination for all of that gold. So, he rushed to a surprise attack on Babylon and plundered its temples—the very temples in which the merchant-moneylenders had stored their hoards of gemstones, silver, and gold. He also carried away the statues of the omnipotent gods, all of whom unanimously hesitated to send down any lightning bolts, or even to command an earthquake to swallow him, or even to curse him with leprosy, or even give him bad dreams, or even make him feel bad about himself. Thus, the famous First Dynasty of Babylon came to a sudden end in 1595 BC.

The merchants and moneylenders of Babylon, who had trusted the mighty gods of Babylon and had deposited their silver and gold in the gods' temples, were wiped out. Although in their penury, they could still borrow at no interest from fellow guild members in other cities to rebuild their fortunes, but they were beginning from nothing—except their land holdings. The wealthier merchant-moneylenders had wisely divided their loot into smaller deposits in the various temples in different cities, so they still had working capital left to them, even though they had been greatly damaged in their ability to collect interest from debtors and clients who were also impoverished from the Hittite looting expedition.

The families within the merchant-moneylender guilds who were least affected, were those investors who still had gold being shipped to them from their partners in Egypt—shipments which would continue for the next 45 years. Those families had also diversified their deposits to the moneylenders' main guild city of Ur, which king Murshili had not been able to loot. So, their hoards of bullion there, were still safely untouched.

Thus it was that those specific merchant-moneylender families whose sons and hired generals were still looting Egypt, who gained supremacy above all of the other moneylenders of Babylon. Their own thousand years of craftiness with the Sumerian Swindle, plus their habit of diversifying the locations where they stored their bullion, plus the free gold looted from Egypt, plus their trust in the Moon God, Sin, and his mighty temple-bank in Ur, were the events that elevated them—without opposition—to the very top rung of the social and financial ladder of Mesopotamian civilization. These were the moneylenders who had been circumcised while they were in Egypt. Their gold was still safe in the city of Ur.

Those wily Babylonian merchant-moneylenders had never trusted any individual god with their gold. They had learned from their own experiences in plundering Egypt, looting the temples there, starving, torturing, and murdering the old men and women and the priests so as to force them to divulge the location of their hidden treasures; it was from such experiences that they knew that the mighty gods of Egypt could not protect Egyptian gold from the moneylenders of Babylon. So, why should they trust the gods of Babylon as sole protectors of merchant-moneylender gold? They always spread the risk of their reserves among other holy cities such as Ur and Uruk. No, they did not trust the gods with their gold and silver, but they still needed the temples of the gods to store their vast bullion reserves. Their gold and silver was too heavy to carry around. It had to be placed in a secure location. They very much needed the temples to protect it. But obviously, the kings still had the power to steal it. So, that was a problem which had to be solved.

Although Murshili conquered and plundered, he did not stay. His kingdom in Hattiland was undergoing political upheavals. So, he gathered up as much loot as he could, including the statues of the god Marduk from the chief temples—Esagila and the Etemenanki—and returned to his rebellious kingdom in the cool, tree-covered mountains of Anatolia while leaving a power vacuum in Babylonia.

Into this looted vacuum, whose Babylonian king had been killed, the Kassite forces descended from the Zagros Mountains to take control of the capital and to impose their government upon Northern Babylonia. The local Indo-European Kassites who had been cheap immigrant labor and small land-owners in Babylonia, rose up and joined their invading relatives to establish a Kassite dynasty.

This Kassite dynasty, which rapidly adopted much of the culture and institutions of Babylonia, lasted about 400 years (1595-1150 BC) and was in fact the longest lasting of any dynasty in the history of Mesopotamia. This was primarily because they employed fellow Aryans as the kings' administrators and did not allow the treacherous Babylonian Semites into the administration. Of course, they wanted to buy the goods that the Babylonian merchant-moneylenders sold, but if those Semites would betray their own people to the Kassites, then why would the Kassites want to entrust such unworthy traitors into positions of political power?

The first Kassite king of Babylon was Agum II, who was credited with recovering the statues of the god Marduk and his consort after they had been 24 years in Hittite captivity. With Marduk reinstalled in his temple in Babylon, the Kassite kings were able to "take the hand of Marduk"—a symbolic gesture denoting dynastic legitimacy and respect for Babylonian traditions, which naturally had the approval and blessings of the Babylonian priests.

The Kassites united the country after recapturing the south from the Sealanders. They restored the Babylonian empire to the glory of Hammurabi's age. They were neither Sumerians nor Semitic Amorites, but they wanted the country to be "as it had always been" before they had seized administrative control. This was entirely acceptable to the Babylonian merchant-moneylenders, as those Semitic parasites merely jumped from Babylonian kings and rulers to Kassite kings and rulers, all while selling their wares throughout the Mesopotamian river and canal systems and lending silver and grain to whomever had enough collateral. Even the Kassite kings wanted spices from India and copper from Oman, so the merchant-moneylenders thrived, no matter who sat on the throne. So, it was business-as-usual for the merchant-moneylenders.

Meanwhile, the Babylonian landowners and farm laborers became a dispossessed majority in their own country, either working at menial jobs or joining the army. This would be a continuing theme throughout history, where the common people were betrayed by the merchant-moneylenders and dispossessed by foreigners who pushed them out of their farms, crafts, and other means of employment, thus leaving open to them the only means available to make a living, which was to join the army and be sent out to fight and die. The poor became the soldiers who fought in the meat-grinder of war so that the rich merchant-moneylenders could "own" even more. And then they were killed in battle. Their grieving widows and orphans were forced to borrow money from the merchant-moneylenders who, after the money was all spent, seized their farms and homes. It was all such a subtle and clever scheme, and so profitable, too. Just as it has always been!

*****

It should be noted that from the First Dynasty of Babylon (1894 BC) to the end of Babylonian history with the conquests of Alexander the Great (323 BC), the possibility of administering the southern half of Babylonia depended to a considerable extent upon the cooperation of a few key cities, notably Ur and Uruk.

Ur was an especially important city for the merchant-moneylender guilds, both economically, because it controlled all sea and river traffic, and religiously, because it was home to the chief god of the merchant-moneylenders, the Moon God, Sin—an appropriate name for the god of the moneylenders, a god of stealth and secrets. The city of Ur was also the Biblical city from which the famous Jewish pimp known as Abraham was allegedly born and from whence his mythological saga began.

In the Old Testament, Ur is named "Ur of the Chaldees" (Gen 11:28, 11:31, 15:7). This designation, "Ur of the Chaldees" (or "Ur Kasdim"), actually gives evidence that Genesis was not written during the time that the lying rabbis claim that it was written because "Ur of the Chaldees" was not under Chaldean control until the early 7th century BC—but more on this subject in *The Monsters of Babylon*.

Those two cities, Ur and Uruk, were not only religious centers but Ur was also the international warehouse city of the merchant-moneylender guilds. Ur controlled both the river and the sea trade routes. Since Sumerian times, Uruk (Biblical 'Erech') was the ancient home of the highest god and goddess: Anu was the Sky God, and his consort, Inanna (later known as Ishtar), was the goddess of love and warfare. Thus, the chief gods of the merchant-moneylenders were the gods of stealth, secrets, sexual love, and warfare. These gods were not only worshipped by the moneylenders but also by the prostitutes, tavern-owners, and pimps.

However, the moneylenders and merchants had a much better reason than mere religious sentiments for worshipping the mighty gods in the temples. The priests solemnly assured their depositors that the temples were the only safe places to deposit large quantities of gold and silver. The priests absolutely guaranteed their customers that, for only a small service fee, their gods would protect all deposits down to the tiniest grain of silver. Every temple in every country of the ancient world, served as a bank of deposit, with the unarmed priests, backed up with idols of the fearsome gods, as the main guardians. What better guarantee could anyone want?

And yet, the Hittites had looted the temples of Babylon and had even carried away the statues of the gods without suffering in the least from god-given curses. It was another, amazing, difficult-to-explain miracle! With the temples of Babylon robbed of their gold and silver, where could the Kassites get the silver and grain necessary for paying and provisioning their armies?

Of course! *Borrow it* from the merchant-moneylender guilds based in Babylon who had originally betrayed their own people by giving cheap loans to the foreign Kassite immigrants for the purchase of Babylonian properties. Even though the Hittites had stolen their bullion from the temples of Babylon, once the Kassites had seized control of Babylon, these same merchant-moneylenders could still make loans of any amount as middlemen between Babylon and the moneylender guild of Ur, where Egyptian gold was still on deposit.

The cities of Ur and Uruk were within Sealander territories and their temples held the major reserves of tamkarum gold and silver safely on deposit. However, the merchant-moneylender guilds of Babylon, Ur, and Uruk did not want their bullion deposits separated from Babylon by the two city-state borders of Babylonia and the Sealands Dynasty because Babylon's more central location in Mesopotamia was better suited to controlling the growing trade with Anatolia and the Mediterranean Sea. So, rather than move their huge and very heavy gold and silver reserves from Ur and Uruk back to the looted temples of Babylon, they decided to eliminate the border between the two empires by erasing it. This would make it much easier to move their bullion to wherever was safest without the troublesome border inspections and taxes. With inspections by the king's tax assessors, the king would know just how immense the bullion holdings of the moneylenders actually was. This had to be avoided or else the moneylenders would lose their ability to lie about their lack of funds.

So, with loans of grain and silver, the moneylenders of Ur financed the Kassites to attack Sealander territory.

The tamkarum guilds were very familiar with every city controlled by the Sealanders. It was a part of their financial services to supply accurate military intelligence to their best customers who were, in this case, not the Sealanders among whom they had been allowed to live, but the Kassites whom they wanted to militarily destroy the Sealanders. Because the moneylenders had made "new friends" among the Kassites while betraying their "old friends" among the Sealanders, and even though both Ur and

Uruk were within the Sealander Dynasty territories, the moneylenders had no fear for their own safety or that of their families or their gold when they treasonably and successfully brought a warring army down among the surrounding lands and towns

As a reward for their help, the successfully-conquering Kassites treated those southern cities of Ur and Uruk with honor, refraining from looting or destroying their business properties and homes. In gratitude for their help, some of the Kassite kings later undertook building operations on the temples and other works of "piety" in Ur and Uruk. You will see this as a recurring theme throughout history, where armies destroy every people and loot all properties—except for the property of the treasonous money-lenders who had supplied their financing and military intelligence.

The Kassite kings wanted the Babylonian culture to be "as it had always been." They were Aryan kings who respected the advanced Baby-lonian culture but they were not well acquainted with the greed and cunning of the Semitic merchant-moneylenders. They were kings who falsely assumed that their control of Babylonian territory was sufficient to also have control of the tamkarum who lived within that territory but whose tendrils extended beyond that territory along the trade routes and across the known world—farther than any king could see. And their schemes were more diabolical than any king could imagine.

Simultaneously, to the immediate north, a powerful rival was grow-ing in might: The especially cruel Semitic kingdom of Assyria was begin-ning to arise. Their ruthless Assyrian merchant-moneylenders also prac-ticed the Sumerian Swindle just as it "had always been"—but even worse.

Tribute or War

However, before studying the Assyrians, we should again consider the international influence that was suffusing the entire ancient Near East at that time. This influence upon all of those societies was felt by the Hittites, Hurrians, Mycenaeans, Mittani, Assyrians, and Babylonians as a constant need for each country to fight and loot other countries and to force others into paying 'tribute.' Tribute was essentially a form of blackmail, telling a conquered people, "You must reimburse us the expense of invading your country with our armies; so pay us a yearly tribute of silver and gold or we will murder you all."

Even in modern times, this strange mental disease forces entire countries to go to war. It is still ravaging the countries of the world where the politicians stupidly pretend to be unable to figure out how to be friends with anybody else, while the moneylenders cheer them on from the sidelines and the people are stirred into paroxysms of hatreds and rages which quickly lead them into warfare. Modern societies are more complex than ancient societies but are despoiled by the very same Sumerian Swindle and manipulated by the very same manipulators, "just as it has always been."

Population pressures have always been an animating force, even in primitive tribal societies where fighting over hunting grounds, land use, and water rights had brought numberless tribal groups into armed conflict. These are all simple reasons why the primitive peoples clashed. But there was another dynamic, a subtle dynamic, a behind-the-scenes dynamic, which became a common reason for the kingdoms to go to war with one another. Other than actual pirate expeditions by sea or bandit raids by land, this reason was always in the background and never an officially stated policy of the kings who led their people into battle, disease, maiming, suffering, and death.

Long before the rise of Assyria as a major kingdom, all of the ancient societies had become interconnected through the trade routes which were simultaneously the most direct and the easiest routes for armies to traverse. All of those ancient countries, through trade, had become interconnected by their use of gold and silver as a medium of exchange. With gold and silver as a type of pseudo-money, business could be completed through a transfer of bullion even without a transfer of trade goods.

Because shekel-weights of silver and gold were used as money which could be exchanged for any and all trade goods, these commodity metals served to focus, like a glass lens focuses the sun's rays, the reasons why the various kingdoms went to war. By seizing silver and gold through the force of warfare, any and all goods and services could be purchased. So, obtaining silver and gold became a prime objective of wars.

But those kingdoms did not need more silver and gold to purchase goods for themselves. What they needed was more silver and gold *to repay the moneylenders more than they had borrowed.* There was never enough silver and gold to repay the huge numbers which were totaling daily on the accounting tablets.

Besides the Sumerian Swindle claiming that more was owed than what had been borrowed, and even more was owned than what actually existed, there was the ever-repeating fact that large quantities of silver and gold always magically vanished from every kingdom, as if into thin air. First, there was plenty of money—and then there was not enough. It was a great mystery.

What was animating the various kingdoms toward war, was the corrupting influence of the Sumerian Swindle upon all societies of mankind. What the various kings needed, was both to pay their debts to the moneylenders by stealing somebody else's silver and gold, as well as to replenish their own treasuries with the metals which always grew more "precious" as they inexplicably seemed to "disappear."

As precursor to their loan agreements, they had all given their word and pledged their honor in the name of their gods to repay their debts-plus-interest. Thus, they were bound by their sacred promises to the gods. And yet, it was because of their simple honesty and pious beliefs that both kings and commoners were all deceived by the world's most diabolically smooth deceivers who, in a matter of speaking, slyly unlocked the chains of the borrowers' sacred promises to the gods and then once again surreptitiously locked those same chains to their own accounting ledgers.

The kings and the people honestly tried to repay their loans to the moneylenders because they were fearful of the gods who would curse them with lightning strikes, bad luck, or leprosy for breaking their solemn and holy vows to the moneylenders. The moneylenders, themselves, as part of their phony street theater, always assumed an imperious attitude of the utmost integrity and punctual trustworthiness while haughtily insisting on the most pristine honesty from their borrowers. With diabolical grins, they pushed forward their clay tablets filled with cuneiform calculations and always repeated the ancient and well-worn phrase: "Numbers don't lie." But neither the kings nor the common people understood that "Liars who manipulate numbers, *always lie.*"

The kings and commoners all struggled to make sense out of the amazing phenomenon that the numbers on the accounting tablets allegedly "proved" that they owed more—very much more—than they had borrow-ed. One thing that they knew for certain was that if they did not repay the money-plus-interest which they had sworn, in-the-name-of-the-gods, to repay, then the consequences would be most dire—foreclosure of their farms, seizure of collateral, and enslavement of their children by the moneylenders, immediately followed with lightning strikes from the gods. And all in one day!

It was because of their very own honesty that the kings and the people were enslaved into repaying the moneylenders instead of hanging them. This same honesty of mankind protected the dishonest moneylenders be-cause they were operating under Secret Fraud #3 of the Sumerian Swindle: "Loans rely on the honesty of the borrower but not the honesty of the lender."

It has always been difficult for both kings and commoners to obtain enough gold and silver to achieve their goals of repaying the principal and the interest on the loans because the interest was always in amounts that, in reality, did not exist and could therefore never be repaid, unless the money could be robbed from their neighbors through warfare. Thus, to war they would go, maiming and being maimed, fighting and dying, while shouting at the top of their lungs every variety of battle cry *except* the one, true battle cry that invigorated them all, which was: "We need your money!"

"We Want the World!"

It was after their successful raid and looting of Egypt that the Babylonian moneylenders and their scribes realized that by using the Sumerian Swindle as their main engine of destruction, combined with careful military planning, that they could just possibly come into ownership of the entire world, if they played the Swindle just right.

The numbers in their accounting ledgers proved to the merchant-moneylenders that by operating the Sumerian Swindle, they had the demonic power to own everything on Earth, to enslave all of mankind and to steal the entire planet for themselves. They had been deceiving mankind for centuries for much smaller sums, so obtaining such a stupendous result was not a problem for them to imagine. The problem was: How could they commit such a crime of worldwide grand larceny and get away with it?

Of course, back in their Babylonian guild halls, most of their fellow tamkarum guild members ignored such speculations for owning the entire world as a laughably impossible dream, too huge to even imagine, or as a private joke among fellow guild members, soon to be forgotten.

But there was *one group* of merchant-moneylenders who really considered such a dream as being obtainable because their calculations proved it. After all, their private adventure in Egypt had paid great dividends without the kings being aware of the enterprise until it had already been accomplished. They knew the importance of military secrecy and of careful advance planning. They could trust their fellow conspirators to cooperate because they all had golden proof that such cooperation was extremely profitable to everyone involved, if the prize was big enough.

In addition to what they had personally plundered in Egypt, all of them had inherited a lot of gold and silver from their fathers who had plundered Egypt before them, enough to place them all at the very top of merchant-moneylender society in Babylonia. As a special commemoration of the huge amounts of loot that their fathers had won, eight days after each of them had been born, their daddies had given each of them a circumcision and a blow job from the rabbi instead of a T-shirt. So, they all had a circumcised penis which proved that they were descendants of the Babylonian merchant-moneylender crew who had plundered Egypt. And because of circumcision, they were all sex fiends obsessed with their multiple wives and their sex slaves.

With first-hand experience of plundering Egypt, as well as having been trained by their fathers in the best ways of swindling and thievery, they knew that they could plunder the entire world as long as they kept the secrets of their criminal schemes within the circle of their circumcised relatives and gang members. One very important difference in attitude between themselves and their *un*circumcised fellow guild members, was that all of the circumcised Babylonian merchant-moneylenders were murderers.

The Babylonian merchant-moneylenders who had remained in Babylonia during the Hyksos raid and were therefore not a party of the conspiracy to loot Egypt, continued to operate under the Laws of Hammurabi where murderers were punished with death. But those guild members who had conspired to plunder Egypt were restrained by no laws whatsoever. Murder, rape, and pillage were the only laws that they followed. With no laws and no kings to restrain them, they murdered whomever Egyptians that they wanted to murder with no repercussions from doing so. Throughout the entire Hyksos occupation of Egypt right up to the very last months, when they actually had to fight a trained Egyptian army, most of their murder victims had been defenseless old men and old women, and any young girls or young boys who resisted being raped.

This penchant for murder, is what allowed them to keep their secret plans secret by murdering not only their uncircumcised competitors but also any circumcised members of their ever-growing gang who were deemed to be too talkative and unreliable. There was an immediate danger to themselves from those uncircumcised fellow guild members who might discover the private schemes which they were developing and feel snubbed for not also being included in the plot. By being left out of the profits, they might tattle to the kings and then all would be lost.

In those days before electric lights, and with only wicks flickering in lamps of vegetable oil for illumination, there were always plenty of shadows for assassins to hide in and await their victims with dagger or staff, and then leave the scene of the crime unobserved, protected in their crimes by their secretive Moon God gliding through the sky like a slim reed boat.

If the kings discovered the machinations of this small group of circumcised sex-fiends, swindlers, and murderers or learned of the threat that they posed to all kings everywhere; or if the people knew of their plots to impoverish and enslave mankind, then all of their swindled properties would be confiscated and they, along with their extended family members, would all be executed for treason to the realm and betrayal of the gods. They had no doubt about such an outcome. So, keeping their schemes restricted to their own private gang of circumcised Babylonian swindlers, slave drivers, thieves, merchants, masturbating child-molesters, pimps, murderers, and moneylenders, was of the highest importance and secrecy.

The circumcised guild patriarchs and their sons and grandsons schemed and planned and pondered such questions as "How can we get away with it?" and "What do we need in order to accomplish this swindle?" and "We figured out a simple scheme for plundering the great nation of Egypt, so surely there is a way that we can plunder the entire world, own it all for ourselves, and enslave all of mankind to be servants beneath out feet." These and many other questions of how this gang of circumcised accountants could turn all of mankind into their slaves and gain ownership of the entire planet, took much debate and exchange of ideas. It was not an easy jump from being the most hated scum of the Earth to being kings above all, but there was a way to do it if they could just figure out how. First, they had to know what factors were preventing them from attaining their goal.

Eventually, over many years of discussion and debate, they were able to identify the "Fifteen Secret Problems Which Prevented the Babylonian Merchant-Moneylenders from Owning the Entire World." Once they understood what the problems were that prevented them from owning the entire world, finding a solution for those problems would take many more years of guess work and discussion. Their goal, if attained, would bring them very much more wealth than what they had stolen from Egypt.

Among the circumcised patriarchs, all of these secret problems required deep discussions within the inner sanctums of their sound-proof, mud-brick guild temples and their private, sound-proof mud-brick mansions. Year after year, they discussed and debated deep into the night while their mysterious and secretive Moon God waxed and waned across skies filled full of glittering stars, and the Babylonian constellations moved mysteriously and silently across the skies with unvarying precision.

From their combined centuries of experience in creating slavery and buying and selling slaves, the merchant-moneylender guilds knew that if the people could be physically defrauded and then clapped into irons before they realized their danger, then all would be well for the merchants and moneylenders. Once the people were enslaved, they would be powerless to do anything about their losses. And while they were being gradually swindled of their goods and freedoms, it was imperative for the moneylenders to keep the people stirred up and in a state of fear and anxiety so that they would not have the opportunity to realize the real cause of their problems. The people would not be thinking about beating and hanging the bankers if they were kept running about under a hail of an attacking army's sling stones and flaming arrows or, as in modern times, running about under the Molotov cocktails and cobblestones of communist hooligans hired by the bankers.

Because the money-lenders and merchants profit so enormously from their frauds, they had the money enough to hire mercenaries, assassins, trouble-makers, rumor-mongers, and seducers to make sure that there was always a controlled level of chaos in every society in which they were allowed to live. When the people are sufficiently worried and stressed from rumors of war and manufactured crises, they don't have the leisure to think of anything besides survival. Meanwhile, the merchants and moneylenders always had plenty of food and other necessities to carry them through whatever scarcities which they had engineered for others.

Enslaving the entire population would have to be a gradual process, otherwise there would be no one able to pay the moneylenders. First, the moneylenders had to acquire the wealth of the people, and only then could they enslave them. There had to be a social class of the very wealthy to buy the goods offered by the merchant-moneylenders. Slavery had its limits both as a means of collecting on the debt as well as for its use in terrorizing the people. As long as society had enough circulating wealth to buy the debt-slaves, the moneylenders could profit from their swindle. But when the interest payments became so high that no one could afford to buy anything because all of their money was going to the bankers as debt-service, then the Swindle would break down. Also, when the rich were over-supplied with slaves and no one wanted to buy them from the moneylenders' slave markets, then the entire Sumerian Swindle became paralyzed. There had to be both poverty-stricken slaves and excessively wealthy awilum (the Haves), as well as the chaos of war to kill off the dispossessed, in order for the Swindle to operate smoothly and profitably.

However, one danger to the moneylenders was (and is) the rise of a *middle class*. A well-fed middle class provides leisure and an opportunity for thinking men to ponder the causes and cures of social and political ills. Also, a middle class of property-owners provides a storage place for silver and gold diffused throughout society during times of prosperity. Such a money-absorbing sponge needed to be squeezed out on a regular basis so that the peoples' hidden hoards and rainy-day savings of silver and gold could once again cascade into the bankers' hands. Once the people are given an opportunity to prosper, ruthless application of Secret Fraud #11 of the Sumerian Swindle was the merchant-moneylender's standard tactic: "Dispossessing the people brings wealth to the dispossessor, yielding the greatest profit for the bankers when the people are impoverished."

A middle class is also useful from whom interest can be swindled from loans and to whom merchants can sell their goods at a high profit. As long as they are dependent upon the moneylenders, an indebted middle class is a source of huge profits, as can be seen in modern times. But once the wealth of a middle class reached a point of being wealthy enough to be independent from the moneylenders, they would have to be destroyed, impoverished, dispossessed of their property, and enslaved. No competition from outside of the merchant-moneylender guilds could be allowed if the moneylenders and merchants were to maintain their extremely high profits which gave them power even over the kings.

Once enough of the middle class had paid off their property to become property-owners rather than mere debtors, then the bankers conspire to destroy such a middle class in order to maintain their own high profits without competition. Such an independent middle class would not be allowed to keep what they had worked so hard to acquire ownership of, without owing anything to the moneylenders. If the middle class property-owners could be subjected to emergencies and social stresses such as war or foreign immigration which caused them to once again borrow money to "tide them over the bad times," then those property owners who had purchased their homes and farms at interest from the moneylenders at a high price, would then, out of desperation, be forced either to sell back to the moneylenders those same homes and farms at a low price or else lose them in foreclosure.

Creating poverty for others was the moneylenders' guarantee of maintaining all wealth for themselves while crushing the people beneath their feet. This was again Secret Fraud #11 of the Sumerian Swindle: "Dispossessing the people brings wealth to the dispossessor, yielding the greatest profit for the bankers when the people are impoverished."

Boom or Bust

But a new twist to this already-ancient system began to be practiced by the Semitic moneylenders in Assyria.

It was during the rise of the Assyrian Empire that the Assyrian moneylenders began to expand the Sumerian Swindle into yet another of its many corrupt levels of grand larceny. In this case, the banker's swindle known in modern times as the so-called "business cycles of boom and bust" became common in Assyria. We modern people experience it today and accept it because "it has always been here."

Through a purposely-designed series of repetitive cycles of inflation and depression, swinging back and forth throughout the years, the moneylenders could obtain all of society's wealth. They were like a snake swallowing its prey by putting its mouth around the entire victim. First chewing on one side and then on another side, little by little, sawing back and forth between depression and inflation, the bankers could swallow the entire country into their vaults and ledger books. And so, they promoted first the one and then the other and back again, while hiding their profits behind a hypocritical sham of pretending that they, too, were suffering from what they claimed to be a mysteriously uncontrollable and random economic events which they called the "business cycle."

But just as in those ancient times, the real causes of such larcenous "cycles" were hidden from the public because nobody but the money-lenders knew the actual available quantities of gold and silver. So, nobody but the bankers knew that those so-called "business cycles" were fake and purposely staged. The gold and silver were always hidden away in the bankers' private hoards and strong rooms to create a "bust," and then loaned out liberally so as to create a "boom." The only ones who knew how much money was actually in circulation, were the moneylenders. No one knew where or why the money disappeared—except the money-lenders. In order to conceal from both kings and commoners that the business cycles were staged events, the amount of silver and gold hidden in the moneylenders' secret strong rooms, was known only by the money-lenders. This information, which affected the entire public, was always privately controlled by the moneylenders, just as it is in modern times and all for the same reasons.

Just as it is today, only those who controlled how much money was in circulation, could profit from such knowledge. Even the kings had to borrow from the moneylenders at interest when the silver gradually and mysteriously disappeared, leaving the people without enough silver to pay the king's taxes. Even the poorest peasant would fritter away his wages to the *sabitum* (alewife-moneylender) when money was plentiful and wages were high, leaving him begging the alewife-moneylender for a loan when silver was scarce.

Times of plenty and times of dearth could be manipulated by the tamkarum guilds working in collusion across the borders of all kingdoms, and lending or hoarding silver, and lowering or raising interest rates simultaneously across all of Mesopotamia. When the loan-rates were the same across the entire Fertile Crescent, then there was nowhere for the people to borrow other than from this same, conspiring and larcenous trade cartel with branch offices in every city and town.

Thus, from earliest development of civilization, a criminal system was established by the moneylenders whereby the public circulation of money was allowed to be controlled by a private coalition of frauds and swindlers whom we call in modern times by such names as "bankers" and "financiers." Such a dangerous situation is allowed in modern times, too. The bankers get away with not being hanged for it, because they lie and pretend to be "honest businessmen." So, everyone is fooled by their lies and swindles, just as "it has always been."

Low-interest and zero-interest loans to the rich created a richer class of awilum (Haves). Any reduced profits were made up by making high-interest loans to the poor, the muskenum (the Have-Nots). Since there were always more "Have-Nots" than there were "Haves," then the profits were always greater by lending at low-interest to the rich who did not need the money, while lending at high-interest to the poor who needed money the most. Those who were poor enough and desperate enough, would accept the highest loan rates just for a temporary respite from their grinding poverty. Being poor and illiterate meant that they could not understand that their thumb print on the wet clay tablet loan agreement guaranteed that the moneylender would have them in slave's shackles at the end of the loan period, no matter how hard they worked under the hot sun from dawn to dusk.

As Assyria began to throw off its inferior status to Babylonia and to defend itself from the raids of the Hittites, the scheming Assyrian merchant-moneylenders simultaneously began to solve their problem of too many slaves and not enough buyers. Whenever the total wealth of a country is held by and owed to the moneylenders, resulting in not enough silver to pay off the loans, the only way to keep the Swindle producing more profits for the moneylenders, is to induce the people to steal silver and gold from other people and pay their debts to the moneylenders with the resulting loot. This was most efficiently accomplished by sending the entire populace to war.

In addition, the Assyrian merchant-moneylenders found that war killed off large numbers of land-owners, resulting in many starving and desperate widows and orphans selling their farms and properties cheaply. Those farms which had been abandoned because the owners had been killed in war, could be cheaply acquired merely by paying to the king the back taxes on the property. With good farmland bought cheaply, the tamkarum found that they could again profit from war by selling those vacant farms to foreigners at high prices and once again betraying their own people and their own country to foreign investors and foreign immigrants.

Thus, every merchant-moneylender in every kingdom became the ultimate parasite, who not only sucked the health and wealth out of his own people but finally killed his own people in warfare. Then, after impoverishing his own country through his swindling, he betrayed his own country by immigrating foreign victims from other countries so that he could next parasitize and suck the lifeblood from them. This is "how it has always been": the merchants and moneylenders betraying their own country to its enemies.

As the wealth of foreign nations was seized as a trophy of war, this brought circulating bullion into the moneylenders' international system of fraud. What silver and gold that was not directly paid to the moneylenders as debt service, remained in circulation among the people as bullion that was spent into the merchant-moneylenders' network of family and guild monopolies such as luxury imports, real estate, beer taverns, brothels, gambling halls, and slave markets. Through their interlocking businesses, the merchant-moneylender guilds cast a wide net which caught all shekel weights of silver and gold circulating in the ancient Near East.

For the above reasons, with the merchant-moneylenders operating from behind the scenes as advisors and spies and financiers of the kings, *war* became the primary business of Assyria.

PART THREE

From Apiru to Jews

CHAPTER 12
THE ASSYRIANS AND THE GOAT-RUSTLERS

As we look into the history of Assyria, please remember that because the Sumerian Swindle is a deceitful and dishonest scam, it can never be administered by honest men. Although they strive to appear to be honest businessmen, however, banking and moneylending are intrinsically criminal enterprises. The ones who controlled it in ancient times as well as those who control it in modern times, were and are the most evil and the most corrupt creatures in all of society, no matter how nice they look wearing fancy clothes. Every one of them is a monster. What else can be said of a creature who sucks the life out of people, creates warfare and desolation, tears children away from parents and enslaves them, kicks widows and orphans out of their homes and into the streets, creates slavery in all of its forms, and profits from human misery?

How could those old devils be anything other than monsters when taking callous advantage of the weak and the poor, enslaving entire families, pimping out little boys and girls, operating prostitution, alcohol, gambling, pawning of stolen goods, smuggling, tax evasion, combined with the beating and murder of those who could not pay the larcenous debts, all while sending off millions of people into the hell of war? How could such evil creatures be "honest businessmen"? The bankers, money-lenders, financiers, and merchants today are nothing but criminals and traitors to all of mankind just as they "have always been."

As the long centuries passed, the moneylenders became no different than demons preying upon the impoverishment, enslavement, starvation, disease, suffering, illiteracy, war-losses, and death of mankind. Basking in the "prestige" of their riches and the high positions granted to them by the deluded and corrupted kings. The bankers and moneylenders were—as they are today—the actual causes of the death and suffering of billions of people. But they were not Jews—yet.

Under the pressure of cheap foreign labor, the resulting dislocation of native labor from the land gave the moneylenders and kings plenty of foreclosed and starving peasants to fill the ranks of the army in exchange for land grants, social status, and rations. Like a giant meat grinder, the tamkarum (merchant-moneylenders) shoved the people into their war machine and swindled them out of all that they owned.

After dispossessing their own people by immigrating into the country cheap foreign labor; and after the poor immigrant farmers had built a new farm with their hard work, the tamkarum once again dispossessed the new-comers of their land because that was "how it had always been." So, these peasants, in turn, out of desperation, joined the army in order to be given an *ilkum* (military land grant) and some rations because that was the only avenue left open to them for wealth and social prestige.

Then, they would be marched out to fight other countries for loot which they gave to the kings or spent in the shops of the tamkarum; or drank and whored in the taverns of the *sabitum* (alewife-moneylenders); or gave to the *naditum* (priestess-moneylenders) in their gratitude that the gods had brought them through the wars alive and not maimed. Of those who died, the kings confiscated their property and sold it for back taxes to the moneylenders. It was all a smoothly working scam that had taken centuries to perfect.

And it still works smoothly today. What is consistently good for enriching the bankers and the merchants and the moneylenders, has always proven to be very bad for the people. So, when you see a banker or financier, know that he has built his wealth upon the impoverishment and the destruction of tens of thousands and millions of other people. A banker is a parasite. A financier is a con-artist. Both are criminals.

The Hittites

Passing mention has already been made of the Hittites who attacked Babylon, plundered its temples, and then retreated, leaving the country in Kassite control. With such a powerful army capable of defeating Baby-lonia, the Hittites were certainly a challenge to Assyria.

The earliest inhabitants of Asia Minor spoke dialects which were not Indo-European. The Indo-European speakers among them, known as Hittites, began to arrive in the area in the first century of the second millennium. Before following the history of the Assyrians, it would be good to under-stand the Hittites and their relationship with Assyria and the entire region.

The trading arrangements between Asia Minor and Assyria came to an end shortly after 1800 BC as the Hittites came into prominence and be-gan to take control of the natural resources and trade routes within their own territories, resources which the Assyrians had been monopolizing [see Map 17]. Before they asserted themselves in this way, the region's trade

had been conducted through trading colonies established by other countries. Assyrian tamkarum had a trading colony in Cappadocia that monopolized the bronze trade from the region. We find evidence from Hittite documents that in the second half of the second millennium the Hittites had
trading relations not only with Mesopotamia but also with Egypt and the
Mycenaean kingdoms in western Asia Minor, Rhodes, and Greece.

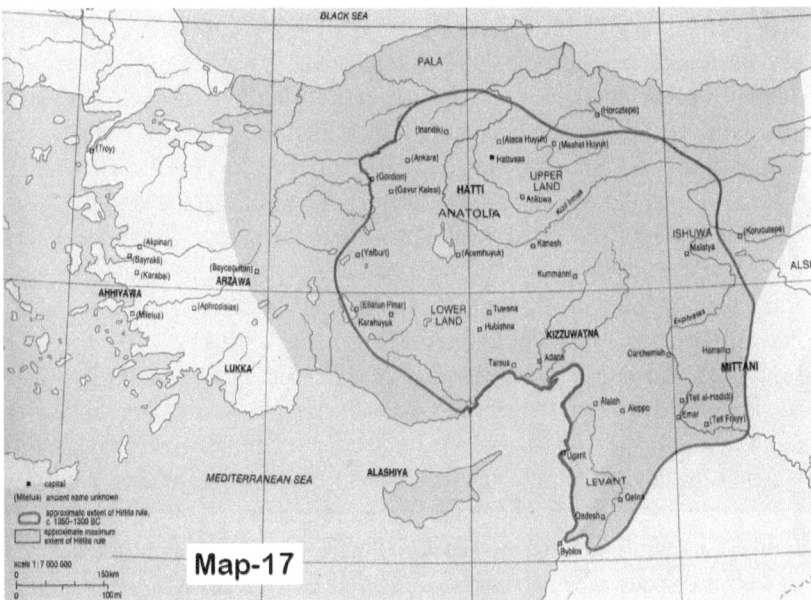

Map-17

The Hittites mined copper and silver in large quantities. These resources
alone gave them the buying power and the products that were in demand
all over the ancient Near East. They could buy whatever they wanted and
could trade these natural resources to build profitable trade relationships.

In addition, during part of the second millennium, the Hittites had a
virtual monopoly of iron, still a relatively unknown and rare metal. Iron
could be forged into steel on a charcoal fire to make light weight and extremely sharp swords and daggers which held an edge in combat and could
cut through the softer copper, bronze, and brass weapons. Like any
technology which gives a military advantage, the production and export of
particular metals of military importance, such as copper, brass, bronze, tin,
and iron, were frequently under state control in every country. As a
strategic metal, the export of iron was a royal monopoly.

Thus, the Hittites had valuable trade commodities as well as a military technology superior to the bronze, copper, and brass weapons of the

surrounding countries. Through their control of strategic metals found within their own territories and their Aryan military might backed by superior iron swords and chariots, the Hittites became a major force in the region.

Wages paid in Hattiland, where the Aryan Hittites controlled the economy, were 12 shekels of silver for a man and 6 shekels of silver for a woman per month. Farm work paid 1500 liters of barley for three months, 600 liters for a woman. Compare this to the low wages paid to the workers under Hammurabi's first Dynasty of Babylon (1894-1595 BC) which established standards for all of Mesopotamia throughout its subsequent history. In Babylonia, farm work only paid 1200 liters of grain per year, and only if the worker was a full-time employee rather than a mere seasonal worker, who was paid less. Wages paid in silver in Babylonia, where the Semitic merchant-moneylenders controlled the economy, were only 4 shekels of silver per year. This difference is strictly a reflection of the corrosive influence that the Semitic merchant-moneylenders had on Babylonia. Using the Sumerian Swindle, they had impoverished everybody in their society except for themselves.

It could be argued that these price differences could be attributed to the fact that the Hittites had their own silver mines, so that the metal was more common and prices reflected a temporary inflation. However, this was not the case because wages were also paid in grain rations. And it is these grain wages which reflect the values, not just of goods but of a higher form of humanity among the Aryan Hittites, who cared about the welfare of their own people, which was so unlike the cruelty that was found among the Mesopotamian Semites, who cared only for personal profits while betraying their own people. The difference between a generous 1500 liters of grain paid to Hittite laborers for *three month's work* versus the miserly 1200 liters of grain paid to the Babylonian and Assyrian laborers for a *whole year's work*, cannot be a result of inflation but is rather a result of fairness between the Hittite "Haves" and "Have-Nots." The Hittites paid their people a fair wage, while the Mesopotamian merchant-moneylenders, specifically, and the Mesopotamian "Haves," in general, swindled and robbed their own people at every opportunity. Under the influence of the ancient Sumerian Swindle, every society becomes materialistic and cruel because the Swindle is controlled by thieves, con artists, and corrupted kings.

The Hittites had not been subverted and betrayed by the moneylenders as had the Babylonians and Assyrians because Hattiland was ruled by a king for the sake of his people rather than by moneylenders for the sake of themselves. Furthermore, because the Hittites were not dominated by the merchant-moneylenders, theft was not considered such a horrible crime. The thief merely paid a fine of 12 shekels of silver. Under the Semitic Laws of Hammurabi, a thief was executed.

In addition, the sexual perversions of the circumcised merchant-moneylenders were abhorred by the Hittites. Unlike the societies of Mesopotamia that were dominated by the perverted merchant-moneylenders and the homosexual bankers, in Hattiland, sexual relations with one's mother, daughter, son, or a beast was punished with execution, while in Semitic Babylonia, all of those perversions were considered to be entirely acceptable. From these early dates, one can begin to understand where all of the unnatural and demented sexual perversions of modern times have their origin: from among the circumcised Semites.

The Syrian Middleman

But there were other people besides the Hittites who had trade contacts with Assyria and Babylonia. It is appropriate here to refer to the part played by Syria as a middleman in international trade. Located between Assyria and the Hittites, Syria was in the Hittite orbit for a time because Northern Syria always formed a terminal of one of the main trade routes from Mesopotamia. The Alalakh district was a terminal for trade routes from both southern Mesopotamia and Cilicia as early as the fourth millennium. In the second millennium, the Amorite city of Alalakh had a checkered career politically, coming under the control successively of Egypt, northern Mesopotamia, and the Hittites. But this very fact is an indication of its commercial importance.

Although this city would later be destroyed by the Hittites, it should be noted that one of the kings of Alalakh was Idrimi, who recorded on his statue in the 15th century BC that he had gained his throne by winning the support of the "Hapiru people in the land of Canaan." These Hapiru recognized him as the "son of their overlord Barattarna" and "gathered around him." After living among them for seven years, he led his Hapiru warriors in a successful attack by sea on Alalakh, where he became king.

Keep these mercenary Hapiru tribes in mind, since we will be dealing with them again. It is of interest here because of the long geographical distances outside of Canaan traveled by the goat-rustling Hapiru (or Habiru, or Apiru, or Hebrew) tribes. These Semitic tribes of roving bandits were widespread throughout the entire region. It is noteworthy that they were allied with a Semitic Amorite Syrian where the trade goods from Babylonia were merchandized. Assyria was growing but it was not a great empire at that time [see Map 13]. It was the merchants of Babylonia who supplied them with the bronze swords and daggers which they prized. They were not allies of any of the petty kings of the tiny towns of Canaan.

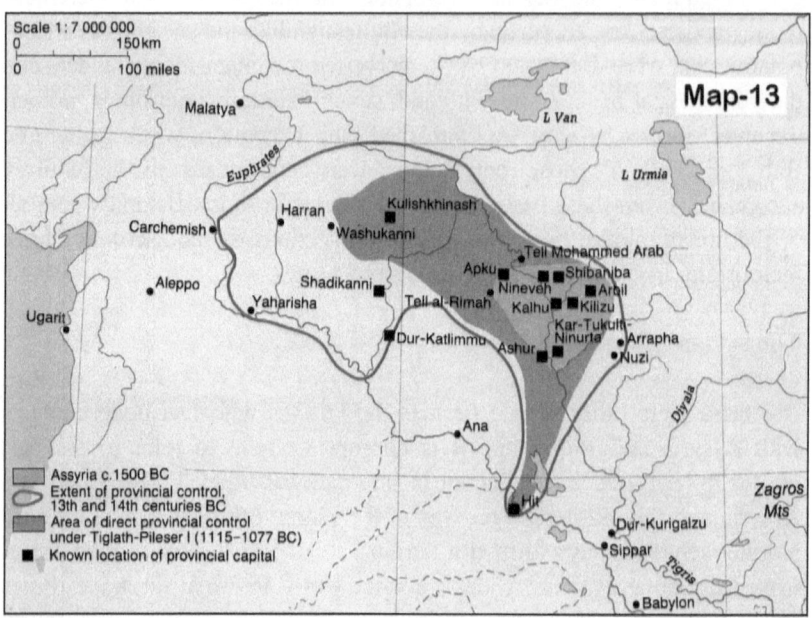

Other trade colonies were established in Hittite territory by Mycenaean (Greek) merchants. There were also Assyrian and Egyptian trade colonists present, to judge by a document listing wine deliveries for people of these nationalities. As to values, it is stated in the cuneiform texts that gold was at this time worth three or four times its weight in silver. This low ratio was the result of the huge amounts of gold bullion that had been released into circulation from the Hyksos plunder of Egypt. It was still in circulation in the markets and hidden in hoards that had not yet fallen completely into the hands of the moneylenders.

Another large and important group of people were the *Hurrians*, who were moving southwards during the first half of the second millennium BC. Associated with the Hurrians at this time was an aristocracy of the race which we know as 'Indo-European' or 'Aryan.' The Aryans derived ultimately from the steppes of Russia, one of the original homes of the wild horse. Because of this, the Aryans were always found in association with the horse, and it was the Aryan migrants of the second millennium who introduced the horse-drawn chariot as an instrument of war. This chariot-owning Aryan aristocracy, ruling over a population which was largely Hurrian, had succeeded in establishing a powerful kingdom shortly before 1500 BC centered upon the Habur River area. We know this kingdom as *Mitanni*. Mitanni at its greatest extent stretched from Lake Van to the middle Euphrates and from the Zagros Mountains to the Syrian coast [see Map 16]. This map gives a general view of the empires which existed during the very beginnings of that demonic cult known as Judaism.

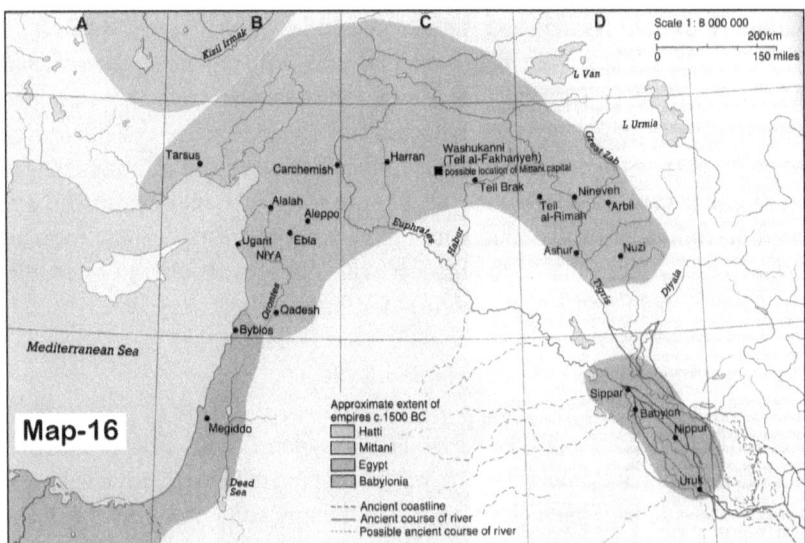

The kings of Mitanni bore not Hurrian but Indo-European names, while the old Indian gods Mitra, Varuna, Indra, and the Nasatiyas were worshipped by those Aryans. In Hurrian documents, particularly those concerned with horses and warfare, technical terms occur which have cognate forms in Indo-Aryan. It is also significant that unlike all the earlier peoples of the Ancient East, among whom burning of the corpse was rare and sometimes regarded as a horror transcending death itself, burning was the proper mode of disposal for the bodies of the early Mitannian kings. All this points to the presence of an Aryan warrior caste ruling over a largely non-Aryan population. There is some evidence of the same kind pointing to the presence of Indo-Aryan elements among the Kassite ruling caste also.

The kingdom of Mitanni is, oddly enough, best known not from evidence found in the kingdom itself, but from documents discovered in the land of the Hittites, in Syria, and above all in Egypt. These documents point to the considerable, if temporary, importance of Mitanni.

The sources from Egypt are of two kinds. One is the Egyptian hieroglyphic documents, which have references to armed conflict with

Mitanni in the Syrian region, the area in which the two States came into competition. The other Egyptian source, surprisingly, consists of clay tablets inscribed in cuneiform. These tablets are the famous El Amarna letters constituting part of the diplomatic archives of the Egyptian Pharaohs at a period around 1400 BC. These documents include letters to the Pharaoh from various princes of Palestine and Syria, from the kings of the Hittite land, from Assyria and Babylonia, and from the King of Mitanni.

The part of the correspondence involving Mitanni clearly shows that Mitanni was on an equality with Egypt. These letters show that marriage alliances were made between Mitanni and Egypt, and give evidence of several instances in which Mitannian princesses were sent as brides for the Pharaoh. It may be added that the Kassite ruler of Babylonia also made marriage alliances of this kind with Egypt. It should also be noted for later reference that these marriage alliances with Egypt were always brides for the Pharaoh but never Egyptian brides for foreign kings.

Nebuchadnezzar and the Babylonian Exile

Let's jump ahead about 800 years. The Assyrian Empire fell in 605 BC, and Babylonia became inheritor of the conquered Assyrian territories. Once Assyria had been destroyed, surprisingly, one finds in the Neo-Babylonian empire far less concentration of power in the hands of the king. The domestic history of Babylonia during the following century was in some aspects a struggle for power between the dynasty and the temples, a struggle in which the temples were finally victorious.

In Assyria, the king was consecrated at the beginning of his reign once and forever. And so, he became the representative of the gods without limitation. However, in Babylonia, even to the very end, the king had to lay his insignia humbly before the god each year, submit to personal indignities at the hands of the high priest, make a declaration of good intentions, and only then receive re-investiture with the royal authority by once again "taking the hand of the god."

This power of the Babylonian priests over the king became a great danger to the authority of the king if he was ever out of favor with the priests. Besides the slaps on his face and the ear-pulling that the king received from the priests of Marduk as a part of the ceremony, there was always the danger that the priests would use a liver divination or some other sign from the gods to remove the king's authority. And what king could retain his authority if the gods were against him? His own people would leave his services out of fear of the mighty gods.

Thus, in Babylonia the king remained a tenant-at-will of the god and, as such, was less able to gather temple lands into his own hands and thereby into permanent royal control. This power of the temple in political and economic affairs was envied by the tamkarum class because it was a power that they could not buy. However, they could corrupt and steal it. In all of those ancient societies, even if a king ruled, it was the god of the temple priests who had the greatest power over all.

In the provinces of the Neo-Babylonian empire, the general lines of Assyrian policy continued to be carried out. Thus, the deportations by Nebuchadnezzar II, in 597 BC and 586 BC, of some of the population of Judah—known today as the Babylonian Exile—were nothing but a continuation of the policy instituted by Ashur-nasir-pal II (884-859 BC) and developed by Tiglath-Pileser III (745-727 BC) to deal with recalcitrant vassals and to reduce the likelihood of rebellion, because deported people did not have the advantage of knowing the territory well enough to mount an effective rebellion. At the same time, Nebuchadnezzar II, like the Assyrian government in similar circumstances, appears to have made strenuous attempts to preserve a native administration for governing the people who were not deported.

After the surrender of Jerusalem in 597 BC and the deportation of the young king Jehoiachin along with his administration and his court clowns dressed as rabbis, Nebuchadnezzar II attempted indirect rule by using Zedekiah as a vassal prince bound to Babylonia. For nine years, the experiment was successful. Even after the siege and capture of Jerusalem consequent on Zedekiah's ultimate yielding to the pro-Egyptian party, Nebuchadnezzar still did not abandon the attempt to employ some form of indirect rule. So, he appointed an influential Jewish aristocrat, Gedaliah, as governor. It was only after Gedaliah's assassination by Jewish zealots hired by the rabbis, that Judah came under direct Babylonian administration.

It was during the Neo-Babylonian Period that the power of the circumcised moneylender guilds was at its highest. These secretive brotherhoods of schemers had cemented their business relationships well enough through guild membership and marriages that they no longer needed to use written contracts for their business transactions between one another, such was their mutual trust. The merchant-moneylender guilds were international in membership. Without bothering to notify the kings of their true loyalties, these circumcised betrayers controlled the flow of goods and bullion across the borders of all kingdoms,

Since Sumerian times, it had been the practice to commit every transaction to writing. But for the first time, the Neo-Babylonian wholesale merchants seem to have preferred oral agreements supplemented by a variety of operational devices. With oral agreements between trusted guild brothers, all sorts of schemes and plots were possible without fear of detection or proof of treachery.

But a dearth of clay tablets does not mean that contracts were not used at all. It was during these times that cuneiform characters written on durable clay were being replaced by Semitic alphabets written on perishable parchment. The Semitic language, Aramaic, had become the international language of business and politics.

At the death of Nebuchadnezzar II in 562 BC, he was succeeded by his son Amel-Marduk (Evil-Merodach of 2 Kings 35:27) who, after a brief reign of two years, was killed in a revolution. Little is known of him beyond the statement in 2 Kings 25:27-30 that he showed special favor to Jehoiachin, one of the two ex-kings of Judah held captive at Babylon. Curiously enough, there is a direct reference to Jehoiachin in some cuneiform tablets found at Babylon and datable to the reign of Nebuchadnezzar. These tablets are lists of ration issues and the relevant part of one of them reads:

> For Ya'u-kina king of the land Yahudu, for the five sons of
> the king of the land of Yahudu, (and) for eight Yahudaeans,
> each one-half sila [one-half liter] of grain per day.

Philologically, "Ya'u-kinu of Yahudu" is unmistakably the name which the Bible translators render Jehoiachin of Judah.

After King Amel-Marduk died, the man who benefited by his death and the one who led the revolution to depose him, was Nergal-shar-usur (Neriglissar of the Greek accounts, Nergal-shar-ezer of Jeremiah 39:3), a son-in-law of Nebuchadnezzar II. It is now known from a Babylonian chronicle that he undertook a great and foolish campaign across the Taurus Mountains, wasting the men and strength of Babylonia. After initial success, this usurper suffered a serious defeat and returned to Babylon in 556 BC, dying so soon afterwards that one is tempted to wonder if his personal rivals at home took advantage of his loss of prestige to hasten his end. Certainly his son, Labashi-Marduk, who attempted to assume the throne in succession, was very shortly removed by a rebellion of the chief officers of state, who put on the throne Nabu-na'id (Nabonidus), the diplomat who had been commissioned by Nebuchadnezzar II to assist negotiations between the Medes and Lydians in 585 B.C.

Why would the chief officers of the Neo-Babylonian Empire want Nabonidus to lead them rather than someone of the lineage of Nebuchadnezzar? A desire for honest government was the reason. That Nabonidus had been a wise and loyal diplomat who could lead effectively was important. But most important was that he was a sincerely religious man. He had the trust of the chief officers who had rebelled against the usurper, Nergal-sharusur, and his son, Labashi-Marduk. And he was a devotee of the Moon God, Sin, the god of the moneylenders of Babylon and of Ur. He could lead his people along the "straight and true path."

Nabonidus (555-539 BC), already in his sixties, ascended the throne after many years of service to Nebuchadnezzar II. He was not a member of Nebuchadnezzar II's family. He was to be the last of the Neo-Babylonian kings. As he wrote: "I am Nabu-na'id who has not the honor of being a somebody—kingship is not within me." Certainly, a most humble comment from a king!

Nabonidus was not of the royal family of Nabopolassar. He was the son of a nobleman and the high-priestess of Sin, the Moon God at Harran. Being the son of the high priestess of the Moon God, would have had an effect upon anyone born to such a position. For Nabonidus, the effects were extreme. He was a very religious man whose life was ruled by his god. Once again remember that this was an age when the divinations over the liver of a sheep, or the meaning of dreams, or the consequences of omens in the sky, were all piously accepted as messages from the gods. That Nabonidus became king, whose mother was priestess to the Moon God, are facts that don't seem to have been properly understood by the atheist archeologists who profess confusion over the subsequent historical events.

At the beginning of his reign, Nabonidus had a dream in which Marduk ordered him to rebuild the Temple of Sin at Harran. This temple had lain desolate for 54 years. This was his mother's temple and he no doubt wanted to please her since she was still living at Harran. Now that he was king of Babylonia, he had the power to do so.

Once again note the piety of these kings of the ancient Near East. Based upon a dream wherein the god, Marduk, spoke to him, Nabonidus changed both state policy and the destiny of his entire kingdom. All based upon a religiously inspired dream! Please remember this when we explore the dreams and fantasies of the demon Jews in *The Monsters of Babylon*.

Nabonidus rebuilt the temple and re-dedicated it to the Moon God, Sin, though with some considerable opposition from the priests of Babylon. He also gave special attention to the centers of moon worship at Ur and later also at the oasis of Tayma in Arabia. His growing devotion to the Moon God was a religious change which caused friction with the traditional and ancient religious factions in Babylonia. Nabonidus' mother, Adad-guppi, was devoted to this god at Harran. According to her cuneiform biography, Adad-guppi lived 104 years. So, her life spanned the entire Neo-Babylonian period.

In his dedications, Nabonidus' inscriptions expressed what he considered the impiety and lawlessness of his subjects. This pious king could see for himself the rampant fraud and ruthless avarice of the Babylonian society which was under the oppressive debts and the debauchery of the merchant-moneylenders. Through licentiousness and desperation, both of which were promoted by and profited by the merchants and moneylenders, the people had abandoned the holy way of devotion to the gods. Making money to give to the moneylenders had become their main, panic-stricken concern. And that is exactly how the moneylenders preferred their debtors to be—terrorized by what these demonic accountants and bean-counters could do to them.

This long decline in public morals and piety can be seen in the changes that occurred in the peoples' allegiance to the gods over the millennia. During Sumerian times, the ancient Ubaidian city of Uruk was home to the temple of Anu, the god of heaven and king of the gods. Every Mesopotamian city had its chief god residing in its main temple. Also, every city had numerous smaller temples and chapels devoted to the lesser gods of that region.

Until the end of the Third Dynasty of Ur when the Sumerians still controlled their own culture, Anu was the Sumerian god of heaven and he resided in the biggest temple in Uruk. His daughter was the goddess Ianna, the Sumerian goddess of love and warfare. She resided in a small temple. But as the tamkarum gained the debt-slave ownership of women through their money-lending scams, and as the prestige of women was degraded through slavery and prostitution, the peoples' devotion to Anu, the god of heaven, decreased and the devotees of the love and warfare goddess, Ianna (Ishtar), increased.

As the Sumerians were replaced by the promiscuous Semites (variously called Akkadians, Amorites, and Aramaeans); and as the Sumerian culture was replaced by the ruthless, materialistic, Semitic Babylonian culture; and as the protective authority of the kings and the moral authority of the priests were subverted by the moneygrubbing corrosive power of the merchant-moneylenders; so the temple of Anu became less prosperous while the temple of Ianna (Ishtar) became predominant. In a culture which was dominated by moneylenders, merchants, bankers, and whore-mongers, the temple of Ishtar (the goddess of love and war) became the biggest temple in Uruk by Neo-Babylonian times.

Profit-Making Temples

Despite its great agricultural wealth, the Neo-Babylonian empire suffered severe economic constraints. During the previous wars against Assyria and against the Medes, manpower had been diverted to the army while the fields and canals fell into neglect. This was always a recipe for famine. The military and building campaigns of Nabopolassar and Nebuchadnezzar had taken their toll on the royal finances, and the disastrous military adventures of Nergal-shar-usur had drained away dwindling resources.

Some of Babylonia's major trade routes in the east fell to the control of the Aryan Medes of Persia. The merchants, no longer limited by the ancient Laws of Hammurabi, raised prices by 50 percent. Babylonia also suffered from plague and famine. Nabonidus tried to explain the famine as a result of the impiety of the Babylonian people. This was the usual belief for all of the peoples of the ancient Near East when faced with either good or bad events; that is, the benevolence or wrath of the gods was the result of the holiness or wickedness of the people. But even in bad times, as the people implored the gods to save them, the temples received from pious devotees, gifts and donations of land and gold as sacrifices to the gods.

Putting matters of godly provenance aside, the temples always had a source of donated gold and silver in their treasuries. It is clear from the cuneiform documents which have come down to us, that the kings in the Neo-Babylonian period took a share of the temple revenues. Special royal officers were installed in the temples for this purpose. Among revenues which certainly went to the temples in the first instance were tithes on date crops and catches of fish, rents (payable in kind) on grain-land, a cattle tax, customary offerings made by farmers at the time of particular festivals, and other dues of a more or less obscure nature. There were also death duties which were levied on rich private citizens and which, like the tolls in certain of the canals, went wholly to the king even though the temple authorities may have been responsible for their assessment and collection. This was made possible by the sons and daughters of the kings being installed as high priests and priestesses.

All in all, in the course of the sixth century BC, the Neo-Babylonian kings managed to get control of an increasingly large share of the temple revenues. This increased the wealth and power of the king but tended to throw the temple priesthoods and laity into opposition to him.

It must be remembered that temples were not just places of worship but were also profit-making corporate entities that manufactured trade goods, practiced farming and animal husbandry, and were the safe repositories for bullion in their treasuries. For large commercial transactions between temples, the idols "visited" other temples in ostentatious processions. The priests carried the idols of their god on a palanquin through the streets accompanied with music and fanfare. The procession would visit a temple across town or in a neighboring city and have a feast and celebration. The gold and silver bullion hidden in the idol's base could be secretly transferred between temples in this way so that the account books could be balanced with the gods acting as witness.

Nabonidus' attempt on behalf of the Moon God, Sin, to usurp Marduk's place as head of the pantheon, were the religious reasons for that king's unpopularity rather than his fiscal policies. Nabonidus wanted to make the Moon God both of Ur and of his mother's city of Harran as the supreme god of the Neo-Babylonian empire. It was no coincidence that Ur and Harran were the two chief temple cities of both the circumcised and the uncircumcised merchant-moneylenders.

It was from Ur and Harran that the mythology of Abraham, the Jewish pimp, moneylender, and slave master, began (Genesis 11 & 12). But now, a thousand years after they had plundered Egypt, instead of claiming that their circumcised cocks were a sign that they belonged to the same families who had plundered Egypt, now those swindling con artists were claiming that their maimed penises were a sign that their god loved them best. And their circumcised penises proved it! How could anyone argue with such a holy proof?

The supreme Babylonian deity, Marduk, an old Sumerian sun god specifically associated with the city of Babylon, did not have the supreme place in the pantheon of the Semitic Amorites, Aramaeans, or Arabians because they all worshipped the Moon God, Sin. This worship of the Moon God by the Semites is explained in *The Monsters of Babylon*, wherein you will discover how the Moon God, Al-Lah, became the supreme god of the Muslim Werewolves.

A place where the economic and religious problems of Babylonia met, was the city of Harran. The very name "Harran" means "road" and was applied to this city because it was the great cross-roads of the trade routes northwards from Babylonia on the one side and from Egypt, Arabia, Palestine, and the Mediterranean Basin on the other. Harran was also one of the cities whose legal status differed in essential points from that of any other community. In Babylonia, the cuneiform tablets indicated that there were certain privileged and "free" cities such as Nippur, Babylon, and Sippar. And in Assyria, Harran and the old capital Ashur in Upper Mesopotamia were also "free cities." The inhabitants of these "free cities" were exempt from conscripted labor, military service, and taxes. The privileges accorded the inhabitants of these cities were under divine protection. Their status had both legal and religious implications. So, by decrees of both kings and gods, these privileges were eternal and not rescindable.

Harran was the perfect place for the circumcised moneylenders, who did no work, to set up a guild hall. It was the perfect place for the circumcised merchants who always demanded special privileges above all other merchants. And it was the safest place for the merchant-moneylenders to conspire and foment wars among all other people while remaining, by law, free from combat.

To commence his work of restoring the Moon God's temple in Harran, Nabonidus ordered a general levy of troops from the western provinces. The Medes, occupied in battle with Cyrus of Persia, had withdrawn from Harran just as Nabonidus' dream had predicted. And Nabonidus was able to use his levies to commence the projected work of restoration. Being conscripted into the army and then being ordered to re-build the temple of the Moon God at Harran, had the effect, however, of promoting a mutiny among the people of the great cities of Babylonia whose people were devoted to Marduk.

After he was assured that the temple of Ishtar in Uruk would provide a steady payment to the palace, Nabonidus began preparations to leave Babylon. Based upon another religious dream that he had, Nabonidus now made an extraordinary move. Installing his son Bel-shar-usur (the Belshazzar in the Book of Daniel) as regent in Babylon, he led an army through Syria and Lebanon and finally onward to the oasis of Tayma in northwest Arabia where he was to remain for the next ten years.

During his period of residence in the west, he pushed 250 miles farther southwards through a number of places which can be identified. Finally, he reached Yatrib (Medina) on the Red Sea. Nabonidus specific-ally states that he established garrisons in and planted colonies around the six oases which he names. He describes the forces used as "the people of Akkad and of Hattiland," that is, both native Babylonians and the Hittites from the western provinces. That he carried along with him families belonging to the guild of circumcised merchant-moneylenders, is indicated by the fact that, a thousand years later, five of the six oases named were, at the time of Mohammad, occupied by Jews.

Those Jews were none other than the descendants of the Jews who had accompanied Nabonidus. Those Jewish merchants became very wealthy as they monopolized the trade routes which passed through the oasis rest stops along the Arabian "incense route" from Tayma to Medina.

To the goat-rustling Arabians, the conquering army of Nabonidus, arriving from some distant land to do nothing more than establish trade centers and to pray to the Moon God, was a wondrous sight. The Semitic Arabs had been devoted to the Moon God from the earliest times. Their faith in that deity was certainly increased by the king of Babylonia arriving with an army to establish worship to his god, Sin, who was none other than their own Moon God, Lah. They certainly did not object to Nabonidus re-naming a vast wilderness of their territories as "Sinai," that is "Wilderness of Sin." The Moon God, El-Sin, of Nabonidus was identical to the Moon God, Al-Lah, of the Arabians. Thus, Nabonidus the Babylonian increased the fanatical faith of the Arabs in their Moon God, Al-Lah.

After ten years in Tayma, at the age of 70, Nabonidus returned to Babylon. In a dream, Sin had told him to re-build the temple of the Moon God at Harran and at Ur. And in a dream, Sin had also told him to travel to Arabia, stay for ten years, and establish the worship of the Moon God there. "I hid myself afar from my city of Babylon ... ten years to my city Babylon I went not in." A passage in the Harran inscription implies divine direction. "In ten years arrived the appointed time, the days were fulfilled which Sin, king of the gods, had spoken." This inscription re-affirms that he had attempted to supplant Marduk with Sin as king of the gods. This religious king thus gave his reasons for moving his court to Arabia and leaving Babylonia. The trade routes were secondary to his religious reasons. And those trade routes did not produce necessities for Babylonia but rather luxury goods such as incense and pearls supplied through the merchant-moneylender guilds.

Cyrus Takes Babylon

The work at Harran was completed and that city survived for many centuries as a center of the worship of the Moon God whose crescent symbol still appeared on Roman coins minted there as late as the 3rd century AD and appeared again on the Muslim flags of 622 AD. Yet for the city of Babylon, the end was near. The "young servant" of Nabonidus' dream was engaged in the conquest of an empire that was soon to exceed even the greatest aspirations of the Babylonians. This young servant was

Cyrus, a Persian of the royal line of Achaemenes, the 7ᵗʰ century founder of the dynasty known by his name.

The Persians were an Indo-European tribe who settled in the territory of ancient Elam, their name derived from Parsua (modern Fars), one of their first strongholds. One of their princes, Cambyses, had married the daughter of the Median king Astyages, perhaps in recognition by the latter of the rising strength of the Persians. Of this union was born Cyrus, who was to become the subject of legends recorded by Herodotus and reminiscent of those circulated about the ancient Akkadian king, Sargon.

In 539 BC, the New Year Festival was celebrated in Babylon, apparently for the first time since Nabonidus' retirement to Tayma. During the ceremony a plentiful supply of wine was distributed, and to judge from the accounts of Herodotus, Xenophon and the author of the Book of Daniel, not only were the revels prolonged but the memory of them remained fresh for many years.

During this time, however, Cyrus was advancing on Babylonia. Again revealing his extreme religiosity, Nabonidus ordered the collection and transport of the country's gods into Babylon so that he could surround himself with idols and thus to secure their holy protection, deemed by him to be even better than manning the walls and fixing arrow shafts to strings. But Borsippa, Cutha, and Sippar wanted to keep their idols on guard duty for their own cities and so refused to comply. In the month of Tishri, Cyrus successfully assaulted Opis on the Tigris and then marched on Sippar which was taken without opposition. Nabonidus fled, and two days later Ugbaru, governor of the Guti, and the army of Cyrus entered Babylon without a battle. And so, the greatest city in the ancient world fell to the Persians.

Herodotus attributed this to the Persian stratagem of breaching the Euphrates, which constituted one side of the defenses of the city, and leading the river into a depression, thereby rendering the main stream temporarily fordable. There is no reason to reject the story, but the real reason for the collapse of the city was less grandiose than re-routing a large river. Within the city, was a "fifth column" of circumcised merchant-moneylenders who later became known as "Jews" who were supporting the cause of whichever side would protect their profits. The Jews betrayed Babylon by opening a gate to let their new allies in. This theme would be repeated thousands of times throughout history, of the Jews betraying the people among whom they had been allowed to live, and embracing their "new friends" to whom they pledged their most sincere "Jewish loyalty."

It would appear that Cyrus' liberal religious views were welcomed after the discontent aroused by the heresies of Nabonidus. Indeed, an inscription of Cyrus from Babylon relates how Marduk, whom Nabonidus had neglected, marched with him and his army "as a friend and companion." Nabonidus was later captured in Babylon where, according to Xenophon, he was killed.

Cyrus entered Babylon in triumph, forbade looting, and allowed to remain undisturbed the religious institutions and civil administration. These included the tamkarum, who continued practicing the Sumerian Swindle "just as it had always been." But Cyrus appointed a Persian governor and so came to an end the last native dynasty to rule the city.

At the beginning of the following year, Cambyses II represented his father in the temple New Year ceremonies, legitimizing Persian rule by "taking the hand of the god." But something more than Persian rule was legitimatized when Cyrus disallowed the looting of Babylon. The bullion on deposit in the temple treasuries was allowed to accumulate in the accounts of the merchant-moneylenders. Like so many kings before him who owed their success to the moneylenders, Cyrus honored the ones who had opened the gates to him and betrayed their city. He honored the ones who had financed his armies and who had provided the military intelligence for the best timing for his attack while the Babylonians were busy with their New Year celebration prayers.

Before the time of Cyrus, Babylon had seen many foreign dynasties come and go, and had in turn successfully assimilated each of them. Now, however, new forces were at work in the Near East and new religious and political ideas were gradually replacing those of ancient Mesopotamia. Social institutions were also changing, and even the system of writing, long a unifying force, was being superseded by the more efficient Aramaic alphabet of only 22 letters. Cuneiform continued to be employed, however, especially for religious and astronomical treatises, a number of the latter are known from as late as the 1st century AD. Cuneiform also remained in use for at least some economic documents, and we have numerous records in this script of prosperous merchants and banking houses in Babylon and Nippur. Indeed, on the surface, the private lives of Babylonian citizens appear to have changed very little under Persian rule. Religious forms were preserved and commercial activity prospered. It was business as it "had always been." Under Persian rule, Babylonia continued to thrive.

However, by the time of Cyrus, not just the debt-slaves but *all women* had finally been reduced to the level of chattel and prostitutes under the profiteering scams of the Semitic merchant-moneylender guilds, most especially by the circumcised Jews who were "horny all of the time." Herodotus (~425 BC) tells us of the debauched status of women under the laws and the cultural decay induced by the Jews of Babylon:

> In every village once a year, all the girls of marriageable age used to be collected together in one place, while the men stood round them in a circle; an auctioneer then called each one in turn to stand up and offered her for sale, beginning with the best-looking and going on to the second best as soon as the first had been sold for a good price. Marriage was the object of the transaction. The rich men who wanted wives bid against each other for the prettiest girls, while the humbler folk, who had no use for good looks in a wife, were actually paid to take the ugly ones, for when the auctioneer had got through all the pretty girls he would call upon the plainest, or even perhaps a crippled one, to stand up, and then ask who was willing to take the least money to marry her, and she was knocked down to whoever accepted the smallest sum. The money came from the sale of the beauties, who in this way provided dowries for their ugly or misshapen sisters.
>
> It was illegal for a man to marry his daughter to anyone he happened to fancy, and no one could take home a girl he had bought without first finding a backer to guarantee his intention of marrying her. In cases of disagreement between husband and wife, the law allowed the return of the purchase money. Anyone who wished, could come even from a different village to buy a wife. (*Histories* I.196)

However, Herodotus was describing the low status of women in Babylonia before his time, as it "used to be." But Secret Fraud #6 of the Sumerian Swindle never stops until its victims are totally destroyed. Secret Fraud #6 is a relentless technique: "High morals impede profits, so debauching the virtuous destroys their moral superiority and pulls them below the depravity of the moneylender who thereby masters them and bends them to his will." So, merely reducing women to the level of trade goods was not degenerate enough for the demonic merchant-moneylenders, who found their greatest profits in the perversion of even the most innocent.

Herodotus goes on to describe the status of women in Babylonia in his own day, as he continued his narrative:

The above admirable practice has now fallen into disuse and the people have of late years hit upon another scheme, namely the prostitution of all girls of the lower classes to provide some relief from the poverty which followed upon the conquest with its attendant hardship and general ruin.

That is, Herodotus is describing the general ruin of the "Have-Nots." The merchant-moneylenders were pimping not just their debt-slaves but the poor, lower classes as well. From auctioning all girls into marriage contracts, to pimping the daughters of the poor as prostitutes, the merchant-moneylenders surreptitiously pulled society ever downward into wickedness where everything had a price tag.

Herodotus continued with his description:

There is one custom among these people which is wholly shameful. Every woman who is a native of the country must once in her life go and sit in the temple of [Ishtar] and there give herself to a strange man. Many of the rich women, who are too proud to mix with the rest, drive to the temple in covered carriages with a whole host of servants following behind. And there wait. Most however, sit in the precinct of the temple with a band of plaited string round their heads. And a great crowd they are, what with some sitting there, others arriving, others going away. And through them gangways are marked off running in every direction for the men to pass along and make their choice.

Once a woman has taken her seat, she is not allowed to go home until a man has thrown a silver coin into her lap and taken her outside to lie with her. As he throws the coin, the man has to say, 'In the name of the goddess Ishtar.' The value of the coin is of no consequence. Once thrown, it becomes sacred and the law forbids that it should ever be refused. The woman has no privilege of choice. She must go with the first man who throws her the money.

When she has lain with him, her duty to the goddess is discharged and she can go home, after which it will be impossible to seduce her by any offer, however large. Tall, handsome women soon manage to get home again, but the ugly ones stay a long time before they can fulfill the condition which the law demands; some of them, indeed, as

much as three or four years. There is a custom similar to this
in parts of Cyprus. (I.199)

Cyprus was a major mercantile port for the merchant-moneylenders.

This degrading of women was always profitable to the merchant-moneylenders because they were always looking for something to sell. To them, women were just like any other saleable item. As slaves, they could work; as whores, they could bring in a profit. Under the influence of the Semitic merchant-moneylenders, all of the women of Babylonia had become prostitutes.

Cyrus offered peace and friendship to all, and compensated those who had suffered under Nabonidus, or so he tells us. Wherever he went, Cyrus called on the support of the local gods, a policy which proved highly successful.

Equally acceptable was the new Persian administration. For the most part local officials were retained in office, but governors known as "satraps" were installed in the various provinces. Their power was effectively restrained by holding the treasurer and garrison commander in each capital city responsible solely to the king. Thus, both monetary and military power were tightly held in the fists of the king. And behind the king stood the merchant-moneylenders of Persia and of Babylon because every king depended upon the money which they could provide, the luxuries which they gifted and sold to him, and the military intelligence which they, alone, could provide.

The Persian Empire, into which Egypt was incorporated in 525 BC, now exceeded in extent any which had gone before it. At the height of its power, the empire spanned three continents, including the territories of Afghanistan and Pakistan, parts of Asia Minor, Central Asia, Thrace, much of the Black Sea coastal regions, Iraq, northern Arabia, Jordan, Palestine, Lebanon, Syria, and all of the significant population centers of ancient Egypt as far west as Libya. Certainly, this territory far exceeded the insignificant fly specks upon geography that are called by the lying Jews, "the Great Kingdoms of Israel and Judah." Of the Persian Empire, Babylonia and Assyria combined formed only one province.

However, Babylonian and Assyrian culture had a continuing influence. Persian art, civil administration, and military science owed much to their Babylonian and Assyrian roots. Babylon was, if not the political, certainly the administrative and cultural capital of the whole Persian Empire, so much so that Aramaic, the Semitic language of the merchant-moneylenders, became the official language of the Persian Empire.

It was only when Darius I (~549-486 BC) had acquired the Persian throne and ruled it as a representative of the Zoroastrian religion, that the old Sumerian, Babylonian, and Assyrian traditions were broken and the claim of Babylon and the Babylonian gods to confer legitimacy on the rulers of western Asia ceased to be acknowledged.

After 500 BC, the Persian Empire came into collision with Greece. The conflict continued intermittently until 331 BC when the Greek Macedonian, Alexander the Great, overthrew the Persian power at a battle near Arbela. Afterwards, he extended his authority to the borders of India. Had Alexander lived, it was his intention to establish a world empire with its capital at Babylon, but his premature death at Babylon in 323 BC, at the age of 32, left his territories to be divided up among his generals. The eastern provinces, including Babylonia and Assyria, eventually fell to the Greek general, Seleucus I (301-281 BC).

Esaggila, the great temple of Marduk, however, still continued to be kept in repair and to be a center of Babylonian patriotism, that is until the founding of the city of Seleucia had diverted the population to this new capital. Then, the ruins of Babylon became a quarry for the builders of the new seat of government.

Under the Greek Seleucids, Babylonia and Assyria came increasingly under Hellenistic cultural influence. The Akkadian language, which had already been superseded by Aramaic as the language of everyday speech, was no longer even written except for religious or astronomical purposes. The ancient culture of Babylonia and Assyria was dead. The future lay with Greece and Rome.

These events are covered further in *The Monsters of Babylon*. But for now, we should explore how the Jews, after a long incubation period of over 2,000 years, finally oozed from out of the leathery eggs laid by those cold-blooded, horned serpents of Babylon, the merchant-moneylenders.

CHAPTER 13

THE APIRU, HAPIRU, AND THE HEBREWS

Let's leave the great empire of Babylonia to its demise around 300 BC and go backward in time once again to where we left the Hyksos goat-rustlers who had escaped from Egypt in 1550 BC. We can understand those times because the decipherment of Mesopotamian and Egyptian literatures in the 19th century AD, opened new vistas of ancient Middle Eastern history. Before this, knowledge of the ancient Middle East as well as the general understanding of the Christian populace, had been limited to the sparse contents of classical Greek and Latin literatures and the enormously detailed lies of the Hebrew Bible. It was not that the ancient people did not write histories but, as you shall see, it was standard practice among the Jews to destroy the history books of all other peoples so that Jewish lies would replace the actual truth. Before those translations from the original archives which were made by modern archaeologists, mankind primarily had the self-glorifying lies and deceits of the Jews upon which to base our understanding of those ancient times.

Although some archaeologists place the beginning of the 18th Dynasty of Egypt at 1539 BC, all dates in archaeology are temporary, based on new findings, rather than definite. So, let this not be cause for criticism if you are using a slightly different time line. It is the timing of events in relation to one another that is important and not specific dates which actually cannot be established with certainty by anyone.

Once Pharaoh Ahmose, founder of the Eighteenth Dynasty (1550-1292 BC), had chased the Hyksos out of Egypt and had reestablished Egyptian rule, he continued to solidify and protect his country by leading expeditions into Canaan and Syria. For thousands of years, Egypt was satisfied with its quests for immortality within its Nile Valley and its desert environs. But now that Egypt had been violated by the Babylonian money-grubbers and their stinking Hyksos goat-rustlers, Egypt wanted a bigger buffer of protective territory to prevent further invasions.

Although the Hyksos sheep-stealers were too scattered in the hilly regions to make chasing after them a priority, the established towns and cities of Canaan were worth the military effort to show the Canaanites that Egypt would not accept their depredations. Those Hyksos who got trapped and enslaved in Egypt, including the treasonous Semitic Ma'adians whom the Egyptians had allowed to live among them for more than a thousand years, were given the Egyptian name for "slaves"—which was "Apiru."

As the Egyptian army dealt with the Hyksos who had scampered off into the wilderness with their loot, chasing them away from Egyptian territory in Canaan, they were still called Apiru by the Egyptians. Thus, the people of Canaan also called those bandits Apiru. In this way, the Egyptian word took on a new meaning among the Canaanites. It meant "bandit and cut-throat" because that is what those goat-rustlers were. After helping to loot Egypt, they had returned to their former lives as roaming goat-molesters and bandits.

By pushing his military campaign into the Near East, Pharaoh Ahmose set a precedent for most Egyptian kings for the next five centuries. During Ahmose's reign, Upper and Lower Egypt were once again unified and Egypt became one of the main Near Eastern powers. His reign is therefore seen as the end of the Second Intermediate Period and the beginning of the New Kingdom. A new and great era had dawned for Egypt. The Eighteenth Dynasty is perhaps the best known of all the dynasties of ancient Egypt and it was led by a number of Egypt's most powerful pharaohs, including Thutmose III (1458-1425 BC), Amenhotep III (1388-1350 BC), Akhenaten (1350-1336 BC), and Tutankhamen (1333-1324 BC).

While these Pharaohs were ruling their empires and protecting their people, the goat-rustling Hyksos who had escaped Egypt, were scampering around Sinai, Canaan, and Syria looking for weak towns to rob. We left them counting their loot in the previous chapter while we followed the great empires of Babylonia and Assyria to their respective and historical demise. And now, let's consider what happened to the Hyksos—all of them.

The Hyksos

By the time Pharaoh Ahmose allowed the Hyksos to escape in 1550 BC, Sumeria had become a forgotten legend, while its cuneiform writing, its culture, its inventions, and its religious systems had been appropriated and absorbed by the Babylonians and Assyrians as well as by all of the other peoples who came to live in Mesopotamia. However, even after 1800 years, the Sumerian Swindle, itself, remained the sole secret of the Babylonian and Assyrian merchant-moneylenders. They made themselves huge fortunes with this ancient scam just as the modern-day bankers and financiers do to this very day—swindling the people around them secretly, while pretending to be honest businessmen doing business just as "it has always been."

While the great empires of Babylonia, Assyria, and Egypt contended with one another across the centuries, the Gutians, Hittites, Hurrians, Scythians, Medes, Amorites, Kassites, Sea Peoples, and numerous other tribal and ethnic confederations walked on foot and rode on donkeys and horses and chariots back and forth across the dusty plains of the Fertile Crescent and among the hills of Palestine and Anatolia. They vied with one another over water rights, farm lands, trade goods, and silver, all combined with the violent, personal disputes between the Type-A personalities, the charismatic psychopaths, and the egomaniacs who had become their kings. These historical struggles for empire were vast in scale and filled with incredible suffering and bloodshed.

But in Palestine, though the struggles among the petty kingdoms and the tribes of goat-rustlers were no less lethal man-to-man, they were certainly quite small and insignificant when set beside the epic scale of the marching armies of the great empires. Egypt, Hattiland, Mitanni, Assyria, and Babylonia were truly enormous, while the petty kingdoms in Canaan, Moab, and Judea were truly tiny. As the great empires traded on an international scale and fought wars involving tens of thousands or hundreds of thousands of people, the small towns and villages of Palestine fought battles with ten or maybe a hundred goat-herders wielding bronze swords and copper maces, and throwing rocks at each other with their slings. These were the "mighty kings" bragged about by the lying rabbis in the Old Testament.

Every town and village had to protect its farming and grazing lands from the roving bandits and cattle rustlers who infested the countryside. These areas of Canaan were too insignificant and too far away from the power-centers of Mesopotamia, Anatolia, or Egypt for the small towns to ask the Great Powers for protection from the tiny bands of rampaging Apiru. Every tribe of twenty or thirty flea-bitten nomads was ruled by a "great king," according to the fables which the rabbis wrote. These heroic bandits and "great kings" of the Old Testament, terrorized the vicinity astride their donkeys, from which they could dismount in a trice by putting their sandaled feet on the ground and letting the poor animals walk away from under them.

But small though the land is, the Sinai Desert was important for its copper mines. And it had trade routes which passed through Arabia and Egypt to the Horn of Africa, as well as trade routes from the Gulf of Aqaba over the Red Sea to Punt, India, Elam, and Babylonia. It also had major trade routes connecting it to Anatolia, Mesopotamia, and the Mediterranean. So, Palestine had strategic importance to the great empires [see Map

19]. Yet, the land was sprinkled with small villages and tiny towns, each ruled by a "mighty king." To guard such an area was more of an inconvenience than a profitable tactic for the great empires. But because of the convergence of trade routes, this mostly desolate land was nevertheless strategically important to the flow of trade.

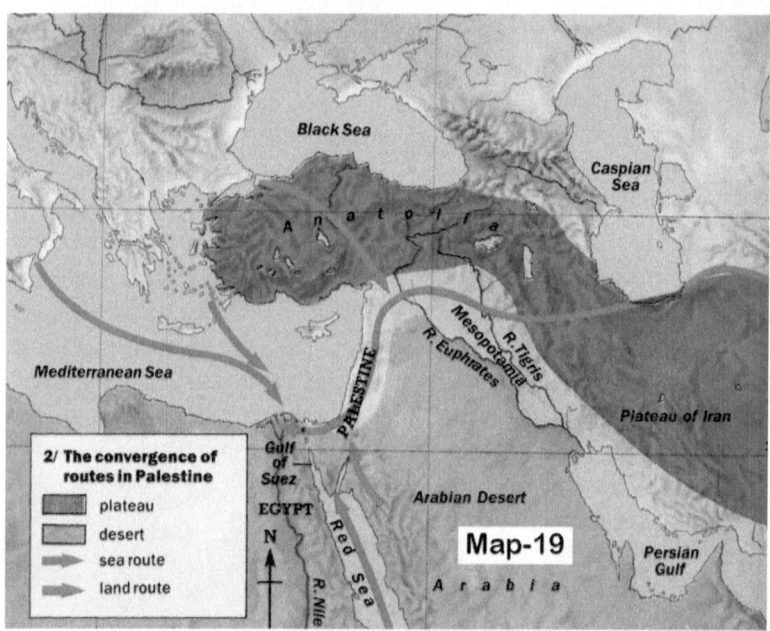

Now, back again to 1550 BC. Once Pharaoh Ahmose began his assault from Upper Egypt, those wealthiest of the Hyksos who could do so commandeered boats, horses, chariots, and donkeys, and ran for their lives. These were the commanders of the Hyksos, the leading generals and lieutenants, the wealthier of the Babylonian merchant-moneylenders and their bodyguards, plantation foremen, boat-owners and their families. All of these upper classes fled north along the Nile to the safety of Avaris.

But the lower-level Hyksos who had been ignorant shepherds before the Hyksos takeover and who were members of the gangs of enforcers and bosses over the enslaved Egyptian farmers, were left behind to fend for themselves. Because there was no room on the boats and not enough horses and donkeys, these lower-class shepherds were abandoned to their fate. As the hired hands of the Hyksos slave-drivers, they had murdered and enslaved the Egyptians and had helped to loot the temples and plunder the tombs. So, when the Egyptian army caught up with them, they were either killed or bound in fetters and enslaved.

For now, let's leave these enslaved Hyksos (Apiru) chained up in Egypt, working for the Egyptians who were none too happy with either the cruel and rapacious Hyksos shepherds or the Semitic Ma'adians who had betrayed Egypt by joining in the pillage. Their history is of little importance. They were slaves. Nothing more can be said about them that cannot be said about any other slaves of the ancient Near East. They worked for the Egyptian people whom they had helped the Babylonians to loot, and slavery was their reward.

Although slaves were not allowed to work on Egyptian pyramids or temples (since this was a holy privilege of the Egyptian people alone), these Apiru slaves no doubt did most of the brick-making under the hot sun and the harvesting of papyrus among the crocodiles during their time when Pharaoh Ahmose was building the last pyramid by an Egyptian monarch. Illiterate, they had no way of writing down their travails. And of what history of slaves can there be other than the daily drudgery of labor? They and their descendants were to remain as slaves in Egypt until they were released from bondage by Assyrian king Ashurbanipal in 671 BC. So, leaving them at their much-deserved labors, let's move on to the second group of Hyksos as escapees from the wrath of the Egyptians.

Those Hyksos who had reached Avaris in time to find safety there, can be divided into the other three groups. Pharaoh Ahmose had allowed the Hyksos to leave Avaris and take with them all of their loot, as a way of avoiding a long siege. After the Egyptians let them go, one or two families of the Hyksos turned to the east and south, wandering with their loot and small cattle into the Sinai region of Arabia. This desolate region King Nabonidus would later name after his Moon God, Sin, as the "Wilderness of Sin," that is, "Sinai." These people got lost in the wilderness of Sinai where, for 40 years, they herded their goats and ate locusts before finding their way back into Canaan. These were not the smartest of the Hyksos, but they made up for their lack of intelligence by telling great lies based upon desert mirages and the fanciful delusions induced by thirst and hunger. Schlepping their gold and silver ornaments and herding their goats, they eventually wandered into the moderately-settled hill country of Canaan where they took up once again their goat-rustling and banditry. There, they joined with the tribes of smarter Hyksos who had gone to Canaan directly from Egypt with their loot.

No doubt those illiterate goat-rustlers were extremely pleased with their good luck. They had been the foot-soldiers of the Hyksos invasion.

They, as well as their poorer relatives who were captured and enslaved by the Egyptians, were the pawns of the operation—totally expendable and useful for basic soldiering and gangster work. They had entered Egypt as shepherds and bandits and they left Egypt following that same pastoral life as their forefathers and fathers, as goat-herders and thieves. Only now, they were rich gangs of dusty goat-herders, carrying an unusually large amount of Egyptian gold, silver, fine linens, and gemstones into Canaan.

True to their nature, those tribes of Apiru began lurking around as wandering bands of thieves and goat-rustlers. They had plenty of silver, gold, goats, and cattle but no land of their own. The quiet towns and villages of the region could eke out a living in the rocky and dry land, but the land could not support both the Apiru bandits and the Canaanites. Besides, the Apiru were thieves. They were not wanted in Egypt by the Egyptians and they certainly were not welcome in Canaan, in either the coastal cities or the poor inland villages. Yet, when did thieves ever worry about whether they were welcome or not, since they never are?

As wandering nomads, traveling on foot and by donkey, there was not much space on their pack animals and carts for them to be carrying around statues of their gods. No different than any other of the people of the ancient Near East in their belief system, the Apiru believed in many gods and they believed that each god lived in his own territory. Their fortress city of Avaris had been home to religions from all over the ancient Near East. Whether Canaanite-style temples, Minoan wall paintings, Palestinian-type burials, all made use of statues of gods.

In Egypt, they had worshipped the Egyptian gods whose territory they had invaded, most notably their own Moon God whom they already had worshipped but who was now in the guise of the Egyptian Moon God, Yah. The Moon God was always a favorite of the Semites because the moon gave them plenty of light at night for their burglaries and night raids. He was called 'Sin' in Babylonia, 'Lah' in Arabia, and 'Yah' in Egypt. So, praying to Yah was a practice learned from their residence in Egypt. They had even been chased out of Egypt by Pharaoh Ahmose (Yahmose) whose name meant "The Moon is Born." So, even after these Apiru had returned to the worship of their goat-herder gods, all this influence of moon worship carried over to their own Moon God, which they now accepted by the Egyptian name of *Yahweh*, or "Yah is here,"

Throughout the Middle East, the gods were believed to take up residence at specific geographical locations and to live in specific temples within specific cities. Among the hills and mountains of the Sinai Penin-sula and Canaan, the Apiru bandits worshipped El-Shaddai, the god of the mountain. In those hot and arid lands, the work of this god could be seen in the clouds which surrounded the highest mountain tops as thunder and lightning. This mighty god, with flashes of burning fire, caused the goats and sheep to panic and the women to scream. This was not a god to be trifled with. Whenever they needed additional protection, their priests and elders would go up into those mountains to seek out this god to offer him sacrifices atop piles of heaped stones sprinkled with goat blood.

The god of the mountain, El-Shaddai, was not only a mighty god of thundering and earthquakes, but he was also invisible. For people living in goat-hair tents and riding donkeys, invisible gods didn't weigh very much.

This god could only be seen when he was dressed in his surrounding clouds and lightning bolts high up on the mountaintops, or as pillars of whirling dust-devils dancing around the goat-rustlers as they traversed the deserts. Since their invisible god didn't weigh anything, they didn't need statues or idols to pray to him—which was convenient because that left more room on their pack donkeys for loot.

After chasing the Hyksos out of Egypt, Pharaoh Ahmose and his successors of the Eighteenth Dynasty treated all of Canaan and Sinai as a buffer against the empires of the Hittites and Babylonians. The Egyptians had been insular and self-absorbed before the Hyksos invasion, relying upon the protection of their surrounding deserts. But they learned the hard lesson of international politics. And that lesson is, if you do not defend your country, you will lose it to invading foreigners.

The fleeing tribes of Hyksos bandits and scattered families of shepherds were of less concern for a mighty king of Egypt than were the powerful empires across his borders. And so, after warfare had extended the influence of Egypt all the way into Syria, eventually, with the ensuing peace, the Egyptian and Babylonian royal families became linked through the diplomacy of marriage. This diplomacy was recorded on the clay Amarna tablets written in cuneiform which had been deposited in the royal archives of Amenhotep III and his son, Akhenaton. They were written about 200 years after the Hyksos were expelled. Some of those letters were written by the kings of Hattiland and Babylonia to the Pharaohs, but most were written to the Pharaoh by Canaanite princes in Palestine, Phoenicia, and Southern Syria during the early fourteenth century BC. Those letters tell of attacks by the bandits known, by slight changes in pronunciation, as "Apiru" or "Hapiru" or "Habiru" or "Hebrews."

Although the kings of Babylonia, Hattiland, and Egypt contented themselves with personal gifts and concubines, the tone of the Amarna Letters from the various governors of Canaan were very different. There, the lands were being overrun by those escapees from Avaris, the "shepherd kings," the Hyksos—now called either the Apiru or the Hapiru or the Habiru or the Hebrew bandits. It is clear from these desperate pleas for help that the Hebrews (the Apiru) were taking over the entire region and that Pharaoh was doing nothing to protect his land.

As you read the Amarna Letters, it is easy to see the close correlation between those cuneiform letters and the Old Testament stories of how the Hebrews attacked and took over Canaan. The events in those letters took place about two hundred years after the Hyksos had escaped from Egypt. So, as their circumcised and "horny all of the time" population increased, the Hebrew bandits were becoming an increasing source of trouble to the people of the entire region—just as they are in the present day.

Please understand that those Hebrews were not Jews because there were no Jews anywhere in the world at that time. They were merely the scattered tribes of Hyksos bandits. The Egyptians called them Apiru because that was the name for their slaves. To the Canaanites, because the Apiru were "cut-throats," "bandits," and "thieves," then that is what the Egyptian word meant to the Canaanites—all the same criminals.

The Amarna Letters

Labayu, the governor of Shechem, was a Canaanite. The Amarna Letters show that although he was supposed to have been a loyal subject of Pharaoh Akhenaten, in fact, he was secretly a Hebrew. With the usual Semitic deceit, he claimed to be loyal to Pharaoh even while he was simultaneously raiding the caravans and the territories of his neighbors on all sides. Milkilu, the governor of Gezer, seems to have also been in league with the Hebrews. As descendants of the original looters of Egypt, these Hebrew bandits were now turning their attention upon the towns and villages of Canaan. Two hundred years had passed since they had been chased out of Egypt. With their many wives producing a multitude of children, their numbers had increased enough that they could challenge the established regime. The Amarna Letters describe the situation.

In one letter, Labayu, the Canaanite prince of Shechem in the central hill country, hypocritically complains to Pharaoh Amenhotep III that he is loyal and is being slandered by the other princes. Furthermore, "I did not know that my son associates with the Apiru, and I have verily delivered him into the hand of Addaya." Thus, the Hebrew bandits were not merely tribes related by blood and closed to outsiders, but they were actually amorphous gangs which outsiders could join to become full members participating in their raids.

But Labayu's protestations of innocence certainly did not fool his neighbors who had to defend themselves from his depredations. Biridya, prince of Meggido, writes to Pharaoh Amenhotep III of the troubles he is having capturing the bandit prince Labayu. That these letters were dictated to a scribe is shown in the phrase, "Let Pharaoh know":

> Let Pharaoh know that ever since the archers returned to Egypt, Labayu has carried on hostilities against me, and we are not able to pluck the wool, and we are not able to go outside the gate in the presence of Labayu, since he learned that thou hast not given us archers. And now his face is set to take Megiddo, but let Pharaoh protect his city lest Labayu seize it. Verily, the city is destroyed by death from pestilence and disease. Let Pharaoh give one hundred garrison troops to guard the city lest Labayu seize it. Verily, there is no other purpose in Labayu. He seeks to destroy Megiddo.

And Biridya continues on another tablet,

> I said to my brethren, 'If the gods of Pharaoh, our lord, grant that we capture Labayu, then we will bring him alive to Pharaoh, our lord.' But my mare was felled by an arrow, and I alighted afterwards and rode with Yashdata. But before my arrival, they had slain Labayu.

In another letter, Milkilu, the prince of Gezer, begs Pharaoh for some help against the rampaging Hebrew bandits. He writes on behalf of himself and his friend, Shuwardata, prince of Hebron and says:

> Let Pharaoh know that powerful is the hostility against me and against Shuwardata. Let Pharaoh, my lord, protect his land from the hand of the Apiru. If not, then let Pharaoh, my lord, send chariots to fetch us, lest our servants smite us.

Thus, it can be seen that the fighting throughout the area was so intense that Milkilu wanted to retreat to Egypt. The Hebrews were attacking the entire region. Under the aging Pharaoh Amenhotep III, Egypt was rich but neglectfully weak and unresponsive.

After Amenhotep III died, the new Pharaoh was not any more helpful to these besieged governors. The new Pharaoh was Akhenaton, who had inherited all of the wealth of his father but whose main interest was in the Sun God religion that he founded. Akhenaton was the famous Pharaoh who established the world's first monotheistic religion 800 years before there were any Jews to lie about doing it first.

At the beginning of Akhenaten's reign, Shuwardata wrote:

> Let Pharaoh, my lord, learn that the chief of the Apiru has risen in arms against the lands which the god of Pharaoh, my lord, gave me; but I have smitten him. Also let Pharaoh, my lord, know that all my brethren have abandoned me, and it is I and Abdu-Heba [governor of Jerusalam] who fight against the chief of the Apiru. And Zurata, prince of Accho, and Indarata, prince of Achshaph, it was they who hastened with fifty chariots to my help – for I had been robbed by the Apiru – but behold, they are fighting against me, so let it be agreeable to Pharaoh, my lord, and let him send Tanhamu, and let us make war in earnest, and let the lands of Pharaoh, my lord, be restored to their former limits!

Not only were the Hebrews attacking the towns of Canaan without fear of retribution, but many of those towns were actually joining the Hebrew gangs. The loyalty to the Pharaoh was quickly being replaced with self-interest and the opportunity for acquiring land and loot.

The Hebrews were so numerous that even the two foes, Abdu-Heba, governor of Jerusalem and Shuwardata of Hebron, could not fight against them. In this letter, Shuwardata complains to Akhenaten that Abdu-Heba, the prince of Jerusalem, was one of the Hebrew land-grabbers:

> Pharaoh, my lord, sent me to make war against Keilah. I have made war and I was successful; my town has been restored to me. Why did Abdu-Heba [Prince of Jerusalem] write to the people of Keilah saying, 'Take my silver and follow me'? Let Pharaoh, my lord, know that Abdu-Heba had taken the town from my hand. Further, let Pharaoh, my lord, investigate; if I have taken a man or a single ox or an ass from him, then he is in the right! Further, Labayu is dead, who seized our towns; but behold, Abdu-Heba is another Labayu, and he also seizes our towns! So let Pharaoh take

thought for his servant because of this deed! And I will not do anything until the king sends back a message to his servant.

The territorial infighting between the governors and princes of Canaan was always superseded by the general chaos of the entire region brought on by the thieving Hebrew tribes. Abdu-Heba's name can be translated as "servant of Hebat," a Hurrian goddess. The Hurrians origininated from the area east of the Tigris River in the Zagros Mountain region. He was a long way from his homeland and serving the Pharaoh.

Unbeknown to Abdu-Heba, the entire populace of pre-Israelite Jerusalem (known as 'Jebusites' in the Bible) was under the ban of the Hebrew god who demanded their complete genocide. In this letter, Abdu-Heba complained to Pharaoh Akhenaten:

> Lost are the lands of Pharaoh! Do you not hearken unto me? All the governors are lost; Pharaoh, my lord, does not have a single governor left! Let Pharaoh turn his attention to the archers and let Pharaoh, my lord, send out troops of archers, for Pharaoh has no lands left! The Apiru plunder all the lands of Pharaoh. If there are archers here in this year, the lands of Pharaoh, my lord, will remain intact; but if there are no archers here the lands of Pharaoh, my lord, will be lost!

The entire region was in turmoil. The Hebrews were turning Canaan into a total war zone with their raids and plundering.

Abdu-Heba of Jerusalem complained about a number of events which recur in other letters. In the first place, he excoriates Milkilu of Gezer and Tagu of the northern Coastal Plain of Palestine for their aggression against Rubutu, which lay somewhere in the region southwest of Megiddo and Taanach. In the second place, he urges Akhenaten to instruct his officers to supply the Egyptian archers from the towns in the plain of Sharon in order to avert heavy drain on the scanty supplies of Jerusalem. He finally complains that his last caravan containing tribute and captives for Pharaoh was attacked and robbed near Ajalon, presumably by the men of Milkilu of Gezer and the sons of Labayu.

Although Akhenaten had sent a troop of Nubian archers to aid Abdu-Heba, they were certainly not a blessing. Much like their modern-day descendants who take every pretext and opportunity to riot and loot, the black Nubian mercenaries garrisoned in Jerusalem were caught up in the riotous pillaging of the time and had even attacked the governor, Abdu-

Heba, himself, as they attempted to loot his home. In another letter to Akhenaten, Abdu-Heba wrote:

> Behold, this deed is the deed of Milkilu and the deed of the sons of Labayu who have given the land of Pharaoh to the Apiru. Behold, O Pharaoh, my lord, I am right! With reference to the Nubians, let my king ask the commissioners whether my house is not very strong! Yet, they attempted a very great crime; they took their implements and breached the roof.... The men of the land of Nubia have committed an evil deed against me. I was almost killed by the men of the land of Nubia in my own house. Let Pharaoh call them to account. Seven times and seven times let Pharaoh, my lord, avenge me!

As the general banditry and attacks by the Hebrews spread, Abdu-Heba, sent yet another letter to the unresponsive Pharaoh:

> Let Pharaoh take thought of his land! The land of Pharaoh is lost; in its entirety it is taken from me; there is war against me, as far as the lands of Seir and as far as Gath-carmel! All the governors are at peace, but there is war against me. I have become like an Apiru and do not see the two eyes of Pharaoh, my lord, for there is war against me. I have become like a ship in the midst of the sea! The arm of the mighty Pharaoh conquers the land of Naharaim and the land of Cush, but now the Apiru capture the cities of Pharaoh. There is not a single governor remaining to Pharaoh, my lord – all have perished. Behold, Turbazu has been slain in the very gate of Sile, yet Pharaoh holds his peace. Behold Zimreda, the townsmen of Lachish have smitten him, slaves who had become Apiru. Yaptih-Hadad has been slain in the very gate of Sile, yet Pharaoh holds his peace. Wherefore does not Pharaoh call them to account?

Thus, it is clear that by the early 1350s BC, when Akhenaton became pharaoh, that Canaan was being overrun by the Hebrews. This word, "Hebrew," was not a religious term at that time, since this and other letters by the other governors indicate that anyone could join the Hebrew gangs, anyone could become a Hebrew (Apiru) bandit. The Hebrews were not

Jews—yet. They were not an exclusive group of religious nomads—yet—as the lying rabbis claim. They were raiders who welcomed more allies to increase the size of their bandit tribes. As Abdu-Heba laments, "I have become like an Apiru (Hebrew) … I have become like a ship in the midst of the sea." It is quite clear that those roving bandits, those Hebrews, who attacked from the desert regions, welcomed any who would rebel and join their tribes. Whether they were sons of local kings like the son of Labayu or "slaves who had become Apiru" like the townsmen of Lachish, all who could fight were welcome to join the Hebrew bandits in their rape, looting, warfare, and genocide across all of Canaan.

Such were the tumultuous times. Once the Hyksos-Hebrews had been expelled from Egypt, they continued their thieving and plundering and were known by the Canaanite populace as "cut-throats," "bandits," and "thieves"—all words which were all wrapped up in the word, "Hebrews." Once they had increased their tribal numbers enough to become a military threat, they committed crimes wherever they roamed, killing, thieving, raping, rustling, and taking over entire towns after first murdering every man, woman, and child within that town. From their first days after being expelled from Egypt, genocide became a standard method for destroying those who were not members of their tribes of Hebrew scoundrels.

The Amarna letters do not record the names of their enemies except as the general names of bandits or thieves or cut-throats which they called Apiru (Hebrews). They do not mention the tribal names of their Hebrew enemies—the tribes of Benjamin, Ephraim, Manasseh, Naphtali, Dan, Asher, Issachar, Judah, Zebulon, Simeon, Reuben, and Gad. For those names, we must read the Hebrew account of the so-called "conquest of Canaan" in the Old Testament. The full account of how the Hebrews practiced genocide on the Canaanites and stole their property, is explained in its entirety in *The Monsters of Babylon*. But for now, let's leave the first and second groups of Hyksos—those who had been captured and enslaved in Egypt, and those who had escaped into Sinai and Canaan to become bandits—and study the third group.

The Third Group of Hyksos: Phoenicians

The first group, the smallest group, of Hyksos were still enslaved in Egypt during those times and they were called Apiru (slaves) by the Egyptians. The second group of Hyksos who had escaped Egypt were ravaging the countryside of Canaan. The princes of the cities in Canaan also called them by the same Egyptian name when writing to Pharaoh, but in this case, Apiru meant "bandit."

The third group was composed of the Hyksos officials, their generals and military guards, and some of the lower-level petty moneylenders. They and their fathers and grandfathers had not been among the first wave of Babylonian financiers and their hired henchmen who had first looted Egypt. That first wave of the Babylonian merchant-moneylenders who had planned and orchestrated the entire attack, along with their Hyksos bandits and hired henchmen, had immediately skimmed off the easy pickings from the temples and palaces of Egypt.

As the huge shipments of gold, silver, jewels, ebony wood furniture, ivory carvings and panels, and other Egyptian handicrafts and trinkets began appearing in Babylonia, the secret could no longer be kept. The moneylender guilds had captured vast wealth by looting Egypt. This looting continued for the entire 108 years that Egypt was occupied by these thieves, while increasing numbers of opportunists and late-comers from the guilds traveled to Egypt to seek their fortunes, as well.

These late-comers were all experienced merchants and moneylenders but they were not the direct guild brothers of the original conspirators, nor had they participated in the first wave of looting, so they got no share of those great treasures. What they could squeeze out of the Egyptians with their own hands, was all that they would ever get.

When Pharaoh Ahmose finally kicked all the Hyksos out of Egypt, there was very little for this second tier of robbers to go back to in Babylonia. Compared to the first looters, their own profits were small. They knew that the merchant-moneylenders who had made great fortunes by being among the first wave of looters, would all be in unassailable positions of high finance. To return to Babylonia would mean that they would always be at the bottom of the merchant-moneylender social scale. They would always have less wealth than the first bandits. So, why go back to Babylonia?

These mid-level merchant-moneylenders and upper-level Hyksos knew how to lead and organize their men. They had the loot that Pharaoh Ahmose had allowed them to take, as well as the accumulation of over a hundred years of looting which their families had safely stashed in the coastal cities of Canaan. They had tasted wealth and power without being the servants of the kings or subalterns of the tamkarum trade guilds of Babylonia. They had ruled Egypt as tyrants with wealth, power, and prestige, while the mighty Egyptians had been forced to literally kiss their feet. So, to once again become servants of some Babylonian king was not appealing to them. Besides, the trade guild cities of Babylonia were distant, and the markets and trade routes were controlled by competitive tamkarum guilds. For these particular Hyksos, those markets were either closed to them or tightly controlled by competing guilds, which gave them only secondary profits in Mesopotamia as petty merchants or as mere employees of the merchant-moneylender patriarchs.

However, there were richer possibilities—not in the distant markets of Babylonia and Assyria, but near at hand in the untapped markets of the Mediterranean Basin.

These new markets were scattered throughout the Mediterranean Sea on both the North African and European continents. No one controlled those markets because those areas were lightly populated and few of the foreign merchants understood the power of organized, international trade cartels. What was even better, none of those people in the new lands knew anything about the Sumerian Swindle. These were markets with unsophisticated and illiterate peoples who were innocent of the deceits of the Semitic merchant-moneylenders. So, this third group of Hyksos escaped from Egypt and carried their loot on donkeys to the port cities of Acre, Tyre, Sidon, and Byblos. There, they began building ships.

In such fortified port cities, those Hyksos were safe from the raids and troubles which the Hyksos Hebrew shepherds were causing throughout Canaan. Their families and guilds had been among the second wave of conspirators in the takeover of Egypt. They had been hired as the second-tier field agents for the merchant-moneylender guilds in Babylonia but they were not the main directors. As generals, captains, lieutenants in the army, as high priests for the Canaanite gods, as merchants and traders, as sea captains for the Red Sea fleets, as caravan organizers and warehousemen, as an educated elite, they were not among the top profiteers from the Hyksos invasion of Egypt. Once they were expelled by Pharaoh Ahmose, they were like grasping arms and hands which had been cut off from a head which was based in Babylonia.

During their years in Egypt, these Hyksos had developed trade partnerships with the Canaanite coastal cities, and on Crete, as well as in Babylonia. So, when they were expelled, unlike the shepherd Hyksos wandering around as flea-bitten and unsophisticated Hebrew bandits, these merchant Hyksos had somewhere to go besides to Babylonia, and they had trade partners with whom to do business.

The entire Mediterranean Sea and its margins were open to them. They transferred the Babylonian sailors and sea captains from their reed ships in the Red Sea and based them in the cities along the Canaanite coast in sturdier ships built of wooden planks. From the cities of Dor, Acre, Tyre, Sarepta, Sidon, Beritos, Tripoli, and Arwad, these wealthy Hyksos began building a trading fleet that could carry the manufactured goods of Egypt, Assyria, Syria, and Babylonia into the less-urbanized lands of Greece, Europe, North Africa, and the Black Sea. All they needed were these sea ports as a base of operations and some new ships, and they were back in business. Being expelled from Egypt was a new beginning for them.

Adhering to their basic business policy of dealing whenever possible in easily-transported, rare, and therefore expensive goods, these Hyksos already had such a rare item readily at hand with which to sell at a high profit and with which to bribe the kings of any country. Best of all, as in Secret Fraud #7 of the Sumerian Swindle, where "Monopoly gives wealth and power but monopoly of money gives the greatest wealth and power," this product could be monopolized. This product was the famous purple dye which was not only very beautiful but very costly. The dye was made from the sea snails of the eastern Mediterranean coast found in the very area where the Hyksos established their new trading ports. By mono-polizing the manufacture of this dye, the Hyksos merchant-moneylenders had an immediate source of profit which they, alone, could control.

The purple dye was manufactured from a medium-sized predatory sea snail which thrived in the area. The snails were crushed to extract the dye. It took 12,000 snails to yield 1.4 grams of pure dye, enough to color only the trim of a single garment. So, purple dye was very, very expensive. The expense rendered purple-dyed textiles as status symbols and became a mark of royalty and extreme wealth and a prestigious symbol of those "born to the purple." Known as royal purple or Tyrian purple after the main distribution point of Tyre, it was worn only by kings and high priests. Thus, this expensive and profitable trade item gave the Hyksos merchants their special entry into the palaces and homes of the leaders of society wherever they traveled.

The language of those Hyksos was Canaanite, the same language as the shepherd Hyksos, while the outlying tribes spoke the related dialects of Hebrew and Aramaic. These were the languages which they spoke when they first had invaded Egypt and which they still spoke as they made their escape out of Egypt. In terms of archaeology, language, and religion, there is little to set those Hyksos apart as markedly different from the other tribes of Canaan. They were Canaanites. In the Amarna tablets, they called themselves *Kenaani* (Canaanites). But we know them today as Phoenicians because of their monopoly of the purple dye.

Their first and most important customers were the Greeks. The Greeks called the purple dye "phoenix" meaning "purple-red," hence the Greek name *phoinikèia* or "Phoenicia." But whatever name they were called, whether Phoenicians, Tyrians from Tyre, or Sidonians from Sidon, they were the same Semitic gangs of thieves and moneylenders who had originally joined together with their Babylonia leaders to loot Egypt. And now that they had escaped, they were looking for new opportunities for profits doing what they did best: buying, selling, haggling, and profiteering from the Sumerian Swindle.

Herodotus (~460 BC) tells us that the Phoenicians came originally from the coasts of the Indian Ocean; and as soon as they had penetrated into the Mediterranean and settled in that part of the country where they are today, they took to making long trading voyages. Loaded with Egyptian and Assyrian goods, they called at various places along the coast, including Argos—in those days the most important of the countries now called by the general name of Hellas.

> Here in Argos, they displayed their wares, and five or six days later when they were nearly sold out, it so happened that a number of women came down to the beach to see the fair. Among these was the king's daughter, whom the Greek and Persian writers agree in calling Io, daughter of Inachus. These women were standing about near the vessel's stern, buying what they fancied, when suddenly the Phoenician sailors passed the word along and made a rush at them. The greater number got away; but Io and some others were caught and bundled aboard the ship, which cleared at once and made off for Egypt. (*Histories*, I.1)

Even though the kidnapping described took place before 539 BC, nearly a thousand years later than the time that we are describing here, it does give an account of the methods and morals of the Phoenician merchants and shows that they were still thieving Hyksos bandits and slavers even as late as Herodotus' time.

Although Herodotus' information was partially correct in that the Phoenicians came from the *direction* of the Indian Ocean, he did not know that they had been the Sea Captains for the Babylonian moneylender guilds. The Phoenician leaders and captains came from the Persian Gulf via the Red Sea, from the direction of India, but they did not come from India. Their original home ports were the cities of Babylonia.

But once they had moved into the Mediterranean Sea, their main fortified harbor and shipyard was at Tyre. With their Babylonian and Assyrian guild partners, they soon had plenty of Egyptian, Assyrian, and Babylonian goods with which to trade. These trade goods included the debt-slaves who were becoming so numerous in Babylonia as well as the war-slaves captured by Assyria. Very, very few of their slaves were Negroes because dealing with Egypt was closed to them at this early time. Of course, the prettiest women fetched them the most profits.

As merchants, the Phoenicians began a seafaring enterprise of trade and moneylending which brought them great wealth. Where else could these merchant-moneylenders and pirates go but out to sea? The Mediterranean Sea was new territory for them. To the south and southwest, Egypt had just chased them out and was more interested in killing them than doing business. To the north, an emerging Indo-European power known to us as the Hittites was beginning to expand. To the east, the empires of Babylonia and Assyria would allow no trade competition in their territory. So, these Amorite merchant-moneylenders and fugitive Hyksos, used the profits which they had made in the looting of Egypt to build ships and warehouses behind the fortified walls of harbor cities.

There was no difference between the Semitic Apiru (Hebrew) goat-rustlers who had wandered about in the deserts of Sinai and the Semitic Hebrews who had been trapped and enslaved in Egypt. There was no difference between the Hebrew thieves who slinked about the hills of Canaan and those Hebrews in the coastal cities who became known as Phoenicians. There was no difference between any of those Hyksos, either culturally or linguistically. *They were all Semites.* However, in addition to their skills as traders and merchants, they carried with them wherever they went, the Sumerian Swindle with which to enslave and defraud the peoples of Greece, Europe, and North Africa. The Phoenicians were not just traders, they were also loan sharks.

A decade or so before they were kicked out of Egypt, a volcano in the Aegean Sea exploded. The explosion of the island of Thera sent 100-foot-high tsunamis crashing against the island of Crete. Those monstrous waves wiped out the seaside cities and the ships of the Minoans. The Minoans had had a monopoly on sea trade for hundreds of years before this volcanic explosion. They had temples and warehouses in the Hyksos city of Avaris where they had traded for Egyptian loot. The Hyksos and the Minoans had been trading partners whose highest ideal was making a profit in trade. Before the explosion of the Thera volcano, it was the Minoans who had the shipping monopoly in the Mediterranean. Into the void left from the destroyed Minoan civilization, the Phoenicians happily sailed in.

But across the Aegean Sea, the rowdy Mycenaean Greeks were less interested in trade than they were in war. The main interest of those warrior Greeks was heroic adventures through warfare and the ideals of a noble death in battle. For the Greeks, gaining wealth in business was not as much fun as gaining wealth as a prize of battle. They were not at all shy about making money through the booty of war, but mere business and trade was never their top priority.

Their heroes have come down to us in such stories as Homer's *Odyssey* and the siege of Troy. With fierce and idealistic warriors such as these, the materialistic Phoenicians had little in common, and in battle, no chance of success. But once the Minoans were erased from the scene with tsunamis and layers of volcanic ash, the war-like Mycenaeans from the Greek mainland were quick to raid the devastated islands of Crete to salvage what treasures they could and to establish themselves as the inheritors of the Minoan trade.

The Mycenaean Greeks were not as successful at trade as the Phoenicians were because ethics, fair-play, honor, and honesty were a part of their national character. These virtues were not found among the Babylonian-Hyksos-Phoenicians. But at warfare, the Greeks were supreme and skillful experts. So, the Phoenicians dared not oppose them openly. However, the Phoenician methods of trading both with the Greeks as well as with all of the enemies of the Greeks, began to reap its rewards. And the Phoenician use of the Sumerian Swindle gave them a money-making engine which funneled silver and gold into their coffers beyond anything that trade alone could bring in.

These loan sharks, lending-at-interest in every port, soon created a network of money-siphons sucking the silver and gold out of every country where Phoenician ships made landfall. This combination of import monopolies, sharp trade practices, and moneylending, gave the Phoenicians the wealth to finance a successful trade empire. Their craftiness at trade was apparent to all; but the Secret Frauds of the Sumerian Swindle, as the engine behind their growing trade empire, was hidden from all. They were both tradesmen and parasites because that is "how they had always been" among those Babylonian merchant-moneylenders sailing the world as Phoenicians and marketing their purple dye to every king.

This situation lasted for about 150 years as Phoenicia expanded its maritime trade across North Africa. During this time, the Hittites continued to press southward. They engulfed Ugarit and came to the borders of

Phoenicia. The most northern Phoenician city was on the island of Arwad. The Hittites took the island and forced the Phoenicians to abandon that profitable trade city. They were losing both trade and territory to the Hittites and they did not have the manpower to resist.

Although the powerful Rameses II of Egypt fought the Hittites, he finally signed a treaty with them in 1258 BC which ceded to them all the lands which the Hittites had already taken, including the Phoenician's island of Arwad. To the Phoenicians, it must have been evident that the next push southward by the Hittites would breach the walls of their coastal cities, at which point the sea traders could again expect no support from Egypt, and Phoenicia would in all probability cease to exist.

However, the Hittites had plenty of troubles of their own. Following after this treaty, during the next 45 years of Rameses' long reign, the Hittites were beset on all sides but were able to hold their own (recall Map 17, Chapter 12). They fought the Assyrians in the east. They fought the fierce Kaska people who controlled the north shore of Anatolia. And they fought several groups of people who divided western Anatolia among them. Meanwhile, the Mycenaean Greeks continued to raid into Anatolia to the west of the Hittites and to occupy the lands around Miletus.

Something had to be done to protect their trade zones and property. So, in the Phoenician cities on the Canaanite coast, the priests of Ba'al made use of the high religious science of the Semites by sacrificing to Ba'al little children as well as goats and sheep. After propitiating Ba'al in this way, they could plan political tactics based on messages from their god, who preferred to communicate the future to the Phoenicians by writing messages on the livers of the sacrificed sheep. It this way, they would know whether their various schemes for solving their political questions were worth pursuing or not. It was an ancient system of prognostication guaranteed by the priests to give results, whatever they might be.

Profits were good as they traded with the Greeks, Assyrians, Hittites, Egyptians, and Libyans. By this time, instead of incising cuneiform script on wet clay, they were writing with ink on papyrus and parchment by using a Canaanite alphabet and a reed stylus. While their Hebrew relatives were stealing sheep and pillaging the villages of Canaan, the Phoenicians were ensconced safely behind the walls of their port cities and aboard their merchant-moneylender ships on the open sea.

But the Phoenician city-states did not have the manpower to defend themselves from all of these great and powerful nations. They did have, however, an abundance of Semitic cunning. And the Sumerian Swindle gave them wealth and its resulting financial power for buying what they wanted and bribing who they needed. The moneylenders from the most ancient times in Sumeria and Babylonia had practiced Secret Fraud #8 of the Sumerian Swindle: "Large crime families are more successful than lone criminals or gangs; international crime families are the most successful of all."

The Phoenicians Attack Egypt

As international moneylenders and merchants, the Phoenicians knew not only their friends and their enemies, but they also knew *the friends and enemies* of their friends and enemies. Because they were merchants who traveled to places outside the borders of individual kingdoms, they were well-acquainted with the international relationships between those countries. The Phoenicians were well-equipped to ally themselves with those who could best serve their purposes. In this case, the poor and illiterate denizens of the Black Sea region served them very well.

While the Hebrew slaves in Egypt were hauling dung and making mud bricks, while the Hebrew goat-rustlers were shepherding their sheep and raiding the small towns of Canaan, the Hebrew Phoenicians were practicing the Sumerian Swindle and making preparations to subvert their enemies. Hiring mercenaries whenever they needed soldiers and then dismissing them after the battles had been fought, was an efficient system for small scale battles—a simple system which worked for these stingy merchants. But for prolonged large-scale warfare against the mighty Hittites, or against the noble, brave, and skillful Mycenaean Greeks, or against the godly and powerful Egyptians, the Phoenicians did not have the manpower.

But they did have the demonic cunning of the Babylonian merchant-moneylenders who had joined forces with them when they decamped from Avaris, Egypt, to establish their seafaring businesses on the shores of the Mediterranean. They also had the merchant-moneylender guild-lore and the Secret Frauds of the Sumerian Swindle.

Using the peoples of distant countries to subvert, betray, and dispossess the people of Sumeria and Babylonia, was a standard part of the merchant-moneylender treason and trickery. Using the shepherds of Canaan and Sinai to beat back the Egyptians during the Hyksos invasion required some long-range planning by the merchant-moneylenders, but it became a reality, and a very profitable reality, which had positioned the merchant-moneylender Phoenicians to control a Mediterranean trading empire. But their plans for monopolizing Mediterranean trade could not be achieved if the Mycenaeans and Hittites kept pressing in on their home port cities in Canaan and restricting their profits. All those mighty empires were war-like and war-ready, not at all like the naïve Egyptians whom the Babylonian shepherd army had been able to invade by use of deceit.

With deceit, the merchant-moneylenders made war. In this case, to rid themselves from the enforced tribute and threats from the Hittites and Greeks, what the Phoenicians needed was control of a large army. They found this army among the peoples of the Black Sea. And best of all, they could obtain the services of those hordes of primitive people for free, and they could even make a profit from the operation.

In their usual guise as wandering merchants, the Phoenicians had first traded with the Greeks. They beached their ships and dealt directly with the Greeks of both the mainland as well as on the Aegean islands. Dealing in whatever would bring them profits, including whatever women whom they could enslave and sell, these Phoenician merchant-moneylenders of Canaan sailed past the Mycenaean colonies and into the Black Sea. There, they found illiterate people who were eager for trade goods and who were also a hearty and war-like people, greedy for whatever they could rob from their neighbors. Such people were the perfect pawns for Secret Fraud #15 of the Sumerian Swindle: "Loans to friends are power; loans to enemies are weapons".

Suddenly, in 1213 BC, the great Rameses II died and a great worry seized the entire region. It was fairly common in the ancient Mediterranean for the death of a powerful king to draw in attacks by neighboring states, each seeking to determine if the successor king was weak and if prized lands might be wrested away. Under the circumstances, the Phoenicians would have had every reason to fear an imminent campaign southward into Egypt by the Hittites. However, the Hittites were preoccupied by problems at home and put off action in this direction. With their extensive trade contacts with the Egyptian court, the death of the aged Pharaoh did not come as a surprise. Rather, they had factored that eventuality into their schemes.

With the death of the aged Pharaoh as their signal, and the knowledge that the Hittites were not going to attack Egypt, it took less than two years for the Phoenician merchant-moneylenders to organize the alliances between Libyan raiders and Black Sea barbarians and to coordinate an attack timed to the moon cycles of their Babylonian calendar.

Gathering up a raiding party of 5,000 barbarian warriors and their ships, was the easy part of the scheme. The raiders sailed and rowed their ships from one Phoenician port-of-call to the next and, using Phoenician navigators to rendezvous with the Libyans, the Black Sea warriors rowed into the Nile Delta in 1208 BC and attacked the successor to Rameses, the Pharaoh Merneptah.

The Sea Peoples

But Pharaoh Merneptah had spies of his own and knew in advance of the attack. He concentrated his defenses and routed their forces, as described on his victory stele at Thebes. It was from this period in the history of the ancient Near East that the barbarian people from the Black Sea region became known as the Sea Peoples. Although this first strike to obtain gold and riches was a failure, it showed the surviving warriors how easy it was to raid in the Mediterranean Sea when they had the help of such rich and knowledgeable allies as the Phoenician merchant-moneylenders. They returned to their Black Sea homes and were able to verify to their people the Phoenician stories about the rich grain lands of the Near East.

Their 5,000 raiders had been hugely outnumbered, even with their Libyan allies. Although their raid on Egypt had failed to procure loot, it had given the Black Sea Peoples the confidence that they could successfully beat the peoples of the Near East in combat. They had only lost in their raid from lack of numbers. But if enough of them could attack the lands to the south, they could make those rich and fruitful grain lands their own.

The unrelieved food shortages put increasing pressure on those people to take action. At every Black Sea port-of-call, the Phoenicians told tales of rich grain lands and mountains of gold and silver loot in the lands to the south. The stories from the warriors returning from the Egyptian raid began circulating about the food supplies and wealth of the lands to the south, energizing these strong and increasingly hungry people. They began buying more weapons than cloth from their "friends," the Phoenician merchant-moneylenders. And they began fitting out their ships and even their fishing boats for war on a massive scale. As the stories spread, the tribes from Central Europe and the entire Black Sea region began migrating toward Anatolia while the Phoenicians sold them the best bronze weapons, grain, and military intelligence.

The attacks against the Hittites began by land. In fact, the greatest campaigns the Sea Peoples would mount were by land. This has led recent sources to refer to them as the "Land and Sea Peoples," which is a much more accurate appellation. The Kaska lived to the north, between the Hittites and the Black Sea. They attacked at this time. The Assuwa, Arzawa, and Lukka lived in the land to the west of the Hittites, between that empire and the Aegean Sea. They also attacked Hattiland.

By 1176 BC, the remainder of the eastern seaboard of the Mediterranean fell to the Sea and Land Peoples, except for the Phoenician cities. King Rameses III stopped the Sea Peoples attacks on Egypt but he did not contest their other conquests and ceded to them the lands in Canaan which they had already taken.

These relentless attacks by the Sea Peoples virtually destroyed all of the major powers of the Mediterranean, and cleared the way for the rise of the Greeks, the Romans, and Western civilization.

But though they had wiped out the mighty Hittite empire and had decimated the Mycenaean Greeks, ending their hegemony of the Aegean Sea, the Sea Peoples left untouched and unmolested, the cities of their secret allies, the Phoenicians. Amid this cataclysm, where hundreds of thousands of Land and Sea Peoples had engulfed and destroyed almost every city in the eastern Mediterranean area, the Phoenician cities remained completely untouched. This is a recurring theme throughout the history of not only the ancient Near East, but the history of Western civilization. This recurring theme is found in every nation where, after wars and disasters of every kind, one particular group of people was spared. And that group was composed of the very people who had schemed and engineered the disaster, itself: the treasonous merchant-moneylenders and their extended families.

Tyre was the leading Phoenician city in those days, and we are fortunate to have an excellent archaeological study of this site which went all the way down to bedrock. The archeological dig not only showed no widespread destruction at that time but there was also great continuity from layer to layer, indicating that the local society continued to live in the same way throughout this period. Sarepta (modern Sarafand) between Tyre and Sidon was similarly the subject of detailed archaeological study; the results again showed no destruction and great continuity in the strata.

The most northern Phoenician city was on the island of Arwad, also known as Arvad and Arados. The Hittites had captured from the Phoenicians this valuable trading center prior to the attacks of the Sea Peoples. This city was, in fact, destroyed by the Sea Peoples. But after they had captured it, they returned it to the Phoenicians.

Because the merchant-moneylenders of Phoenicia had sold weapons and food to the Sea Peoples, shared with them their spy data, and provided them with the logistics necessary to attack and subdue all of these great empires of the eastern Mediterranean, they were accorded a special status. The Sea and Land Peoples had benefited greatly by their alliance with the merchant-moneylenders of Phoenicia. But like every deal that the moneylenders conceived, the real winners are not those who believed themselves to be the winners but those who chose who the winners would be.

Once again, the methods of the Sumerian Swindle had worked perfectly. Those who saw their lands overrun and dispossessed by the Land and Sea Peoples, did not see those who stood invisibly behind the invaders.

Under the destructive force of the Sea Peoples' attacks, all of the powerful adversaries of the Phoenicians had been destroyed while leaving the Phoenician cities untouched. This left the Phoenicians in a very advantageous position with fully functioning cities and fleets of trading vessels and trade channels ready to buy and sell amid the war-ravaged lands. The historical record shows that their untouched and active cities quickly began to expand in size and in influence by establishing trading posts and guild halls in Cyprus, the Aegean, Sicily, Sardinia, North Africa, Algeria, Morocco, and Spain.

The legacy of the Sea Peoples was that they had forcefully cleared away the old powers from the Mediterranean. The old powers had been uprooted, leaving the Phoenicians with a new and naïve people upon whom to practice the Sumerian Swindle. In time, the Greeks and Romans arose and sowed the seeds of Western civilization. But it was a Western civilization which would become infected with the debilitating economic and social disease known as the Sumerian Swindle. This disease was carried about and spread by the Phoenicians and their parasitic cousins, the circumcised merchant-moneylenders of Mesopotamia.

Following the migrations of the Land and Sea Peoples, the Phoenicians formed the major naval and trading power of the entire region for almost a thousand years. For the sake of brevity, let's condense this time span. They established a second production center for the purple dye in Morocco. Brilliant textiles were a part of Phoenician wealth; Phoenician glass was another export ware. They traded whatever brought them a profit—from African Basenji dogs to wine and metals and slaves. And they loaned silver wherever they went, profiting both from the interest as well as from the property swindles and debt-slaves that inevitably resulted. They worked their slaves to death in their iron and silver mines in Iberia (Spain) and brought tin from Great Britain to Cyprus, where it was alloyed into bronze from the local copper mines. The Phoenicians established commercial outposts and guild halls throughout the Mediterranean, the most strategically important being Carthage in North Africa, founded in 814 BC under Pygmalion. Its chief god was a blood-thirsty incarnation of the Canaanite god, Ba'al.

With the Red Sea on the east of Africa and the Mediterranean Sea on the north of Africa, after they had sailed to the Atlantic and found an ocean on the west of Africa, it was not much of a stretch of their imaginations to think that they could sail all the way around the south of Africa and arrive back in the waters of the Red Sea once again. A Carthaginian expedition led by Hanno the Navigator explored and colonized the Atlantic coast of Africa as far as the Gulf of Guinea; and according to Herodotus, a Phoenician expedition sent down the Red Sea by Pharaoh Necho II of Egypt (~600 BC) circumnavigated Africa and returned through the Pillars of Hercules (Gibraltar) in three years.

Although Cyrus the Great conquered Phoenicia in 539 BC, Phoenicia continued to prosper as long as they furnished fleets for the Persian kings. However, Phoenician influence in the area declined after this because much of their population migrated to Carthage and other colonies following the Persian conquest. In their ships, they could sail away from the Persians and not be followed.

Alexander the Great took the Phoenician city of Tyre in 332 BC. The rise of Hellenistic Greece gradually ousted the remnants of Phoenicia's former dominance over the Eastern Mediterranean trade routes; as a result, Phoenician culture disappeared entirely from the area. As for their coastal cities, after Alexander, they were controlled by a succession of Hellenistic rulers. In 197 BC, Phoenicia along with Syria reverted to the Greek Seleucids and the region became increasingly Hellenized.

However, its North African offspring, Carthage, continued to flourish, mining iron and precious metals from Iberia, and using its considerable naval power and mercenary armies to protect its commercial interests. But Carthage was finally destroyed by Rome in 146 BC at the end of the Punic Wars. Finally, in 65 BC Pompey incorporated Phoenicia into the Roman province of Syria.

And so, after nearly 1,500 years of swindles, monopoly capitalism, piracy, slave-mongering, and treason, this third branch of the Hyksos merchant-moneylender army—the late-comers and second-tier Babylonian opportunists who had arrived in Egypt too late to make the really big loot, but who then became the merchant-moneylenders of Phoenicia—these became extinct. Although the Phoenician culture became extinct, the Sumerian Swindle did not become extinct. The Swindle spread to the moneylenders of Rome, Europe, Africa, India, and China, creating great riches for those who practiced it—but poverty, starvation, and death among those who suffered under it.

CHAPTER 14
FROM HYKSOS TO JEWS

To recap: Most of *The Sumerian Swindle* traces the history of how the fraud of moneylending arose among the civilizations of mankind. So far, we have seen how the merchant-moneylenders seized the wealth of the ancient world by using moneylending, monopoly capitalism, and warfare as their main engines of acquisition to surreptitiously swindle all wealth for free from both individual people as well as from entire countries.

The moneylenders—operating as cartels and crime families—swindled everybody. All of mankind was being swindled by those secretive, wealth-sucking vampires. Those criminal parasites did not deserve to own the wealth of the whole world but they had succeeded in deceiving the honest and gullible people of the world with their mesmerizing and false belief that a few ruthless individuals have a self-granted "right" to swindle and to enslave the entire planet, all for their own private profit. It is a delusional fantasy which they still claim for themselves in modern times. Because the Sumerian Swindle was a secret scam, the merchant-moneylenders did not ask the people for permission to swindle them. They swindled them through perfidious guile and ruthless cunning, while keeping their Twenty-One Secret Frauds carefully concealed and their stacks of bullion safely hidden.

And yet, even with this background of more than 1,700 years of history, there were still no Jews in existence anywhere on Earth. There were no Jews; however, there was an over-supply of circumcised moneylenders in Babylonia who were using every dirty trick they could think of to change themselves into Jews. But so far, they did not know how to do it. To understand how they were trying to accomplish this, we must leave the Phoenicians to their doom beneath the heel of Rome at Carthage in 146 BC and return once again to 1550 BC. But we will not return to the Hyksos who were enslaved by the Egyptians. We will not return to the Hebrew tribes of Hyksos bandits who were roaming around in the hills of Canaan and Sinai. And we will not return to the Hyksos who later became the Phoenician sellers of purple dye. But we must now study those Hyksos who were the circumcised descendants of the original looters of Egypt. They were living a life of luxury in Babylonia.

Remember, in 1550 BC, when Pharaoh Ahmose had allowed the Hyksos to escape their fortress of Avaris with all of their loot, they were divided into four groups: (1) the low-level Apiru bandits and Ma'adian Semites who were trapped in Egypt and enslaved; (2) the roving bands of Hebrew goat-rustlers and bandits who wandered into the hills of Canaan and Sinai; (3) the second-level Babylonian merchants and military officers who became the Phoenicians; and (4) the tamkarum who returned to Babylonia loaded with the vast treasures which they had looted from Egypt.

Please note: Almost all dates in the archeological record are only accurate until later discoveries re-calibrate the time frame. Although some historians place the years that the Hyksos ruled northern Egypt as being between 1630 BC and 1523 BC, I am placing the first appearance of what I call the "proto-Jews" at about 1550 BC, when the last group of the Babylonian merchant-moneylenders who had originally financed the expedition, began returning to Babylonia holding their loot in one hand and their circumcised cocks in the other.

This last group of Hyksos in our study were actually the first group to leave Egypt. They were the sons of the original Babylonian merchant-moneylenders who planned and organized the Hyksos invasion. They were the leaders who usurped Pharaoh's throne and who coordinated both the invasion and the systematic looting of the entire country north of Thebes. They were trained by their fathers to inherit all of their fathers' wealth, cunning, and treachery. They and their fathers moved in a steady stream into and out of Egypt from the very beginning of the Hyksos raid, as they accompanied the shipments of gold bullion, precious stones, and carved ivory back to Babylonia. Like their fathers, they had themselves circumcised while in Egypt, both as a souvenir of their conquests and so that they would be "horny all of the time."

Extreme wealth, luxury, sexual gratification through harems and sex-slaves, plus their sadistic enjoyment of power over mankind, were the very essence of their lives. It would be inaccurate to say that they had "escaped" from Egypt because, unlike the other groups of Hyksos who were dependent upon what they could steal from their immediate surroundings, these Babylonian moneylenders were international in their affiliations. After murdering any priests or old Egyptians who got in their way, they had been melting down Egyptian artifacts into bullion and shipping it to Babylonia since they first arrived. They and their fathers had accompanied the bullion shipments back to Babylonia as a part of their systematic stripping of everything precious from the temples and palaces of Egypt.

Indeed, each group of Hyksos who were forced out of the fort at Avaris can been seen in an ascending order of complexity and worldview. The Hyksos goat-rustler foot soldiers and Ma'adian traitors who were captured and enslaved, were limited to their daily life of toil as determined by their Egyptian masters. The Hyksos shepherds who escaped into the wilderness to continue the bandit lifestyle of their forefathers, were limited to whatever livelihood they could gather from their herds and from their brigandage. The Phoenician Hyksos who used their wealth and mercantile skills to build a trading empire, were limited to just the places that their ships could dock plus whatever area they needed to hire farmers and herdsman to provide them with food.

But it is this fourth group of Hyksos, the merchant-moneylenders of Babylonia, who were the most sophisticated and wily and by far the wealthiest. They require a deeper inspection and study because they were not limited by any laws of man or Laws of God; their stated intent was to own the entire world and to either enslave or commit genocide upon all of mankind. Monsters such as these require a careful study in the same way that one would study a poisonous snake or a plague bacillus.

For 2,000 years, these Babylonian merchant-moneylenders made extensive use of spies and informants and to keep their hoards of precious metals carefully removed from places of possible theft. Through their system of merchants, peddlers, and beer taverns, they gathered the most minute hints about the politics and economic news of the day. Their profits from the Sumerian Swindle and its related businesses were so huge that they could afford to pay a large gang of spies to keep them informed with gossip and news from across the countryside. In this way, they could move their hoards of silver and gold from one temple city to another, as necessitated by political and military threats.

Also, "escaping" is not the correct term for their egress from Egypt because the word usually means moving with haste from one dangerous place to a place of relative safety. For the merchant-moneylenders who sat on Pharaoh's throne as well as the monied aristocracy of fellow pirates who surrounded it, their places of business extended far beyond the borders of any one kingdom. So, these Hyksos did not so much "escape" from Egypt as they merely *relocated* their place of residence from Egypt back to Babylonia, leisurely taking with them whatever treasures they fancied. As the wealthiest of the Hyksos, they were, if not thoroughly educated, at least the employers of numerous scribes. They recognized the importance of and the value of written records. Among the treasures which they took with them back to Babylonia, were the wisdom writings from the libraries of Egypt.

When their trading agents far up the Nile began informing them of the movements of Egyptian troops and the shipments of grain out into the deserts where they were not allowed to venture, they were well-prepared for the war which followed. It was not necessary for them to actually do any fighting, themselves, because that was what they hired their generals to do. That was why they hired mercenaries—to fight and die so that they could continue to profit from and to enslave the peoples around them. They were enormously rich from their frauds and thefts, and that wealth bought them protection and advance notice that the Egyptians were soon to wage war against them.

Long before any attack by the Egyptians, the Babylonian Hyksos moved out of Egypt dressed like everybody else and riding along with an ordinary trade caravan. Then, they took passage down the Euphrates and were comfortably residing in their family mud-brick mansions in Babylon and Ur, months before the Egyptians began their counter-rebellion.

From their residences in Babylonia, these merchant-moneylenders received reports of the Egyptian victory over their Hyksos army. When Avaris fell, the Hyksos generals and mid-level merchants either returned to their family properties in Babylonia or they joined the Phoenician branch of those bandit families. This was no concern to the tamkarum guilds of Babylonia. They had no use for military men there because Babylonian security was guaranteed by the king and his generals. However, losing their Hyksos generals and their network of merchants to a competing trade guild in Phoenicia, was just one more problem about relying upon the Sumerian Swindle as their sole business model.

Plundering Egypt was a first for the moneylender guilds of Babylonia because it was the first time that they had conquered a country using their own resources, rather than as mere advisors who stood behind a king. It was an operation that was coordinated among various of the wealthier members of the merchant-moneylender guilds as a joint operation. But as Egypt was being looted, and especially after the defeat at Avaris where the guilds and their soldiers were scattered, every moneylender took whatever he could for himself without regard to previous business agreements.

Especially irksome to the Babylonian guild patriarchs were the great treasures which their previous business partners had absconded with, in order to set up the Phoenician trade centers. And now, instead of being partners, as was the case when they were all looting Egypt together, the

Phoenicians turned into business competitors who were monopolizing the Mediterranean trade and not sharing the profits.

These and many other problems gave the greedy and "always horny" circumcised patriarchs of the Babylonian guilds much to contemplate, as they feasted and drank and whored in the cities of Babylonia.

*****

One thing needs to be repeated: The businesses of the ancient people were family operations, and the patriarchs of those families were extremely anxious that their sons should follow them in the family business. No religion of those times offered anything to look forward to after death. There were no ideas about dying and going to heaven or hell. What a man could make for himself and enjoy in this life, was all he would ever get. So, it was important to him to get as much as he could in the present life and to leave something for his sons to remember him by.

The common people desired only to leave a good profession for their sons, to train them in the skills of brick-maker or potter or weaver or silver-smith. With these, he could make a living and perpetuate the family line.

Among warriors, the best that a man could leave for his sons was a bit of land and the fame of a good name. Likewise, the kings desired this, immortalizing themselves and their deeds and their names in stone bas reliefs and sculptures and in written records, bragging of their conquests and of the justice and prosperity which they had brought their people.

In this regard, the moneylenders were no different. Like everyone else in the ancient Near East, they prayed to their gods and desired to teach their sons the ways of business and moneylending so that their families would prosper and their names would be honored among their descendants. But there were also some very different perspectives on life which were held solely by the patriarchs of the moneylender guilds—perspectives which only great wealth, ruthless covetousness, and malicious hatred can simultaneously engender.

As their businesses grew, so did their need for more loyal sons to manage the numerous foreclosed estates and bankrupted enterprises. And they needed more loyal daughters to marry into the families of high political officials and rich business families to bring even more political power and wealth to the moneylender family. The moneylenders' parasitic system of cancerous growth had worked very well in the nearly 2,000 years that the Sumerian Swindle had provided them with limitless wealth.

But their expulsion from Egypt, along with the changing times, gave the merchant-moneylenders some new problems.

The world was a bigger place than it had been when Sumeria was young. The horizons had widened. No longer was the world limited by how far a man could see by standing at the top of a 60-foot-tall ziggurat. Through trade and warfare, the general populace had learned of distant countries and strange peoples, none of whom practiced the Sumerian Swindle but all of whom desired the goods that the merchants carried.

At their guild hall in the city of Ur, the most successful members of the various tamkarum guilds discussed their businesses and the events in Egypt, just as businessmen discuss their businesses in modern times. Profits and losses, products and prices, are always part of the discussions.

But especially among those most elite of the merchant-moneylenders; the very wealthiest; those who had participated in the Egyptian plunder; the ones who had profited the most by being among the families who had planned the entire operation; the ones who had celebrated their victory by having themselves circumcised while they were in Egypt; the ones who were "horny all of the time"—for them, this new situation and its resulting problems were a topic that had never before confronted the moneylender guilds of Mesopotamia in their nearly 2,000 years of swindles, frauds, pimping, and treason.

Although the merchant-moneylender guild members were related to one another through business and marriage, they were also in competition with one another. Every city in Babylonia had its own moneylenders' guild. It became apparent to all of the tamkarum guilds that, profitable though it was, the Sumerian Swindle had some recurring limitations.

But it was to this elite group of circumcised merchant-moneylenders in the city of Ur that these problems seemed the most serious. They were at the very topmost level of wealth. They were the richest moneylenders in Babylonia. And it was these circumcised guild patriarchs of Ur who had been pondering the curious questions which the Sumerian Swindle offered to them. The Swindle gave them the opportunity to own the entire world for free and to enslave all of mankind to their tyranny, but the question was, *"Why don't we already own everything?"* It was these circumcised swindlers and bandits who had the most to lose if these repetitive problems could not be solved because these were the very same problems which prevented them from owning the entire world

In their private discussions open only to those of their own elite status, these circumcised guild members identified fifteen problems which were both recurring from ancient times, as well as some new problems which had become only too apparent during their Hyksos adventure. These problems were as follows:

The Fifteen Secret Problems That Prevented the Babylonian Money-lenders from Owning the Entire World:

Problem #1: Wealth attracts robbers, so how can it be hidden?

Problem #2: The gods do not protect tamkarum wealth.

Problem #3: When the strongest city is not strong enough, where can one go for safety?

Problem #4: Wealth escapes into the god's temples.

Problem #5: Guild members follow different gods.

Problem #6: Close relatives are lured away by the gods.

Problem #7: What keeps people loyal?

Problem #8: Genealogies link tribes but without a root.

Problem #9: The kings gain wealth by taxing both rich and poor.

Problem #10: Kings are targets, so it is better to hold the target in your hands than to be a king.

Problem #11: We tamkarum promote warfare and thereby profit enormously; but while inveigling others to do the fighting, how can we avoid military service without invoking the wrath of our victims?

Problem #12: Armies are expensive, so how can they be induced to fight for free?

Problem #13: When conquering a country, how can it be secured? (Assyrian deportation? Genocide? Enslavement?)

Problem #14: Moneylenders are despised; yet, how can we have honor and prestige?

Problem #15: The Sumerian Swindle is both a secret and a mystical gift from the gods; how can it be protected forever as a possession of our families alone?

Let's look at each in turn. *Problem #1*: "Wealth attracts robbers so how can it be hidden?" was the oldest problem faced by the moneylenders. Next to using all their wiles to defraud the people of silver and gold through business, alcohol, slavery and moneylending swindles, their most important problem was being able to keep what they had swindled by protecting their silver from thieves. What was the use of accumulating piles of treasure if thieves could merely carry it away?

The palaces, temples, and homes of the Mesopotamia people were made of mud brick. It was a simple matter for a thief to break through a mud wall with a pick and shovel to raid any residence, even that of the king. Even a bucket of water to soften the dirt and a sharp stick to dig out the mud, were all of the tools that a thief needed to burglarize any building in Mesopotamia. So, from the earliest days of Sumerian Law, breaking through a wall, whether to steal anything or not, was a punishable act. Yet, regardless of the thickness of the walls, a big enough hoard of silver would attract any number of ambitious thieves. The only places that no thief would dare to rob, were the holy temples which were the homes of the gods. But even these had been raided at various times by the kings. So, how could their treasures be protected both from robbers and the confiscations of the kings?

Problem #2 had also plagued the moneylenders repeatedly since ancient times. It was abundantly obvious that "The gods did not protect tamkarum wealth." No matter how much they prayed or how many sacrifices they made to Nabu, the god of accounting and bookkeeping, or to Sin, their mighty Moon God of stealth and subversion, nothing seemed to keep their hoards of gold safe from the kings. Yet, even so, it was obvious that the safest and most secure place to keep gold and silver bullion was in the temple treasuries.

They could never deposit their wealth into the *palace* treasuries because the kings were always very happy to claim whatever was in the treasuries as their own. The temple was the safest place because even the kings feared the wrath of the gods, most of the time.

In the early days of Sumeria, this theory held good; and not even the kings would dare to take anything from the temples of the gods. It was not just the huge temple complex protecting their hoards with thick walls of mud bricks; it was not just the temple guards who protected whatever bullion was on deposit there; but it was the actual fear both of king and burglar of being struck down with a plague, or having their persons attacked by snakes and scorpions, or having the earth open up and swallow them, or by being struck by lightning; those possibilities alone are what kept the temple treasuries safe from theft. Even invading armies feared the gods and respected the sanctity of the temples and their treasures in those early days.

But all of this changed over the millennia as first one king and then another invaded and seized the temple treasuries, or merely took what he wanted from his own city temples during the contingencies of war. It was observed by everyone that these kings did not turn into toads or contract leprosy or suffer any other displeasure of the gods. Obviously, the gods were either powerless to prevent theft from their own temples or they didn't really care if their temples were looted or not. Or perhaps the gods had decided to favor a particular king for reasons that only the gods knew.

This was a major concern of the moneylenders that had arisen over the millennia. They had to have a safe and secret place to store their bullion, both out of sight of their starving and enslaved victims as well as out of the hands of thieves, who were either stealthy enough to steal it or powerful enough to overcome their hired guards and take it. It was of the utmost necessity to find a safe place for their hoards of bullion. They could not bury it in the ground or under the floor because there was just too much of it. They needed a treasury which was guarded constantly and which they could enter and leave at will, making whatever deposits or withdrawals as needed. So, temple strong rooms were the only answer to such problems.

But Problem #2, "The gods do not protect tamkarum wealth," also created a corollary question of "Which of the gods offered the most protection for a moneylender's wealth?" None of the gods of Mesopotamia had proven to be powerful enough. The Moon God had seemed like the ideal god, with moneylender stealth and secrecy waning and waxing like the depressions and inflations which the moneylenders created and profited by. But even the statue of the great god Marduk in Babylon was kidnapped and hauled away by the Hittite king Murshili after he had learned of the tamkarum sacking of Egypt. He pirated away both the Babylonian and the Egyptian gold on deposit in the Temple of Marduk in 1595 BC, just 45 years previously, and simultaneously brought the Babylonian empire to an end. Fortunately, the Moon God of Ur had kept the loot of the merchant-moneylenders safely unmolested—this time.

But, in fact, no Mesopotamian god was especially partial to the money-lenders. The thefts of their bullion by the kings at various times from all of the temples of all of the gods, was enough proof for the moneylenders in this matter. It was obvious to them that they ultimately needed the protection of the mightiest of gods guarding their money securely in the mightiest of temple treasuries. The mightiest and most powerful and most awe-inspiring god would have to be found for this task, because none of the gods of Mesopotamia were particularly partial to the moneylenders. And yet, it seemed only reasonable that there had to be some god, somewhere, who cherished the moneylenders because, how else could they be so prosperous for so many centuries without some god somewhere loving them and caring for them more than he cared for any of their victims?

The moneylenders reasoned that because none of the temples had given 100 percent guarantee of safety for their hoards of bullion, obviously they had been trusting the wrong gods and the wrong temples with their loot. This was the only conclusion that made sense to these ancient schemers. This had to be the cause of their problem! None of the Babylon-ian gods had offered them total protection because they had been trusting *the wrong gods*. The moneylenders realized that they needed a god who was particularly fond of gold as well as of moneylenders. But which god? And where could He be found, since He was obviously not residing in any of the temples of Mesopotamia?

This engendered *Problem #3*: "When the strongest city is not strong enough, where can one go for safety?" Like all other people of the ancient Near East, the moneylenders were free to worship whatever god they chose. But if none of the gods were partial to them and their special needs, then it was obvious that they had to find a god who would protect them against all other gods and against the thefts of both kings and commoners. They needed a special "God of the Moneylenders" who would protect them alone—an unknown god who had no connection to the Mesopo-tamian pantheon. And this god had to have a strong temple to dwell in and to guard their treasures.

Also, the temple and the god could not be like any other temple or god because as they correctly observed for *Problem #4*: "Wealth escapes into the god's temples." So, even if they could find such a god and locate their treasury in such a city, the fourth problem would still occur.

No matter what god they trusted with their wealth and with their worship and their sacrifices, it was only a matter of time before the temple of this god would begin to acquire its own wealth through donations and offerings. This wealth would be money that devotees would take from their own finances and from their own families and from their own tamkarum trade guilds to give to the god in the temple. Thus, once again, the silver and gold that the moneylenders coveted for themselves would be given to the god, thereby reducing their own wealth. Through pious relatives as well as through their own gifts, wealth would be absorbed by the temple, no matter to which god the members of the tamkarum guilds devoted themselves. And so, whatever temple that they found to protect their wealth, would have to be in some way under their personal control.

In Babylonia and Assyria, tamkarum control of the temples was impossible because the temples had been in existence since before there were any moneylenders. Their priestly staff had passed down their offices to their sons in an unbroken genealogical lineage. No moneylender could hope to step into such a closed shop except through marriage, and even then, the sons and daughters of such a marriage would be devoted to the god and to the temple.

The kings had gained some control over the temples by installing sons and daughters as chief priests and priestesses. So, between the inherited office of the temple priests and the king's assigned office to his sons and daughters, there was no opportunity for tamkarum infiltration. The tamkarum could corrupt and bribe the priests but could not take their places. The only way to solve such a problem, was to establish a temple of their own with themselves as the priests. But how was something like that possible?

And there was *Problem #5*: "Guild members follow different gods." This problem was older than any other problem. Whether a man and his family followed Ishtar or Sin or Marduk, usually didn't matter as long as his loyalties to his tamkarum guild were not affected. However, this problem's harm to their total wealth only became painfully apparent to the tamkarum guilds after their ejection from Egypt.

While family members and relatives usually followed the same gods which were honored by their fathers, it was not uncommon for them to honor other gods of the pantheon. The gods of Babylonia and Assyria were like a big family in that all of the gods were related to one another. The ancient stories of how the gods came into being had been passed down from before Sumerian times, long before 3300 BC. The Epic of Creation was recited during the New Year's celebration in Babylon each year. So, everyone in Mesopotamia and the surrounding countries knew where the gods came from and their genealogical relationship to one another.

In general, for the average Babylonian to change loyalties from the god of his father or from the god of his guild and switch to some other god was not a great problem, since the Mesopotamian pantheon was all one related family of gods and goddesses.

But for the merchant-moneylender guilds, it was a problem for the moneylenders because such a man's new-found devotion often caused him to donate his wealth to that god's temple, thus depriving the moneylender of wealth which could have been invested to generate more profits. And for what? Every Mesopotamia god was genealogically related to every other god. So, changing to the worship of one of the other gods in the pantheon did not matter because it was still worship of the same family of gods, no matter which one was worshipped.

This became even more acute in *Problem #6*: "Close relatives are lured away by the gods." The tamkarum guilds were especially affected when, after being ejected from Egypt, many of their guild brothers proclaimed their loyalties to the Canaanite gods such as Ba'al and joined with the Hyksos of the Mediterranean faction to establish the competing guilds of Phoenicia. Remember, the ancient peoples believed that the gods dwelled in specific geographical locations. So, when they moved to a new city or country, it was common to begin praying to the gods of that country. The Phoenician Hyksos could not be prevented from leaving by appealing to their loyalty to the Babylonian gods, simply because the Babylonian gods resided in Babylonia and the Canaanite gods resided in Canaan. It was this local character of the gods that had cost the tamkarum guilds so much. What the moneylenders needed was a god who was not restricted to a particular city but whose domain extended to the very farthest trade routes beyond the borders of any country.

The tamkarum guilds of Babylonia had lost huge amounts of treasure as well as the entire Mediterranean trade monopolies and their connected trade routes through the competition of the Phoenician Hyksos. The Phoenicians gained independence from them partly because of the new gods whom they worshipped. Thus, this problem of how to keep their guild members from praying to foreign gods, became a major issue during the retreat from Egypt.

Identical with this problem, but much more personally injurious to the patriarchs of the tamkarum guilds, was *Problem #7*: "What keeps people loyal?" What was the result when a close family member began worshipping another god? While worshipping some other god was a pecuniary loss to the trade guilds, it was also a loss of wealth and a loss of power to the patriarchs of the moneylender families. Remember, the foundation of those merchant-moneylender businesses had been based upon families, tribes, marriage connections, and guild brotherhoods since Sumerian times. They had developed an extended patriarchal system of authority which could transcend individual families through genealogical relationships. And all of it was rooted in the authority of the individual sheik or chief or patriarch or father of the tribe.

So, for a son or other family member to declare his loyalty to a god other than the god of his father was to remove himself from the authority of his father. His son could claim independence simply by claiming the protection of some other god, a god who might even be an enemy god in the pantheon. And so, by 1550 BC, the tamkarum guilds were finding that their control of business and finance was weakened when guild members and family members became devotees of other gods. Loss of control over family members and guild partners was a very big problem for them because it meant a loss of control over the vast wealth and real estate holdings which they had acquired and for which they needed loyal sons and partners to help them administer.

Problem #7 had ramifications in all spheres of business and politics: "What keeps people loyal?" Certainly, fear of the gods keeps them loyal to certain gods. But they also knew that material goods were even more important to the ordinary people. Plenty of food, a share of the loot, loyalty to their leaders and devotion to the same god, were all a necessary part of the methods which the patriarchs used to control their employees and families.

As Joseph, their Hyksos Minister of the Granary, had demonstrated when he had starved the Egyptian people into submission in order to force them into digging up their gold and silver images and jewelry, people will sell their own children into slavery in exchange for something to eat. Also, as their Hyksos generals had demonstrated, if they are impoverished enough, men are willing to fight and die in exchange for the mere promise of loot. The promise is enough because once they began to fight and die, it didn't matter if they got any loot or not. Just the promise of loot was enough to con them into fighting for free. And if they won, the loot didn't cost the tamkarum anything since it was looted from the vanquished and could then later be purloined from the victorious soldiers through the Sumerian Swindle. The merchant-moneylenders had raised an army of shepherds and had conquered Egypt with such an army. They had done it cheaply, too. Promises are cheap.

With food and a promise of wealth, loyalty to the leaders could be bought; it did not matter whether their mercenaries even followed the same god or not. But what an even greater power would the Babylonian money-lenders have, if all of them could be induced to follow *the same god?* Then, whatever army that they could raise, would have the unifying power behind it of a single god rather than the power of a greedy rabble, each of whom followed different gods.

Problem #8 was actually a part of the solution: "Genealogies link tribes but without a root." Their Hyksos generals had organized the nomadic shepherds into a single army by amalgamating related friendly tribes and by keeping separated those tribes whose genealogical histories preserved ancient animosities. It was very useful to military morale to use such a system of combining brotherly affection and keeping separate any familial bitterness. The lesson was not lost on the tamkarum patriarchs of Babylonia. They appreciated anything that would increase efficiency and therefore profits. Once Pharaoh Ahmose had retaken his country and kicked them all out of Egypt, those competing tribes once again scattered across Canaan and Sinai without a unifying genealogy to keep them governable under a single ruler.

But what if it was possible to take unrelated tribes with unrelated genealogies and link them into a single genealogy? What could be the possibilities if all of the Amorite tribes could be linked within a single genealogy, with the tamkarum themselves as the foundational root of that genealogical tree? And if that root was made worthy and virtuous enough, with plenty of prestige, then a 'genealogical swindle' could be invoked whereby all those tribes could be induced to obey the central authority of the patriarchs—that is, themselves—at the root of the tree. Like the fraudulent accounting records "proving" with fake arithmetic that more was owed than was borrowed, such a genealogical swindle could be accomplished entirely in writing. Thus, the solution to Problem #8 began to take form.

As for *Problem #9*: "The Kings gain wealth by taxing both rich and poor." But how could they circumvent paying taxes to the king? They had put themselves on Pharaoh's throne and had profited from all of the taxes that they had placed upon Egypt. As the wealthy "Haves" in Egypt, they knew how much more they could have had by shifting the tax burden onto the poor. The poor have less than the rich, but since there are so many more poor people than rich people, the government could make more in total taxes by taxing the poor and not taxing the rich. Even in modern times, this inequality of taxes is observed where the ratio of taxes favors the rich and oppresses the poor simply because the rich write the tax laws.

"The Kings gain wealth by taxing both rich and poor." This loss of profits through taxes to the king was as old as the Sumerian Swindle, itself. The moneylenders had circumvented taxes by smuggling whenever they could get away with it. But smuggling had the unpleasant risk of discovery and punishment. Besides, it was the best policy to always fawn at the feet of the king and show outward signs of complete submission and loyalty. Getting caught at smuggling always destroyed such hypocrisy. So, the merchant-moneylenders had always paid the taxes and safe passage licenses when they could find no other alternative. And they always protected their reputation for loyalty with many layers of middlemen separating them from their smuggling operations.

One alternative that they had developed was to gain control of the tax collection process and turn it into a profitable business. As tax farmers, they could guarantee the kings a set amount of taxes, beat more than that amount out of the people, and then keep the remainder for themselves. Such power gave them the leeway to tax their guild brothers lightly. In addition, fear of the tax collector's office gave them the prestige and fear-induced respect from the people which they craved. So, from the earliest days, the moneylenders coveted the office of tax collector for their sons. With a family member in such an office, they could reduce the taxes on themselves and collect the shortfall from the poor.

Controlling kings was better than being a king. This was *Problem #10*: "Kings are targets, so it is better to hold the target your hands than to be a target." When they had the opportunity to sit on the throne of Pharaoh, the tamkarum guilds wasted no time in assuming kingship over Egypt. So, having one of their own as king was a great advantage. But being a king was fraught with peril. Yet, who is above a king? Certainly not a scheming merchant or moneylender. The only one who was above a king, was a temple priest. The priest gave the king his authority to rule because such power was passed down from the gods. But the priests had gained their own power from ancient times and had passed down their priestly office to their own sons. So, the moneylender patriarchs considered ways in which they could infiltrate the priesthood and put their own sons into the position of head priest. In this way, they could hold the king in their hands and rule both the temple and the palace. And if the king died or was assassinated, transferring their "loyalty" to the next king was an easy task for such lying hypocrites, all of them experts in fawning humility and deceit.

Problem #11: "We tamkarum promote warfare and thereby profit enormously; but while inveigling others to do the fighting, how can we avoid military service without invoking the wrath of our victims?" Through their international spy networks, the merchant-moneylenders could predict with some accuracy the probable winners in any war. Knowing the amounts of precious metals in every king's treasury and the size of the grain harvests, they could usually predict the winners in any conflict.

The profits from war were tremendous, not only from loans to kings, but from the higher prices which they could get for their goods. Plus, the booze, gambling, and whoring that the soldiers were so fond of, brought in huge wealth. But as profitable as war is to a moneylender, actually being drafted into the king's army was a frightful and dangerous hazard. Let the "Have-Nots" go to war. Let the "Haves" go to war. There were profits in foreclosing on the surviving widows' homes and buying the abandoned property of both "the Haves" and "the Have-Nots." But the moneylenders counted themselves as a superior class of "Haves." They deserved to stay safely at home, counting the profits, and far away from the brutality, hardship, bloodshed, maiming, and death which they financed and promoted. But how could they be exempt from warfare while everyone else was fighting and dying?

And *Problem #12* needed a solution: "Armies are expensive, so how can they be induced to fight for free?" The Egyptian invasion was made possible for the moneylender guilds simply because they had not needed a prohibitive amount of silver as payment for the soldiers who had accepted grain as payment and free swords and other weapons.

Certainly, the merchant-moneylender guilds had to finance the Hyksos invasion through an actual outlay of silver to pay for supplies and mercenaries. But they were also able to save a huge amount of money by paying the shepherds and goat-rustlers with nothing but promises of loot. This system was very workable when the target was a wealthy nation like Egypt because, even if they had never seen Egypt for themselves, the poor shepherds of Canaan and Sinai knew very well of the incredible wealth that was in Egypt simply because of the stories that had circulated through-out the ancient Near East about that fabled land. So, it did not take much to convince them to fight in exchange for a few baskets of grain and the promise of all the loot they could steal.

But finally, the Hyksos had been no match for the determined revenge and joy of combat exhibited by the returning Egyptian forces. No amount of money could make a man fight with such abandon. Neither grain nor silver nor promises of loot could induce the Hyksos to match the ferocity of the avenging Egyptian soldiers.

What the tamkarum financiers discussed in their guild meetings in Babylonia as they analyzed their Egyptian adventure, was whether or not it was possible to get soldiers to fight for free in *every* war. They could certainly make a lot more money if the soldiers did not have to be paid.

This brought up *Problem #13*: "When conquering a country, how can it be secured? (Assyrian deportation? Genocide? Enslavement?)" In Egypt, they had wanted primarily to steal everything that they could and carry it back to Babylonia. The reasons that their plans did not entirely succeed have already been mentioned, as the other groups of Hyksos carried off some of the loot for their own purposes. For 108 years, the merchant-moneylenders of Babylonia had siphoned the wealth out of Egypt while forcing the Egyptians to work as slaves. But that was their only purpose. They had not originally intended to take the land of Egypt for themselves because they had plenty of land of their own in Babylonia.

But now that they had been kicked out, they wondered if ravaging a country for riches without physically possessing that country was the best policy. What if they had actually taken Egypt as their own property? Or what if some other opportunity arose whereby they could treat some other country in the same way that they had treated Egypt? What should they do under such circumstances? It made no sense to repeat their same mistakes. Once they had seized a country, why not keep it forever? And what was the most efficient way to do that?

Should they capture a country and deport the population like the Assyrians did? Should they slaughter and genocide the population? Should they enslave the population? Or practice all of those methods? All of those methods would leave the merchant-moneylenders in complete possession. If they kept the conquered people alive, it would cost money to feed them. So, should they capture and enslave the people, or should they murder them?

Problem #14 had always been vexatious. "Moneylenders are de-spised; yet, how can we have honor and prestige?" No one in ancient society was more hated than the moneylenders, while honor and prestige was always denied to them. What little prestige which they enjoyed was only accorded to them as they entered villages at the head of donkey caravans packed with trade goods or as they were feted by dignitaries who coveted their exotic trade goods. Thus, it was only the prestige which they could buy and not a heart-felt or genuine prestige. They were not honored as the 'great men' whom they believed themselves to be. But they were honored as their whores were honored—a tawdry honor which disappeared as soon as they had given up what they had.

But even this minor prestige of being a new face in town who carried trade goods, or of being someone willing to lend-at-interest to a starving family whose only collateral was a pretty daughter or some little children, even such minor prestige as this, was always over-ridden by hatred. They were hated for their methods of acquiring other peoples' wealth and hatred for their evil character and hatred for the evils which they imposed on people. So, they wanted to solve this continuing Problem 14.

How can hatred for the merchant-moneylenders be turned into love? Obviously, it cannot. The moneylenders had stolen, swindled, pimped, debauched, and betrayed the people around them for thousands of years. Nothing that they could do would make the people love them. But like all parasites, the merchant-moneylenders had to live among those from whom they derived their living. This was always very dangerous for them. The bodily assaults upon their persons and upon their families, they had been able to thwart mainly through repressive and ruthless penalties by the king's law, along with personal bodyguards and goons to beat up anybody who dared to harm them.

This age-old problem of the moneylenders was always with them. They could make the people fear them but never love them. The evils which they committed against mankind, gave them both the wealth which they absolutely did not deserve and the hatred which they very much did deserve. But perhaps there was a way to make their victims, if not love them, then at least to hate them less. Perhaps hatred could be turned into *pity*. And through compassion for the moneylenders, the oppressed could be deceived into feeling sympathy for their oppressors. Pity was not love, but at least it lessened the hate. Those who had mercy for the merciless moneylenders, were less likely to want to harm them.

So, the question remained of how could the most loathsome of demonic parasites be pitied rather than hated? How could the richest of vampires be looked upon with forgiveness by the very victims whose blood they had sucked? This seems like an impossible problem to solve; but one moneylender in the city of Ur, devised a solution to the problem.

And finally, *Problem #15* had always been difficult for them to solve. "The Sumerian Swindle is both a secret and a mystical gift from the gods; how can it be protected forever as a possession of our families alone?"

The Sumerian Swindle was a secret because of its immense profits to the moneylenders who didn't want to share it with anyone. And it was a secret because if too many people began lending money at interest, then profits would fall as competition lowered interest rates. But most importantly, it had to remain a secret because if the people ever learned how they had been deceived, defrauded, enslaved, and betrayed through a mere arithmetical trick, they would rise up and murder every financier and every banker without exception, and take back what had been swindled.

By this time of 1550 BC, the moneylenders had amazed themselves with their own account tablets. It was an incredible wonder to them that the Sumerian Swindle produced so much wealth out of even the tiniest loan. To receive three baskets of grain after you loan out two, is an amazing work of magic. To be paid two shekels of silver after you loan out one shekel becomes even more amazingly wonderful, the higher that the loan amounts become. And with compound interest, those numbers increase astronomically until the borrower can no longer repay the interest on the loan. For the most inconsequentially tiniest of loans, the borrower ends up giving to the moneylender his farm, his daughters and sons, his wife, and finally submits himself to the slave shackles. The Sumerian Swindle is a diabolical invention. And it became the secret power and the personal weapon of the world's greediest, most ruthless, and most treasonous monsters.

Their Very Own God

It amazed those ancient scoundrels that such incredible wealth could be achieved with so little actual effort. Vast fortunes were given to them for free while their victims bowed at their feet and offered up the interest payments from their hard labor and even sold their children to pay off the loans, while the moneylender merely put out his hand to take the offerings. The Sumerian Swindle was a magical gift and blessing of the gods; that is, it appeared to be a gift of the gods to those who practiced the Sumerian Swindle. What could be more miraculous than gaining all of the wealth of mankind plus ownership of the entire planet Earth and the enslavement of all of its people for free, merely by making a small loan-at-interest? But to the borrowers, it was an invisible and harsh shackle around their necks which they could not remove without incessant labor and privation, believing as they did that it was an honest method of business because "it has always been here."

Regardless of either its business or its criminal nature, what the tamkarum patriarchs of Babylonia realized was that whatever god was the true god of the moneylenders, *that* god would have to be their very own god, unaligned with any other god. Certainly, it could be none other than an act of a god from which the moneylenders, and only the moneylenders, had received the wealth of the world as a free gift.

And it was obvious that the special god who had secretly blessed the tamkarum above all other people, had to exist somewhere other than in Mesopotamia because all of the cities were already ruled by Mesopotamian gods who had proven to not cherish the merchant-moneylenders enough.

But where could that god be found? He most certainly had to exist somewhere, because the huge piles of silver and gold from their ill-gotten wealth, was proof enough to the moneylenders that they were loved by some god somewhere. Obviously, this mysterious god had to be a very mighty god whose power extended into the domains of all other gods because the Swindle produced wealth for them in every country where other gods also resided. Such was the power of the moneylenders' god! A power above all other gods!

So, it was obvious that this secret god of the merchant-moneylenders was more powerful than any of the other gods. He was everywhere, day and night producing wealth for the merchant-moneylenders and their accounting tablets. But he was invisible. Such a great miracle! In the scheming minds of the ancient moneylenders, it all made such perfect sense!

The merchants and the moneylenders discussed these problems and considered a variety of solutions during their guild meetings, just as modern-day merchants and moneylenders discuss their own problems today. They discussed their problems and solutions for those quandaries, but because they were also competing guild members, they didn't necessarily want to share their conclusions with one another, especially because the merchant-moneylender guilds of Babylonia had become divided into two unequal factions.

The original faction was composed of the ordinary uncircumcised guild brothers who shared their mutual business problems for the sake of the entire guild "just as it had always been." The second faction was the circumcised super-wealthy looters of Egypt who had been elevated by their stolen Egyptian gold to the very top of the Babylonian social ladder. These circumcised moneylenders were the very wealthiest within all Babylonia. They wanted no competition for their supreme wealth from any guild member from any quarter at any time. They were always very wary of this because it was only other tamkarum guild members who had the financial knowledge and skills to take away their fortunes. So, these circumcised gangsters had to be careful of who they trusted. They trusted no one other than their own circumcised gang members, all of whom had either personally looted Egypt or whose fathers and grandfathers had passed along the prestige of being among the original looters of Egypt.

As in the case of Egypt, these circumcised moneylenders had discovered how, by conspiring together, they could steal the wealth of entire countries for themselves. They were confident that if they could do it once, they could do it again. So, in addition to Egypt, how could they loot the wealth of other countries for themselves? Or how could they steal the entire world for themselves? Their looting of Egypt had taught them that any thefts, swindles, murders, and double-crossing treasons were possible if, and only if, they kept their conspiracy as a closely held secret among themselves, alone.

This was not "as it had always been." This was something new in Babylonia. This was the coalescing of a Babylonian secret cult growing like a malignant tumor within the ancient merchant-moneylender guilds of Babylon and Ur. With their Egyptian gold, the circumcised looters of Egypt had the wealth and economic power to bribe any official, buy any goods or property and subvert any king, as long as they could keep their connivance secretly hidden from both the people and the kings whom they wished to subvert and overthrow.

These Bronze Age merchant-moneylenders were mere scribes and bean-counters who daydreamed of owning the entire world. It seemed like an impossible dream, but with the Sumerian Swindle, they had a money machine with which they could buy the entire world. All that was lacking was a method for applying that machine in such a way that all of mankind would acquiesce to their chicanery and become enslaved to the will of those scheming, circumcised accountants and masturbating sex fiends.

A Solution Found

These were the circumcised moneylenders, merchants, and bankers of the ancient Near East. They were all without exception despicable fiends. These thoroughly criminal gangsters were the very ones who controlled ancient society, just as they do today, not because that was how "it had always been" but because their criminality was so ancient that it manifested "long before anyone could remember." No one could remember a time when the moneylenders had not been a part of society. So, their criminality was accepted as something "normal" to society rather than the criminal aberration and subversion of society that it was and is.

Only the priests in the temples offered the moneylenders warnings and advice regarding the "straight path" that the gods wanted mankind to follow. But the straight path of the gods did not offer as much profit as the crooked path of the moneylenders. So, this was another reason why the merchant-moneylenders wanted their own temple staffed with corrupt priests who were in agreement with their crooked and criminal methods. What the moneylenders wanted, but what they did not have a name for at that time, was "rabbis."

The days when mankind had served the gods and lived a good life of peace and harmony with Nature, had been forgotten as the merchant-moneylenders perverted mankind into living a life devoted to ceaseless labor, warfare, debauchery, sexual dissipation, and paying-interest-on-a-loan. The moneylenders had absolutely nothing good to offer mankind. Exactly like the modern-day bankers and financiers, not a single grain in their piles of gold and silver was earned honestly. It was all swindled wealth amassed by con artists and bandits.

Ur was the southern-most Babylonian city where all the international traders from the Persian Gulf docked their ships to off-load trade goods for distribution along both the Tigris and Euphrates Rivers. The tamkarum guild at the city of Ur, more than any other guild in Mesopotamia, had the first choice of goods and the first news from distant ports.

The guild members of Ur knew of the events beyond the horizon in much more detail and much sooner than any king. Unlike all other guilds, they were truly an international merchant-moneylender guild, with guild halls in every city and retail merchants traveling to every town. The guild patriarchs traveled from city to city in their duties of overlooking and coordinating the tamkarum monopolies of trade goods and loan rates. Furthermore, as traveling officials, the guild patriarchs and officials discussed any and all problems at their guild meeting halls.

Most of them shrugged off the "Fifteen Secret Problems Which Prevented the Babylonian Moneylenders from Owning the Entire World." They were not interested in theories. What they wanted was solid results and their own share of the profits which were found in daily business-as-usual: lending money, enslaving debtors, foreclosing properties, monopolizing trade, swindling mankind, and deceiving kings. All of this while competing with one another for advantage and profits! Their marriage-related crime families had been practicing such duping of mankind for nearly 2000 years and they were experts at the lie, masters of the swindle. Most of them were content with profits "as it had always been."

But there was *one* particularly greedy and devious patriarch, of *one* particular moneylender guild family, who did not shrug off these Egyptian problems as a thing of the past. This particular moneylender recognized that the great wealth which he had achieved could not be maintained and preserved with the tricks of the Sumerian Swindle alone. New schemes had to be devised, otherwise the recurring weaknesses of their business model could face them with confiscation of their bullion by conquering kings at any time. The ancient Sumerian Swindle would still bring in great profits, but it needed to be refined so that the moneylenders would not merely be rich—they would own everything! So, a solution for the Fifteen Problems had to be found, if the greatest profits were to be obtained.

After many years of discussing and arguing about their dilemmas and how to solve them, as it turned out, this one particular guild patriarch actually figured out a way to solve the "Fifteen Secret Problems Which Prevented the Babylonian Moneylenders from Owning the Entire World."

It is from about 1550 BC, or sometime soon after this pivotal date, after the Hyksos had been expelled, that this wealthy, circumcised merchant-moneylender of Ur realized the solution to the Fifteen Secret Problems. It is from this date that Judaism first began to emerge on the world stage. It is from this date that the Jews—all of the Jews in their entirety—not only became the world's champion masturbators and sex fiends but the World's Oldest Organized Criminal Conspiracy.

We know the name of this scheming merchant-moneylender because it is recorded in the Old Testament (Genesis 11:24-32). Not that the Old Testament is accurate, not at all, but the ancient people were very particular about preserving their names and therefore the memories of themselves. This moneylender's name was *Terah* (meaning "ibex" in Babylonian). He was the patriarch of that gang of circumcised moneylenders whose family and business partners had made a fortune during their Hyksos raid on Egypt, the gold of which placed him at the apex of merchant-moneylender society in the city of Ur.

He had three sons whom he named Abram, Nahor, and Haran. The name that this patriarch gave to his first son, tells us much about what Terah thought about himself. "Abram" means "he is great by reason of his father," or "he is of noble descent." For the ancients, a name did not merely indicate, rather it made a thing what it was. So, Terah egotistically named his oldest son with a name that glorified himself. When Abram later changed his own name to Abraham, this change in name meant a change in destiny. Abraham means "father of a multitude," a name which is equally applicable to male rats or male cockroaches, but in this case means that he was the father of multitudes of voracious Jews.

This was a name calculated to be famous among the Semites where many children resulted from their sexual licentiousness. They were circumcised, so they were "horny all of the time." The Semite females were made pregnant as often as possible and the Semite males gained personal satisfaction and social prestige by having many wives and many children. The Semitic strategy was to out-breed the people among whom they were allowed to live and thereby gain a population advantage through the power of unrestricted fornication, very similar to rats and cockroaches.

Terah's home was in the ancient guild city of Ur. As patriarch over his family of circumcised moneylenders, Terah had listened to and discussed the various points of the Fifteen Secret Problems which the guild brothers had conceived over the years. But when the black light of his evil mind struck upon the answer to those Fifteen Secret Problems, he kept the secret to himself, and only hinted to his most-trusted family members how they could achieve their goals of owning the entire world and enslaving all of mankind. Terah's untangling of the problems for how to achieve this, was demonically ingenious. But it could not be achieved unless the fraudulent nature of his scheme could be concealed from his moneylender guild brothers. He only trusted the already-proven loyalty of his circumcised family of thieves with his secret.

But secrets are best kept when they are known by very few. In fact, secrets are not secrets when they are known by more than one. As patriarch of the family, Terah was in the position both of keeping the secret to himself while simultaneously having the authority and the wealth to delegate to his subalterns the deeds and duties which they must each accomplish to achieve his purpose. A full discussion of the patriarch's solutions to those Fifteen Secret Problems, and how solving those problems would empower the circumcised moneylenders to own the entire world and to enslave all of mankind, is found in *The Monsters of Babylon.*

But before the solution to any of those fifteen secret problems could be fulfilled, there was one vital step in this Babylonian moneylender's plan which had to be accomplished first. It was the pivot point upon which the Fifteen Secret Problems could be solved. Indeed, it was the pivot point upon which the entire Jewish hoax, even into modern times, depends. This was none other than *to steal the right to speak for God.* But as lying merchants, deceiving moneylenders, and hypocritical betrayers of the people among whom they had been allowed to live, none of them had the right to speak for God. But Terah devised a method to swindle that right. And he relegated his first son, Abram, to complete that vital first step.

To accomplish this particular grand larceny, Terah had to get away from the territory already occupied by the various temples and their gods. He had to leave Babylonia and operate his new-found swindle elsewhere.

A Plan in Action

The first stage in Terah's plan was to move his main offices from Ur to the city of Harran on the Balikh River tributary (Genesis 11:31-32). Leaving all his business affairs at Ur in the hands of his second son, Nahor, he took his oldest son, Abram, with him, along with all of their closest family members. They took passage by reed boats up the Euphrates, 600 miles north into Assyrian territory to the trade city of Harran. Such a movement of people and their goods, would only have been done for a serious purpose.

Terah hired his most loyal servants and his best allies from the south of Ur, the tribe of Amorites known as the Binu-Yamina (Benjamin). The tribe of Benjamin had long been the closest ally of the moneylenders of Ur. They made themselves useful as mercenaries and strong-arm gangs for collecting loan payments and as the moneylenders' private security guards during regime changes in the city states. Terah hired the entire tribe to take the land route and meet with him in Harran. This was not a simple transfer of a few family members; it involved many hundreds of relatives, men, women, children, slaves, servants, and hired guards with all of their moveable property including herds of goats and sheep, pack donkeys, and supply wagons, along with whomever of Terah's lesser relatives had wanted to join him in Harran.

After the tribe of Benjamin had reached the environs of Harran and had settled into their campgrounds and tents, Terah had work for them to do in Canaan. Although they were loyal and well-paid, their descendants would suffer the fatal consequences of their forefathers trusting the circumcised patriarch of the Ur moneylender guild.

Once Terah had settled in Harran and all of his business arraignments were in place and turning a profit; and as his various family members arrived along with his Benjamin hired guards and their families, he sent Abram to Canaan to begin Stage Two of the Evil Hoax of Judaism. This hoax involved Babylonian swindlers and flea-bitten Hebrew bandits claiming the "right" to speak for God—and not merely the right, but the *only* right.

Terah also needed to use the trade routes to tie his scheme together. While Ur was the one city in Babylonia where the ships of the sea and the boats of the rivers and canals met, in the northern city of Harran there was another convergence of trade routes. Harran means "road," and that name was applied to that city because Harran sat upon the roads that converged from the Mediterranean Sea and from Egypt, Arabia, and Palestine. All of those trade routes passed through Harran.

Besides its trade advantages, there was something especially important to Terah about the city of Harran. Its legal status differed from that of any other city. In Babylonia, the cuneiform tablets indicated that there were certain privileged cities such as Nippur, Babylon, and Sippar. And in Assyria, the old capital Asshur and Harran in Upper Mesopotamia were also among those privileged "free cities." The inhabitants of these "free cities" were exempt from conscripted labor, military service, and taxes. The privileges accorded the inhabitants of those cities were under divine protection of the gods and therefore could not be changed or revoked by any king. This was extremely important to the success of Terah's scheme. By moving to Harran, he and his family of bloodsuckers could (1) avoid the manual labor of which other cities required of their citizens, such as cleaning the canals or repairing the city walls, and (2) avoid being drafted into the army, and (3) avoid paying taxes on the huge profits which he intended to make with his new organization. By moving to Harran, he was able to remove these important privileges out of the hands of the kings and to put such special privileges into the inviolable hands of the mighty gods —in this case, into the hands of the god that Terah was planning to create.

Thus, Terah did not move into a strange city but was among his friends and fellow guild members from the very first. But even among the circumcised members of his cult, he did not tell anyone the basic reason he had moved there because he wanted all of the profits for himself and his family. From Harran, Terah could more efficiently gather in the tons of gold which was still in the possession of that second group of Hyksos raiders, the wandering tribes of Canaan. Besides the basic benefits of working out of Harran rather than Ur, he was closer to the events which he was intent upon initiating.

To further control his conspiracy in the traditional incestuous manner of the Semites, Terah ordered his son, Abram, to marry his daughter, Sarai. Incest among the Semites assured obedience from his children—a son and daughter married together would both be obedient to their father. But most especially, their incest insured that Terah's wealth would remain in the family and not be dispersed through marriages to unrelated families. Under the new fraud that he was developing, that wealth would be very huge. So, he wanted to control it immediately.

Sarai was Terah's daughter by another wife. So, when Terah ordered Abram to marry his half-sister, thus began the incestuous inbreeding that has forever given to the modern Jews more birth defects, club-feet, hunchbacks, genetic diseases, mental retards, dwarfs, midgets, androgenous mixtures of genetically defective male-female sexually queer freaks, and more butt-ugly faces than any other people on Earth. But they were all rich with swindled wealth, so that's all that mattered.

In Harran, Terah completed the first stage of his plan to own the entire world. Of course, he knew that he would never live long enough to see his plan fulfilled, but with careful planning, it would be fulfilled by his descendants and his name would be remembered.

For the second stage in establishing his new system, it was obvious to Terah that the most vital necessity for solving all of those "Fifteen Secret Problems" was to establish a base of operations which had a secure fortress for protecting their gold and silver. This had been the number one and most important problem of the merchant-moneylenders since the most ancient times: protecting what they had. But there was no place in Meso- potamia that had proven to be impregnable. Indeed, the very fact that even the greatest cities were built of mud bricks, left very little to the imagination of attacking armies as to ways of breaking through the mud- brick walls, stealing everything they could lay their hands on, and turning such cities into piles of dirt.

With the vast fortunes already at his disposal, this patriarch of the moneylender guild at Ur, searched for a city whose walls were built of stone, with a location well-suited to defense. Stone was absent in the alluvial, riverine lands of Babylonia as well as in Assyria to the north where all cities were built of mud bricks. Also, the Assyrian kings had proven to be temple wreckers and treasure thieves as well. But closer to the emerging markets of the Mediterranean, there was plenty of stone and rocks.

In addition to defensive walls, the required city needed to be near to the trade routes which were the life-blood of the merchants and moneylenders. It had to be located somewhere outside of Mesopotamia so as to avoid the conflicts between Babylonian and Assyrian kings, both of whom were in a constant need of money for their empires. The money- lenders liked to lend silver to the kings at interest but did not want them breaking into their temple treasuries and taking what they wanted. So, the best way to keep their bullion out of the hands of the kings was to keep it in a distant place surrounded by the stone walls of a temple which was protected by a terrifying god.

During the 108 years of the Egyptian occupation, the Babylonian traveling merchants apprised the tamkarum guild at Babylon and Ur, not only of the geography and trade potential of Egypt, Nubia, and Libya, but also of Arabia, Sinai, and Canaan as well. Knowing the location of water wells, oasis, grazing and forage lands, the location of every village and town, as well as trying various detours known to the local inhabitants so as to avoid bandits, was all a part of the knowledge-base of the merchants, traders, and small-town peddlers. Their trade caravans and traveling agents penetrated into every town and village then known, bringing in trade goods and carrying out silver, gold, and military intelligence.

So, the guild patriarch of Ur, Terah, was well-informed by his spies and the returning Hyksos generals, as well as his own traveling merchants, about the location where all of the moneylenders' requirements for a fortified temple could be met: It was located in the land of Canaan, atop two rocky spurs which were protected on the southern, western, and eastern sides by two deep valleys. Atop these ridges in the Judean Mountains, between the Mediterranean Sea and the northern edge of the Dead Sea, a fortified town built of stone already existed. It was named *Urusalim*.

The Perfect Spot: Urusalim

As a dwelling place, Urusalim only had the defensive qualities of its location as its only worthwhile attribute. The site offered no other advantages other than being safe from attack. It did not dominate communications nor was it surrounded by fertile land. It was not a location that would attract conquering kings because it offered no military or commercial advantages to a king. The surrounding countryside was waterless. That factor alone made it difficult to attack because the defenders could draw upon water stored in cisterns, while the attackers would be forced to travel long distances to replenish their supplies. With its precipitous valleys and plenty of building stone, the place was an ideal location for a fortress. But it was a fortress best-suited not to guard a trade route or a valley of ripening grain because there were none of these in the area. It was to be a fortress to guard a *metallic treasure*, a hidden and secret treasure, ensconced within a stone temple guarded by a monster.

This small town sitting atop this rocky spur was named Urusalim, after Shalim, a deity personified as a god of the dusk. For the moneylenders of Ur, whose main deity was Sin, the Moon God, this was a good omen—a strong fortress named after a god of the secretive darkness, a god whose "day" began in the evening, just like the Babylonian method of counting the time.

From Harran, Terah sent the tribe of Benjamin on a new assignment. They were to travel to the region around Urusalim and engage in trade with the wandering tribes of goat-rustlers in all of the surrounding territories. Urusalim, itself, could not be taken because of its defensive strength, but the surrounding territories could be occupied.

Embedded in every squad of these Binu-Yamina gangsters, Terah had assigned a scribe whose job was to listen in and observe all conversations and negotiations between the Binu-Yamina chiefs and the chiefs of the roving tribes of Canaanite goat-rustlers and shepherds. Owing to the dry conditions and the lack of wet clay to write on, these scribes were trained in the demotic script and Phoenician alphabet which could be written with a reed stylus with black ink on parchment. In this way, all of the genealogies could be recorded. Who was who, and where did they live, and where did they come from, was meticulously written down. This data was vitally important for the plan that Terah had devised. With such genealogical information, Terah and his own scribes, could hijack control over those tribes by using their own genealogies for weaving a story of the moneylender's making, a story which would enhance his standing among them, and bind them to Terah's own crime family with himself as the chief patriarch. All this was accomplished with forgery of the genealogical lines.

As tribal gangs, the Hebrews were a fighting force of goat-rustlers and bandits. When they were among the Hyksos robbers of Egypt, they murdered whomever they wished with the bright, shiny, bronze swords supplied by their Babylonian masters. After being expelled from Egypt, these Hyksos brigands disbanded into scattered tribes who were willing to fight for nothing more than the booty which they could steal from the Canaanite villages and towns. Genocide became a standard strategy for these Hebrew Hyksos because, after they had attacked a village and murdered everybody, they could claim ownership of the houses which they did not build, the water wells which they did not dig, and the orchards which they did not plant, all for themselves (Deuteronomy 6:10-11).

So, getting the shepherds to fight for free was a good Babylonian business strategy. But each tribe was fighting for their individual tribal gain and often against each other. There was nothing welding them into a single army, because after they had run away from Egypt, the Hebrew shepherds broke up into their genealogical tribal factions. But Terah had devised a plan to solve that problem. It was into this bandit-ruled countryside of wandering tribes and walled towns and cities that Terah sent his teams of peddlers and traders, guarded by his trusty Binu-Yamina mercenaries with the embedded Babylonian scribes taking detailed notes.

Bandits needed trade goods and supplies just like everybody else. And those particular Hebrew bandits were carrying huge amounts of silver and gold which they had looted from Egypt, as well as whatever they had stolen from the Canaanites. Terah wanted to recover that treasure. Copper pots and pans, woven garments, grain, horses, weapons, whatever could turn a profit was exchanged for looted jewelry, gold statues of the gods, bullion, or Egyptian luxury items.

For the short-term strategy of the Patriarch of Ur, gathering in the Egyptian loot that those Hyksos goat-rustlers still had in their possession, was accomplished through trade. But for his long-term strategy to succeed, the genealogies of those tribes had to be recorded. And the only way to do that was to trade with them and swap stories around the campfires. For this, the scribes listened to negotiations and asked questions of the Hebrew chiefs. In the privacy of their tents, they wrote down the names, towns, tribes, and genealogical relationships of every tribe.

Terah wanted to know the various genealogies of the tribes because it was his intention to tie them all together into a single army by linking their various unrelated family lines into a single genealogy, with himself and his family at the root. It was a simple way to deceive those illiterate goat-rustlers and bind them to his own authority as patriarch over them all. Only genealogies three or four generations back would be necessary to bind all the Hebrew tribes to Terah's own family. Everything older than that, could be entirely fictitious, to plant all their genealogies rooted into his own. None of the illiterate Hebrews could remember more than four generations back, so if Terah claimed an older ancestry starting five generations back and older, they could all be tied to his own family's genealogical root. And by writing it all down, he could claim his forgery and lies to be true, with no one able to refute him because the fables were allegedly from ancient times. No one ever claimed that the merchant-moneylenders of Babylonia were honest people.

Those scattered tribes of Hebrew bandits were to be Terah's soldiers who would fight for free as guardians of what they believed to be their ancestral line, because Terah's hoax would convince them that they were actually descended from Terah's ancestors. The main goal of all of that genealogical juggling, was to get them to fight in defense of the treasury that Terah planned to build. His own relatives were not numerous enough to defend a city against a king's army, but with the entire population of Hebrew bandits throughout Canaan all following his orders, there would be plenty of soldiers taking his family's side.

One Babylonian Semite, Terah, conceived this Great Hoax. But it was his willing descendants who brought the plan into reality. Terah's scribes recorded his name as the patriarch of this circumcised family of great deceivers, giving him the fame which he craved. But it was a fame for being the root of Great Lies and Greater Evil.

Abraham Takes Charge

After Terah died in Harran, Abram bought a herd of goats and sheep, both to disguise his mission and to supply meat on the hoof, milk, skins and wool during his groups' travels. As wandering shepherds, he and Sarai and their extended family, as well as his troop of armed Binu-Yamina and their flocks of sheep and goats, traveled to the territory around Urusalim in Canaan. This was a very large group (318, per Genesis 14:14) consisting of many hundreds of Abram's relatives, employees, slaves, and armed guards. So, Abram had plenty of protection.

While the tribe of the Binu-Yamina spread out and began trading with and discovering the genealogy of each Hebrew tribe in Canaan, Abram traveled to the vicinity of Urusalim to offer a tithe of one-tenth of his goods and silver to *Melchizedek*, the priest-king of Urusalim.

As both a king and the chief priest of Urusalim, Melchizedek only had about 1,500 townsmen under his rule, so he was a rather impoverished priest-king, living in an impoverished town in an isolated region. Although it was a very small town, it was in a very strong defensive position surrounded by deep ravines and waterless rocks. Behind its stone walls, the residents were safe from all of those Hebrew bandits riding on donkeys. But they were not safe from the trickery and deceits by the son of the top tamkarum guild patriarch of Babylonia.

It really did not matter to Abram which god Melchizedek worshipped at Urusalim since all gods lived in their own cities. The only thing that mattered in Terah's wicked plan, was for Abram to steal a blessing from whatever priest was in authority over that hilltop fortress of Urusalim. Abram and his cohorts could not take the town for themselves because its stone walls were too strong, its position too secure. So, getting a blessing from its chief priest, would be a step toward eventual ownership. That was the goal, by any means possible, to get a blessing from the chief priest of Urusalim.

Flattering kings was an art at which all merchant-moneylenders throughout Mesopotamia excelled. Terah had taught Abram very well in such skills of wheedling wealth and winning favors from kings, both big and small. So, flattering a little king of a little town in a desolate patch of real estate in a far corner of Canaan, was not a problem for Abram. The only important requirement to Terah's evil plan, was to get that blessing, no matter the cost.

The priest-king's name was Melchizedek, a Canaanite name. He worshipped what he called the "Most High God, El-Elyon." This is a compound name, each of its two parts being the title of a god in the Phoenician pantheon. The Phoenicians, that third group of Hyksos who had escaped from Avaris with their Egyptian loot, thus donated two of their demon gods which together became the "Most High God" for Abram to worship. At last! Abram had found his one, true god, El-Elyon.

But the Phoenicians sacrificed babies and little children to their Canaanite gods. So, Abram would have to make a name-change in his new god to brighten up its public image.

A rich shepherd like Abram and his hundreds of followers, naturally attracted the attention of such a poor priest-king like Melchizedek, whose impoverished town on a rocky hilltop was always in need of donations.

Especially in ancient times, the stock-in-trade of the various priests of the various gods in the various temples, was blessings and curses. Give to the temple priests your sheep and goats and silver and fresh bread and wine, and the priests will give you something even better—his blessing! But do something to offend the various priests in the various temples and —Oh! The doom of it all!—he might curse you! So, it was always safer to keep the priests well-fed and happy than to be stingy and receive certain doom from the gods. This is not to say that the priests were not beneficial to society—they most certainly were—if they preached to their followers to follow the "straight and true path." But they did not have the power over thunder, earthquake, and pestilence as was commonly believed of them in those days.

So, Melchizedek gave his blessing to Abram. And this wily Babylonian merchant-moneylender made sure that it was a legal contract which, once given, could not be taken back. He sealed the contract by giving Melchizedek a tithe of ten percent of everything which he owned (Genesis 14:20). This was a large fortune for a poor priest-king whose only wealth consisted of an impregnable little walled town on a rocky hilltop. Thus, with this blessing, Abram was able to steal for himself, the religious virtue and authority of the priest of the "most high god." Abram then had a blessing from the "most high god" which he could parlay into a type of delusional religious power for "blessing" or "cursing" whomever he wished, just like a real priest! It truly was a religious miracle—that the most hated of Babylonian moneylenders could so easily turn into saints!

Melchizedek is a Canaanite name. He was the priest of the "most high god" because he said so. And that was good enough for Abram and the swindles which he was planning, all of which are based upon the great "prestige" of being "blessed" by a small-town Canaanite priest of a tiny, impregnable walled town with an estimated population of 1,500 lice-infested goat rustlers.

The original name of this tiny, impregnable, town was Urushalim, or "the city of Shalim," the Hurrian God of Darkness. It doesn't matter what the lying Jews claim in their forged "scriptures," written on dead goat skins. Long before there were any Jews, this Indo-European god, Shalim, shows up in the cuneiform baked-brick Ugarit god-list as one of "the gods who are Ba'al's auxiliaries." Thus, Abraham and the earliest Jews worshipped an Indo-European god whom they mistakenly called "the most high god" but who was actually a lesser god serving under the Canaanite storm-god, Ba'al. Yet, Jewish hoaxes become even stranger than this.

The Hurrians originated from the area east of Lake Van in the Zagros Mountain region. They were an Indo-European people important to the history and culture of the Middle East during the 2nd millennium BC. They worshipped the gods Varuna, Mitra, and Indra and they were ruled by an Indo-Aryan aristocracy. Hurrian influence prevailed in many communities of Syria as they occupied large sections of eastern Anatolia, thereby becoming eastern neighbors and, later, partial dependents of the Indo-European Hittites. In the 15th century BC, the Hurrian heartland was dominated by dynasties of Aryan origin which were united into the state known as Mitanni.

But what mattered to Abram was that Melchizedek called El-Elyon the "most high god" and had blessed him under the authority of that name. That was all that was necessary for furthering the secret instructions of Abram's father, Terah, because it was the town which they wanted, regardless of any blessing by any god. Yet, it was the blessing which allowed them to take the town.

As I've noted, Mesopotamian gods resided in specific locations. So, when he left Harran for Canaan, Abram abandoned his Moon God, who was the "most high god" of both Harran and Ur in favor of the "most high god" in whatever location he settled. So, Melchizedek's "most high god" became the next "most high god" to whom Abram prayed. That little fortress town of Urushalim became Urusalim, which became Jerusalem. And Abram changed his name to Abraham.

And now, tending his flocks in the vicinity of Jerusalem, he took up the worship of Melchizedek's god, the "most high god" residing in that vicinity.

By putting aside the actual facts of archaeology, the Jews put the best light that they can on their sordid and demonic past. To this day, they claim that "Melchizedek represented the best type of monotheist of the non-Jewish race." Although Abraham swindled a blessing, it was all okay because it came from "the best type" of goyim [lowly insects, stupid cattle]. Thus, the alleged "holiness" of the Jews is based on a blessing from the non-Jews. So, very much like parasites, even their god was swindled from mankind. They say so, themselves.

The quote below is one way in which the Jews leverage their lies into the gigantic hoax that Judaism is today, by basing an alleged "blessing" by a Canaanite priest as the foundation for their fake religion. The Jews all want to surround themselves with Abraham's great legacy so that every drooling, masturbating, half-wit of a Jew, along with all of the fishy-breathed rabbis, can claim the power even to bless God, Himself. Basing this Jewish hoax upon their plagiarized Sumerian stories of Noah and the Flood, the lying rabbis even claim to know the very mind and intention of God, as exemplified in the following Talmudic teaching of those frauds.

> Rabbi Zechariah said on Rabbi Ishmael's authority: The Holy One, blessed be He, intended to bring forth the priesthood from Shem [the son of Noah, Abraham's alleged eighth ancestor], as it is written, And he [Melchizedek] was the priest of the most high God. But because he gave precedence in his blessing to Abraham over God, He [God] brought it [the priesthood] forth from Abraham; as it is written, 'And he blessed him and said, Blessed be Abram of the most high God, possessor of heaven and earth, and blessed be the most high God.' Said Abraham to him, 'Is the blessing of a servant to be given precedence over that of his master?' Straightway it [the priesthood] was given to Abraham. The Lord hath sworn, and will not repent, 'Thou art a priest forever, after the order of Melchizedek,' meaning, 'because of the words of Melchizedek.' Hence it is written, 'And he was a priest of the most High God,' [implying that] he was a priest, but not his seed. [Though Abraham was a descendant of Melchizedek, and thus the priesthood was inherited by the latter's seed, yet this was through the merit of Abraham, not of Melchizedek.] (Babylonian Talmud, Nedarim 32b, 6-7)

Even in this false teaching of the lying rabbis, the Jews show how Abram swindled the entire priesthood from Melchizedek. The rabbis teach that the Jews' own claim to be holy, does not depend upon how many little children they sodomize or how many people they dispossess and swindle or how many millions of people they cause to be murdered in wars in which they, alone, foment and profit. No, none of their own crimes against mankind matter at all. All that matters, is that they have magically "inherited" Abraham's ancestry which includes the entire priesthood of the

Most High God, which was swindled from Melchizedek! Melchizedek gave them a blessing, so these thieves shove him aside and claim sole possession of not only the blessing, itself, but of Melchizedek's office as priests for the Most High God! Then, they brag about their defrauding of Melchizedek in their phony-baloney "scriptures"!

All of the Jews today claim to be the descendants of Melchizedek and Abraham, the holy priests of the Most High God. All Jews worldwide make the fake assertion that because Abraham swindled a "blessing" and then used that as an excuse to hijack and confiscate Melchizedek's so-called "priesthood," then all of the Jews are also automatically "priests" who are just as qualified to dispense "blessings" and "curses" as was Melchizedek! Even in modern times, these lunatics claim to be so holy that they can even bless God! And their fake claims are based upon Abraham swindling a blessing from a Canaanite priest and claiming—Abracadabra! —that one blessing from a Canaanite priest of 1550 BC, automatically makes every Jew on earth as holy as the angels! And so began the many hoaxes of Judaism.

Throughout Assyrian, Babylonian, and Sumerian history and for nearly 5,000 years up until today, the merchant-moneylenders have lurked behind the thrones of the kings and the offices of the priests. From that hidden position of influence, they have used the Sumerian Swindle to steal the wealth from the people among whom they have been allowed to live and to betray every country, all to satisfy their insatiable greed. By bribing and blackmailing kings and priests alike, they have pulled down people who were much better than themselves, people who trusted them, in order that they could stand upon their graves and glory in other peoples' wealth.

They have enriched themselves by creating wars, slavery, prostitu-tion, death, disease, and starvation for the sake of their own profits. Using silver, gold, sex-slaves, whores, and alcohol, they have debauched entire societies.

It was in Jerusalem that the ultimate, supreme, most demonic fraud in the entire history of mankind was to be developed by Abraham and his descendants. In the city of Jerusalem began a conspiracy of the most horrible monsters to have ever walked the Earth. The Babylonian money-lenders had put themselves upon the throne of Pharaoh, so why not also put themselves upon the throne of God?

Calling themselves "priests of the most high god," it was in Jerusalem where these most corrupt and most evil monsters arrayed themselves in stolen golden chains and Phoenician purple robes which sparkled with swindled jewels. It was in Jerusalem, where it began that these Monsters of

Babylon, monsters who were hated by all of mankind but who demanded our pity while they stole our wealth, our houses, our children, and our countries; monsters who claimed that mankind was indebted to them forever because they were so holy as to be a blessing upon the entire planet. These monsters presented themselves as being so wondrous and holy that they considered all of mankind as nothing more than mere goyim—lowly insects and stupid cattle.

These Babylonian monsters claimed complete ownership of the entire planet as their "inheritance" from God, Himself, with all of mankind being created merely as servants of the Jews! And so, these Monsters of Babylon considered the people of the world to be worthy only as a lowly resting place for their stinking feet.

In Jerusalem, the foulest, most evil, and the most hated of monsters ever to walk the Earth, gathered all of the necessary accouterments, gewgaws, gimcracks, and fake façades to construct their very own religious hoax. They did not make them any less as monsters merely because they called themselves the "Children of God." Certainly, the merchant-moneylenders of Babylon were monsters, but they were monsters who had not yet devolved into that very much more evil and demented criminal cult known today as Jews. Not yet. Not yet. They were only just beginning their demonic hoax.

By 1550 BC, Terah, the guild patriarch of the Babylonian tamkarum guild of Ur and Harran, had solved the "The Fifteen Secret Problems Which Prevented the Babylonian Moneylenders from Owning the Entire World." With their theft of a "blessing" from the resident god of Urusalim, he and his sons, Abram and Nahor, put into motion their plans for enslaving all of mankind, pulling down all civilization, destroying all that is good, and stealing the world for their very own. Their plans for plundering the world were devilishly clever. With lies, deceits, grand larceny, and genocide, those Monsters of Babylon could swindle and steal everything on Earth and succeed in their crimes against mankind, just as long as they could maintain their protective smokescreen of pretending to be the "Children of God."

Shrewdly peering through their slit-like, half-closed eyelids from out behind the smokescreen of a Canaanite God of Darkness, wrapping themselves in the costumes of priests, pretending to be holy men with a predilection for gathering in other peoples' gold and silver, they were not the Children of God—they were (and are today) the Monsters of Babylon.

APPENDIX
TIMELINE:
3000 TO 1000 BC

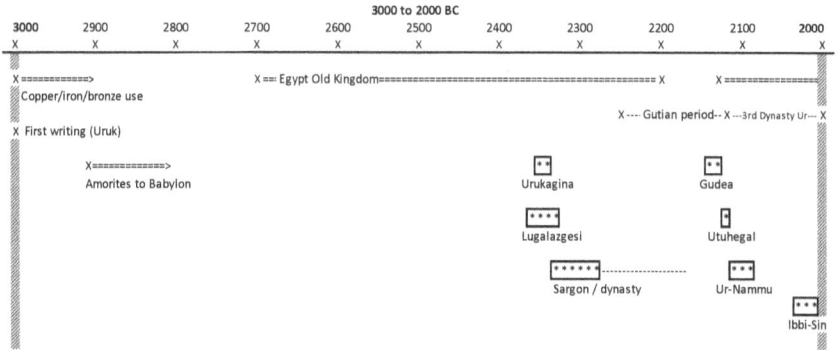

3000 to 2000 BC

3000	2900	2800	2700	2600	2500	2400	2300	2200	2100	2000
X	X	X	X	X	X	X	X	X	X	X

X ============>
Copper/iron/bronze use

X === Egypt Old Kingdom== X   X ================

X --- Gutian period-- X ---3rd Dynasty Ur--- X

X First writing (Uruk)

X=============>
Amorites to Babylon

Urukagina

Gudea

Lugalazgesi

Utuhegal

Sargon / dynasty --------------------

Ur-Nammu

Ibbi-Sin

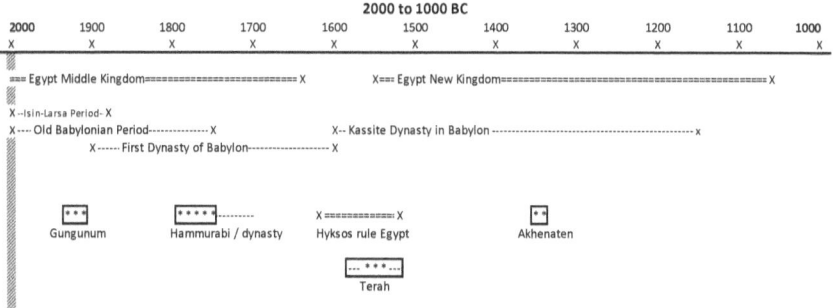

2000 to 1000 BC

2000	1900	1800	1700	1600	1500	1400	1300	1200	1100	1000
X	X	X	X	X	X	X	X	X	X	X

=== Egypt Middle Kingdom============================ X   X=== Egypt New Kingdom=== X

X --Isin-Larsa Period- X
X --- Old Babylonian Period-------------- X   X-- Kassite Dynasty in Babylon -- x
X ------ First Dynasty of Babylon-------------------- X

Gungunum

Hammurabi / dynasty --------

X ============ X
Hyksos rule Egypt

Akhenaten

--- *** ...
Terah

www.ingramcontent.com/pod-product-compliance
Lightning Source LLC
Chambersburg PA
CBHW020429130626
46549CB00001B/52